2nd
edition

A History of American Business

Keith L. Bryant, Jr.
University of Akron

Henry C. Dethloff
Texas A & M University

PRENTICE HALL, Englewood Cliffs, New Jersey 07632

Library of Congress Cataloging-in-Publication Data

Bryant, Keith L.
   A history of American business / Keith L. Bryant, Jr., Henry C.
Dethloff. -- 2nd ed.
      p.   cm.
   Includes bibliographies and index.
   ISBN 0-13-389255-7
   1. United States--Economic conditions.   2. United States-
-Commerce--History.   3. United States--Industries--History.
I. Dethloff, Henry C.   II. Title.
HC103.B7888   1990
338.0973--dc19   89-3725
                                                  CIP

Editorial/production supervision and
   interior design: Marianne Peters
Cover design: Ben Santora
Manufacturing buyer: Carol Bystrom/Ed O'Dougherty

© 1990 by Prentice-Hall, Inc.
A Division of Simon & Schuster
Englewood Cliffs, New Jersey 07632

Printed in the United States of America
10 9 8 7 6 5 4 3 2 1

ISBN 0-13-389255-7

Prentice-Hall International (UK) Limited, *London*
Prentice-Hall of Australia Pty. Limited, *Sydney*
Prentice-Hall Canada Inc., *Toronto*
Prentice-Hall Hispanoamericana, S.A., *Mexico*
Prentice-Hall of India Private Limited, *New Delhi*
Prentice-Hall of Japan, Inc., *Tokyo*
Simon & Schuster Asia Pte. Ltd., *Singapore*
Editora Prentice-Hall do Brasil, Ltda., *Rio de Janeiro*

Contents

| 14 | Foreign Trade | 238 |

| 15 | The Modern Corporate Image | 255 |

| 16 | Government and the Economy | 272 |

Preface

When we began to do the research for the first edition of this book in the late 1970s, the nation's business leaders faced an uncertain future. Rampant inflation reached 13.5 percent in 1980, interest rates soared to 20 percent, and unemployment climbed to 7–8 percent; "stagflation," the economists called it. The federal deficit seemed much too large at $60 billion, but the price of petroleum appeared to be a greater worry as a second fuel shortage in 1979 sent oil prices skyrocketing; in the booming "oil patch" the exuberant wildcatters talked of oil at $40 or even $50 per barrel. The "sick industries" of the Northeast and Midwest, notably automobiles and steel, brought to those regions the derisive term *rust belt.*

Now as we prepare a second edition of the volume, businessmen and women face an entirely different set of problems. Inflation has fallen to 4 percent, interest rates are in single figures, and unemployment at 5.4 percent is the lowest since 1974. While hundreds of thousands of workers in the Midwest and Northeast lost their jobs in heavy industry, those areas are making a major economic recovery even as the petroleum-producing states sink into an economic morass as oil prices plummet to less than $15 per barrel. Declining consumption and the failure of the OPEC cartel devastated portions of the economy even as industrial production in 1988 exceeded that of 1980 by more than 25 percent. Yet the price being paid was extraordinary. Federal deficits of incredible magnitude in the 1980s produced a national debt measured in trillions of dollars, and huge trade deficits had made the United States the world's greatest debtor. The world's banker of 1945 had become the global prodigal in the 1980s. Confidence had been further shaken by a stock market crash in 1987 and by corporate raiders engaged in megamergers. But the men and women of business persevered, the economy continued to function, and to grow, and many of those traits most common to the history of American business served to maintain a commitment to a system now being emulated by even Marxist states.

This book remains a modest effort to provide a general survey of American business history. We have emphasized individuals because we believe that the signal contributions of the few have given direction to the larger whole. Similarly we have emphasized certain firms that have innovated or pioneered in the creation of administrative structures, technology, or managerial practices. We also acknowledge that not all areas of American business have been described and analyzed. We have emphasized such traditional subjects as heavy industries, transportation, and banking, while also adding topics such as war and business, retailing, and the multinationals. The overall focus is on evolving American enterprise and the emergence of a technologically sophisticated, if financially troubled, business structure in the 1980s.

There has been an effort to describe businesses both large and small. As sons of small businessmen in the Southwest we have observed first-hand the triumphs and struggles of entrepreneurs attempting to sustain enterprises in an economy that seemed to be moving inexorably toward bigness. We have not sought to romanticize the small entrepreneurs, only to try to suggest their importance to the total economy. If we have found a commitment to the work ethic, a belief in the basic economic order, and fulfillment in our personal experiences, we have also noted the presence of "Babbitts" and "Dodsworths" as well as "Robber Barons."

We believe that America is essentially a business society. The nation's economy is based on a capitalistic structure that has generally been supported by the other major institutions—political, religious, and educational. Through prosperity and depression, the American people have placed their faith in an economy based on private ownership of the means of production with some regulation by the state and federal governments. That faith has been neither blind nor unwavering. Criticism of business practices, profits, and avarice from politicians, consumers, and laborers has been an ongoing aspect of the rise and maturation of capitalism in this country, and rightly so.

The authors view the business structure with awe for its productivity and its bounteous contribution to the economic well-being of the majority. We are not unaware, however, of the "warts" on the nation's economic visage. Throughout this book we have attempted to strike a balanced view of the successes and failures of our capitalistic economy and to provide a hearing to the critics who also have given shape to the nation's business just as have the entrepreneurs and managers. Nevertheless, we believe that despite its many faults, the evolving economic order in this country has provided most of the American people with a material well-being that has been and continues to be the envy of the rest of the world.

Ironically, few Americans understand how the business system operates, know how it has changed over time, and appreciate the complexities of capitalism as it exists in this country. This lack of understanding is particularly pronounced among young people, many of whom eagerly seek positions in American businesses without any substantial knowledge of either their internal operations or the role of those firms in the total economy. Thus we hope that this study will serve to enlighten, to provide a basis for responsible criticism of business practices and a better understanding of the workplaces of most Americans.

We would like to acknowledge the following reviewers for their suggestions and comments: Ronald Edsforth, Skidmore College; Joseph J. Holmes, College of the Holy Cross; and Robert Freeman Smith, University of Toledo.

"The Business of America *Is* Business"

Did President Calvin Coolidge really tell the American Society of Newspaper Editors in 1925 so bluntly that "the business of America *is* business"? No! Despite the ridicule heaped on the president by some politicians and many intellectuals in the more than half century since his speech, that is not what he said. Quoted in context, Coolidge's words take on a more thoughtful meaning. "After all," he declared, "the chief business of the American people is business. They are profoundly concerned with producing, buying, selling, investing, and prospering in the world."[1] And of course he was, and still is, correct. From the period of discovery and exploration in the fifteenth century to the present, those who came to this land and most of their descendants have been engaged in some aspect of a business enterprise. The result of this constant economic activity has been tremendous growth. The United States, with less than 7 percent of the world's population, generates almost 40 percent of the world's income—at a time when nearly two-thirds of the peoples of the world live at or below the poverty level. Social commentators, economists, foreign observers, and many others have emphasized the significance of business in the American culture. One of the nation's leading philosophers, Ralph Waldo Emerson, declared in the early nineteenth century that "the greatest meliorator of the world is selfish, huckstering Trade," a fact that he found unpalatable but true.[2] The astute British observer Lord James Bryce would note later that "business is king in America," that is, the use of labor and capital to produce goods and services profitably. This book attempts to describe and explain the processes by which business came to dominate American society, to examine the business leaders and their firms—both the successes and the failures—and to explore the relationships between business and government and the larger society.

The United States is the leading example of a business civilization in the world. Between 1929 and the mid-1980s the real Gross National Product (GNP) increased at an average rate of 3.1 percent yearly. This means that the output of goods and services doubled nearly every twenty years. No wonder the world has stood in awe of this enormous economic engine that underlies all our lives, to paraphrase another president, Woodrow Wilson. The American people have been the most affluent in the world, and the open structure of their society has made dreams of success believable to the majority. Even as per capita incomes in some of the Arab emirates, Sweden, Switzerland, and West Germany came to exceed those of Americans, faith in the system continued among most of our people.

The search for economic profit has dominated the nation's culture. Society's measure of well-being is the amount of goods and quality of services one obtains. Clearly the distribution of goods and services is not equal. The system presumes, in fact, to allow people to acquire goods and services in unequal proportions. There are areas of abject poverty in both urban and rural America, and only governmental programs keep more families from falling below the poverty line. Raw materials in vast abundance in the nineteenth century became scarce in the closing quarter of the twentieth. The squandering of resources has been matched only by the use of government to further the interests of some segments of society. Yet the capitalistic system in America has worked for the benefit of the many. Individual efforts in enterprise have created opportunities and gain for the majority. The societal goals have made business expansion and success possible as the

A Radio Shack outlet, one of America's franchise businesses.   (Courtesy: Radio Shack, a Division of Tandy Corp.)

American people developed an almost universal interest in business. The society created a role structure that encouraged business leaders to manipulate the production of goods and services to create profits. The reinvestment of a portion of those profits has fueled the great engine of capitalism.

The American economy evolved over two hundred years. The evolution occurred slowly until the 1830s, then gained momentum as a railroad-based transportation system tied together a network of booming cities. Vast urban markets for construction materials, food, and raw resources helped small firms grow into industrial giants. Technology, ever the handmaiden of industrial development, provided new products and, as important, more efficient means to manufacture and distribute goods. Business leaders constantly sought and found new techniques and methods to deal with a changing society and economy, and they emphasized efforts to save time and use less energy to produce more goods and services, meaning lower cost to consumers and higher profits to the firm. Great corporations expanded in size, integrated their operations, and diversified their activities. For most Americans, business came to mean these giants of capitalism, those firms now to be found on the *Fortune* 500 list. But the nation also remained a land of small-scale enterprise.

SIZE AND STRUCTURE OF AMERICAN BUSINESS

In the 1980s, businesses with fewer than five hundred workers employed nearly 60 percent of the nation's labor force, and half of all businesses had three or fewer workers. Yet those companies with more than five hundred workers dominated the manufacture, distribution, and sales of most products. The owners, proprietors, and partners in 13 million small firms do not, and have not, had the power to make the decisions that alter the course of the nation's economy. It is also important to make distinctions between types of business activities. While almost 60 percent of all firms are engaged in retail sales and services, the 12 percent of companies in manufacturing and transportation have far greater impact on the national marketplace. If McDonald's raises the price of a Big Mac by a dime at thousands of outlets, there is scarcely a ripple on the economy; but if Ford, General Motors, and Chrysler lay off or furlough 150,000 workers, there is a massive splash in the economic pond. In describing the history of business in America, it should be evident that not all firms, or their leaders, are of equal importance or have had the same influence on the shape of the national economy.

The size and structure of a business often reflect the changing nature of those who manage the firm. Most businesspersons are managers, not owners. Large enterprises are administered by salaried employees who in the late nineteenth century replaced the traditional family owners of firms. Thus, managerial capitalism is an outgrowth of the rise of large-scale enterprise. The corporate managers allocate resources and establish the direction of the economy, rather than the marketplace, which at an earlier time made such determinations. Adam Smith's "invisible hand" of the market has been replaced by what Alfred Chandler has called the "visible hand" of the corporate leaders.[3]

Both the structure and size of business units in America reflect innovations made by individuals and firms as they sought efficiency and profits. Small enterprises could not sustain the economies of scale of larger firms, where the quantity of output meant lower per-unit costs and, therefore, lower prices for the goods sold. As production units increased in size, managerial hierarchies replaced the owner-foreman-worker structure of small firms. Increasing output required greater concern for the distribution of goods, and market coordination became yet another element that added to the scope of the structure. The managers became more professional and technologically proficient, and also more isolated from the owners, that is, the bond and stockholders. Managers sought profits to keep the owners happy; they also sought stability, which enhanced their own employment. And so a structure emerged that facilitated the decision-making processes related to production, marketing, maximization of profits, and to stable relations with governments and the society.

The structures that became commonplace by the mid-twentieth century developed in response to the need to manage larger and larger units of production. Corporate leaders sought to create and sustain demands for their products and services. Manufacturing skills were simply not enough; firms needed more than technology and efficiency to sustain growth and development. Simultaneously, corporate executives had to motivate employees who had no direct profit sharing in the enterprise. Size and structure produced a business *bureaucracy* with all the problems that word suggests. Over time the industrial giants of America created multidivisional organizations that were highly decentralized to carry out diverse functions. The corporate headquarters established broad policies that the lower-level divisions executed. Once the managers established a plan or strategy to carry out their goals for production and marketing, they then created structures or organizations to administer the firm. The growth in volume of output, the national geographical dispersion of larger firms, and product diversification led to the formulation of what are now the typical structures of American business.[4]

The modern American economy rests on large industrial corporations where high levels of integration and efficiency produce and distribute a vast array of goods. These firms have accumulated huge capital resources, which their managers use to enter markets with new or altered products. The corporate leaders seek to maximize the use of these sources in order to enhance profits for the owners, who, however, have little voice in the day-to-day operations of the firm. The owners are individual security holders, pension funds, banks, insurance companies, and foreign investors who seek a high rate of return on their capital. While the financial magnitude of this process is almost incomprehensible, the roots of American business structures can be found on a small scale in Western Europe even before the age of discovery and exploration. The basic business concepts that we so often assume to be *American* have in fact evolved from the practices and ideas of the Italian Renaissance, the German Reformation, and English common law. Our material success may be unique; our capitalist ideology and legal processes are not.

THE EUROPEAN BACKGROUND

The economic development of Western Europe provided the conceptual basis upon which the American economic order was established. Western Europeans from the time of ancient Greece and Rome sought to escape from poverty and famine. Family units, villages, cities, and nation-states attempted to raise the quality of life through economic growth, that is, to expand the quantity of goods and services in order to increase per capita consumption. They created an economic order to achieve that goal based largely on the concept of private property rights. That order provided rewards for individual incentive, and the desire for additional goods and services stimulated demand. The long-range increase in per capita wealth demonstrated the importance of the presence of raw materials and technological change. In providing more goods for growing markets, Europeans discovered the significance of economies of scale when per-unit production costs declined. The emerging market society also emphasized thrift and the reinvestment of savings to increase the pool of capital. Groups of individuals combined their capital in order to engage in even larger enterprises, and they developed more efficient economic organizations to maximize profits.[5] The achievement of these ends required almost a thousand years.

The history of trade and commerce can be traced to ancient times, and small-scale businesses emerged even before the Golden Age of Greece and the Roman Empire. Commerce in the Mediterranean reached fairly substantial levels in the days of Rome, with trade in foodstuffs, metal goods, and slaves. Merchants and traders, acting alone or in temporary partnership with others, provided a wealthy urban elite with luxury goods. But mass consumption in a largely agrarian society remained at a primitive level. Nevertheless, the Romans developed an intricate body of law to govern commercial activities throughout the empire as well as a uniform currency system coordinated by a central government. The order and stability that allowed for this commercial development began to collapse, however, long before the fall of Rome in 476.

From the fifth through the ninth centuries, Western Europe was largely a vast underpopulated wilderness. The stability of Roman rule disappeared to be replaced by governmental chaos and invasions by eastern tribes or Norsemen from Scandinavia. The agrarian economy of Charlemagne's Holy Roman Empire failed to produce enough food for the population, and a weak and often disrupted distribution sytem contributed to the constant threat of famine. Slowly a social, political, and economic system called *feudalism* emerged, and the major formative period in Western civilization began. Some people built fortifications at strategic transportation points to become rulers of the immediate countryside. An agricultural system, the manor, emerged, which organized the farm population into large estates. The farmers, or serfs, worked the land for the lords, who protected them from the ravages of war and invasion with small groups of knights. The manor was also a social structure, as the serfs who worked the land owed personal allegiance to the lord as well as rent. Around the castles or manor houses emerged communities based at first on self-sufficient agricultural production. Eventually a more complex economy developed as demands for harness, flour, luxury goods, armor, and other products brought craftsmen to the larger towns. There and in the towns and cities that had survived from Roman times they formed guilds or professional organizations that controlled entry into the trade and often output and prices. Skills such as weaving, masonry, metalworking, and dyeing were closely held monopolies by the guilds, with lengthy training periods required for apprentices and journeymen before they could become master craftsmen. The guilds sought to preserve a way of life, not just to enhance profits. With the emergence of commerce based on substantial population increases and the rise of some cities, the European economy made major gains in the twelfth and thirteenth centuries. The Crusades established trade routes in the eastern Mediterranean and exposed Europeans to spices, silk, and other luxuries; and the commercial activities they generated brought great wealth to some cities, such as Venice. This developing market economy was snuffed out between 1347 and 1351, however, when the plague, or Black Death, ravaged the continent and at least one-third of the population perished.[6]

THE HANSEATIC LEAGUE

Following the ravages of the Black Death in Europe, cities began to grow and prosper as trade increased and small-scale manufacturing revived. In the northern German seaports, merchants and traders sought protection for their business transactions and the transport of their goods. The city of Lubeck had made a treaty with the city of Hamburg in 1230 that established free trade between the two and guaranteed that the road linking the North Sea and the Baltic Sea would be guarded. The absence of a strong central government in Germany allowed the cities to make such treaties, and soon other communities asked to join the arrangement. The cities in Germany north of Cologne became part of the emerging Hanseatic League, but as the league sought to protect long-distance trading routes in the Baltic, non-German cities joined as well. The mutual protection and free trade which the league provided proved appealing to Riga, Danzig, and other Baltic ports. As the Hansa cities prospered, their traders sought access to commerce in southern Germany, England, and even Russia. The Hansa established a trade center in London in 1266, and its representatives opened a market in Novgorod in Russia. They sent German grain to Scandinavia in exchange for dairy products, furs, fish, and ship timbers. Salted fish and furs were then sent south along the Rhine, Elbe, and Oder rivers to be traded for wool, metal goods, and spices. Thus the ancient trade routes from the towns at the mouths of the rivers south into the northern European plain were reestablished by a loose federation of merchants. The league's power peaked in the period between 1356 and 1377; it then declined.

The gradual collapse of the Hanseatic League in this precapitalist era can be traced to both internal and external factors. The business methods of the Hansa lagged two hundred years behind those of the Italian bankers and merchants. The traders of the league remained petty capitalists long after the Italians developed commercial capitalism, as the former sought only to spread or reduce risks. The Hansa businessmen created partnerships for only a single venture, sending a ship from one port to another and then dissolving the organization. Their bookkeeping techniques were crude, and they constantly fought over the division of profits and the calculation of losses. Elected merchants held the keys to a common chest that contained all commercial deposits. Although a democratic process, this method failed to develop a sophisticated system of exchange such as the Italians had created.

Even if the internal difficulties of Hanseatic business had been resolved, the face of Europe had already begun to change in the fourteenth century. The Hansa failed to respond to the rise of nationalism. As powerful rulers created national states in England, France, Russia, and Sweden, the rimlands of the Baltic and Germany remained weak city-states or minor kingdoms. Wars between England and France cut off the Hansa from Bruges in Flanders, one of its major centers. The rise of a strong Swedish nation terminated some of the trade relations in the north. The Hansa had raised funds by levying dues, and the cities began to lose the privilege of an independent taxing system to central governments. The rise of nationalism meant the loss of trading rights; for example, Elizabeth I revoked the Hansa's privileges in England. The absence of a strong German nation left the cities with no political base, and by the fifteenth century the Hansa entered into sharp decline. The success of capitalistic ventures depended upon political and economic stability and order; a loose federation of merchants simply could not succeed as modern nation-states emerged. Businesspersons had to create more innovative techniques if they were to conduct their activities in a changing environment; when the Hansa failed to do so, it lost its economic viability.

The catastrophic population losses disrupted society, but slowly the trends that had emerged earlier began to be reestablished. The rural areas remained decimated, but the cities recovered, commerce revived, and a more systematic economic order appeared that stressed labor-saving devices, mechanization, and trade. While 90 percent of the people still depended on agriculture for a livelihood, the nonagrarian sector of the economy altered substantially. Prior to the twelfth century, the Roman Catholic Church had dominated the religious life of Western Europe and made major decisions that affected the secular society as well. The Church theoretically opposed usury, that is, the collection of interest on loans. Usury was a mortal sin, and those who defended it were guilty of heresy. The Church also opposed the accumulation of wealth and ostentatious display and, in general, the concept of profit. Merchants were enjoined to sell goods at "just prices," that is, at a price which only covered costs. These positions changed over time as the Church itself became a significant landholder and prospered greatly in the era of the Crusades. The Church also became a borrower, and thereby a payer of "fees" in lieu of interest. Too, most of the Church's major efforts to prevent profit making had been directed at holding down the cost of food during times of famine. Church leaders accumulated wealth for themselves as well as for the institution, and the differences were often obscure. While not sanctioning the charging of interest or the making of profits, stringent enforcement of edicts against both all but disappeared.

By the fifteenth century, trade and business revived to reach levels higher than those that had existed before the Black Death. Small bands of merchants traveled from manor to town, holding fairs and selling wares gathered from over the continent and the Middle East. Individuals formed commercial organizations that fostered long-distance trade. The Hanseatic League developed in northern Europe and helped stimulate trade in the Baltic. In Italy banking houses, such as that of the Medici family, developed modern business practices, new accounting procedures, and a monetary system based on credit, loans, and bills of exchange. Powerful craft guilds in growing cities became participants in this new commercial world, and as their output of goods and services increased an incipient market society emerged. In the absence of a way to dispose of surplus crops, the lords had not encouraged extraordinary agricultural production; but with the rise of urban markets, land values advanced as the demand for foodstuffs increased. Thus the economic structure of feudalism began to change even as the political order was drastically altered.

With the maturation of feudalism, groups of lords banded together for mutual protection and profit. Slowly, powerful leaders emerged to create nation-states far larger than the political fragments that had existed earlier. Population growth not only stimulated the economy, but also provided more troops, which were levied by the barons or lords for the kingdom. The development of strong national governments in England, France, Spain, Sweden, and elsewhere created secular competitors for the Roman Catholic Church. Economic, social, and political issues developed between rulers of the nation-states and the prelates of the Church. Disputes over taxes, lands, and power with the Church triggered wars between the kingdoms. As the cultural Renaissance bloomed in Italy, Holland, and England, wars of nationalism and religion tore apart the fabric of postfeudal Europe.

Efforts by the nation-states to acquire wealth—with which to pay the armies that protected the kingdom and added new territories—caused them to seek more profitable trade outlets. Improved transportation, the growth of fairs, and the rise of the great port cities all contributed to commercial expansion. The Portuguese, Spanish, French, and English began to seek additional trade in Africa, the Middle East, and eventually in the New World. The great merchants of these nations accumulated resources and advanced the concepts of capital formation. They came to rival the nobility in economic if not political power, and their financial contributions to the nation-states added yet another significant aspect to the social structure. The need for more tax revenues forced rulers to define property rights with greater precision and to codify what until then had been common law. Clearly it was economically more advantageous for the monarchs to further the prosperity of the landowners and merchants, and thus provide long-term tax revenues, than it was to engage in a one-time confiscation of property of wayward vassals. The society changed dramatically as the role of the nobility declined and as the commercial classes came to dominate the secular governments.[7]

THE MEDICI AND THEIR BANK

The generally accepted idea that Europe's great cultural outburst, the Renaissance, rested on a solidly prosperous economy is not the case. While there were wealthy rulers, merchants, and princes of the Church, the continent generally was quite poor. One of the more profitable businesses was banking, and the bankers of Florence, Italy, in the fourteenth century had been among the leaders in the Western world. They collapsed, however, when the kings of England and Naples refused to pay their debts. A new group of lenders arose in the fifteenth century among whom the Medici family became the most powerful as well as the greatest art patrons of the Renaissance. The rise of the Medici was part of the urban growth and development of northern Italy in the late Middle Ages. Italian merchants became Europe's leading businessmen with contacts throughout the continent. The size of their commercial activities, the need to exchange a myriad of coins, and the constant demand for loans from the Roman Catholic Church and the emerging rulers of larger national states generated a demand for international banks. The Medici responded with a modern commercial and investment banking house that used superior business organizations and techniques.

In 1397, Giovanni di Bicci de'Medici established a bank in Florence that loaned money to Church leaders, established rates of exchange for various currencies, and created a system whereby merchants could transfer funds to pay for goods in other cities. Under Cosimo de Medici the bank expanded rapidly in the fifteenth century. He found partners for the bank in Rome, Venice, Naples, and Pisa who opened branches or served as correspondents. The branches were partnerships that existed independently of the bank in Florence; thus the structure was not a corporation, but a holding company. The holding company's principal business was ownership of the securities of other firms that carried on commercial activities. By establishing general policies in Florence and a decentralized management in the branches, the bank flourished. Risks were extraordinarily high, but so too were the profits. Soon branches opened in Geneva, Bruges, Avignon, London, Basel, and even Tunis and Rhodes. Under the strong and effective leadership of the Medici, the bank became a powerful economic and political force, and in the Florentine Republic the Medici achieved princely status.

With increasing wealth from the bank, land, shipping, the silk and wool trade, and an alum monopoly, the Medici became the leading art patrons of the era. They made Florence the greatest center of the Renaissance with commissions for the day's master painters, sculptors, and architects. Under Lorenzo the Magnificent (1449–1492), Florence blossomed, but the bank withered. Engaged in political intrigue in the Republic and in artistic endeavors, Lorenzo had little interest in or time for the bank. He placed its adminis-

Lorenzo de Medici (1449–1492). Ruler of Florence and patron of the arts. Andrea del Verracchio. (Courtesy: National Gallery of Art, Washington, Samuel H. Kress Collection.)

tration in the hands of outsiders, and a rapid decline ensued. Coordination with the branches deteriorated, several of the correspondents failed financially, and ill-advised investment policies and generally adverse economic conditions brought the bank to collapse by the time of Lorenzo's death. Two years later, in 1494, Charles VIII of France invaded Italy, and when his army reached Florence, the Medici family was expelled from the city.

The Medici left a handsome legacy to Western civilization in the form of palaces, churches, and libraries containing some of the greatest art treasures the world has known. They also helped to create a modern business system upon which capitalism rests. The Medici used bills of exchange and double-entry bookkeeping, which the Italians had developed. They employed the concept of limited partnerships to spread financial risks in large transactions, and the branch banks and correspondents served as a model for the holding company. New accounting procedures and insurance contracts also aided in the establishment of modern commercial practices. The Medici's contributions to the Renaissance and to business history were significant indeed.

Simultaneously the Roman Catholic Church found its position in much of Europe undermined by the power of the rulers of strongly nationalistic states and by the Protestant Reformation. The refusal of monarchs such as Henry VIII of England to submit to the Church on matters of diplomacy and economics led to clashes and ruptures. Excesses by the Church caused some, such as Martin Luther, to rebel and to demand internal change and reform. Others, who came to be called Protestants, sought to alter the relationship of individuals to the religious institution. For economics and business the most important aspect of the Protestant Reformation was the concept that has been called Calvinism. The Protestant reformer John Calvin believed in a harsh and angry God who had predestined that only a few of the world's people would be saved. While all had to live a life of hard work, piety, and diligence, few would escape damnation. Calvin urged that individuals dedicate themselves to their endeavors to demonstrate their membership in the elect. One should be committed to work, accumulation, and economic success; worthiness and material possessions became synonymous. The Calvinists believed that wealth was not for ostentation, but rather to be used as capital. Thrift, not poverty, became a major virtue, and prosperity a key to God's kingdom. This body of doctrine, known as the Protestant Ethic, came to dominate the secular attitudes of many European Protestants. The Calvinists of Switzerland and France, the Lutherans of Germany and Sweden, and the Anglicans of England shared in this new doctrine. While little of the Protestant Ethic would have struck a Renaissance Italian banker as "new," these beliefs were soon held, not only by the wealthy upper class, but also by virtually the whole society. They provided a philosophical basis upon which a capitalistic economic structure could be erected.[8]

By the sixteenth century, when the period of discovery and exploration began in earnest, the situation in western Europe could best be described as volatile. The Protestant Reformation had led to wars of religion and counter-reformation that produced intense national rivalries. The authority of the Roman Catholic Church had been challenged and destroyed in some areas. A new philosophy had come to dominate northern Europe that urged greater commitment to worldly endeavors. The accumulation

John Calvin (1509–1564). Theologian and founder of Presbyterianism. (Courtesy: Presbyterian Historical Society.)

and use of capital had become a virtue; to save and invest became both individual and national goals. The rise of nationalism furthered these concepts that brought economic progress to nations desperately in need of tax revenues to support continental wars and expansion abroad. Materialism, which emphasized physical comforts and the accumulation of goods, became a dominant characteristic of the society. Significant advancements in science and technology enhanced these nationalistic and materialistic ambitions even as long-distance commerce in staple and luxury goods stimulated the European economy. The employment of movable type after 1450 enhanced communication, and significant advances were made in navigation and surveying. More capital, larger investments, the development of trading companies, and the application of greater units of savings to commercial ventures brought about economic growth. Thus the exploitation of North America was simply part of a much larger maturation process by which Western Europe developed a capitalistic society.

CAPITALISM

A good place to begin a discussion of capitalism is the work of economist Werner Sombart, who spent much of his career attempting to define the term, its evolution, and the stages of its growth. While never achieving an all-encompassing definition, Sombart emphasized aspects of capitalism that can be carefully analyzed. The spirit of capitalism included rationality, acquisition, and competition, and the system in which capitalism operated was generally free, individualistic, private, and aristocratic. It utilized occupational specializations, separated economic functions, and existed in a decentralized political and social environment. In order to be successful, capitalism needed technological advances to generate higher levels of productivity. The economic order in which capitalism operated had to grant businesses an independent existence, and the leaders of the enterprise were required not only to produce profits, but also to motivate workers and create an atmosphere that encouraged thrift, industry, and stability.

Sombart's theory of capitalism emphasized the role of individuals who through initiative and perseverance created enterprises. Neither the enterprises nor the environment in which they operated were static. As the political economy grew and matured, the atmosphere became less free, restrictions by government and the society reduced the range of choices available to the capitalists, and innovation and creativity waned.[9]

Although Sombart's major work was published over half a century ago, it still provides insights into the evolution of capitalism in the United States. The need to see that the system is not static, and that the roles of individuals and firms change over time, is crucial to understanding *free enterprise* in America. Internal and external factors have altered capitalism as practiced in this country, and wars, wage-price fluctuations, the degree of competition, and the monetary policy of the central government have brought about drastic changes in the economic order. The petty capitalists of the 1790s and 1830s who operated small shops, forges, and mills rose in an environment far removed from that which fostered the great industrial firms of the 1890s. Henry Ford could create an automobile giant in the first two decades of this century, but Henry J. Kaiser failed to build another in an entirely different post–World War II economy. The mercantile capitalists who created the first department stores would be replaced by financial and commercial capitalists who erected great chains of stores, and they in turn would be succeeded by vast conglomerates which absorbed the chains. And yet enough elements of Sombart's dynamic capitalism remain to allow the emergence of innovators with new products and technology even in an era of heavily regulated capitalism with less freedom, restrained competition, and greater centralized authority. The capitalism of the 1980s was a far cry from that of the 1780s, but certain dominant characteristics continued to provide the basis for a business society in America.

CONCEPTS BASIC TO AMERICAN BUSINESS

Private enterprise requires a stable and orderly environment to be successful. There must also be a balance between individual self-interest and the welfare of the larger society. The latter can provide the stability and the freedom for economic action that the businessperson seeks, but if the potential entrepreneur perceives that the social order will be disrupted, or that there is the likelihood of instability that will heighten economic risks, then opportunities will be ignored and entrepreneurship will diminish. The classical economist Adam Smith emphasized the need for "order and good government, and along with them, the liberty and security of individuals." Both the Declaration of Independence and the Constitution, once amended, sought to protect the rights and liberties of individuals and to maintain an orderly society. While the Constitution expressly guaranteed the sanctity of private property, an entire body of custom, practice, and law existed to provide entrepreneurs with an environment that attempted to minimize risks for the development of enterprise.

From English common law came the precedents that established the rights to and sanctity of private property. In the 1620s a common law relating to commercial development emerged in England. Efforts to reduce the power of the monarch to create trade monopolies led to the Statute of Monopolies of 1624, which encouraged innovation even as larger economic opportunities for trade appeared—a victory for the rising merchant and commercial class. As early as the thirteenth century, English courts established the concept of exclusive property rights in land, and those courts also acquired jurisdiction over free individuals. The English colonists, then, would bring with them the intellectual and legal baggage that became basic to the rise of enterprise in the United States—that government should protect private property and guarantee due process of law.[10]

While a structure of government would be erected to protect property, the system was never based on pure free enterprise in the sense that no governmental regulation existed. The French term *laissez faire,* or hands off, did not apply in that English common law, colonial charters, the Articles of

Confederation, state constitutions, and the Constitution of the United States all specifically provided for governmental intervention in the economic order to protect the welfare of the people. Common law feared monopoly whether granted by the crown or created by entrepreneurs. Though there have always been rhetorical claims of free enterprise in the United States, government intervention has been a constant theme, both in terms of legal restrictions on business and governmental support for it. State laws encouraged the incorporation of firms and limited the liability of investors. Supreme Court decisions, especially under Chief Justice John Marshall, gave the federal government powers to aid business while preventing the states from hindering commerce. Efforts to create and erect a federal system with specific powers granted to the national and state governments produced a decentralized framework that enhanced entrepreneurship.

Thus a society emerged in which a legal structure undergirded a body of belief in economic growth and development. Thoroughly imbued with the Protestant Ethic, the first settlers believed in saving, thrift, and investment. Capitalism, a system of production in which capital predominates, came with the colonists of 1620 if not with the explorers of 1492. While much capital came from abroad well into the nineteenth century, Americans generated surpluses for investment internally even before 1800. In that year there were over three hundred corporations in the United States while England and France each had only a handful. Enterprises retained earnings to provide capital in an era of low or nonexistent taxation, and additional capital came from governmental sources as well as through private accumulation, though largely the latter. Americans saved, planned, accumulated, and advanced economically in an environment secured by legal protection for property. But accumulation represented only one step. Capital, to be productive, had to be mobilized and applied, and in that step risk became a significant factor.[11]

Capitalism and enterprise begin with the actions of businesspersons who assume and accept the risks of initiative. What must be understood at the outset is that over the years as many have failed, perhaps more, as have succeeded. And state and federal laws have protected the failures as well. Bankruptcy proceedings and geographical mobility have aided the unsuccessful entrepreneur. The failed merchant or tradesman of colonial times could enter bankruptcy proceedings and then move on to reenter the realm of business. Then, no less than in the present, ordinary and legitimate risks were high, and business strategies involved attempts to manage and reduce risks. The projected rate of return on investments must compensate for the risks; and if they do not, capital will not be readily found. An entrepreneur operates in a world characterized by a large element of uncertainty, so that he or she is not only an inventor, discoverer, organizer, and merchant, but also a gambler.

The corporation is a key to the reduction of risk. It can issue securities in the form of stocks (equity) or bonds (debt). Often the former are of low face value in order to encourage widespread sales. The liability of the stockholders is limited to the assets of the firm, thus protecting their personal holdings. Many potential investors might avoid a partnership because of risk but would seek the relative safety of the corporation. If the firm fails, it can enter into receivership and continue to operate, thus holding out the possibility of the recovery of portions of the investment. The savings of many small investors can be used as venture capital to embark on a new enterprise or expand an existing firm so that it can market a product or technological innovation. Without entrepreneurs, however, the corporations have limited opportunities as well as liability.

The American entrepreneur functions in an environment where social controls over economic behavior, as opposed to governmental controls, have traditionally been few. As a leader, organizer, and motivator, the businessperson is the central figure in modern economic history. Operating in a society in which rewards, monetary and nonmonetary, are granted for achievement and success, profit maximization is not the only goal of the entrepreneur. Business leaders determine the objectives of the venture, and in so doing must be both creative and innovative. The aspect of creativity generally separates those who develop a firm and its basic concept from those who simply manage. The economist Joseph Schumpeter emphasized the concept of creativity in defining the classical entrepreneur. He applied that term only to individuals who responded to an economic problem outside of existing practice. For Schumpeter the business leader was an individual who challenged the status quo, who found the means to commercially utilize an invention or technology, and who relished the taking of risk in the marketplace. Schumpeter's model immediately calls to mind a Henry Ford or John D. Rockefeller. But few successful enterprises are products of one individual.

Other scholars, such as Arthur H. Cole, noted that creative entrepreneurship of Schumpeter's kind in the American economic system is too rare to be the only basis for the development of a successful firm; rather, many people are involved.[12] Cole emphasized the purposeful activity of an individual, or group, who initiated and maintained a profit-making enterprise for the production and distribution of goods and services. For Cole and many other students of American business, the concept of management and the role of managers are as important as that of the creator or innovator. Too, in the twentieth century, society has given management not only an authority role in the economy, but also far greater social responsibilities. As a result, business leaders have developed a different view of their functions that limits their willingness to assume risks, and to exercise innovation, while accepting, albeit reluctantly, far greater responsibilities in the society and the culture. The business enterprise does not exist in a vacuum, and as the larger society alters its goals, concerns, and demands, the entrepreneur must redefine the aspirations, methods, and economic activities of the enterprise.

For over three centuries the business of America has been business, but the characteristics of the society, the economy, and the culture have been in a constant state of change. Business leaders have operated in a generally friendly environment in times of prosperity and depression. A relatively open society has benefited from an economy that has for a century doubled its output of goods and services every twenty years. Yet the "free enterprise" system, as its defenders call it, or "unrestrained capitalism," as some of its detractors refer to it, is still not widely understood. It is accepted by the majority, though neither seriously questioned by those who do not share fully in it nor adequately defended by those who do. The historical evolution of business in America needs to be understood if the nation desires to comprehend its origin, successes, failures, and future prospects. It is especially vital that those who soon will be in the driver's seat of this great economic engine have an historical highway map before they take to the open road.

NOTES

1. Calvin Coolidge, "The Press under a Free Government," in *Foundations of the Republic: Speeches and Addresses* (Freeport, New York: Books for Libraries Press, 1968; originally published, 1926), pp. 187–188.

2. Ralph Waldo Emerson, "Works and Days," in *Society and Solitude* (Boston: Fireside Edition, 1909), p. 159.

3. Alfred D. Chandler, Jr., *The Visible Hand: The Managerial Revolution in American Business* (Cambridge: Harvard University Press, 1977), pp. 1–2, 6–12.

4. Alfred D. Chandler, Jr., *Strategy and Structure: Chapters in the History of the American Industrial Enterprise* (Cambridge: MIT Press, 1962), pp. 2–3, 13–16.

5. Douglass C. North and Robert Paul Thomas, *The Rise of the Western World: A New Economic History* (Cambridge, England: Cambridge University Press, 1973), pp. 1–18.

6. The best survey of European economic history is Shepard B. Clough and Richard T. Rapp, *European Economic History: The Development of Western Civilization* (New York: McGraw-Hill, 1975); see particularly pp. 4–11 and 38–97.

7. North and Thomas, *The Rise of the Western World*, pp. 71–119.

8. The debate over the importance of Calvinism and the rise of capitalism continues. The best analysis remains the classic study by Max Weber, *The Protestant Ethic and the Spirit of Capitalism* (London: Allen & Unwin, 1930), which contains a foreword by R. H. Tawney.

9. Werner Sombart, "Capitalism," in *Encyclopedia of the Social Sciences* (New York: Macmillan, 1930), III, pp. 195–208.

10. North and Thomas, *The Rise of the Western World*, pp. 146–156.

11. Although his theories are often rigid and deterministic, N.S.B. Gras's pioneer work is still the starting point to understand the role of capital. See *Business and Capitalism: An Introduction to Business History* (New York: F.S. Crofts & Co., 1939).

12. The following works succinctly express these differing views: Joseph A. Schumpeter, "The Creative Response in Economic History," *Journal of Economic History*, 7 (November 1947), pp. 149–159; and Arthur H. Cole, *Business Enterprise in Its Social Setting* (Cambridge: Harvard University Press, 1959).

SUGGESTED READINGS

BRUCHEY, STUART W., ed. *Small Business in American Life*. New York: Columbia University Press, 1980.

CHANDLER, ALFRED D., Jr. *Strategy and Structure: Chapters in the History of the American Industrial Enterprise*. Cambridge: MIT Press, 1962.

———. *The Visible Hand: The Managerial Revolution in American Business*. Cambridge: Harvard University Press, 1977.

CLOUGH, SHEPARD B., AND RICHARD T. RAPP. *European Economic History.* New York: McGraw-Hill, 1975.

COCHRAN, THOMAS C. "The Business Revolution." *The American Historical Review* 79 (December 1974): 1449–1466.

———. *Challenge to American Values: Society, Business and Religion.* New York: Oxford University Press, 1985.

GRAS, N.S.B. *Business and Capitalism.* New York: F. S. Crofts & Co., 1939.

HIDY, RALPH W. "Business History: Present Status and Future Needs." *Business History Review* 44 (Winter 1970): 483–497.

LARSON, HENRIETTA M. *Guide to Business History.* Boston: J.S. Canner & Co., 1964. Reprint of 1948 edition.

LIVESAY, HAROLD C. *American Made: Men Who Shaped the American Economy.* Boston: Little, Brown, 1979.

PORTER, GLENN, and HAROLD C. LIVESAY. *Merchants and Manufacturers.* Baltimore: John Hopkins University Press, 1971.

TAWNEY, RICHARD H. *Religion and the Rise of Capitalism.* New York: Harcourt, Brace & Co., 1926.

WEBER, MAX. *The Protestant Ethic and the Spirit of Capitalism.* London: Allen & Unwin, 1930.

2 | The Merchant Capitalists

The merchant who handled the exchange of goods between people and places was well on the way to becoming the central, dominating force in the composition and dynamics of the rising nation-states of Europe at the time when Christopher Columbus first voyaged to the new world. Indeed, the necessities of trade and commerce partly dictated the rise of nations, and the merchant provided the political and economic sinews of the new nationalism. In the seventeenth and eighteenth centuries mercantilism became a political-economic policy of European governments in their efforts to convert from predominantly agricultural states to modern commercial-industrial nations. Mercantilism involved the state's encouragement and direction of economic activity through patents, charters, monetary subventions, and military support. The state sought to enhance the wealth of the merchant in order, through taxes, to enrich the realm. Thus, colonial ventures in particular tended to become adjuncts of state policy. The state desired colonies as a source of raw materials and a marketplace for finished products. The object was to establish a favorable balance of trade and to accumulate gold within the realm. The colonial businessperson was subservient both to the interests of the state and to the prerogatives of the European and British merchants.

Spain, France, England, and Holland led in the commercial revolution that embraced the era of American colonization, and which was made possible, in part, by the influx of gold, silver, and raw materials that those colonies provided. The business interests of Europe and America, however, quickly found the constraints of mercantilism bothersome, and the Americans especially—anticipating Adam Smith, who in 1776 advised nations to leave people to their natural inclination to accumulate wealth—came to believe in the dynamics of individual acquisition and in *laissez faire*. The Spanish conquistador, the French merchant-adventurer, and the English proprietor are interesting prototypes of the independent-minded American businessperson of the Revolutionary era.

They came to America seeking fame and fortune, and extolling the glory of God. The search for profit motivated the voyages of exploration and the founding of the English colonies in America. Profit in fifteenth-century and early sixteenth-century Europe derived largely from the spice trade, which involved the transporting of such condiments as ginger, pepper, and cinnamon from the East Indies by dangerous and expensive overland and water routes to the west. One Englishman estimated in 1621 that 3,000 tons of spice purchased for $227 in the Indies would sell for nearly $2 million by the time it reached Alleppo, on the eastern end of the Mediterranean, and at that point the cargo was still distant from the ultimate consumer. No wonder, then, that Louis de Santangel, keeper of the Spanish privy purse, encouraged Ferdinand and Isabella to underwrite Christopher Columbus's proposed voyage to the Indies, which as historian Samuel Eliot Morison wrote, offered "so little risk for so great a gain."

CHRISTOPHER COLUMBUS

In 1492 Christopher Columbus crossed the Atlantic and discovered a new world. A number of historians have since speculated that this individual venture was of no great consequence, usually citing one of several reasons: (1) The New World would have soon been discovered anyway, (2) it was an accident, or (3) it had been discovered long before Columbus's time. None of these speculations disturbs the central historical feature of what, in fact, Columbus did, why he did it, or the even more crucial economic significance of the motivations and business structures behind the voyage. Christopher Columbus was a businessman, perhaps more accurately an entrepreneur, who operated within the context of his time and society to accomplish a thing which few had conceived of and none had achieved. He assumed great personal risks, both physical and fiscal, in pursuit of enormous fame and fortune. The former he acquired. Others, following his lead, obtained the latter.

Columbus seems to have developed a reasonably mature plan to "pass over to where the spices grow" as early as 1474.[1] It is almost impossible to say when the Portuguese sea-captain's plans had reached the point of his actually "doing something about them," as Morison has put it, but certainly he had submitted a proposal to the king of Portugal in 1484 to reach Japan by sailing west—without success. Over the next four years he made inquiries and alliances in Spain, obtaining an audience with Queen Isabella in

1486 and winning an offer of support from the influential merchant Count Medina Celi. His efforts ended, however, only with the receipt of a very modest retaining fee, approximately equal to a seaman's annual wage. His brother Bartholomew apparently obtained an interview with Henry VII of England and with Charles VII of France, but he failed to win more than polite interest and some ridicule from the courts of those sovereigns. Columbus renewed his applications with Portugal in 1488, and was in Lisbon when Bartolomeo Dias returned from the Horn of Africa. "The King of Portugal," suggests Morison, thereafter "had no more use for Columbus, who returned to Spain."

Finally, in 1492, after years of fruitless effort, Columbus received word from the Court of Madrid that his enterprise was rejected. He left Madrid, only to be retrieved from the road home and brought back to court. Thanks to the last-minute intercession of Louis de Santangel, the court was convinced to undertake the enterprise. The government found 1.4 million maravedis (Spanish currency of the time) to outfit the expedition; Columbus invested 250,000 maravedis, most of which he obtained from friends and supporters. The total cost of the voyage is estimated by Morison at 2 million maravedis, or $14,000.[2] It is interesting that Christopher Columbus spent almost ten years in promotional efforts, selling himself and his idea to a reluctant and sometimes hostile world—and succeeded.

The contractual negotiations were concluded in April 1492. "Don Cristobal Colon" and his heirs received the designation of Admiral in and over all islands and mainlands "which shall be discovered or acquired by his labor and industry." He was appointed viceroy and governor-general over the mainlands and islands. Ten percent of all gold, silver, pearls, gems, spices, and other merchandise "whatsoever" produced or mined within his domain were to be his, tax-free, and he obtained the option of receiving

Christopher Columbus (1451–1506). Skillful mariner, adventurer, and explorer. (Courtesy: *Dictionary of American Portraits.*)

one-eighth of the profits of all voyages into the new dominion in return for a one-eighth investment in those ventures.[3] Columbus's failures, if such they were, could only be in returning a profit from the new dominions over a period of ten years sufficient to cover the costs of the four voyages and to satisfy too-eager creditors. In this failure Columbus was not alone. As an entrepreneur, he succeeded, albeit on behalf of others, in establishing the new and ultimately lucrative business of colonizing the Americas.

SPANISH ENTREPRENEURS AND CONQUISTADORS

It is, perhaps, difficult to identify Hernando Cortes, Francisco Pizarro, and Hernando de Soto as preeminently entrepreneurs and businessmen, but they differed little from Christopher Columbus. Each sought wealth, preferably instant wealth. Each assumed considerable risk and operated from a similar financial structure. For Columbus, the key to instant wealth meant a short, direct trade route to the Indies; for the conquistadors, the key was conquest and plunder. Soldiering became but a means to an end. For the conquerors life was too short to think about long-term economic development. They sought to accumulate wealth as rapidly as possible.[4]

Private individuals and armies carried out the conquest of New Spain usually under a contractual arrangement with the Spanish crown much like that obtained by Columbus. Under the terms of the contract part of the profits, a *Quinto*, the royal fifth, went to the government, with the remainder to be divided according to the arrangement of the "proprietors." The actual business structure of the conquest ordinarily involved the creation of a partnership or company (*compañia*) for investment in New World expeditions. One of the partners would be the leader of the actual expedition, as were Cortes, Pizarro, and de Soto. Another main partner usually served in a managerial role, obtaining financing, outfitting ships, purchasing supplies, and recruiting the company of men (*or compaña*) who actually comprised the expedition. Lesser or equal partners met certain supply or military obligations, providing ships, men, horses, and equipment, in return for which proportionate shares were received.[5] This business structure foreshadowed the joint-stock arrangements that became increasingly common among the Dutch, British, and French.

The compañia, representing the financial partnership and leadership of the expedition, usually received one-half of the rewards or plunder. The remaining half, in theory, went to the fellowship or compaña who accompanied the expedition. The men of the compaña received proportionate shares according to their participation. For example, a horseman received twice the share of a footman; a notary or accountant, somewhat more than the horseman. Horses, in fact, were entitled to an individual share, and some "investors" in expeditions supplied only horses and received appropriate shares. In practice, most of the profits of an expedition went to the outfitters who often advanced the necessary equipment to the men and collected most of their profits or shares. Leaders of expeditions often hoarded supplies, which were later sold to their men in times of need at exorbitant prices. Great fortunes were made, and lost, by the conquistadors. The risks were great, but then, too, so could be the rewards.[6]

Hernando Cortes

Cortes, in the opinion of two modern historical researchers, stands out as the "great encomendero and capitalist of New Spain," who had a "better head for business than most of the Spaniards around him."[7] Arriving in Santo Domingo in 1504, Cortes accompanied Diego Vasquez in the conquest of Cuba in 1511, where he was awarded an *encomienda,* or grant of Indian labor, and there he turned to raising cattle and horses and to mining. Only after accumulating considerable capital and influence did he elect to invest in an expedition to the mainland. He gathered a force of 550 men, including some Cuban Indians and Blacks, sixteen horses, a few light cannons, enormous debts, and the enmity of Governor Velazquez, and sailed for the mainland in February 1519. By August 1521, Cortes and his troops had completed the conquest of the mighty Aztec empire. Cortes had defeated competing Spanish interests and established his supremacy in Mexico.

The first phase of the Spanish conquest, the looting of the Aztec empire, quickly ended. The second phase, mining, soon followed; it lasted for several hundred years, joined concurrently with and gradually superseded by the third phase, the production of agricultural commodities or, in the case of Mexico, cattle raising. Cortes, unlike the other conquistadors who usually ended their careers and their lives with the looting of their conquered empire, initiated and supervised each phase of the conquest in Mexico, including the looting, the mining, and the commodity-production phases.

Cortes began importing livestock and chickens from Cuba almost immediately after the conquest. Obtaining a large *encomienda,* and purchasing additional lands, such as the valley of Oaxaca, Cortes organized large cattle and horse ranches reminiscent of the later *hacienda.* By the 1530s Cortes and other ranchers were exporting livestock to South America and providing hides to the mining operations there and in Mexico. On other large plantations he raised wheat, produced silk, and became most successful with sugar operations including the development of a refinery near Vera Cruz. His efforts to profitably produce grapes and olives generally failed. Although Cortes fell into political disfavor, and ultimately into historical disrepute, according to Michael C. Meyer and William L. Sherman his career provides "no greater example of rise to fame and fortune in the New World."[8]

Francisco Pizarro

Pizarro, an illiterate and probably illegitimate son of a poorer branch of a large commercial family in Trujillo, Spain, arrived in Hispaniola in 1502—aboard the fleet that would have carried Cortes had he not suffered injury during an escape from a compromising "affair of the night." In 1513

Pizarro accompanied Balboa as a captain in the conquest of Panama. He formed an early business association, or partnership, with Diego de Almagro, who later served as business manager and agent for recruiting and financing Pizarro's commercial and military operations in Colombia and Nicaragua in the 1520s when Spain was probing toward the Pacific. In 1528 Pizarro and Almagro began the expedition that would result in the conquest of Peru four years later and the plunder of a treasure trove that made the Aztec pale by comparison. Along the way the partnership was broadened to include Bertolomé Ruiz and Hernando de Soto, who arrived at a critical moment with men, horses, and supplies, and who most often led the vanguard of Pizarro's conquests.[9]

Unlike Cortes, Pizarro was much less the capitalist and more the plunderer. His small force of about 160 men captured the ruler of the Inca nation, Atahualpa, and looted an estimated 1.5 million pesos of treasure, of which the King of Spain received his fifth, and the remainder, most of it, went to Pizarro and, in unequal portions, to the partners. Subsequently Almagro and Pizarro fought over Peru, a rivalry ending with Almagro's execution in 1537. De Soto, who was slighted in the disposition of spoils, brought his case to Spain and received a commission to conquer Florida. Pizarro was assassinated by an Almagro partisan in 1541.[10] Pizarro, perhaps, took greater risks and won greater wealth than all of the conquerors, but, like some spoilsmen of a later day, he plundered rather than built.

Hernando de Soto

De Soto arrived in the West Indies in 1513, with Pedrarias de Avila, and quickly achieved distinction as a rider, scout, and Indian fighter. He organized a partnership with Francisco Compañon and Ponce de Leon; and although de Soto was literate, most of the management of his enterprises came under the auspices of Compañon, or Ponce de Leon. In the 1520s de Soto associated with Pizarro for the first time in the conquest of Nicaragua, where he usually led the advance party while Pizarro headed the main troop and distributed supplies. Receiving a large *encomienda* in Nicaragua, de Soto conducted mining and limited cattle operations.

His compañia had begun making plans for the conquest of Peru when Pizarro opened negotiations with them for participation in his own expedition. De Soto reached an agreement by which he provided two ships and supplies, one hundred men, and twenty-five horses, and joined and reinforced Pizarro when the latter penetrated the heart of the Inca empire. De Soto first made contact with King Atahualpa and was instrumental in the subjugation of the Incas. He received one-third of the treasure, lost a political struggle with Pizarro, but apparently extracted a good part of his profits from the Indies. He arrived in Spain with at least 100,000 pesos, not only sufficient to make him one of that nation's wealthiest men, but also enough to more than outfit his final private venture in Florida, which ended in disaster.[11]

The Spanish conquistadors took great risks for great profits. In this they were like entrepreneurs of a later day; but unlike businesspersons and entrepreneurs, the conquistadors, with the possible exception of Cortes, sought only immediate returns or plunder and had little intent to develop and manage a business operation. Although the government of Spain did institutionalize the conquests into a well-organized and elaborately bureaucratic structure, those institutions were of the Church and state and not private enterprise. France on the other hand, used the structures of business to accomplish the mission of the state.

FRENCH ENTERPRISE IN AMERICA

French enterprise is significant in the development of business history, if for no other reason than the global scale of its activities, the distinctive influence of government on the business structures of French enterprise, and the guiding influence of Jean-Baptiste Colbert.

Jean-Baptiste Colbert and the Company of the West

Colbert has been seen as the embodiment, if not the creator, of mercantile capitalism. He envisioned the role of the merchant and the function of trade as the central, dominating, dynamic forces of society. In Colbert's mercantile world, the mother country provided the capital and manufacturing goods; colonies provided raw materials and the marketplaces for finished products. Specifically, the French West Indies produced sugar and tropical fruits; Africa (Senegal) provided slave labor for the colonies; and North America produced sugar, tobacco, grain, and furs. Trade was confined in theory, and most often in practice, to French ships and French merchants, and the whole economic system was to be self-sufficient and closely regulated.

Colbert gave structure to this grand scheme of empire by the organization of the East India Company and the West India Company in 1664. He was inspired, in part, by the spectacular success of the Dutch East India Company and was certainly motivated by what he regarded as ruinous competition by the Dutch with French trade. The West India Company received all rights to trade and colonization in French territories in South America, the West Indies, Canada, Acadia, Newfoundland, and West Africa. The company could build forts, manufacture ammunition, levy troops, build ships, appoint governors and officials, declare war and make peace, and it enjoyed a monopoly of trade for forty years.[12] It was, in effect, to be a sovereign state within the state.

The company, organized as a joint-stock venture, had no fixed capital but returned stockholders their prorated shares or dividends on the basis of their subscriptions. The minimum subscription was 3,000 livres. A 10,000-livre subscription entitled a shareholder to vote in the general assembly of the company, and 20,000 or more livres qualified one for membership on the board of directors. The company absorbed the older Cayenne Company, which operated in the West Indies, as well as the Company of

New France, which by 1672 had some 6,700 colonists and a thriving fur trade and fisheries industry in Canada.[13]

Contrary to Colbert's design, however, the West India Company reflected, not the mercantile interests of France, but rather the governing bureaucracy. Of the 5.5 million livres subscribed, 3 million came from Louis XIV, and much of the remainder from officials such as Colbert himself, who subscribed 30,000 livres. Company policy was set by governing officials, not by merchants. Many of the original subscribers were crown officials, who, during the early operations of the venture, authorized expenditures greatly in excess of subscriptions. Some would-be investors from the commercial ranks were frightened by the possibility of being held liable in excess of their participation. Despite government assurances to the contrary, the company failed to attract the merchants. Moreover, war with England, and subsequently with the Dutch, forced the company to spend "millions in defense" rather than in profit-making ventures. Property losses, especially from shipping and from wars in the West Indies, were enormous. French citizens were reluctant to leave their homeland for an uncertain colonial venture in the West Indies, or subsequently in Louisiana; and Colbert, who essentially administered the company's affairs, was unrealistic in assuming that the colonies, or the framework of the mercantile empire, could be truly self-sufficient and independent of the rest of the world. His efforts to exclude Dutch and other foreign traders from the Indies undermined the production and distribution of goods and services within the empire. By 1674 the West India Company was bankrupt and the crown assumed its assets and liabilities, which had been largely that of the king anyway.[14]

The company, to be sure, achieved limited successes in colonizing French holdings and in promoting the production of sugar, tobacco, timber, naval stores, and furs. But these industries were already initiated by the private corporations of pre-Colbert days and would most likely have thrived without the inducement of the West India Company. Ultimately, perhaps Colbert's concept was not at fault. But in reality the company "was maintained and controlled by the state to perform a national service and to make possible the success of a national policy," rather than to generate commercial profits.[15]

Sieur de La Salle

Private venturers such as Robert Cavalier, Sieur de La Salle, and his business associates, Louis de Buade, Comte de Frontenac, and Henri de Tonty, most often worked within the context of Colbert's grand scheme as free agents. La Salle, born in Rouen of a wealthy family, arrived in Canada in 1666. He established a trading post on a large estate which he purchased near Montreal, and he did well in the fur trade. In 1669 La Salle sold his holdings and led a small expedition into the Great Lakes and southward along the Ohio River, possibly as far as present-day Louisville. On his return from the interior, La Salle and Governor Frontenac formed a business association that led to the establishment of a French fort on Lake

Ontario, ostensibly to deter the western fur trade from shifting to the British in New York, and more specifically to channel the business into the pockets of La Salle and Frontenac.

Frontenac authorized a probing expedition deeper into the interior in 1673, sending Louis Joliet, a fur trader, and Father Marquette, a Jesuit priest, to search out the "Great River." Marquette and Joliet launched their canoes on the Mississippi in June and followed the river south as far as the mouth of the Arkansas. Father Marquette remained with the Indians around Green Bay, but Joliet hurried back to Canada with his report. Frontenac, through his personal representative La Salle, petitioned the king to establish colonies and trading posts in the territories explored by Joliet. Colbert, however, advised against the plan, preferring to maintain a compact and defensible French settlement in Canada. La Salle received a title of nobility and a grant of land in Ontario, but little else. Finally, by 1678, when La Salle again returned to France, Colbert grudgingly accepted Frontenac's plan to fortify the Mississippi valley and to develop the fur trade south and west of the Great Lakes. Colbert was more interested in the water route through the continent and blocking of British expansion in North America than in the fur trade. Frontenac and La Salle sought the profits from the furs.[16]

La Salle began his meticulous exploration and mapping expedition in 1680, when he founded Fort Crevecoeur near Peoria, Illinois. In 1682 he established Fort St. Louis, leaving in command Henri de Tonty, who had joined La Salle when the latter visited France in 1678. De Tonty and others had become financial backers and partners in La Salle's fur interests, and they suceeded in monopolizing the fur trade south of the Great Lakes, particularly with the Miami and Illinois Indians. Frontenac, in 1682, was recalled from office having been constantly at odds with the Jesuit order and with Colbert's policies.[17] La Salle continued his expedition, in 1684 claiming for France all of the lands drained by the Mississippi River. Finally, on the ill-fated expedition to found a colony at the mouth of the Mississippi, La Salle was assassinated by his own crew.

The fur trade proved highly profitable to the La Salle and Frontenac interests—but very bothersome and expensive to the French government, which provided nominal protection. The trading posts themselves were rendezvous points both for Indians and for a host of lesser traders and trappers, the *courier de bois*, who as independent agents conducted the fur business at the tribal level and sold their wares to the posts. In 1696 France specifically forbade trapping and trading in the western country, although it granted certain patents and exemptions from the prohibition, such as tò Henri de Tonty. The proscriptions, however, served to stimulate rather than end the fur trade with the British, and they may ultimately have contributed to the loss of the Hudson's Bay region to the English following Queen Anne's War. The transfer of the bay to the English can partly be explained by the intervention of French fur interests in international diplomacy. By the 1690s, independent French traders were openly defying French imperial policy.[18]

John Law

La Salle, nonetheless, initiated a policy of colonial expansion in North America that the government of France was determined to pursue largely as a point of imperial policy rather than for trade and profit. To this end, France sought to secure the Mississippi and its tributaries with a string of fortifications from Quebec to New Orleans. The southern approaches to the Mississippi River were secured by colonies planted on the Gulf Coast in 1698 by Pierre Le Moyne, Sieur d'Iberville, and by his brother de Bienville, two of the eleven sons of a Quebec fur trader. But war and the financial excesses of Louis XIV were more than the French treasury could afford, and France turned its Louisiana colonies over to a proprietor, Antoine Crozat, in 1712.

Crozat received a monopoly on all trade in the French territory between the Great Lakes and the Gulf of Mexico, free of any import or export duties. All gold and silver found, less the king's fifth, were to be his, and he had exclusive rights to the sale of slaves and to manufacturing. Despite Crozat's heavy injections of people, money, and supplies, the Louisiana venture failed, and by 1716 Crozat was financially ruined. In that year John Law, an exile from Scotland, obtained a charter for a remarkable national bank, the Banque Générale, which restored order to the chaos of French finances. Through Law's intercessions a giant commercial conglomerate, similar to Colbert's West India Company, was established, and the Banque Générale became the major shareholder.

Originally established as the Company of the West (or Mississippi Company), the corporation received exclusive rights to the commerce of Louisiana and to the beaver trade of Canada. Law then began to accumulate the resources and privileges of lesser companies through mergers and stock issues, which ultimately brought under the control of his company the tobacco, slave, China, African, and East Indies trade. The Mississippi bubble burst in a frenzy of speculation in 1719, and Law escaped from France, destitute and condemned. The Company of the Indies, as it had been renamed, survived, and it continued to operate the Louisiana colony unprofitably until the colony was returned to the crown in 1731.[19] The French colonial experiment in America failed to return financial profits, but that experiment undoubtedly served French imperial policy. French territorial expansion in North America was designed not only to generate profits, but also to convert the Indians and block British and Spanish expansion in the New World. France experienced partial success on all three counts. For France, as for England, the colonies existed to serve the interests of the mother country, and when they came into conflict, interests were expendable.

THE UNITED EAST INDIA COMPANY

The charter of the United East India Company, as historian George Masselman has observed, "ranks among the historic documents of all time."* Established in the Netherlands by an act of the States General on March 20,

1602, the company became the first joint-stock company of consequence, establishing a Dutch empire in Asia that survived for 350 years.

The charter eliminated ruinous competition among Dutch trading companies for profits from the spice trade, and it created a giant trading company that presented a united front against Spanish and English competition. Credit for the consummation of the trading hegemony is given Johan van Oldebarnevelt, born in 1547 in Ameersfoort, east of Amsterdam. Oldebarnevelt fought against Spain and became a jurist and principal architect of the Dutch Republic. His great expertise lay in mediating between the many states and city factions, an ability critical to the formation of the Republic and the East India Company.

The company received the right to all trade and commerce east of the Cape of Good Hope and west through the Strait of Magellan. All other Dutch ships were specifically excluded. It could establish forts and garrisons and appoint governors and civil officials. Unlike later French and Spanish trading companies, the Dutch government obtained no interest or shares in the company and appointed none of the directors. The company constituted an independent merchant republic. Capital was set at the very large figure of 6.5 million guilders, and the company's affairs were directed by six chambers headquartered in six different cities, each with its own board of directors. Each chamber retained some autonomous control over its trade, directing the dispatch of ships and cargo and receiving return freight. Profits, however, went into a single account administered by a committee of seventeen chosen from the directors—the Lords Seventeen—with seats allocated approximately on the basis of participation. Amsterdam, for example, held eight of the seventeen seats. The Seventeen comprised the real authority in the company. They entrusted administrative management to a solicitor or executive officer.

The embarkation of company troops at Amsterdam. Abraham Storck.   (Courtesy: Collection Amsterdam Historical Museum.)

The directors, who qualified for their position with a subscription of not less than 6,000 guilders, received a commission of 1 percent of the cost of each voyage, and 1 percent of the return cargo. The ordinary stockholders exercised no voice in management or in the selection of directors, but they received their proportionate share of profits as soon as they equalled or exceeded 5 percent of the capital. Shareholders had no liability beyond the limit of their investment. The company, in effect, encouraged wide participation, and the Dutch government did not presume to preclude the possibility of competition from foreign governments. The result was the creation of the world's largest and most competitive mercantile firm without hazarding the security of the government.

*George Masselman, *The Cradle of Colonialism* (New Haven, Conn.: Yale University Press, (1963), p. 146, and see pp. 135–137, 141–150.

THE BRITISH MERCANTILISTS

English colonization derived more clearly from individual interests, both commercial and religious, than from public spirit or national goals. England in the early seventeenth century regarded America as a depository for "surplus" populations, a means to employ the merchant marine, a source of raw materials, a marketplace, and possibly a route to the Indies. The British were quite pragmatic about it. Much of their information about America—and reasons for colonizing it—came from the pen of Richard Hakluyt, a man who had much to do directly, and indirectly, with the colonizing of Virginia, Massachusetts, and South Carolina. Commercial enterprise stimulated the founding of Virginia and the Carolinas and provided the initial impetus behind the Massachusetts venture.

Jamestown

In 1606 King James I granted letters of patent or charter to a joint-stock company that was later to be designated The Treasurer and Company of Adventurers and Planters of the City of London. Shareholders received the right to colonize and trade in the part of America "commonly called Virginia" between the thirty-fourth and forty-fifth degrees of north latitude. The company divided into two groups of associates. The first, comprising London merchants and Richard Hakluyt and designated the First Colony, was to establish a plantation between the thirty-fourth and forty-first parallels; and the Second Colony, comprising Plymouth merchants, was to plant a colony between the thirty-eighth and forty-fifth parallels. Three ships bearing 143 persons left England in January 1607, arriving at the James River in May. The colonists received specific letters of instruction about choosing a site, building a fort, storing supplies, dealing with the natives, and exploring for minerals and gold. Food and supplies

Jamestown, Virginia, as depicted by Sidney E. King.   (Courtesy of Virginia State Library.)

were to be distributed to the colonists from a common storehouse, and produce obtained by the colonists from planting or gathering was to be deposited in a central storehouse for shipment back to England. The enterprise, from the colonists' point of view, was a collective, with no distinction or reward for individual effort or productivity. Five weeks after their arrival in Jamestown, the *Susan Constant* returned to England with specimens of minerals and timber, but no gold or silver, and with a report that the colonists were being harassed and killed by the natives. Indeed, affairs in the colony went from bad to worse.

Quarreling among the leaders and the colonists, disputes over the distribution of dwindling supplies, starvation, disease, and deaths from Indian attacks brought the colony to almost hopeless straits by 1609. The returns to the company were insignificant, including little more than shipments of "sweetwood" and 17 tons of metal smelted from ore that brought £68. Despite a reorganization and redirection of efforts by the new "Company of Virginia" in 1613, which sought to establish a firm agricultural basis for the colony and to entice settlers with outright grants of land, by 1621 the company had invested, and lost, some £200,000 in the enterprise. In 1624, the charter was withdrawn and Virginia became a royal colony. Despite these early adversities, Virginia's exports of tobacco, which began in 1613, rose from 20,000 pounds in 1618 to over 500,000 pounds in 1627.[20] But it was a case of doing too little, too late for the Company of Adventurers.

Massachusetts Bay

The inspiration behind the settlement of Massachusetts Bay was much the same as that for Virginia in terms of people and purpose. Captain John Smith and Richard Hakluyt provided promotional efforts in both ventures. The predecessor of the Massachusetts Company, the Dorchester Adventurers, wrote Samuel Eliot Morison, were a "group of public-spirited men who wished to do something for their country, a little for the Indians, somewhat for the fisherman, and a good deal for themselves."[21] Their effort to establish a fishing and trading post on Cape Ann soon folded. After several reorganizations (lastly as the New England Company), the Massachusetts Bay Company was officially born in 1629. The Puritans, who became the stockholders and the colonizers of the company, historian Bernard Bailyn contends, "looked to the New World not only as a haven but for profits, the more satisfying in that their extent would measure the success of a godly enterprise."[22]

The Massachusetts colonizing venture was unique in two ways: First, it was a religious enterprise that proposed to establish a Puritan commonwealth in America; and second, the company transferred its charter and its governing offices to the New World. In March of 1629 Charles I elected to disband Parliament and imprisoned its Puritan leaders, who had won a resolution declaring the supporters of the high church and royal prerogative enemies of the kingdom and commonwealth. Impending civil war prompted many Puritans to remove themselves and their families from England. If the stockholders of the Massachusetts Bay Company were to leave, should not their company offices leave with them?

In August the stockholders of the Massachusetts Bay Company agreed to remove the charter and the government of the company to New England. The Massachusetts Bay Company, like the Virginia Company, was a joint-stock enterprise with profits to be prorated according to the value of one's participation. The stockholders, or freemen, elected their board of directors, called assistants, and the company president, called the governor, as is done today by business corporations. The company charter specified that there should be quarterly meetings by the stockholders and provided for the election of officers, but the charter did not, perhaps through oversight, say *where* such meetings would be held. By transferring the business offices from London To Massachusetts, the colonists at once eliminated a canker which had plagued the early colonies. Governing officials in London really could not implement effective colonial policies simply because they knew nothing about colonial conditions. Even if they did, the months or years required in resolving a problem or testing a policy often meant that however well-advised a company decision was when made, it was often not applicable once the decision arrived in America. John Smith had already publicly commented from his Virginia experiences about "meddlesome orders and instructions from English businessmen who knew nothing" about America.[23]

JOHN WINTHROP—GOVERNOR OF THE MASSACHUSETTS BAY COMPANY

John Winthrop by training and temperament was something of a self-made businessman, although his philosophy and purposes were basically religious. He was the secular and spiritual leader of the Puritan church in Massachusetts. Born in 1588, in Suffolk, England, he attended Cambridge University before assuming his duties as Lord of Groton Manor, the family estate. As lord of the manor Winthrop supervised the economic, political, and religious affairs of his estate. He served as justice of the peace and also as steward, directing the planting, reaping, and marketing of crops, and the general business affairs. He was much in earnest in his Calvinist persuasion and highly disturbed by the frivolity, excesses, and immorality of English society. The leadership of the Massachusetts colony was a station he accepted as a God-ordained obligation of public service. Winthrop served as the sometimes controversial and at times autocratic governor of the colony for ten years before his death in 1649.

Extravagance, sloth, and idleness had no place in God's secular world, Winthrop believed. God forbade indolence and a lack of industry by either the rich or the poor. God "called" one to perform tasks or to enter business and the "elect" were those blessed and favored by God. People proved their election or state of grace by adherence to religious observances prescribed by the Bible and by their being and their doing. Calvinism, American Puritanism, and John Winthrop provided a powerful stimulus to the "work ethic" that had much to do with the success of the Massachusetts colony.

The Protestant Ethic, which derives in part from the Puritan experience, became a powerful stimulus for the American business system. Americans increasingly came to believe that God's blessing included the material comforts. A good indicator of one's state of grace was the quantity of material

John Winthrop (1588–1649). Puritan, governor of Massachusetts, and businessman. (Courtesy: *Dictionary of American Portraits*)

goods that a person accumulated. Although it was certainly a modification of Calvinism, the ideal that God helped those who helped themselves, and that wealth was evidence of one's salvation, provided a strong incentive to hard work, thrift, and the accumulation of profit.

In October 1629 John Winthrop, who peculiarly was not a stockholder of the company, was elected governor, and by June 1630 sixteen ships carrying over a thousand, well-provisioned colonists arrived in Massachusetts. The Massachusetts colonists had yet another advantage over those in Virginia. The Virginia colonists were for the most part financed by the stockholders who remained in England. They arrived, in other words, indebted to the company and obligated to the company's will. The Massachusetts Bay colonists *were* the stockholders, who financed their own colonizing, leaving them not only free of debt when they arrived but substantially reducing the cash outlays of the company and the necessity of a large profit margin.

The Massachusetts colony prospered. Farming, timber, fishing, furs, and, by 1649, even shipbuilding became mainstays of colonial development. Fifteen thousand Puritans transferred their homes and industry to the New World over a fifteen-year period. The Massachusetts venture worked, in part, because the colony became an autonomous division of the British economic order. Decentralization and diversification appeared to be good business rules in the seventeenth century just as they would in the twentieth. And the success of the Massachusetts colony also hinged in part on the Puritan ideology that held that God required hard work, thrift, and faith.

The South Carolina Proprietors

As it worked out, the Carolina enterprise developed with considerable autonomy and independence, although that was not the intent of the proprietors. The proprietors' motive was to make money. In 1663 Charles II granted "Carolina"—in theory, an enormous territory stretching between both oceans and lying between the thirty-first and thirty-sixth parallels—to eight court favorites: the Earl of Clarendon, the Duke of Albemarle, Lord Craven, Lord Berkeley, Lord Ashley, Sir George Carteret, Sir William Berkeley, and Sir John Colleton. Interestingly enough, the charter provided for a measure of home rule by the colonists. All laws made by the proprietors were with the advice and consent of the freedmen of the province. The famous, or infamous, "Fundamental Constitutions" that would have established a feudal estate were never approved by the colonists, who were of an independent spirit. More significantly, the proprietors' practice of awarding a headright (50 acres of land) to every freeman and member of his family, including slaves and servants who settled, served to attract considerable numbers of colonists before 1690. Many of these were experienced New World settlers from overcrowded Barbados or French Huguenots who had taken refuge in England during the French wars of religion.[24]

Lumbering, naval stores, and hides provided an early source of revenue for the colonists, most of whom, however, depended more on subsistence from the wild harvest than on money income. By 1679 the proprietors had invested some £18,000 in the colony, with reportedly nothing to show for it but "vexation and poverty."[25] Slavery became an early adjunct of the Carolina colony, and with the introduction of rice culture in 1685, a highly profitable industry developed which thrived with the importation of slave labor.

The population grew from a few hundred to almost six thousand people, including slaves, in 1700. The production of rice and rice exports rose steadily after 1700, reaching 1.5 million pounds in 1708, and 10 million pounds in 1726. A Charleston merchant, Richard Splatt, wrote in 1726—on the back of an invoice consigning thirty-seven barrels of rice and two chests of deer skins to the *Lovely Polly*, bound for London—that the port was crowded with vessels seeking rice while "there is not rice to load the 1/2 of'em." They would have to be loaded with pitch and tar, he said.[26] Each year between 1726 and 1730 rice exports from South Carolina doubled, and soon thereafter indigo became an important adjunct of the rice trade. By the turn of the eighteenth century, New England–made vessels were plying a steady trade along the Atlantic seaboard, to the West Indies, and to London. Tobacco, rice, furs, hides, naval stores, timber, and fish were the major articles of commerce.

As the wealth and population of the colonies increased, the proprietors began to impose greater controls over imports, exports, land distribution, and the payment of debts. This "interference" finally led in 1719 to an armed but bloodless rebellion by South Carolina colonists and the institution in 1721 of a royal government largely subservient to the local assembly. Thus South Carolina, and the American colonies generally, enjoyed during their approximately 170 years of development under English rule a surprising degree of autonomy and self-determination.

The business of America during its incubation, despite the weight of imperial rule from abroad, is best characterized as a decentralized and individualistic effort. While the business structures were by no means as highly developed as the modern corporate structure, the motives and mechanics of operation were much the same. Profit, or perhaps more accurately in the case of the conquistadors plunder, was the primary motive behind colonization. Speculation and the demand for quick returns by investors brought about many more business failures than successes. The very real hazards of weather, Indians, and disease were sufficient to thwart the best-planned, best-led colony. Undercapitalization, misinformation, and poor leadership plagued business enterprise then as now. Overcentralization—that is, efforts to direct business affairs in America from the cities of France, England, and Spain—often inhibited and undermined local economic development and was a chronic problem of the colonial enterprises as it has come to be of the present business structure. Decentralization developed early and most conquistadors and the later American colonies came to exercise considerable independence and self-rule within the broad context of charters, grants, and laws. Despite the enormous risks and losses of the colonial ventures, the gains ultimately proved greater still.

NOTES

1. The following discussion of Columbus is based largely on Samuel Eliot Morison, *Admiral of the Ocean Sea: A Life of Christopher Columbus* (Boston: Little, Brown, 1942), pp. 63–91.

2. Ibid., pp. 101–104. It is estimated that 12,000 maravedis is equal to $80 to $90, or the equivalent of a year's pay for an able-bodied seaman.

3. Ibid., pp. 104–108.

4. Murdo J. MacLeod, *Spanish Central America: A Socioeconomic History, 1520–1720* (Berkeley: University of California Press, 1973), p. 47.

5. James M. Lockhart, *The Men of Cajamarca: A Social and Biographical Study of the First Conquerors of Peru* (Austin: University of Texas Press, 1972), pp. 67–71.

6. Ibid., pp. 47, 67–71.

7. Michael C. Meyer and William L. Sherman, *The Course of Mexican History* (New York: Oxford University Press, 1979), pp. 95–129.

8. Ibid., pp. 130–148; and see Francois Chevalier, *Land and Society in Colonial Mexico: The Great Hacienda* (Berkeley: University of California Press, 1963), pp. 30–31, 75–77, 82, 89–91, 127, 130.

9. Lockhart, *The Men of Cajamarca*, pp. 135–157.

10. Ibid., pp. 4–16.

11. Ibid., pp. 190–201.

12. Stewart L. Mims, *Colbert's West India Policy* (New Haven: Yale University Press, 1912; reprinted, New York: Octagon Books, 1977), pp. 67–71.

13. Ibid.

14. Ibid., pp. 68–71, 75–81, 96–97, 142, 322ff.

15. Ibid., p. 82.

16. Andrew Trout, *Jean-Baptiste Colbert* (Boston: Twayne Publishers, 1978), p. 165.

17. Marcel Giraud, *A History of French Louisiana*, vol. I: *The Reign of Louis XIV, 1698–1715* (Baton Rouge: Louisiana State University Press, 1974), pp. 6–7; Trout, *Jean-Baptiste Colbert*, pp. 164–165.

18. Giraud, *The Reign of Louis XIV*, pp. 11–13.

19. John G. Clark, *New Orleans, 1718–1812; An Economic History* (Baton Rouge: Louisiana State University Press, 1970), pp. 1–45.

20. See Edward D. Neill, *History of the Virginia Company of London* (Albany, New York: n.p. 1869; reprinted, New York: Burt Franklin, 1968).

21. Samuel Eliot Morison, *Builders of the Bay Colony* (Boston: Houghton Mifflin, 1930), p. 28.

22. Bernard Bailyn, *The New England Merchants in the Seventeenth Century* (Cambridge Harvard University Press, 1955), p. 17.

23. Ibid., pp. 65–69.

24. David Duncan Wallace, *South Carolina: A Short History, 1520–1948* (Chapel Hill: University of North Carolina Press, 1951), pp. 1–36.

25. Ibid., p. 37.

26. Richard Splatt, Charles Towne, to William Crisp, London, January 17, 1726, South Caroliniana Library, University of South Carolina.

SUGGESTED READINGS

CHEVALIER, FRANCOIS. *Land and Society in Colonial Mexico: The Great Hacienda.* Berkeley: University of California Press, 1963.

CLARK, JOHN G. *New Orleans, 1718–1812: An Economic History.* Baton Rouge: Louisiana State University Press, 1970.

DUSENBERRY, WILLIAM H. *The Mexican Mesta.* Urbana: University of Illinois Press, 1963.

GIRAUD, MARCEL. *A History of French Louisiana.* Vol. I: *The Reign of Louis XIV, 1698–1715.* Baton Rouge: Louisiana State University Press, 1974.

LOCKHART, JAMES M. *The Men of Cajamarca: A Social and Biographical Study of the First Conquerors of Peru.* Austin: University of Texas Press, 1972.

MACLEOD, MURDO J. *Spanish Central America: A Socioeconomic History, 1520–1720.* Berkeley: University of California Press, 1973.

MIMS, STEWART L. *Colbert's West India Policy.* New Haven, Connecticut: Yale University Press, 1912; reprinted, New York: Octagon Books, 1977.

MORGAN, EDMUND S. *The Puritan Dilemma: The Story of John Winthrop.* Boston: Little, Brown, 1958.

MORISON, SAMUEL ELIOT. *Admiral of the Ocean Sea: A Life of Christopher Columbus.* Boston: Little, Brown, 1942.

———. *Builders of the Bay Colony.* Boston: Houghton Mifflin, 1930.

NEILL, EDWARD D. *History of the Virginia Company of London.* Albany, New York: n.p., 1869; reprinted, New York: Burt Franklin, 1968.

WALLACE, DAVID DUNCAN. *South Carolina: A Short History, 1520–1948.* Chapel Hill: University of North Carolina Press, 1951.

3 The Colonial Merchants

Colonial merchants became an indispensable link in the British trade system. An American merchant class developed almost of necessity, but certainly without the conscious planning or support of British mercantile interests. The proprietors considered lands and the fruits of colonial labor to be the collective properties of the company, and profits, should there be any, accrued to British investors. This state of affairs left little individual incentive among the colonists and precipitated considerable friction between them and the proprietors. It is very significant that in Massachusetts Bay the proprietors and the colonials became one and the same; that with the reorganization of the Company of Virginia, proprietary interests in land, and in the produce of the land, became available to the settlers; and that in South Carolina, and eventually in all of the colonies, the governments became largely subservient to local interests. Thus an American merchant class developed, reached a business accommodation with its British counterparts, provided the sinews for colonial economic growth and progress, and was instrumental in making the British system of mercantilism work.

The emerging independence of American business and proprietary interests can be attributed to many things. Physical and geographical factors contributed to the advent of political and economic freedom within the colonies. Close control of the internal affairs of the colonies from the board rooms of England was a physical impossibility. Moreover, the concepts of personal liberty and private property in America were logical extensions of British traditions and values. American colonists came to believe that liberty meant the right to acquire, manage, and dispose of property. In America, those values flourished because there were no social class restrictions and no institutions, either governmental or bureaucratic, to confine them. The "self-made man" evolved more readily in the New World than in the old. British political and religious developments concurrent with the era of colonization supported the idea of local autonomy and home rule in business, congregations, and government. More specifically, the English Revolution (1642–1649) halted the flow of colonists to America, disrupted commerce and provisioning, and if they had not already done so, forced the colonists to strike out on their own. Already predisposed to independence, the colonists preferred it that way.

FOUR PHASES OF EARLY COLONIAL BUSINESS

By the close of the first century of English colonization, the business relationships of the colonies to the mother country had gone through four general phases. In the first phase the joint-stock companies created colonies and trading posts in pursuit of quick profits for the investors. This phase usually led to an impasse between the home company and the colonists and ended with the bankruptcy or abdication of authority by the company. Reorganization of the colony under either royal or proprietary interests followed, but with a considerable degree of home rule and local autonomy.

The second phase, after the disruption of company authority, was generally a short-lived transition period that brought the colonists near economic anarchy. It was also characterized by the rise of colonial business opportunists. These included the independent fur traders, such as Roger Williams, who opened the first fur-trading post in the Narragansett region, lived as a free-spirit among the Indians, and generally defied the authority of church and state. The Arnold family of Pawtuxent pursued "free trade" to the extent of dealing in liquor and firearms with the Indians.[1] The era of economic anarchy in the Carolinas might be equated with the rise of such pirates as William Rhett, Steed Bonnett, and Richard Worley, who preyed upon legitimate commerce. By 1720 piracy had essentially been eliminated.[2] In all of the colonies another form of anarchy, never completely resolved, involved the acquisition of land without titles (squatting).

The third phase was characterized by the restoration of stability and order with authority vested largely in the colonial government. In this period a legitimate colonial merchant group developed from the ranks of farmers, laborers, and craftsmen, or often, as in Massachusetts and Pennsylvania, they were transplanted English merchants. Most of these, by British standards, would have been considered pretentious upstarts. The colonial merchant primarily engaged in the gathering of domestic products for export and in the import of British products for domestic distribution.

Major export items from the colonies included furs, timber, wood products (such as barrels, staves, hoops, and shingles), tobacco, bread, flour, rice, fish, and indigo. The last five items were the most valuable export commodities. Colonial imports, 90 percent of which came from England and Ireland, included manufactured goods (prominently iron products), textiles (largely woolens), coffee, tea, paper, sugar, molasses, wine, glass, and earthenware. In the earlier period of this third phase, the colonial merchants tended to serve as the supplier to the British merchant who possessed what the colonists lacked—capital, shipping, and established markets. The British merchant usually assumed ownership of the goods at the point of loading and unloading in the colonies and advanced the colonial merchant or factor the necessary credit for accumulating or distributing goods. With the passage of time a fourth stage of colonial business developed.

The fourth, or mature, phase witnessed the rise of the independent colonial merchant. As colonial merchants acquired capital, goods remained in their own account at the point of loading or unloading in England. Colonial merchants also organized trading consortiums or became partners with British merchants. Business relationships often extended across the Atlantic through family ties or religious affiliations. Quakers or Puritans in America tended to do business with their counterparts in England. A considerable secondary trade developed among the colonies and directly between the colonies, the West Indies, the "Wine Islands" near Spain, and southern Europe. Merchants widened their commercial contacts, including trade with French territories, and operated a sizable fleet of colonial vessels. They established some fairly sophisticated business structures including partnerships limited to a specific term of years (usually two to seven and joint ventures between partnerships, as well as letters of credit, accounting systems, agents, invoices, bills of lading, and other paraphernalia of commerce. Regional specialization and a more distinct division of labor developed. As the colonial economy matured the British mercantilist system tightened and became more constraining.[3]

British Mercantilism

Although the American merchants developed as remarkably free and independent agents, their liberty encountered two important constraints. The first was that created by dependence on British creditors. The second resulted from British laws affecting trade and commerce.

The legal foundation of the British mercantilist system rested on the Navigation Acts. A pilot act approved by Parliament in 1650 restricted all British trade to British ships. There were, however, not enough British ships to accommodate the trade, and the restrictions proved too onerous. Parliament had intended to eliminate Dutch trade with the English territories, but it virtually starved England in the process.

Subsequently, the Navigation Act of 1660 developed a more suitable formula. Foreign ships might trade with England, but only if they came directly from the country of origin. Only English-built ships could carry goods to or from the colonies and England. Thus, a Dutch ship could bring goods to England, but it could not accumulate a cargo of foreign goods and sell them on the English market, and it could not carry goods to or from the colonies. The act effectively rid the British of competition from the Dutch merchant marine and "closed" British markets to outsiders.

An amendment in 1661 added the "enumerated articles clause," which required that certain goods and commodities, including sugar, tobacco, indigo, and cotton, must be exported from the colonies only to England. Rice and molasses were added to the lists in 1704, naval stores in 1705, and later beaver skins and copper. This preserved the colonial raw materials exclusively for British interests and guaranteed the colonists a market for their products, albeit at a price sometimes lower than world prices.[4]

The Navigation Act of 1663 required that all European goods destined for the colonies, even on English-built ships, must transship through England, guaranteeing English, rather than colonial, merchants control over the colonial import business. An act of 1673 provided that all duties or taxes be levied at the port of clearance, rather than at the port of arrival, assuring that taxes were collected but also, more importantly, that goods were not off-loaded at foreign ports before entering British harbors.[5] The laws protected the integrity of the British trade monopoly with the colonies.

The Navigation Acts generally supported rather than hindered colonial business expansion. The acts gave the colonists favorable access to English markets, stimulated the rapid expansion of colonial maritime industry, contributed to an increase in the supply of English manufactured goods and services, established a supportive legal framework that eased credit for colonial trade, and provided colonial trade and commerce the protection of the Royal Navy.[6] The greatest impact of the Navigation Acts was to promote rapid expansion of colonial as well as the English shipbuilding business and the carrying trade. Indeed, that was their primary purpose.

John Winthrop launched the first colonial-made vessel, a fishing boat, in Massachusetts Bay in 1631. By 1776 the American maritime fleet was the third largest in the world. Although reliable data about American shipbuilding and shipping for the colonial period is limited, John Lord Sheffield's *Observation in the Commerce of the American States,* published in London in 1784, offers fascinating insights. Despite his repeated statements about the inferiority of American-made ships, Sheffield acknowledges that the American colonies were "rapidly robbing us of the ship-building business."[7] His tabulation of the number and tonnage of vessels built in the provinces in 1769 indicates that in one year American shipyards launched 274 sloops and schooners and 113 ships rigged with topsails comprising about 30,000 registered tons (or 25,000 real tons). Massachusetts launched the largest number of ships with 40 topsails and 97 sloops and schooners. New Hampshire produced the second highest tonnage at 2,452 tons, and Rhode Island, Connecticut, Pennsylvania, Maryland, and Virginia each launched between 1,200 and 1,500 tons. Presumably, all of the square-rigged ships with topsails were intended for transoceanic trade while most of the sloops and schooners would be engaged in coastal and West Indian trade. All but

1,369 tons of vessels built in British provinces in 1769 were built in the colonies that became the United States. The data very clearly disturbed Sheffield, for he argued that if American shipbuilding received any encouragement of support from the British after the revolution, "it will be ruinous to the country."[8]

Throughout his study Sheffield made repeated references to the importance of British credit to colonial merchants. In this he was absolutely correct. It is likely that had there been no Navigation Acts, the necessities of British credit, markets, and manufactured goods would have tied the commerce of the colonies inextricably to England. While the acts tightened their relationship, they did not entirely preclude trade between the colonies and foreign nations. Indeed, in an act of 1731, Parliament specifically sanctioned the direct sale of rice to southern Europe.[9] England could never halt the illicit trade in furs, molasses, and other commodities, and adopted a policy of "salutary neglect" or looking the other way. Essentially, the realities of trade and commerce were in harmony with the law, at least until 1763.

The general framework of the British mercantile system, which basically sought to utilize the colonies as a source of raw materials and a market for English manufactured goods, was supplemented by the passage of trade regulations designed to solve particular problems. The Wool Act (1699) forbade the export of raw wool or finished woolen goods from the colonies to England or to another colony, thereby protecting the English sheep-raising and woolen-textile industries from colonial competitors, who would have been poor competition anyway. The Hat Act (1732) banned the sale of hats by any colony to England or to another colony. The colonies provided the pelts, the English manufacturers the hats. The Molasses Act (1733) attempted, without great success, to halt the import of French molasses from the West Indies to the American colonies. The Iron Act (1750) banned the manufacture of finished iron products in America, which it was ill-equipped to do, but stimulated the production of raw iron, which the colonies could do more efficiently.

Generally, British trade regulations stimulated rather than stifled colonial economic development and business expansion. The British mercantile system did not interfere with the development of an independent merchant class. American merchants began as the agents of the English merchants. As they obtained capital, experience, and expertise, the colonial merchants became increasingly independent from, and at times coequals with, their British firms. Population growth alone encouraged the expansion of colonial businesses. Although the traffic volume is unrecorded, a lively exchange of goods and services among the colonists stirred the internal expansion of businesses, crafts, shipping, and domestic manufactures. By the time of the American Revolution the colonies had developed a high degree of regional specialization, with each region being interdependent upon the other, and all dependent upon England. The northern colonies specialized in commerce and shipping, shipbuilding and fishing. The southern colonies focused on tobacco, naval stores, rice, and indigo.

THE CITY AND RISING COMMERCE

The three major trade and population centers in the northern colonies were New York, Boston, and Philadelphia. These cities in the wilderness became the commercial depots for interregional and transatlantic trade. As a general rule each began as a collection point for the accumulation and transshipment of goods from their hinterlands. Furs, fish, and timber constituted their staple products. When local resources diminished, suppliers easily widened their spheres of operation by ranging up and down the Atlantic seacoast and into the navigable rivers from Canada to the Caribbean. By the eighteenth century the northern colonists largely exported goods gathered elsewhere. Flour, ships, and whale oil replaced furs, fish, and timber as major locally produced items. The importation and redistribution business rivaled the export business by mid-century as populations throughout the colonies expanded.

NEW YORK

Strategically situated with an excellent natural harbor and easy access to the interior by inland river, New York competed fiercely with Boston and Philadelphia for foreign and domestic trade. The Dutch had founded New Amsterdam on the Isle of Manhattan in 1626, but the British captured the city in 1664 and renamed it New York. By 1700 New York had a population of 7,000 and was the busiest port in North America.

The city established a virtual monopoly on flour milling and shipping by refusing to handle milled or packed flour from the interior. The New York Assembly broke the monopoly in 1700 by approving legislation allowing any person in the colony to mill, bake, or pack flour and wheat products. Boston, too, retaliated against New York by refusing to buy New York flour, and it established its own flour mills. Competitive Boston and Philadelphia merchants undercut the initial advantages New York enjoyed in foreign trade.[10] Although New York maintained a dominant position in the flour and grain export business, the westward shift of population tended to favor Philadelphia, and to a lesser extent Boston, over New York. New York failed to overcome this disability until the opening of the Erie Canal in 1825.

REVERE COPPER

Paul Revere was an artist, craftsman, innovator, and businessman of the first order. Already a master silversmith, Revere became a goldsmith and, in 1788, opened a hardware store importing English trade goods. He decided to begin manufacturing goods, not merely to retail them, and established a furnace and foundry for manufacturing iron and brass products—pots, pans, cannon, and church bells. In 1795 he began making copper and brass fittings

Paul Revere (1735–1818). Silversmith, foundry owner, and revolutionist. (Courtesy: *Dictionary of American Portraits*.)

for ships, and in 1800 at the age of sixty-five he established a rolling mill for sheet copper. "I have engaged," he said, "to build me a Mill for Rolling Copper into sheets which for me is a great undertaking, and will require every farthing which I can rake or scrape." He invested twenty-five thousand of his own money, and borrowed ten thousand dollars and nineteen thousand pounds of copper from the United States government. If he failed, he would be ruined. But in 1803 the USS *Constitution* sailed with a Revere-clad copper hull; Revere Copper prospered.

Paul Revere's son, Joseph Warren Revere, ran the business until his death in 1868. The business passed through several generations under the name Paul Revere and Son, which in 1900 merged with the Taunton Copper Manufacturing Company and the New Bedford Copper Company. In 1927 E.H.R. Revere became president of the company, known as the Taunton New Bedford Copper Company.

In 1928 this company merged with five others: Baltimore Copper Mills, Rome Brass and Copper Company, Michigan Copper and Brass Company, Higgins Brass and Manufacturing Company, and Dallas Brass and Copper Company. The name of this new organization was changed to Revere Copper and Brass, Inc. Over the years the company produced copper and metal alloys for ammunition, tanks, armored cars, trucks, airplanes, kitchens, radios, television sets and appliances, computers, telephones, plumbing, insulation, electrical systems, washing machines, and the traditional pots and pans.

Revere Copper provides an interesting study in the longevity of the American business firm. Survival in Paul Revere's time and in modern times depends upon continuing innovation and adaptation by the firm and its managers.

Source: Esther Forbes, *Paul Revere and the World He Lived In* (Boston: Houghton Mifflin, 1942; Sentry Edition, 1969), pp. 377–397, 424, and note 50 on p. 481.

BOSTON

Boston business in the colonial era primarily involved foreign trade. Those who entered the business required capital, connections, and an enterprising spirit. Roger Williams, the son of a London shopkeeper, sought refuge among the Indians of the Narragansett region because of his position on separation of church and state and as a trader of furs. Thomas Hancock, to whom we will return shortly, epitomized the successful Boston merchant, with his trials and tribulations characteristic of those other colonial merchants engaged in foreign trade. Paul Revere, artisan and inventor, founded an industry that still survives today. But perhaps one of the earliest and most interesting of the Boston businessmen was John Winthrop, Jr., who attempted to establish America's first iron works.

Winthrop traveled to England in 1641 with samples of ore from the colony and succeeded in convincing a group of investors headed by Lionel Copley, a leading English iron manufacturer, and John Bex, a London merchant who owned blast furnaces and forges in Gloucestershire, to underwrite his venture, The Company of Undertakers for the Iron Works in New England. Winthrop also negotiated with the Massachusetts General Court for a charter of incorporation to include the grant of a 3,000-acre tract of land to the company, a twenty-one-year monopoly of iron manufacture, a proviso that the company build a forge for the manufacture of finished products (not simply a "bloomery only" for the production of raw iron), exemptions from taxation, and the right to use private property with suitable compensation to the owners. Winthrop immediately found it difficult to reconcile the interests of the colonial leaders with those of the investors. The colonists wanted production for home consumption, and they required the inclusion of a clause in the charter allowing participation by colonial investors—which proved to be extremely meager.[11] As Bernard Bailyn observed:

> The heart of the matter was that ownership of the works was in the hands of absentee businessmen who could judge the wisdom of their investments by the profits they earned and not by contributions they made to the welfare of the community.[12]

This intrinsic conflict between colonial and British interests was eventually met by the appointment of a resident plant manager and business manager, an accommodation that would hopefully prove beneficial to both. In the case of the Massachusetts Iron Works it did not.

Production began in a furnace constructed at Hammersmith that in 1648 produced a ton of raw iron a day. As business expanded, costs and losses seemed to rise more than proportionately. Timber for fuel was plentiful, but labor for harvesting it was not: Skilled workers were unavailable in the colonies and almost impossible to lure from England. Machinery and tools had to be imported from England at high costs; local merchants charged the company exorbitant prices for supplies. Production, which the

Reconstruction of the Saugus Iron Works in Massachusetts. (Courtesy: United States Department of the Interior, National Park Service.)

magistrates specified should first satisfy local demands before exports were allowed, could be paid for by the colonists only in commodities. Despite inventories in 1650 of 106 tons of pig and scrap iron and 7.5 tons of cast-iron pots, the total assets of the company equaled only £4,302. The investors first fired John Winthrop, Jr., and replaced him with Richard Leader, then fired Leader in 1650 and replaced him with a business manager and a plant manager. Then the merchants refused to accept drafts on their London accounts, and by 1652 the company was bankrupt.[13]

A Boston merchant, William Paine, eventually obtained control of the company and achieved a rather impressive production record between 1658 and 1663, but gradually the enterprise sank into debt. Home rule had not solved the problem; perhaps Paine's more limited financial status had aggravated it. American merchants simply could not meet the capital requirements of large-scale manufacturing enterprises. Paine's creditors foreclosed in 1676, and thus ended the Iron Works of New England.[14]

Lord Sheffield may well have identified the chronic problem in early American manufacturing enterprises—"whatever they make is at an expense of at least three times the amount of what the same article could be imported from Europe."[15] The scarcity of capital, shortages of skilled and unskilled labor, and distances to markets meant that the primary occupation of the colonies would be in the exploitation of the abundant natural resources and the transfer of raw materials to European markets. The "natural laws of supply and demand" shaped the British mercantile system more than legislation. The rapid growth of the colonial population and of a domestic market alleviated but did not offset (until well into the national period) American manufacturing and trade disadvantages.

Boston merchants achieved some success in developing home spinning and weaving industries that became the basis of the later textile industry, and their flour and grain shipments sometimes competed favorably with New York. Boston came to excel in the fishing industry and in the carrying trade, and in providing the ships for those enterprises. Most ship tonnage built in America before the Revolution came from Massachusetts. The shipbuilding, fishing, distillery, and flour-mill industries that developed in Boston were ancillary to the necessities of foreign trade.

The colonial merchant was less a specialist and more a jack-of-all-trades who often invested in shipbuilding, flour milling, rum manufacture, fishing and fur expeditions, and real estate, and who also made loans. The merchants' expertise lay in management rather than in money and shrewd bargaining, for they were terribly dependent upon others for the successful conclusion of a venture. They took a calculated risk on people, the weather, and the market. The experiences of Thomas Hancock illustrate the vagaries and diversities of foreign trade.

Hancock began his import-export business by obtaining a consignment of books from an agent in England. Their sale in the colonies netted him enough to pay his indebtedness and pocket a profit. By the 1740s Hancock concentrated on trade with the West Indies and Holland. He sent fish to the West Indies, bought molasses there for shipment back to Boston, and shipped logs, indigo, rice, or anything of value to Holland in exchange for cash, credit, and cargoes of paper or any consumer goods, most of which were contraband, since direct shipments between European ports and the colonies were forbidden by the Navigation Acts. Most interestingly, Hancock rarely specified what his cargoes should comprise but entrusted this vital decision to his principal agent, the ship captain, or occasionally to his "supercargo," usually a young apprentice who accompanied the cargo to its market. Hancock himself, and merchants like him, stayed home.[16]

Hancock's instructions to Captain Simon Gross in December, 1743, granted the captain one-eighth interest in the proceeds of the out-cargo, and one-eighth of the return cargo. Gross received full power-of-attorney, or "liberty," to dispose of the cargo in any way he saw fit and to go wherever he desired, including the French Islands "if he thought it safe." But he should proceed first to St. Eustatius and get the advice of "Mr. Godet," who could best advise him on market possibilities and return cargoes. If Captain Gross could sell the entire cargo and the vessel at "a good price," he was free to do so, or he could take on a cargo directly for Holland or England and sell the cargo and/or the ship there; but Hancock presumed that a load of molasses from the West Indies would be the most likely return cargo.[17] Trade in the colonial era was as uncertain as Noah's sending out a dove to search for land.

Nevertheless, there was a system and a structure for trade—and it worked. The merchant traded on his own account, and as a commission agent he obtained or disposed of goods belonging to others for a fee or percentage. He might also serve simply as a consultant or confidant for a foreign merchant in return for a fee or for similar services. If he had a partnership with a London or West Indies merchant, as many did, the American merchant might consign the goods to a vessel for receipt by the partner. He might also consign goods to the ship captain for receipt by a commission agent. The merchants of Philadelphia utilized essentially the same trade patterns and structure and handled the same commodities as the Boston merchants.

THE HOUSE OF HANCOCK

Thomas Hancock, destined to become one of New England's greatest mercantile businessmen, opened a bookshop on North Street in Boston about 1725. He rapidly diversified into other lines, including cloth, tea, paper, and cutlery; and by the 1740s moved heavily into the export of whalebone, fins, and oils, which remained the Hancocks' primary business until almost 1770. Thomas died in 1764, leaving an estate estimated to be in excess of $100,000 and a thriving import-export business to the direction of his adopted nephew, John Hancock, who had served as Thomas's partner during the previous ten years.

John assumed direction of the business at a perilous time in colonial affairs. The recent French and Indian Wars had disrupted normal commerce while creating opportunities for both large profits and disastrous losses. Postwar relations with England brought new disruptions, higher taxes, and commercial instability.

John Hancock continued Thomas's oil business, which involved an association with the Nantucket firm of Folger Company, the supplier, and a London firm, Barnard and Harrison, which marketed the oil and bone and shipped Hancock his orders for merchandise. By this time the profitable whale-oil business was controlled by relatively few colonial firms, prominently Hancock and William Rotch & Company, who competed bitterly. Hancock became dissatisfied with the quantity and quality of oil obtained from Folger and began building and buying interests in his own whaling ships to assure supplies. In 1766, with the financial support of his London associates, John Hancock entered the Nantucket market with the intent of securing control of all of the available oil while ousting Rotch from the competition. Hancock paid top prices for oil and bone, expecting rising prices in London, and an effectual monopoly on the market. Rotch and all comers were outbid by Hancock, who invested some $25,000 in oil in 1766, only to discover that by the time his oil reached British markets prices had begun to slide as Dutch, English, and German oil began to reach the market. Hancock had, in fact, obtained control of the colonial oil supply, but this was not enough to establish the international oil cartel which apparently he and his associates envisioned. His losses are estimated at $3,600 from the oil venture, and thereafter Hancock's exports of whale oil declined sharply each year.

Hancock's relations with his London contacts similarly became strained, and Hancock shifted associates in the following years, never entirely alienating Barnard and Harrison. In the colonies, Hancock's relations with British officials, once cordial, became considerably less so, as Hancock first vigorously opposed the Stamp Act, then entered politics, threw British inspectors off of his ship, the *Lydia,* only to have another, the *Liberty,* seized by British authorities. Although John maintained intermittent commercial relations with London, his business, and his interest in it, declined. When the Revolution began, John Hancock had a small credit with his London associates and considerable esteem among the British merchants, but he had, in effect, closed the House of Hancock to become a patriot, president of the Second Continental Congress, and literally the boldest signer of the American Declaration of Independence.

Source: W. T. Baxter, *The House of Hancock: Business in Boston, 1724–1775* (New York: Russell & Russell, 1965).

PHILADELPHIA

Pennsylvania produced few products for the British market; goods needed to exchange for manufactured items in England came from elsewhere. Grain came from New York and Maryland; rice and indigo from the Carolinas; sugar, wine, molasses, and dyes from the West Indies. Grain, flour, bread, pork, beef, barrel staves, hoops, and shingles, as well as British manufactured goods, left Pennsylvania aboard a colonial vessel for the southern colonies and West Indies. The ship sold or exchanged those items along the way for new cargo until the ship was loaded for a voyage to England or back home, whichever might be appropriate. The domestic trade resembled more a rolling store, or a peddling-and-barter operation. It was necessarily an uncertain and risky, but usually lucrative, business.

Real estate, manufacturing, and mining offered diverse investment opportunities for the Quaker merchant. In the 1720s the Free Society of Traders, a British-owned joint-stock venture, invested £10,000 in a diversified manufacturing venture near Philadelphia. Obtaining a 20,000-acre grant from the Penn family, the company recruited settlers and erected a tannery, sawmill, gristmill, glass factory, and brick kiln and sent out whaling vessels. But its underfinanced efforts were short-lived. The direction of the company's affairs from abroad proved to be a liability as with the Massachusetts iron venture. Some colonial proprietors succeeded in their manufacturing ventures, as did Samuel Carpenter, who with three partners built the first colonial paper mill in 1690. Carpenter also built and operated sawmills and gristmills. Sybilla Masters, a most innovative woman merchant of Philadelphia, developed and patented a process for cleaning and curing Indian corn. She also perfected a technique for weaving hats from palmetto leaves and manufactured a hominy called Tuscarora rice, which she marketed as a cure for consumption.[18]

Benjamin Franklin, a Philadelphia businessman before venturing into science, politics, and diplomacy, established *The Pennsylvania Gazette* in 1729, and, as he later wrote, "It proved in a few years extremely profitable to me."[19] Franklin secured the public printing contracts for Pennsylvania, including the printing of paper currency, "a very profitable job."[20] He opened a stationer's shop, became a bookseller, publisher, and the largest dealer in paper in the colonies.[21] "Poor Richard's" philosophy was simple: work, save, grow wealthy. While the merchants of New York, Boston, and Philadelphia prospered, the merchant-planters of the southern colonies often did even better.

THE SOUTH AND THE TOBACCO TRADE

Tobacco produced more revenues for the colonies than any other single commodity. Exports most often went directly from the plantation to London markets, and in the earlier years the planter usually consigned tobacco directly to a British merchant who served as the planter's agent or factor. The factor credited the planter's account for the sale and charged that account for goods purchased in England, always adding a commission and charges for cash advanced. Later the consignment system gave way to the sale of tobacco directly to resident English or Scottish mercantile houses or their agents located in Virginia, Maryland, and the Carolinas.

The larger tobacco planters often functioned as planter-merchants rather than simply as growers of tobacco. Planter-merchants such as William Boyd and William Fitzhugh served as agents for smaller farmers, directly purchasing tobacco from them or accepting their shipments on consignment as agents. They loaned money, imported goods, and maintained stores for the sale of goods and supplies. Some operated coastal vessels for trading. William Byrd and others owned iron mines. Some imported slaves for their own use and for sale, and many, such as George Washington, dealt in land.[22]

Other than Baltimore, the upper-south colonies developed no trading and commercial cities. They remained distinctly planter-farmer, rural, frontier regions, directly dependent upon the merchants, markets, and bankers of England. New England merchants and shippers made little serious inroad into British domination of the tobacco trade. The vagaries of tobacco prices and the high costs of shipments and credit resulted in the planter-merchant of the tobacco regions being often indebted to the British merchant. Incongruously perhaps, the planter-merchants of Virginia developed a greater sense of independence. They were essentially alone in their enterprise, having few direct business associations and relatively few social contacts or an urban focus. They developed the characteristics of the English country squire. The lower-south colonies developed along similar lines, but they differed significantly in that Charleston, South Carolina, became the hub for commercial activities and that colonial, rather than British, merchants handled overseas trade.

Once the home of a successful silversmith in eighteenth-century Williamsburg, the James Geddy House has been restored and opened to the public. The Geddy House is furnished to reflect the period when Geddy lived here and had his shop in an adjoining wing. Costumed silversmiths work in the shop, using methods and tools of Geddy's day to turn out examples of silver popular in the 1770s. (Courtesy: Colonial Williamsburg, Williamsburg, Virginia.)

CHARLESTON AND THE RICE TRADE

Henry Laurens, an independent businessman of Charleston, owned plantations in South Carolina and Georgia, but his major occupation was that of a factor or business agent for other Carolina and Georgia rice planters. A partner in a firm with George Austin, Laurens ordinarily earned a 10 percent commission from the planters for handling rice or for marketing indigo, and a similar commission as the agent of English mercantile houses from whom he received shipments of finished goods on consignment. Occasionally Austin and Laurens made direct purchases of goods in England on their own accounts, but they rarely made purchases of rice from the colonial planters. The factor ordinarily functioned solely as the agent or broker for a number of planters. This basic system of trade appears to have changed very little from the early 1700s until the Civil War. Generally, South Carolina exported rice, indigo, hides, lumber, and naval stores(and cotton after 1800); it imported iron products, textiles, earthenware, furniture, consumer articles, and slaves. Charleston merchants provided exchange services as did their New England counterparts, but, unlike northern merchants, they obtained export goods from the local region rather than ship-shopping the Atlantic seaboard and Caribbean.

Laurens visited England in 1749, the year in which he and Austin established their import-export firm, and opened accounts with London, Bristol, and Liverpool merchants. He offered to serve his correspondents as their commission agent in Charleston. He described the particular trade articles that "usually turn to advantage" as being nails, linen and cotton checks, Irish linens, sail cloth, assorted earthenware, lump and double-refined sugar, wines from Madeira, pipes, quality rum, and slaves. He obtained a standing order to ship rice directly to Lisbon on the account of Seel and Knight of Liverpool, letters of credit or security bond from James Crockatt, a London merchant, and tentative arrangements to act as the agent for several English firms shipping slaves to Charleston.[23]

The Ball family of South Carolina functioned as planter-merchants for more than a century. In 1698, Elias Ball inherited several plantations from his father's half-brother, Captain John Coming, including Commingtree Plantation, St. John's Parish, and Berkeley. Additions to the family estates included Kensington, Limerick, Midway, Hyde Park, and St. James plantations. During the Revolutionary era, a son, Elias Ball, and grandson, John Ball, born in 1760, operated the plantations and conducted their business through a family member, Elias Ball of Bristol, Connecticut. The Connecticut firm maintained the Carolina business records, received rice and lumber from the plantations, and arranged for marketing and shipping. The Carolina Balls sometimes shipped directly to England, as agents for Elias Ball of Connecticut, and sales were credited to the Bristol firm.[24] English goods seem to have been most often shipped directly to Connecticut and then transshipped to the Carolinas. There is some evidence of increasing business connections between northern and New England colonial merchants and Charleston merchants toward the later eighteenth century.

For example, Thomas Morris, a commission merchant of Charleston, served as agent for Alexander and Nesbitt, a Philadelphia firm, and had correspondence with Nicholas Law of New York. Morris handled shipments of rice, indigo, and beaver and otter pelts. A letter from Morris to Philadelphia in 1783 indicates that the Revolutionary War considerably disrupted the export business. Planters, he said, no longer made direct shipments to Europe on their own account, and they asked cash payments for their crops at the wharf. Captains "loaded in their own account," which meant that the exporter immediately had to assume ownership of the cargo and liability for it—and needed specie or currency, both of which were undoubtedly scarce.[25] The war halted vital British credit, cut the lines of transatlantic trade, and hastened the shift of the burden and profits of foreign trade from British to American merchants.

By the early nineteenth century the Carolinian merchant, more so than the Virginian, appears to have developed as an entity separate from that of the planter. The planter produced the crop—rice, indigo, or cotton—and the merchant marketed the crop, made the planter's purchases, supervised the import-export function, and served the planter as accountant and banker. As William Johnston advised his Charleston factor, his business was to "make a crop, *you* must sell that which is made."[26]

One of the most interesting entrepreneurs in the Carolina rice industry neither grew nor marketed rice, but instead perfected and sold rice mills. Jonathan Lucas was the Eli Whitney of the rice industry—and financially more successful than Whitney. Existing milling processes included hand milling with mortar and pestle, a pendulum device for husking rice developed by Peter Jacob Geuraud who received a patent from the South Carolina Assembly in 1698, and a cog mill, none capable of producing more than 3 to 6 barrels per day. In 1789 Lucas built his first mill for a planter named Bowman who owned Peach Island Plantation on the Santee River. He combined the beating and cleaning processes into an integrated system using cogwheels, pulleys, conveyors, mortars and pestles, and cleaning screens and fans, powered by huge water wheels. A crew of three could mill 100 barrels of rice (600 pounds per barrel) in a day. The Lucas mill revolutionized the industry.[27]

Lucas built mills for Thomas Pinckney, Henry Laurens, William Horry, and William Alston, among others, and in 1792 completed the first mill in London and Liverpool in 1822, some of those mills being shipped as far as Egypt. He died shortly after moving to London, but his son and grandsons continued to build most of the rice mills in South Carolina and Georgia.[28]

COLONIAL BUSINESS DEVELOPMENT

There is, as was noted earlier, an identifiable pattern to colonial business development. Colonial enterprises began simply as extensions of British company efforts to make a profit overseas. A conflict of interests quickly developed between the colonizers and the company. The conflict contributed to the bankruptcy of the company, a breakdown in English authority over the colonists, and a short-lived era of near anarchy in the colonies that brought to prominence the freelance fur trader, the pirate, and the land grabber. The restoration of order and stability was achieved by a virtual transfer of authority from England to colonial governments, and from the British company to the colonial business agent who increasingly functioned as a free agent, but one nonetheless subservient to British business interests.

British laws, such as the Navigation Acts, and traditions affecting property rights and commerce, supported the development of the colonial business person as a free and independent agent. Moreover, geography, time, and circumstance almost required that an American doing business with England have very wide discretionary powers, or as Thomas Hancock termed it, "liberty." Colonial population growth and the development of domestic markets also encouraged the emergence of the colonial merchant as an autonomous and independent agent. The increased accumulation of capital by merchants broadened their discretionary powers. In effect, merchants began to ship American goods in *American* ships, rather than English goods from America in English ships. As this occurred, greater profits accrued to American, as opposed to British, business interests. This development, however, did not necessarily mean conflict or competition between British and American business interests. It does suggest the establishment of a new relationship between the two. The British and American merchants became partners in a flourishing transatlantic trade wherein the merchants of the mother country remained the senior partners because of their greater capital, markets, and political power. But the point is that the British mercantile system actually worked better because of the increasing independence and proprietary interests of the colonial merchant in that system.

The colonial merchant and colonial enterprise also developed regional characteristics. The northern colonies specialized in the gathering and distribution of goods throughout America and in the West Indies. Their specialty was trade, supplemented by shipbuilding, fishing, and limited manufacturing. Virginia and Maryland produced tobacco, supplemented by grain, furs, and timber. The planter-merchant of the tobacco regions maintained direct relations with British firms or, later, British agents in America. Trading centers and the independent merchant did not develop in this region as they did to the north and south. In the Carolinas business structures paralleled those of the northern colonies except that the domestic trade zone of the Charleston merchant was confined to a much smaller geographical region. Although smaller in physical size, the production of rice, indigo, naval stores, and furs made this one of the wealthiest colonial areas.

As a general rule, by the time of the American Revolution the colonial merchant became the vital New World link in a thriving transoceanic trade. A fairly complex system of agencies, partnerships, correspondents, creditors, and instruments of trade supported the framework of commerce, and the American merchant marine became an international economic force. The unusually rapid expansion of American business threatened the authority and "liberty" of the English merchant.

NOTES

1. Bernard Bailyn, *The New England Merchants in the Seventeenth Century* (Cambridge: Harvard University Press, 1955), pp. 58–59.

2. John Drayton, *A View of South Carolina* (Charleston: W.P. Young, 1802), pp. 113–117.

3. See Gary M. Walton and James F. Shepherd, *The Economic Rise of Early America* (Cambridge, England: Cambridge University Press, 1979), pp. 5–88; and Bailyn, *The New England Merchants*, pp. 33–35, 78–143.

4. See Lawrence A. Harper, *The English Navigation Laws: A Seventeenth-Century Experiment in Social Engineering* (New York: Columbia University Press, 1939); and Oliver M. Dickerson, *The Navigation Acts and the American Revolution* (Philadelphia: University of Pennsylvania, 1951; reprinted, New York: A.S. Barnes, 1963).

5. Ibid.; and Thomas C. Barrow, *Trade and Empire: The British Customs Service in Colonial America, 1660–1775* (Cambridge: Harvard University Press, 1967).

6. William Appleman Williams, *The Contours of American History* (Cleveland: World Publishing Company, 1961; reprinted, Chicago: Quadrangle Books, 1966), p. 66.

7. John Lord Sheffield, *Observations on the Commerce of the American States* (London: J. Debrett, 1784; reprinted, New York: Augustus M. Kelley, 1970), p. 87.

8. Ibid., p. 86.

9. *Acts of Parliament: Anno Tertio Georgii II, Regis*, pp. 559–64 (1731).

10. See Curtis Nettels, "The Economic Relations of Boston, Philadelphia and New York, 1680–1715," *Journal of Economic and Business History* 3 (February 1931), pp. 185–215, reprinted in Ross M. Robertson and James L. Pate, eds., *Readings in United States Economic and Business History* (Boston: Houghton Mifflin, 1966), pp. 140–149.

11. Bailyn, *The New England Merchants*, pp. 62–63.

12. Ibid., p. 64.

13. Ibid., pp. 64–70.

14. Ibid., pp. 70–71.

15. Sheffield, *Observations*, p. 14.

16. See Edward Edelman, "Thomas Hancock, Colonial Merchant," *Journal of Economic and Business History* 1 (1928–29), pp. 77–104, reprinted in Robertson and Pate, *Readings in United States Economic and Business History*, pp. 149–159; and Stuart W. Bruchey, *The Colonial Merchant: Sources and Readings* (New York: Harcourt, Brace & World, 1966), pp. 169–173.

17. Bruchey, *The Colonial Merchant*, p. 179.

18. Frederick B. Tolles, *Meeting House and Counting House: The Quaker Merchants of Colonial Philadelphia, 1682–1763* (Chapel Hill: University of North Carolina Press, 1948; reprinted, New York: W.W. Norton & Co., 1963), pp. 48–98.

19. Verner W. Crane, *Benjamin Franklin and a Rising People* (Boston: Little, Brown, 1954), p. 23.

20. Ibid., p. 26.

21. Ibid., pp. 28–29.

22. Bruchey, *The Colonial Merchant*, pp. 119–145.

23. See Ball Family Papers, South Caroliniana Library (Columbia, South Carolina: University of South Carolina).

24. Ibid.

25. See Thomas Morris Papers, and Morris to Alexander Nesbitt, August 24, 1783, South Caroliniana Library.

26. William Johnston, Mill Brook, to William Allan, Portmanteau, March 31, 1818, South Caroliniana Library.

27. See Lucas Family Papers, South Carolina Historical Society, Charleston, South Carolina.

28. Ibid.

SUGGESTED READINGS

BAILYN, BERNARD. *The New England Merchant in the Seventeenth Century.* Cambridge: Harvard University Press, 1955.

BARROW, THOMAS C. *Trade and Empire: The British Customs Service in Colonial America, 1600–1776.* Cambridge: Harvard University Press, 1967.

BOORSTIN, DANIEL J. *The Americans: The Colonial Experience.* New York: Random House, 1958.

BRUCHEY, STUART W., ED. *The Colonial Merchant: Sources and Readings.* New York: Harcourt, Brace & World, 1966.

DETHLOFF, HENRY C. *A History of the American Rice Industry, 1685–1985.* College Station: Texas A&M University Press, 1988.

DICKERSON, OLIVER M. *The Navigation Acts and the American Revolution.* Philadelphia: University of Pennsylvania, 1951; reprinted, New York: A. S. Barnes, 1963.

DOERGLINGER, THOMAS M. *A Vigorous Spirit of Enterprise: Merchants and Economic Development in Revolutionary Philadelphia,* Chapel Hill: University of North Carolina Press, 1986.

NORTH, DOUGLASS C. *Growth & Welfare in the American Past.* Second edition. Englewood Cliffs, New Jersey: Prentice Hall, 1974.

SCHLESINGER, ARTHUR MEIER. *The Colonial Merchants and the American Revolution, 1763–1776.* Reprinted, New York: Frederick Ungar, 1957.

SHEFFIELD, JOHN LORD. *Observations on the Commerce of the American States.* London: S. Debrett, 1784; reprinted, New York: Augustus M. Kelley, 1970.

TOLLES, FREDERICK B. *Meeting House and Counting House: The Quaker Merchants of Colonial Philadelphia, 1682–1763.* Chapel Hill: University of North Carolina Press, 1948; reprinted, New York: W. W. Norton & Co., 1963.

VER STEEG, CLARENCE. *The Formative Years, 1607–1763.* New York: Hill and Wang, 1964.

4 Early American Manufacture

Before the American Revolution, British policy as well as American preferences caused the workshops to remain in Europe while the colonists engaged chiefly in agriculture and commerce. The Revolution, however, drastically altered the realities of international trade. American foreign commerce suffered from the dissolution of ties with British firms, from the destruction of traditional lines of credit, and from the competition and sometimes harassment by the businesses and governments of these nations. Moreover, the Revolution stimulated the expansion of household manufacturing. The American Constitution, the policies of Alexander Hamilton, and most especially the Napoleonic Wars and the development of an interdependent relationship between the cotton and iron industries, contributed to the inception of what would become the industrial revolution in the United States and the origin of a distinctive "American system of manufacturing." Manufacturing replaced foreign trade as America's major business enterprise in the first half of the nineteenth century, adding a bold new dimension to the economic order and altering popular attitudes toward business enterprise.

ON GOVERNMENT AND MANUFACTURING

The Revolution resulted in the growth of household industries such as weaving, candle and soap making, tanning, and leather crafts, and it promoted expanding iron-, copper-, and tin-fabrication industries. Shipbuilding and agricultural markets, adversely affected by the Revolution, recovered rapidly after the war only to encounter new and greater difficulties during the Napoleonic Wars. On the positive side, the Revolution removed some of the artificial obstacles to economic expansion, specifically the onerous British regulations and taxes. On the negative side, it cost the colonists money, lives, commercial alliances, banking and credit associations, and the protection of British law and naval power. The organization of government, first under the Articles of Confederation and then under the Constitution, substituted American law for British law, but it could not substitute for British power, which had for so long protected American foreign trade.

The Constitution did create a more favorable domestic climate for business enterprise as well as for agriculture. The new government now possessed title to the western lands previously held under British authority. The government created an embryonic national economic order that established the world's largest geographic free-trade zone wherein goods, services, and people could move without restraint under the "equal protection of the law." The Constitution afforded greater protection to rights in property than had existed under the Articles of Confederation, and perhaps greater even than under the authority of British law, which tended to support British rather than colonial property rights. The development and expansion of the national judiciary, the strengthening of the federal monetary system, the adoption of standard weights and measures, and the creation of the national postal system facilitated business expansion.

Alexander Hamilton clearly regarded the Constitution as a tool for the stimulation and direction of economic enterprise and for the encouragement of manufacturing. Hamilton, in his 1791 *Report on Manufacturing,* attacked the conventional wisdom which held that economic development

Alexander Hamilton (1755–1804). Lawyer, politician, secretary of the treasury, and Federalist. (Courtesy: *Dictionary of American Portraits.*)

was best left to "natural forces" and that the scarcity of labor in the United States precluded manufacturing.[1] He admitted the preeminence of agriculture but argued that it should not be given "exclusive predilection." Industrial workers, because of the division of labor and the application of machinery to multiply the products of labor, could provide goods for themselves and for farmers at a lower cost than the agriculturists could provide. Laborers not only produced goods for farmers and for themselves, but they also created a profit for their employers. Moreover, he said, domestic manufacturing consistently resulted in lower prices for goods.[2]

Manufacturing opened employment opportunities to those not ordinarily engaged in the existing pursuits of labor. Hamilton believed that women and children provided an underutilized and enormous labor pool for manufacturing, and that the growth of manufacturing would not create labor shortages or retard the settlement of new lands. In addition, manufacturing offered opportunity for occasional employment for those presently engaged in seasonal work and provided greater opportunities for the diverse talents of humankind. Besides, he noted, "we have a genius for mechanic improvements." The opportunities afforded by manufacturing, he believed, would promote immigration (why would skilled workers come from England when there was no use for their skills in America?) and a spirit of enterprise and new opportunity. Most pointedly, he argued that domestic manufacturing would create new, more certain and steady demand for the surplus produce of the soil. Manufacturing created new uses and greater value for commodities and raw materials.[3]

His strongest argument on behalf of manufacturing and the government's support of manufacturing had less to do with domestic preferences than with world realities. Hamilton suggested that if there were indeed a system of "perfect liberty to industry and commerce in the prevailing system of nations," then there might be less reason for the zealous pursuit of manufactures. But there was, he said, no such thing. While Americans could obtain manufactured goods from abroad with little difficulty, we "experience numerous and very injurious impediments" to the sale and transfer of our own commodities and goods, including staples. And after 1793, when Europe plunged into war, America's difficulties in obtaining manufactured goods from abroad increased rapidly. Hamilton believed that the expansion of domestic manufacturing would result in improved markets for American raw commodities and a lower cost for manufactured goods. Private interests, he said, struggle against unequal terms. Foreign governments create impediments to trade and our government must help establish trade on more equal terms.[4]

Congressional legislation, formulated by Hamilton, created a considerable degree of fiscal order and financial credibility in the new nation, but Hamilton had little immediate impact in bringing about industrial development. Congress approved bills to fund the debt of the government under the Article of Confederation, to assume the debts of the states, to create a national bank, and to impose tariff duties and a whiskey tax to maintain the solvency of the national government. Although these measures created a more favorable environment for business, the movement into manufacturing came as a result of external rather than internal pressures. The Napoleonic Wars, beginning in 1793, set the stage for the transition from foreign commerce into manufacturing, and the War of 1812 directly stimulated investment in manufacturing. As Henry A. Miles wrote in 1846, the war "turned the attention of monied men . . . to manufactures."[5]

American reexport trade—that is, the value of goods brought to this country for transshipment to foreign markets—expanded sharply in 1796, three years after the Napoleonic Wars began, and it continued to rise. Between 1801 and 1810, reexports equaled 50 percent of total foreign sales. They fell precipitously after 1810, however, to about 10 percent of total foreign sales. Although there was some recovery after the close of hostilities with England, the reexport business declined to only 6 percent of total foreign sales by the decade 1841–1850.[6] The great increase in the reexport business between 1793 and 1812 thus may be attributed to the wars in Europe. Maintaining a precarious neutrality, the United States became a major supplier and shipping agent for England and Europe; the Dutch carrying trade virtually ended. Despite high losses from capture and confiscation, and the effects of Jefferson's 1807 embargo on all foreign shipments, American merchants made enormous profits from the war trade.

That situation ended abruptly in 1812 with America's entry into war against England. During and after the War of 1812, American merchants had large capital surpluses with no traditional avenue for profitable investment. Moreover, the Napoleonic Wars, embargoes and blockades, and the diversion of British industry and British labor to war efforts almost halted the importation of manufactured products from abroad. As the prices of European manufactured goods soared, American manufactured goods became more attractive and returned higher profits. Thus, by 1815 American merchants had surplus capital swollen by war profits to invest, and manufacturing offered a far more profitable opportunity than formerly.

A surge of investment into manufacturing enterprises followed, but not without some problems and adjustments. England in particular, and Europe in general, still enjoyed certain manufacturing advantages: Labor was more plentiful and cheaper, capital was far greater, and existing plant and equipment and specialization within industry allowed for greater economies of scale and efficiency. England and Europe possessed greater technology and, in some instances, cheaper raw materials.[7] America suffered particularly from a lack of skilled labor and technological knowledge, but it compensated by "borrowing" the latter and emphasizing the volume production of a standardized product, thus reducing the "finishing" processes and the requirements of labor. Despite their predilection for agriculture, Americans did have, as Hamilton suggested, an aptitude for mechanics and innovation, and a strong aspiration for profit, wherever it might lie.

Changes in the social and political structures between 1815 and 1840 denote the shift from foreign trade to domestic industry. While many of the old seaboard cities remained trade oriented, most developed a substantial manufacturing base, and the new cities located in the inland rivers within reach of ores, raw commodities, and power sources developed distinctly industrial bases. Cheap raw materials drew populations westward like a magnet. Between 1840 and 1860, when the total United States population increased about 250 percent, the population of the cities rose by almost 800 percent even as the frontier expanded to the Pacific.

Traditional attitudes about tariffs, taxes, and business also changed. Few northern merchants supported protective tariffs before the War of 1812; tariffs were believed to discourage foreign trade. By 1816 these same merchants began to advocate protection and convinced the cotton South that they too would benefit from moderately protective tariffs on imported cotton fabrics. Tariffs would help sustain an American textile industry that could provide a more stable and reliable market for raw cotton.

The old hostility toward commerce seemed to diminish with the new association developing between business and manufacturing, and with the rising interdependence between manufacturing and agriculture, typified by the close relationship between the cotton producer and the textile industry. The manufacturer, a businessperson who produced goods, obtained greater public favor than the traditional "Yankee trader" who merely trafficked in the goods produced by others. Benjamin Franklin, himself an astute businessman, reflected the old view when he said: "There seems to be but three ways for a nation to acquire wealth. The first is by war. . . . This is robbery. The second, by commerce, which is generally cheating. The third, by agriculture, is the only honest way." Yet no sooner had the new business enterprise, manufacturing, achieved some acceptance in the public mind, than manufacturing itself created the corporation to make possible large-scale manufacturing and transportation enterprises; and the corporation, in turn, came to represent "a new, strange and unwelcome power in the business world."[8] Thus the power of the machine on the one hand took hold of the public imagination as a device for progress and productivity and a symbol of man's authority over nature, and on the other hand it conjured up the imagery of perpetual conflict between civilization and nature, between good and evil, between the "Machine and the Garden."[9] While Americans reflected on these things in their literature, in their public addresses, and in their conversations, the new industrial force had become a reality.

Douglass C. North argues that cotton became the major expansive force in the growth of the American economy after 1815. Cotton was strategic to the development of manufacturing industries and to the concomitant expansion in income derived from those industries. Cotton and cotton textiles comprised the principal cargo for the wagons, railroads, and steamboats that developed to service the industry; they in turn stimulated expansion in the iron and coal industries. The demand for cotton and cotton goods accelerated the pace of westward expansion and expanded the market economy.[10] The cotton industry laid the foundation for American industrial expansion.

THE TEXTILE INDUSTRY

The establishment of the cotton textile industry is central to the story of the development of manufacturing in the United States. It also illustrates the conversion of merchant-shipowner wealth into manufacturing capital, the disruption of the traditional economic alliance with England, and the role of the entrepreneur, or economic innovator, in business. At first America produced little cotton or woolen cloth, relying almost exclusively on imports. During the Revolution and for several decades afterwards, domestic spinning and weaving industries proliferated. Near the turn of the nineteenth century small-scale manufacturing began, characterized by Samuel Slater's mills in which labor, management, and household industries were closely related. Beginning in 1813 with the Waltham mill, modern, large-scale integrated corporate manufacturing came of age and spread rapidly, spinning off supporting industries and the nucleus of the machine-tools industry, which became the heartbeat of industrial expansion.

Samuel Slater arrived in New York from England in 1789 and was employed by the New York Manufacturing Society, a promotional organization inspired by Alexander Hamilton for the purpose of developing manufacturing industries in America. But Slater, for whom the underfinanced

Slater's Mill in 1793 initiated the development of the New England textile industry. (Courtesy: Library of Congress.)

and ill-directed association offered little opportunity, was soon in contact with Moses Brown of Providence, Rhode Island. Moses and his three brothers had developed a prosperous West Indies and rum trade before the Revolution and also operated candle-manufacturing plants in Providence, Newport, Boston, and Philadelphia. After the war Moses diverted his efforts to manufacturing, and other family members soon followed.

Brown and Slater, with the aid of the Wilkinsons, a Pawtucket, Rhode Island, family of artisans, designed and constructed a small textile mill on the Arkwright design. The latter had been patented by Richard Arkwright in England in 1769. Arkwright's water frame produced a cotton thread strong enough to be used as warp on a power loom. Slater, who formerly managed an Arkwright mill in England, evaded the British prohibition on the emigration of mechanics, and he avoided the restrictions on transferring plans and blueprints of machinery by memorizing the details of the mill machinery, which he reconstructed in America on a smaller scale and with some mechanical improvements. His 72-spindle, water-powered mill, the first mechanical weaving process in America, began operation in 1790. In 1793, a new partnership—Almy, Brown, and Slater—opened a second mill in Pawtucket. Nicholas Brown, Jr., established the Blackstone Manufacturing Company near Providence in 1808, and David Anthony, trained in the Slater mills, initiated the organization of textile mills along the Fall River in Massachusetts in 1813. The Slater operation remained relatively small, and although Samuel Slater is estimated to have accumulated a fortune of $690,000 by 1829, the operations of Francis Cabot Lowell, rather than Slater, established the model for the future expansion of the textile industry.[11]

Francis Cabot Lowell, born in Boston in 1775, enjoyed extended family connections among the the merchant-shipowners of Massachusetts. The Revolution, which the merchant-shipowners had supported, followed by the Napoleonic Wars and the Embargo of 1807, circumscribed opportunities for foreign commerce and disrupted vital overseas commercial alliances. Lowell went to England in 1810 for the purpose of studying English textile manufacture. Having a photographic memory and a talent for mathematics, he returned and began building and perfecting what would soon be the Waltham power loom, an improved version of Cartwright's 1784 loom. During the War of 1812, Lowell received ready financial support from Boston merchants who were looking for new opportunities, since foreign commerce was at a standstill. This is not to say that Lowell had no detractors, for many thought his scheme could only fail. Had it been a period of "business as usual," Lowell would have had far greater difficulties in attracting investors. As it was, Nathan Appleton, Patrick Tracy Jackson, and Lowell founded in 1813 the Boston Manufacturing Company at Waltham, Massachusetts, with a capital of $400,000, a sum probably greater than that of the combined Slater and Fall River operations. Lowell's organizational innovations were also striking.[12]

The Waltham system created an integrated process for manufacturing cloth at a single plant. Whereas in England the spinning and weaving and the dyeing and printing processes were performed by separate firms,

Lowell combined them in one establishment. Labor, mostly women, was divided into specialized functions and organized by departments. The product was standardized and, compared to English production, unrefined. Lowell introduced a cost-accounting system, and he systematized the purchase of raw cotton and the sale of finished cloth. Although Lowell died shortly after the Waltham mill began operation, by 1822 the enterprise had returned profits in excess of the capital outlay, and the investors desired to expand.[13]

The search for additional water-power sources led them to investigate the Pawtucket Falls area of the Merrimack River. About 1790 a merchant, Moses Hale, built water wheels on the nearby Concord and Merrimack rivers to generate power for grist mills, saw mills, carding machines, and for the manufacture of gunpowder. Local investors completed construction of a canal around Pawtucket Falls in 1797, and another canal, the Middlesex Canal completed in 1804, diverted trade from the Merrimack above the falls directly into Boston Harbor. This left the original "Proprietors of the Locks and Canals on Merrimack River" with a nearly worthless property. About 1822 Thomas M. Clark, the director of the Locks and Canals Company, became the agent of the Waltham group and purchased the 600 shares of canal-company stock and almost 400 acres of adjoining farmland for about $100,000. An additional $160,000 was spent in enlarging and deepening the canal around the falls, and a new and virtually untapped power source became available for manufacturing.[14]

The Waltham group incorporated the Merrimack Manufacturing Company in 1822, began construction of a plant on the "Waltham system," and appointed Ezra Worthen the first superintendent or manager. Cotton buyers stationed in the South made direct purchases of raw cotton and arranged for shipment to the mill through Boston. Briefly, the milling process involved passing the baled cotton into a "whipper" for loosening the compacted fiber, then to a "conical willow" that opened it more, and to a "picker" that removed trash and lumps. A "lapper" wound the fiber around a wooden cylinder into sheets. Women took over most of the remaining processes. In the carding room the fiber sheets were finished and passed to a drawing room where the fiber was twisted into ropelike sheets. A "double speeder" formed the roving and a "stretcher" drew the roving out before passing to the throttles in the spinning room where the yarn was made. The yarn was sized and dressed in the dressing room and became available for the looms. In the cloth room a red-hot copper cylinder singed away the nap, and workers trimmed and measured the cloth. In the last department the finished cloth was bleached, washed, and printed.[15]

The Waltham system involved not only compartmentalization and the specialization of labor, but it also depended largely upon the labor of women and children—a hitherto underutilized labor pool. The proprietors specifically sought to attract female employees of good character from rural communities. The company offered what was then attractive wages, good hours, and comfortable accommodations in company-built boarding houses. "Learners" received fifty-five cents per week and could work up to average levels of $1.93 per week plus room and board. For most women in

America, who had almost no opportunity to earn cash wages, the mills offered a unique opportunity and, paradoxically, may have marked the first step in liberating women from household employment. Working hours varied with the hours of daylight and averaged a little over ten hours a day for a six-day workweek. The boarding houses, and the "Lowell girls," were carefully supervised.[16] Child labor and the "Lowell girls" provided the mill owners with a relatively abundant and cheap labor supply—and ultimately introduced a pernicious system of exploitation.

The Merrimack Company proved an immediate financial success. By 1845 it operated five cotton mills and was capitalized at $5 million. The company produced 250,000 yards of cloth a week on 41,600 spindles and 1,300 looms. Employees included 1,250 females and 550 males. But the Merrimack Company was only the first of a coterie of cloth and manufacturing firms located in and around Lowell, Massachusetts.[17]

In 1825 the Locks and Canal Company reorganized with 1,200 shares of stock issued at $500 per share. The company sold "mill-powers," or water rights, with a mill-power roughly equivalent to the power necessary to operate 3,584 spindles. Shares were allocated to new companies on an essentially nonprofit arrangement. Beginning with the Hamilton Manufacturing Company in 1825, ten new cotton and woolen mills located in Lowell by 1839. Most of these remained in operation through World War I, but many disappeared before 1930. Supporting industries quickly sprang up around the new industrial center: a flannel mill, blanket mill, paper mill, planing mill, card and whip factory, and foundry; loom, lock, carriage, and sash-and-door manufacturers; and grist and saw mills. In 1825 the Merrimack Manufacturing Company established an independent machine shop with an investment of $150,000 under the supervision of Paul Moody. This and other shops established in Lowell a machine-tools capacity that became integral to industrial expansion throughout the region. The machine shops that serviced the textile industry became the nucleus of the American machine-tools industry, making possible the mass production of machinery parts and, in turn, facilitating the creation of mechanical devices of an endless array and variety including steam engines and railroad equipment. The mechanical or industrial revolution in America sprang largely from the machine shops of the new textile centers of Lowell, Taunton, and Worcester, Massachusetts; Providence, Rhode Island; Wilmington, Delaware; Paterson, New Jersey; and Richmond, Virginia.[18]

THE IRON INDUSTRIES

The expansion of the iron and transportation industries complemented the growth in manufacturing. Each interacted with the other. Growth in one both necessitated and made possible growth in the other. Economic progress became a cumulative process wherein innovation or invention had a reciprocal impact upon existing knowledge and enterprise.[19] The rise of manufacturing increased American exports, produced new savings and capital investments, generated rapid expansion of the rail and steamboat transportation industries, and created enormous demands for coal, iron, and steel.

Iron ore making and smelting were among the earliest industries of the American settlers. Virginia colonists sent ore samples on the first ship to return to England, and they shipped commercial quantities in 1609. The first American blast furnace entered production at Lynn, Massachusetts, in 1645. Furnaces for extracting iron from the ore existed in every colony except Georgia by the time of the American Revolution. Indeed, by 1776 the American colonies produced 14 percent of the world's supply of iron and exceeded the combined output of England and Wales.[20] The Revolution stimulated greater production, but, more significantly, it provided an impetus for the development of foundries and rolling mills—conspicuously few before that time because of British prohibitions on the manufacture of finished iron products.

The technology of iron production in America remained behind that of Europe until a few decades before the Civil War—the changes deriving from the great and growing demands of the railroad industry. The production of crude or "pig iron" involved melting the ores at high temperature in heavy pyramid-shaped stone or brick kilns or furnaces that measured 25 to 35 feet at the base and ranged from 20 to 50 feet in height. The heavier metal trickled to the bottom of the furnace and was tapped into a trough or "sow" on the sand-casting floor. With smaller troughs scooped along the main sow, the arrangement "resembled the outline of a mother pig feeding her sucklings"—hence *pig iron*. The "slag" or waste that collected at the top of the crucible was drawn off and discarded. A huge bellows powered by a waterwheel forced air into the "blast furnace." The furnaces burned charcoal until almost 1840, when anthracite and then bituminous coal were used. The pig iron was further refined in a smaller forge where the cooling metal was formed into bars with a tilt hammer or trip-hammer operating on a cam. Most of the bar iron then went to a blacksmith or metal worker for hand fabrication or for casting into kitchen utensils and hand tools. Little of the iron went into machine parts or guns until after the Revolution.[21]

Changes in the business organization of the iron industries also occurred after the Revolution. Although British merchants made sizable investments in American iron manufacture from early colonial times until the eve of the Revolution, the returns to English proprietors had been painfully small, and often the ventures were financial disasters. As a general rule, British capital had abandoned the production of crude iron to small colonial proprietors who operated their furnaces in the manner of a large-scale household industry. Capital investment in a furnace was minimal; ores, fuel, waterpower, and stone for construction were gathered locally. The proprietor was often the ironmaster, the supervisor of the labor force, and the one who peddled or contracted with a merchant for the sale of the product. After the Revolution the independent proprietary furnace gave way to a more integrated manufactory financed by the incorporation of stockholders. This managerial transition can be glimpsed in a brief historical view of the ironworks in the Ramapo Mountains area and in Virginia.

The Ironworks of the Ramapos

The Ramapo Mountains on the New Jersey–New York border include Orange and Rockland Counties in New York and Passaic and Bergen counties in New Jersey. Iron manufacture began there in the early eighteenth century but virtually ceased by 1900. James M. Ransom's *Vanishing Ironworks of the Ramapos* offers a vivid, introspective tale of this "shining chapter of early American individual endeavor and ingenuity." A few episodes illustrate the transitory character of early iron manufacture—and the financial hazards of those enterprises.

The Ramapos are dotted with the ruins of extinct forges, furnaces, and mines. The Ringwood Iron Company, founded in 1742, while one of the longest-lived, characterizes the typically erratic fortunes of early American iron manufacture. Founded by the Ogden family of Newark, New Jersey, Ringwood operated the first blast furnace in the area. Nicholas Gouvernour of New York joined the partnership and apparently served as a distributor of the iron until the operations were closed and offered for sale in 1764. The properties then included a furnace, iron mines, two forges, a saw mill, and dwellings. Peter Hasenclever, a German who obtained British citizenship in 1763, headed a group of British investors who sought iron properties in America. Styled "the American Company," Hasenclever acquired the Ringwood properties and initiated plans for the development of an industrial estate devoted primarily to the production of iron, but which would include the cultivation of hemp, flax, and madder (a plant used for red dyes) on 50,000 acres purchased for the company.[22]

> Confident of his ability for making a success of any mining venture, Hasenclever made plans to build a total of 5 furnaces and 7 forges with hammers and 23 fires—a tremendous undertaking in those times. He estimated that the ore in the Ramapo Mountains was so plentiful that each furnace should be able to make 700 tons of pigs a year, about 3,500 tons. Computing the possible yield from future as well as present forge fires, he was sure he could turn out at least 1,250 tons of bar iron a year. He estimated the profits from this large annual volume at over 13,000 pounds sterling, a huge sum indeed in the eighteenth century."[23]

Importing over five hundred workers from Germany, Hasenclever set about constructing furnaces, roads, and dams, and opening mines. The addition of new partners in England and the bankruptcy of one of the old partners brought charges, countercharges, suits, and confusion. Hasenclever returned to England and received the assurances of the investors, only to discover shortly after his return to America that a new manager had been named to replace him. Over the next few years the Ringwood properties produced small quantities of pig iron, and, in 1772, the works were offered for sale by the British proprietors. But the properties failed to sell, and when the Revolution came the manager, Robert Eskine, produced iron for the colonists.

Although the New Jersey legislature gave control of the mines to Robert Lettis Hooper in 1782, Hooper abandoned the works the following year. Production resumed under Martin J. Ryerson in 1807, but after his death in 1839 debts began to accumulate; the properties were offered at sheriff's sale from 1842 until they sold for $100,000 in 1853 to Peter Cooper, a New York financier and industrialist who transferred the properties to Trenton Iron Company. Production resumed, but severe problems with transportation and marketing created constant hard times. The company was saved by the Civil War and the spectacular efforts of the manager, Abram Hewitt, who obtained federal contracts and delivered gun carriages to General Grant's army in thirty days when the chief of ordinance had estimated nine months for the job. Financial losses after the war, however, resulted in suspension of all foundry operations. The mines continued to operate until 1893, and some were reopened and operated between 1900 and 1931. During World War II the Defense Plant Corporation bought the mines, but no profitable commercial production developed. In 1958 the Ringwood properties were sold at government auction to Pittsburgh Pacific Company of Crosby, Minnesota, for real estate development.[24]

The Virginia Ironworks

Interest in iron manufacture in Virginia dates from the first shipment of ore samples to England five weeks after the colonists arrived. By 1610 The London Company received £68 from the sale of metals smelted from Virginia ores—marking the end of the Virginia iron industry for one hundred years. Alexander Spotswood built the first furnace in Virginia in 1720; Colonel William Byrd operated four furnaces, using about one hundred slave laborers for each, after 1732. Augustine Washington, George's half-brother, operated a furnace on Accokeek Creek, and a partnership, including John Taylor, John Ballendine, and Presly Thornton, opened an iron works on the Occuquan, near Mount Vernon, in the 1750s. During the American Revolution the Virginia legislature funded the operation of a small-arms manufactory at Fredericksburg and a foundry at Westham, but results proved negligible. The assembly founded a state-owned arms and cannon factory at Richmond patterned on Eli Whitney's New Haven plant and on the Springfield armory. Musket manufacture began in 1803, and thirty cannons were bored in 1810, but the plant suspended in 1815 with the close of the War of 1812. John Clarke, who managed the plant until 1809, purchased the machinery for use in his private Bellona Foundry just outside of Richmond.[25]

Despite the desultory history of iron manufacture in Virginia, Richmond, where coal, ores, and waterfalls converged, comprised an excellent site for the industry. Moreover, the development of cotton mills in Fredericksburg and the construction of railroads in the 1830s would provide a stimulus for its expansion.

TREDEGAR IRON WORKS

Francis B. Deane, the owner of a forge and rolling mill, created the modern iron industry in Virginia when he organized the Tredegar Iron Works in 1837:

It was his intelligence that launched the Tredegar forge and rolling mill, and then expanded them into a corporation; for, a true son of this dawning age of organization, Deane had been quick to see that the forge and rolling mill and the foundry, each initiated to supply the new railroad needs, would if amalgamated gain in the economies of management and produce ultimately a greater volume.*

The Virginia legislature approved the incorporation of the Tredegar Iron Company on February 3, 1837, with a capital stock of $275,000, of which $150,000 comprised the property and equipment of Francis Deane's Tredegar forge and rolling mill, $75,000 represented the properties of the Virginia Foundry Company, and $50,000 comprised capital from the sale of 5,000 shares of stock at $100 per share, payable in monthly installments of $10 per share. Tredegar earned $9,715.14 in the first four months of operation, but old debts, assumed by the company, problems with water supplies, and bad management by Deane plagued the venture.

Joseph R. Anderson joined the company management as commercial agent in 1841; Deane left the active management of the company to John F. Tanner, but, as a business depression struck, Nicholas Mills assumed the presidency. The enterprise could not solve its debt problems, however. Finally, Anderson assumed control by leasing the business from the directors for five years for an annual rent of $8,000 payable quarterly, the rent payments to be applied to the company's debt. In 1848 Anderson purchased Tredegar for $120,000 payable in six annual installments of $25,000.

In the 1850s Anderson merged with the Armory rolling mill, owned by his father-in-law, and Tredegar and Armory concentrated on the manufacture of U- and T-shaped railroad rails, and in metal fabrication for the railroad industry. During the Civil War, Tredegar became the chief ordnance works of the Confederacy, manufacturing cannon, boiler plate, shells, shrapnel, and even iron plates for the *Merrimack*. Anderson not only supplied the Confederacy, but also served as a brigadier general, commanded troops in the field, maintained a labor force of hired laborers, slaves, and prisoners, and only ceased operations at Tredegar with Lee's evacuation of Richmond.

In 1867 Anderson reorganized the Tredegar Company and maintained effective direction of the business until his death in 1892. The organization of Tredegar Iron in 1837 reflected the classic financial and legal structure of the early American corporation. It was also characteristic in having inadequate liquid capital. Moreover, the company's eventual success can be attributed to Anderson's managerial expertise, his financial restructuring through his purchase and merger arrangements, and the advent of the age of the railroads.

*Kathleen Bruce, *Virginia Iron Manufacture in the Slave Era* (New York: The Century Company, 1930; reprinted, New York: Augustus M. Kelley, 1968), p. 150.

THE AMERICAN SYSTEM OF MANUFACTURING

Modern manufacturing, that is, the conversion from household, labor-intensive production to large-scale, corporate, machine production, derived from a concatenation of events. Iron manufacture was central to the

Factory chimneys and smoke appear above Philadelphia by 1836 as industrial growth accelerates. (Courtesy: Library of Congress.)

scheme. Natural resources, including iron ore, water, and coal, were integral to iron manufacture. The demand for iron products, nursed by the ever-present arms industry and invigorated by the textile and railroad industries, brought the modern age of manufacturing to America. The machine-tools industry grew out of the textile, arms, and railroad shops and created the capacity not only to build machinery for cotton factories, armories, and railroads, but also to build machines and machine components that could be assembled in a variety of ways to produce diverse products. The American system of manufacturing involved machines that made standardized or interchangeable machine parts that, in turn, could be assembled by semiskilled labor to produce a new machine—such as a gun or a cotton gin, a steam engine, or later, an automobile.

The catalyst in all of this was the innovator and entrepreneur, who accumulated the capital and provided the insight, the organizational structure, and the management expertise that made manufacture on a large scale possible. Samuel Colt and Eli Whitney are interesting prototypes of the innovators who conceived and formulated the American system of manufacture.

ELI WHITNEY

Eli Whitney, born in 1765, grew up on a farm near Westborough, Massachusetts, and at an early age developed a propensity for things mechanical. At fourteen, Whitney sensed an opportunity to earn extra money by making nails, which had become scarce during the Revolution. He installed a forge in his father's workshop, hired himself an apprentice, and entered business. When the market for nails evaporated, he made hatpins and walking sticks. In 1783 he accepted a job as a schoolmaster, determined to obtain a college education, and alternated between studying at Leicester Academy and teaching school. In 1789 he "matriculated"—that is, passed the admission requirements—for Yale, where he completed his studies in 1792.

At twenty-eight Whitney left Massachusetts for prospective employment as a tutor on a Georgia plantation. He became the house guest of widow Catherine Greene on Mulberry Grove plantation. There he developed a working model of a cotton gin employing rolling cylinders—one of which was studded with wire teeth to tear lint away from the seed—and a set of rotating brushes to brush the lint from the wire into a hopper. Simple but effective, it revolutioned the cotton industry and brought Whitney frustration, disillusionment, and a myriad of lawsuits in which he tried to maintain patent rights. Unfortunately for its inventor, the machine was simply too simple. According to Whitney's biographer, Constance McLaughlin Green, "Anyone who saw it could understand its workings; anyone equipped with simple blacksmith's and carpenter's tools could build a rough copy."* And practically everyone did.

Phineas Miller, who managed the estate for Mrs. Greene, quickly entered into a partnership arrangement with Whitney to provide financial support for the "patenting making, vending, and working" of cotton gins. Whitney returned to New Haven, Connecticut, applied for patents, and outfitted a machine shop and began work on his patent model. He contracted for six large gins for delivery to Miller, who proposed to conduct a ginning operation for 40 percent payment in kind. Whitney, suffering from recurring illnesses, found it almost impossible to meet the demand for his gins, and he confronted disaster when his shop burned in 1795. He quickly rebuilt, and within seven months of the fire delivered twenty-six gins. The partnership, however, constantly tottered on the verge of bankruptcy, and soon Whitney found his gin being copied, and often improved upon, by countless others. He became embroiled in costly, and most often fruitless, litigation.

Despite his inability to protect his patent, few dispute his title as the inventor and father of the cotton gin. Whitney's efforts to manufacture gins, and to create a monopoly by obtaining a royalty on all cotton ginned, led him to a much more controversial venture. Whitney needed money, and what better way to get it than a government contract to manufacture small arms? The contract included $10,000 in cash advanced before the production of a single piece! On June 14, 1798, Whitney contracted to deliver 4,000 stands of arms to the United States government by September 30, 1799, and 6,000 pieces by September 30, 1800. Although he failed to meet the terms of his original contract, delivering his first 500 muskets in September of 1801, his New Haven Armory maintained government contracts and produced inexpensive, quality weapons in large numbers until his death in 1825.**

Eli Whitney is not the father of the American system of manufacture. The American "system" was the culmination of many diverse social, economic, and technological forces—and the work of many—one of whom, most certainly, was Eli Whitney.

*Constance McLaughlin Green, *Eli Whitney and the Birth of American Technology* (Boston: Little, Brown, 1956), pp. 48–49.
**Ibid., 97–175; Edwin T. Layton, Jr., ed., *Technology and Social Change in America* (New York: Harper & Row, 1973), pp. 47--63.

Samuel Colt (1814–1862). Manufacturer and inventor of the revolver. (Courtesy: *Dictionary of American Portraits*.)

Samuel Colt

Born in Hartford, Connecticut, in 1814, Samuel Colt perfected a pistol with a revolving cylinder at the age of seventeen, and he secured a patent in 1836. He manufactured his revolutionary "rapid-fire" weapon at Paterson, New Jersey, but found little or no market for it, lost his patent, and ceased manufacture in 1842. During the Mexican War and subsequent Indian battles, army officers and Texas Rangers found the "revolving pistol" remarkably effective, and in 1847 the Department of the Army placed an order with Colt for revolvers. Having no plant for manufacture, Colt contracted with Eli Whitney's New Haven Armory for the manufacture of the first 3,000 pistols. In 1848 he regained his patent rights, opened a plant at Hartford, and manufactured his revolvers on the assembly-line system using interchangeable parts.

In 1853 Colt opened an arms factory in England and introduced the "American system of manufacture" there. European weapons, while of very fine workmanship, were essentially custom-made and "fitted" for the user. Mass production of a standardized product, in guns as in cloth, revolutionized and modernized the manufacturing process. Between 1856 and the close of the Civil War, Whitney's Hartford factory produced over a half-million revolvers. By the close of the Civil War, guns, clothing, shoes, textiles, farm machinery, and railroad equipment were being mass produced using interchangeable parts on assembly lines, in plants or factories using departmentalized and specialized labor.

Within approximately fifty years (1815–1865) manufacturing developed from a rather primitive and somewhat questionable enterprise into a new industrial and economic force that became the primary interest and pursuit of business. The number of manufacturing establishments reached over 250,000 by the close of the American Civil War, and the number of industrial employees rose from several thousand to over 2 million. The value added by manufacture exceeded $1.25 billion per year by 1865. The rise of manufacturing in the United States may be attributed in part to the severing of traditional supply lines with England and Europe as a result of the American Revolution and the Napoleonic Wars. These wars left the United States politically, and somewhat economically, isolated. The Napoleonic Wars also resulted in the accumulation of new capital that after the war found domestic manufacturing, rather than foreign trade, a more attractive investment.

The American cotton producer and the textile manufacturer entered into a new economic alliance that in effect created a "cotton kingdom." It included not only the South, but also began to weld the nation into a true national economic order, and it stimulated expansion in supportive industries such as iron, transportation, coal, clothing, and machine tools. Whatever broad overview of the development of manufacturing one might take, the industrial revolution and the refinement of a distinctive American system of manufacturing may be attributed to the independent and largely unrelated efforts of a host of inventors, mechanics, and business managers such as Samuel Slater, Francis Cabot Lowell, Eli Whitney, Samuel Colt, and Joseph Anderson. All of those, in one way or another, seized the opportunity afforded by time, circumstance, markets, or technology to profitably produce and market a product. No less so were the suppliers of raw materials, the farmers, turning their efforts from subsistence to large-scale commercial production and becoming—if they had not already been—business entrepreneurs.

NOTES

1. Alexander Hamilton, "Report on Manufacture," (December 5, 1791) in *The Reports of Alexander Hamilton,* Jacob E. Cooke, ed., (New York: Harper & Row, 1964), pp. 116–128.

2. Ibid.

3. Ibid., pp. 117–128.

4. Ibid., pp. 141–158.

5. Henry A. Miles, *Lowell: As It Was, and As It Is* (Lowell, Massachusetts: Nathaniel L. Dayton, Merrill L. Heywood, 1845; reprinted, New York: Arno Press, 1972), p. 18.

6. *Historical Statistics of the United States, Colonial Times to 1970,* Series U187–200, pp. 885–86.

7. Victor S. Clark, *History of Manufactures in the United States, 1607–1860,* vol. I (New York: McGraw-Hill, 1929), p. 243.

8. Ibid., p. 281.

9. See Leo Marx, *The Machine in the Garden: Technology and the Pastoral Ideal in America* (New York: Oxford University Press, 1964).

10. See Douglass C. North, *The Economic Growth of the United States, 1790–1860* (Englewood Cliffs, New Jersey: Prentice Hall, 1961), pp. 46–65; 68–69.

11. Clark, *Manufactures,* pp. 374–375; Robert K. Lamb, "The Entrepreneur and the Community," in William Miller, ed., *Men in Business: Essays on the Historical Role of the Entrepreneur* (Cambridge: Harvard University Press, 1952; reprinted New York: Harper & Row, 1962), pp. 96–102.

12. Lamb, "The Entrepreneur and the Community," pp. 106–107.

13. Ibid., pp. 106–107; Clark, *Manufactures,* p. 450.

14. Margaret Terrell Parker, *Lowell: A Study of Industrial Development* (Port Washington, New York: Kennikat Press, 1970), pp. 59–63, 73–74, 118–119; Miles, *Lowell,* pp. 14–28.

15. Miles, *Lowell,* pp. 76–110.

16. Ibid., pp. 69–70; 101, 112–134.

17. Ibid., p. 48.

18. Clark, *Manufactures*, pp. 434–435; Parker, *Lowell*, pp. 67–74, 118–119; Miles, *Lowell*, pp. 31–43, 58.

19. See W.W. Rostow, *The Stages of Economic Growth*, 2nd ed. (Cambridge, England: Cambridge University Press, 1971).

20. James M. Ransom, *Vanishing Ironworks of the Ramapos: The Story of the Forges, Furnaces, and Mines of the New Jersey–New York Border Area* (New Brunswick, New Jersey: Rutgers University Press, 1966), p. 6.

21. Ibid., pp. 9–11. See also James M. Swank, *History of the Manufacture of Iron in All Ages* (Philadelphia, n.p., 1892; reprinted New York: Burt Franklin, 1965), pp. 80–99.

22. Ransom, *Ironworks of the Ramapos, pp. 17–19.*

23. Ibid., p. 19.

24. Ibid., pp. 26–69.

25. Kathleen Bruce, *Virginia Iron Manufacture in the Slave Era* (New York: The Century Company, 1930; reprinted, New York: Augustus M. Kelley, 1968), pp. 10–136.

SUGGESTED READINGS

BRUCE, KATHLEEN. *Virginia Iron Manufacture in the Slave Era.* New York: The Century Company, 1930; reprinted, New York: Augustus M. Kelley, 1968.

BRUCHEY, STUART, W. *The Roots of American Economic Growth, 1607–1861.* New York. Harper & Row, 1965.

CLARK, VICTOR S. *History of Manufactures in the United States, 1607–1860.* Vol. I. New York; McGraw-Hill, 1929.

COOKE, JACOB E., ED. *The Reports of Alexander Hamilton.* New York: Harper & Row, 1964.

DEW, CHARLES B. *Ironmaker to the Confederacy: Joseph R. Anderson and the Tredegar Iron Works.* New Haven, Connecticut: Yale University Press, 1966.

GREEN, CONSTANCE McLAUGHLIN. *Eli Whitney and the Birth of American Technology.* Boston: Little, Brown, 1956.

KINDLE, BROOKE AND STEVEN LUBAR. *Engines of Change: The American Industrial Revolution, 1790–1860.* Washington, D.C.: Smithsonian Institution Press, 1986.

LAYTON, EDWIN T., JR., ED. *Technology and Social Change in Amerrica.* New York: Harper & Row, 1973.

MARX, LEO. *The Machine in the Garden: Technology and the Pastoral Ideal in America.* New York: Oxford University Press, 1964.

MILLER, WILLIAM, ED. *Men in Business: Essays on the Historical Role of the Entrepreneur.* Cambridge Harvard University Press, 1952; reprinted, New York: Harper & Row, 1962.

MITCHELL, BROADUS. *William Gregg, Factory Master of the Old South.* Chapel Hill: University of North Carolina Press, 1935.

NEVINS, ALLAN. *Abram S. Hewitt.* New York: Harper Bros., 1935.

NORRIS, JAMES D. *Frontier Iron: The Merrimack Iron Works, 1826–1876.* Madison: State Historical Society of Wisconsin, 1964.

RANSOM, JAMES M. *Vanishing Ironworks of the Ramapos: The Story of the Forges, Furnaces, and Mines of the New Jersey–New York Border Area.* New Brunswick, New Jersey: Rutgers University Press, 1966.

SWANK, JAMES M. *History of the Manufacture of Iron in All Ages.* Philadelphia: n.p., 1892; reprinted, New York: Burt Franklin, 1965.

TAYLOR, GEORGE ROGERS. *The Transportation Revolution, 1815–1860.* New York: Rinehart, 1951; reprinted, New York: Harper & Row, 1968.

TUCKER, BARBARA M. *Samuel Slater and the Origins of the American Textile Industry, 1790–1862.* Ithaca, New York: Cornell University Press, 1984.

WALSH, WILLIAM DAVID. *The Diffusion of Technological Change in the Pennsylvania Pig Iron Industry, 1850–1870.* New York: Arno Press, 1975.

WARE, CAROLINE F. *The Early New England Cotton Manufacture.* Boston: Houghton Mifflin, 1931.

5 | Agribusiness

The rapid growth of cities and manufacturing created new markets and opportunities in agriculture. Improvements in transportation and farm machinery plus the continuing availability of good, fertile land facilitated the change from subsistence farming to commercial agriculture. The biggest business in America in the nineteenth century, and the one occupying the most people, was farming, but by the end of the century farming had become almost exclusively a market-oriented, specialized business. Moreover, the production of the crop had become but one aspect of the business of agriculture. The merchandising, processing, shipping, packaging, canning, packing, and refrigeration of commodities and foods added as much value to the product as did the original production of the raw commodity. Only by examining the rapidly expanding agricultural economy through the perspective of the businessperson and the profit motive can one feel the pulse of the national economic expansion.[1] In no commodity was the change so spectacular, and the urban-agricultural connection so evident, as in the cotton industry.

The antebellum cotton kingdom comprised more than 384,000 slave-owning planters producing cotton. The cotton kingdom stretched from the farms of Mississippi and Georgia to the country storekeeper, to the southern coastal cities of Galveston, New Orleans, Mobile, Charleston, and Baltimore, to the shippers and bankers of New York and Philadelphia, to the manufacturers of Boston and Lowell, and to the factors, bankers, shippers, and merchants of England, France, and Holland. Cotton was the world's business before the Civil War in the same way that petroleum has become the world's business in recent decades.

Plantations and slavery fed the world's seemingly insatiable demand for cotton. Between 1800 and 1860 the consumption of raw cotton in the United Kingdom alone rose from 52 million pounds to over 1 billion pounds. In the same period American production of cotton climbed from 152,000 bales to 4.8 million bales, or two-thirds of the world's supply, handled largely by American merchants and shippers. In 1860 American manufacturers consumed one-third of the total world's supply. Income from cotton, and inescapably from slavery, was shared by businesspersons from the South and from New York and New England, who earned profits from the freight, the sales commissions, the insurance premiums, the warehousing of raw cotton, and from the manufacture and distribution of finished cotton goods, as well as from the sale and transportation of slaves.

The slave trade from Africa to the New World lasted almost four hundred years. That trade produced a unique system of slavery, certainly more exploitative than anything preceding it. Some 400,000 to 500,000 Africans were imported and sold into slavery in American colonies and states before 1808, and an estimated 50,000 to 270,000 may have been imported illegally thereafter. Herbert Gutman estimated that at least 1 million slaves were sold in domestic markets between 1820 and 1860. The slave trade, as a distinctive institution in the slave system, proved lucrative to Europeans and Americans alike. Most of the slaves provided the labor forces of the southern cotton plantations.[2]

Cotton, to be sure, was not the nation's only agribusiness before the Civil War. The tobacco, rice, sugar, livestock, lumbering, and wheat industries accounted for more dollar income than cotton, but not one of them alone before 1860, or even 1900, approached the dollar value of cotton. Each of these commodities involved hundreds of middlemen for every single producer, creating an intricate web of trade and commerce that stretched across North America to Europe. The cotton plantation employing slave labor marked only the first stage in the business of producing, marketing, and distributing cotton products.

THE PLANTER AS BUSINESSPERSON

The southern plantation system reflected the commercialism, capitalism, and specialization of the industrial revolution. The plantation was a capitalistic agricultural organization utilizing slave labor under unified direction and control to produce a staple crop.[3] The small, nonslaveholding farmer of the South differed from the planter much as the craftsman or artisan (household manufacturers) differed from the factory owner. Both sought to accumulate wealth: The small farmer and craftsperson derived profit from their own labor while the planter and industrialist derived profit from the labor of others and from the capitalization of labor and machinery. The small farmer and the artisan remained small businesspersons in part from choice, for there was greater risk in adding land or factories and in hiring or buying labor. Moreover, labor was scarce, and for the artisan and the small farmer often unavailable. In the South, among the small slaveowners, there seems to have been a direct correlation between the size of a farmer's family and the number of slaves acquired. Up to an indeterminate size, a farmer could maximize profits by having no, or few, slaves. Only when farmers could acquire approximately thirty slaves and hire a manager or overseer could they enjoy the economies of scale offered by the plantation system.

At this point the planter lost the relative security of subsistence agriculture and entered almost wholly into the market economy. Slave labor was likely no more efficient than free labor, but it did reallocate output from nonmarket to market commodities. While the farmer's strategy was to produce as much bread and meat (corn and hogs) as possible and "afterwards as much cotton as possible," the planter could only efficiently utilize labor and optimize profits by maximum output of cotton (or sugar, tobacco, or rice).[4] The smaller the farm, the larger the allocation of land and labor to corn; and while the planter derived efficient economic returns from subsistence crops or corn, beyond a certain point the cultivation of subsistence crops resulted in diminishing returns of land, labor, and capital, although, to be sure, some plantations achieved a high degree of self-sufficiency in terms of food production.[5] Thus, there was not only some truth but considerable economic justification for the statement that "in their great eagerness to get money, the planters have brought themselves into a state of dependence on their neighbors for many of the necessaries of life which formerly were raised at home."[6] A large-scale industrial estate with a specialized product, the plantation utilized the division of labor and managerial functions.

The planters served as owner and frequently the business manager of the plantation, although they often shared the latter role or delegated certain authority to a factor or business agent. The overseer was the production manager who most frequently allocated his labor on the basis of tasks rather than hours. The slave labor force was divided into task groups or gangs headed by a driver or crew boss, also a slave. The field gangs performed specialized functions such as plowing, hoeing, and seeding. The plow gangs were most often men; the hoe gangs largely women. Skilled craftsmen, such as bricklayers and blacksmiths, were assigned individual tasks and the assistance of helpers who were trained in those crafts. Women, and some men, were assigned as domestic servants, cooks, and weavers. The elderly and young often served in "trash gangs," cleaning, carrying water and provisions, and in lesser tasks. Men, women, and children worked as "pickers." When the field work was done, the slaves worked as teamsters, barrel and stave makers, ginners, or cooks, or they were simply "laid-by," but the interval between the fall harvest and spring ground breaking was short.

The profitability of slavery on the cotton plantation has been much examined and debated. Some studies estimate that southern slave agriculture was 35 percent more efficient than the northern system of family farming, while others conclude that slavery was inherently unprofitable. The results are inconclusive.[7] The better judgment might be simply to observe that slavery could provide a very profitable and efficient system of agricultural production and that as in any business, there were those who did well, those who did less well, and those who failed. The vagaries of climate and disease, the fallibility of the manager and the owner, and the total independence of the market in terms both of prices and credit costs made commercial agriculture then, as now, a hazardous but potentially profitable enterprise. Much of the profit from farming, in any era, has always gone to the middleman, the banker, the processor, the distributor, and the shipper.

WILLIAM JOHNSON—THE BARBER OF NATCHEZ

Free "men of color" lived and worked within the pale of black slavery in the South, and some achieved distinction and wealth as planters and business people. William Johnson, born a slave, was freed by his white father at the age of five and apprenticed to his brother-in-law, James Miller, the black proprietor of a Natchez barbershop. At the age of nineteen William opened his own shop in Port Gibson, Mississippi, and at the end of twenty-two months reported an income of $1,094.50. In 1830 William purchased the lease and equipment of Miller's shop in Natchez when Miller moved to New Orleans. In 1833 Williams purchased the building for $5,500, paying one-half in cash. The next year Johnson's annual income exceeded $2,500, and he had acquired three slaves of his own. At twelve and a half cents for a shave, and two bits for a haircut, Johnson's shop stayed busy.

In addition to his barbering, Johnson loaned money to his white customers, bought and sold anything of value, operated a toy shop, a coal and sand business, and speculated in farm land. He traveled extensively, including visits to Philadelphia and New York, with frequent excursions to New Orleans, where he gambled, played billiards, entertained "the ladys," and traveled about in hired carriages. Johnson married in 1835, and the couple eventually had ten children. In 1839 he built a three-story brick building to replace his shop and rented a portion of it to a businessman for $1,000 annually. He opened several "branch" barbershops around the city, and established a separate public bathhouse. He built two additional commercial buildings in Natchez that were leased variously to a bootmaker, druggist, grocer, and tenpin alley operator; these returned about $600 in annual rentals.

While Johnson primarily bought and sold farm land, he operated farms at different intervals, leasing them to white tenants on shares, hiring white and black laborers, and using a few slave laborers. During "slow" periods Johnson hired out his slaves to other planters. Johnson usually raised corn, vegetables, fruit, cordwood, wool, hogs, and cattle for the local market, rather than cotton.

William Johnson maintained a daily diary about his business affairs from 1835 until his death in 1851. He recorded the financial and social activities of Natchez, and the local gossip of blacks and whites. He left behind a substantial estate, ten children, and a good reputation in the Natchez business community.

Source: Edwin Adams Davis and William Ransom Hogans' *The Barber of Natchez* (Baton Rouge: Louisiana State University Press, 1954).

THE COTTON FACTOR

The marketing of the cotton crop involved a diverse assortment of middle-men and processors. After the harvest, the planter, if he owned a gin, ginned and baled his crop. If he did not, he took his crop to a neighbor-hood gin where the crop was ginned on a toll basis with payment in cash or kind. The cotton was then delivered in wagons, which might or might not be hired, to a factor or commission merchant, whose business was to market the crop and supply goods on credit to the farmer or planter. In smaller communities the country store often served as an intermediary between the farmer and the factor, the merchant taking cotton at an agreed-upon price in exchange for cash, or more often simply crediting the planter's or farmer's account. The factor, located in inland cities such as Augusta, Macon, Atlanta, Nashville, Columbia, or Shreveport, accumulated cotton from his customers' accounts, including storekeepers, planters, and farmers, and marketed the cotton on a commission basis, frequently at 2.5 percent of the gross receipts, sometimes directly to a buyer, but most frequently to an associate or factor located in a coastal city such as New Orleans, Savannah, or Charleston, where a cash market existed. The inland factor added to his costs the insurance and freight charges to the port city.[8] A factor in New Orleans might buy the cotton outright as an agent for mills in Massachusetts or England, or for the account of yet another merchant or factor in New York who bought or accepted a consignment with the intention of obtaining a better price in England or Europe. Again, shipping, insurance and handling, and credit charges were costs of doing business.

Since the production and marketing of cotton involved a long-term process, credit and financing were generally of lengthy duration, ranging from six to twelve months. Thus, the inland factor who advanced credit to the farmer, planter, or merchant borrowed from the coastal factor, who in turn received credit from his New York or Liverpool merchants. New York merchants were particularly successful in dominating the cotton trade because they were able to extend long-term credit to the southern factors, whereas English and European credit, and that of major southern banks such as in New Orleans, was usually available only on a 60- to 90-day basis. Moreover, imports of finished and manufactured goods were received at New York and northern ports for redistribution to southern and western markets. Therefore northern capital and northern businesspersons and shippers remained as crucial to the cotton trade as such merchants had been integral to colonial commerce, and much of the "income from cotton flowed to the North and West."[9]

Cotton receipts, derived from the actual sale, transport, commission fees, insurance, or finance charges, comprised a major portion of the banking business of the United States in the North and the South before the Civil War, and both necessitated and facilitated the rapid spread of commercial banking. These banks usually loaned money to the factor, rather than directly to the planter, although the planter's notes, endorsed by the factor, often served as the collateral for the loan. The factor effectively served as the planter's business agent and banker, maintaining the planter's accounts, advising him on markets and prices, and serving as well as the planter's purchasing agent for goods, supplies, and often land. It is a role the factor continued to fill throughout the nineteenth and into the twentieth century.

OTHER SOUTHERN AGRICULTURAL INDUSTRIES

Despite the omnipresence of the cotton economy, the "cotton kingdom" requires a sobering perspective. Tobacco, sugar, and rice in most of the antebellum years retained a market value at least equal to one-half of the receipts from cotton. Corn, in fact, was the chief staple crop of the South, usually exceeding three times the acreage in cotton. In 1855, for example, the value of the southern corn crop ($209 million), exceeded that of cotton, tobacco, sugar, and rice combined. Unlike the other commodities, little southern corn reached the marketplace; the bulk was consumed by the people and their animals. On the typical antebellum nonslaveholding farm, corn constituted the principal crop.

Rice production and marketing in the antebellum period changed little from the practices of the colonial era. The industry did expand from South Carolina into Georgia, and on the eve of the Civil War considerable rice production existed in Louisiana along the Mississippi River. Louisiana, too, was the primary source of sugar, with some planting existing in Florida, Georgia, and Texas. A Louisiana sugar plantation was in reality both a farm and a factory where the cane was raised and the sugar refined. Investments in sugar plantations paralleled and often exceeded the investment in rice plantations, and both far exceeded the capital requirements of cotton production. Charles Roland estimates the average value of sugar houses at $50,000, with many exceeding a $100,000 investment.[10] Ditching, drainage, and harvesting required more arduous and expensive labor, and often special or dangerous tasks were assigned to hired labor gangs, rather than hazard valuable slaves. While the risks from weather, disease, and capital investment were large, the sugar planter often accumulated substantially greater wealth than the cotton planter.

The tobacco industry remained the mainstay of the economies of Virginia and Maryland as it had been during the colonial period. Tobacco was a labor-intensive crop compared to other staples; and as a laborer could most efficiently be assigned to two or three acres of tobacco as compared to ten or twenty acres of cotton, tobacco plantations were correspondingly smaller, and family farms produced a considerable portion of the total tobacco crop. Overproduction and fluctuating prices of tobacco, in contrast to the generally stable and upward trend for the price of cotton, created relatively higher risks and lower returns for the tobacco planter. The greater depletion of soil nutrients by tobacco, as opposed to cotton, necessitated crop rotation and diversification. As time passed more of the tobacco crop entered the domestic market for manufacture and consumption. Plug, snuff, and cigar manufacturing employed some 11,000 workers in Virginia in 1860.[11]

Many southern farmers, particularly in Virginia but throughout the antebellum South, raised wheat as a commercial crop before the Civil War. Most of the wheat entered local markets, but Virginia produced large surpluses for export. Like wheat, the corn-hog industry was a widely diversified, small-farm enterprise in the South; but again, most of the pork entered local markets rather than being a factor in interregional or international trade.

The cattle industry became a more viable commercial enterprise in the decades before the Civil War on the prairies of southwest Louisiana and southeastern and central Texas. There, the range-cattle industry, where herds were grazed by family groups on open ranges, provided slaughter cattle for New Orleans and the eastern markets. Edward Pipes foreshadowed the great drives of later days by driving a herd of Texas cattle to Illinois in 1846, and herds moved with some regularity from Texas to Missouri and Illinois in the 1850s. Earlier, cattle moved eastward along the Old Government Road to Fort Smith and Little Rock, Arkansas. Other trails led from Dallas to Shreveport, with extensions to Natchez and Vicksburg. The Opelousas Trail started near San Antonio, Texas, and followed a coastal route to New Orleans and Mobile. Cattle ranching in the Americas began with the conquistadors and continued to be a large-scale business in Mexico and Texas. Richard King, a steamboat captain, began the famous King Ranch in 1852. The foundations of the lucrative range-cattle industry were well-established before the Civil War.[12] While cotton dominated the antebellum South, the southern agricultural economy contained a diversified and many-faceted agribusiness. Many southern and northern farmers did not participate in the market economy, but were more typical of the Jeffersonian yeoman, self-sufficient farmer.

NORTHERN AGRIBUSINESS

Commercial agriculture in the Northeast remained more diversified and on a smaller scale than in the South until the 1850s. Arable land was often scarce, and farm labor, outside of the immediate family, even more so. Wheat, hogs, flax, wool, and dairy and meat products enjoyed intermittently good markets. Northeastern farmers generally prospered throughout the Napoleonic Wars, and into the 1820s, when northern agriculture became increasingly market oriented and farming became more specialized. By the 1830s eastern and New England agriculture largely succumbed to the competition of midwestern farmers, or diversified into vegetable, fruit, and dairy farming for the rising urban markets. The development of commercial agriculture in the Midwest directly affected the rise of manufacturing in the East, and the expansion of the cotton kingdom into the Old Southwest.

The relatively low cost of shipping grain and meat down the Mississippi River and its tributaries allowed the cotton and sugar plantations of the Southwest to devote more land and labor to growing products for the commercial market and less to provisions. This resulted in the production of larger quantities of cotton at lower prices for the New England textile market and facilitated the expansion of manufacturing. The more favorable costs of production in the Southwest, deriving from lower-priced food-

Bucolic agricultural scene by Currier & Ives depicts a New England farm in autumn. (Courtesy: Library of Congress.)

stuffs and land, not coincidentally made the fertile southwestern cotton lands more competitive witih the older eastern cotton plantations and stimulated the western movement of cotton. In turn, settlement and agricultural expansion in both the lower and upper Mississippi River valley established new markets for manufactured goods from the Northeast, promoting an interregional flow of trade from Midwest to South to East.[13]

The opening of the Erie Canal in 1825, and the growth of steamboats and railroads in the 1840s, facilitated the basic counterclockwise flow of trade from the Midwest to the South to the Northeast and opened new arteries of trade, particularly in allowing the bulk products of the Midwest, predominantly wheat, pork, and beef, to flow directly to eastern markets and ultimately to enter European trade. Once grain and farm products from the Midwest entered eastern markets at competitive prices, commercial agriculture in the East could no longer compete. This, coincidentally, freed eastern labor for employment in the manufacturing centers where the growing urban populations created yet greater demands for the farm products of both the South and the Midwest.

Country merchants in the northern as in the southern states served as the principal contact between the farmer and the marketplace before 1820, and they continued to play a significant role until the Civil War. A merchant who accepted produce in exchange for commodities usually assembled small lots of produce and consigned them to a commission merchant in a larger city or sent them to the wholesale supplier for credit on his account. As transportation to interior points improved, commission firms and mills began to send cash buyers to farm communities, and the country merchant's exchange services declined accordingly.[14]

Hog and cattle marketing developed from a local barter economy into a mass-marketing structure by the 1850s. Integral to large-scale marketing was the drover, who might be a local dealer or a buyer from the city. The drover obtained financing, assembled herds from scores of small producers at a few cents per pound, drove the herds to such packing centers as Chicago or Cincinnati, and sold at a profit to a packer or buyer. The railroad replaced the drive, but not the drover, who became the local livestock dealer shipping the herds by rail.[15]

Specialists in the handling and warehousing of grain appeared in Rochester, St. Louis, Cincinnati, Chicago, and other points in the Midwest by the 1840s. As large-scale commercial farming developed, and rail service to milling centers became available, farmers were able to make direct carload shipments to a commercial warehouse or elevator.[16] Because of the expansion of canals and railroads, improved agricultural technology, and the growing urban markets in America, wheat became the North's greatest agribusiness.

THE WHEAT INDUSTRY

Until about 1815 Pennsylvania, Virginia, and New York led in the production of wheat, and New York City emerged early as the leading milling center. The opening of the Erie Canal first stimulated the expansion of wheat production in New York, but soon it contributed to the rapid shift westward, with Illinois becoming the leading wheat producer in 1860, while Rochester, New York, had become the principal milling center. By the 1870s wheat production had shifted farther westward with Ohio, Indiana, Minnesota, and California the leading states, and by the turn of the century the heaviest volume came from the Dakotas, Nebraska, Kansas, and Minnesota. The westward movement of wheat involved not only the development of improved transportation systems but also new agricultural technology.

Prior to the 1840s wheat farming remained largely a small-scale family-farm enterprise, partly because of the necessity and expense of clearing land, and partly because of the expense of hiring labor for the harvest. Wheat, unlike cotton, required harvesting in a very brief period, usually five days from ripening. One person with a cradle could harvest almost three-quarters of an acre in a day, and if hired, received wages of $1 to $3 per day. In addition, the person using the cradle had to be followed by someone raking the wheat into sheaves and another binding the sheaves. Thus, the real scarcity and the high cost of labor greatly circumscribed the scale of wheat farming until mechanical harvesting began to replace hand labor.

McCormick's Reaper

Cyrus P. McCormick's invention of the reaper did for the wheat industry what Eli Whitney's gin did for cotton. McCormick developed his reaper in 1831, and he entered into mass production of the machine at a plant established in Chicago in 1848. The reaper could harvest up to 15 acres of wheat per day, and this efficiency allowed large-scale wheat farming to develop. The reaper, followed by mechanical binders, steam threshers, and harvesting machines, revolutionized the industry, and it in turn created new agribusinesses such as the farm-implements business that McCormick-Deering (International Harvester) long dominated.

Cyrus McCormick, born in 1809 in Rockbridge County, Virginia, grew up while observing his father's repeated failures at perfecting a mechanical reaper. Following an unsuccessful field trial of his father's last attempt in 1831, Cyrus developed a machine utilizing a saw-toothed cutter bar and a reel, rather than beaters, to force the stalks into the cutter. Although he perfected the machine over the next few years and secured a patent in 1834, he made no attempts to produce it for sale but instead farmed and built a furnace for the production of pig iron. The business prospered for a while, but in 1839 it failed. Hard times drove him to attempt to market his reaper, and he made his first sale in 1840. In 1844 he sold fifty reapers, all of which he built in the blacksmith shop on his farm. McCormick soon encountered opposition from a rival machine built by Obed Hussey, and after some skirmishing over patents (which Cyrus lost) Hussey retired from the field, being overwhelmed by McCormick's business genius.[17]

McCormick began production of his reaper in Chicago in 1847 when he contracted with a wheat-cradle manufacturing firm, Gray and Warner, for the construction of the reaper. Gray became a partner of McCormick's, and a new plant was built the next year. The partnership soon dissolved, however, and Gray sold his interests to William B. Ogden and W. E. Jones. In 1849 McCormick bought Ogden and Jones's interests for $65,000. By 1850 at least thirty firms manufactured reapers utilizing many of McCormick's features. Unable to extend or protect his patent rights, McCormick's success came through manufacture and sale of machines, rather than from control of patent rights, licensing agreements, and royalties. McCormick adopted standardized parts and mass production on an assembly line. His Chicago plant, which had the capacity to manufacture forty reapers per day, succeeded in producing 4,000 machines in 1856. He heavily employed advertising, guaranteeing satisfactory performance or the money back, and he staged competitive field trials against all comers. And he offered easy credit terms, with $35 down plus freight from Chicago, with the balance of the $125 due December 1, at 6 percent interest from July 1. Credit, then a novel and risky marketing device, proved tremendously successful.[18]

At the close of the Civil War, the Marsh harvester challenged and overwhelmed McCormick's reaper. McCormick regained a competitive stance in the implement business with the production of the wire binder, invented by Charles B. Withington in 1877. The binder removed the last vestige of hand labor in the harvesting of wheat. Cyrus McCormick died in 1884, leaving behind a thriving business and a market war between the Deering Plow Company and McCormick's Harvesting Company, which was resolved by the intercession of J. P. Morgan and Company and the organization of the McCormick-Deering International Harvester Company in 1903.[19]

Equally important to advanced harvesting technology were the improvements in plows and cultivators. John Deere perfected the steel-faced, mold-board plow in 1837, and James Oliver produced a less expensive but equally good chilled-iron plow in 1868. The improved plows made possible the breaking of large acreages of tough prairie sod in the Midwest and great plains, where the sticky sod either broke or clung to conventional iron plowshares. Concurrent with better mechanical devices, improved plant varieties made possible larger yields in the more arid plains.

Most of the wheat grown before the Civil War was a variety of "soft" wheat that required more moisture, was easily milled by traditional stone mills or "burrs," and milled a very white, soft flour. The soft wheat varieties were generally susceptible to disease, such as rust, and to drought. Daniel Fife of Ontario, Canada, first introduced "hard" spring wheat to America about 1841. The hard varieties, which had been grown first along the Volga River in Russia and then in Scotland, were particularly drought and disease resistant and suitable for cultivation on the western plains. Although use of hard wheat varieties spread rapidly in the 1840s and 1860s, the flour had a dark color and was not easily milled. Flour from hard wheat sold at a 10 to 15 percent discount below soft-wheat flour until improved milling techniques lightened the color of the flour and gave hard wheat an advantage over the soft. Flour from hard wheat retained higher protein and vitamin content and absorbed more water, making the flour particularly attractive to bakers.[20]

John Deere (1804–1886). Inventor and manufacturer of farm implements.   (Courtesy: *Dictionary of American Portraits*.)

Inception of the Rolling Mill

The first porcelain (later steel) rollers in the Washburn-Crosby flour mills in Minneapolis—introduced by Minnesota Governor C. C. Washburn in 1878—solved the problem of milling hard wheat and removed the final obstacle to its cultivation on the great plains. The total dollar value of such commercial crops as corn, hogs, vegetables, dairy products, hay, and wool exceeded the value of wheat, but no one crop matched the profit from wheat. In the twenty years between 1849 and 1868, annual wheat production rose from 100 million bushels to 288 million bushels, and it continued to expand.[21] By 1860 the subsistence homestead had all but given way to farm businesses that stressed specialized agriculture for the marketplace. The expansion of the railroad and food-processing industries provided the vital link between the city and the farm. In 1860 northern urban markets consumed about one-third of domestic wheat production, southern markets about 20 percent, and local markets about one-third, with the remaining 15 percent exported. During the Civil War foreign sales rose markedly and continued thereafter to absorb an increasingly large percentage of total output.

The number of mills and the production of flour grew dramatically after the Civil War. By the 1880s severe competition and a real excess of milling capacity created convulsions in the milling industry that led to bankruptcies and the consolidation of mills. In 1889 British investors accomplished the merger of C. A. Pillsbury and Company with the Washburn Mill Company (owned by W. D. Washburn and not to be confused with the Washburn-Crosby Mills), creating the then-largest flour concern. Size, however, proved no assurance for profit, and the company failed to declare a dividend during most of its twenty-year existence.[22]

The Pillsbury group triggered the consolidation of six Minneapolis mills into the Northwestern Consolidated Milling Company in 1891, and the organization of the Minneapolis Flour Milling Company in 1892. In that year major New York mills merged as the Hecker-Jones-Jewell Milling Company, and six California mills created the Sperry Flour Company. Thomas A. McIntyre, a New York miller and promoter, attempted to organize a trust in 1898 designed to control the production and prices of spring-wheat flour. His United States Flour Milling Company sought to acquire thirty-one mills producing 200,000 hundredweight of flour daily. McIntyre did obtain control of companies having a combined capacity of 77,000 hundredweight, but he failed to acquire control of the Northwestern Consolidated and Hecker-Jones-Jewell enterprises. The would-be trust went into receivership in 1900 and was subsequently reorganized as the Standard Milling Company.[23]

At the close of the nineteenth century some four or five hundred milling companies existed. Most of them were family-owned and located in or near the major production areas. All were fiercely competitive, and none marketed more than 5 percent of the trade. But the trend toward consolida-

The Pillsbury Company's first flour mill in Minneapolis.   (Courtesy: The Pillsbury Company.)

tion had become clearly evident and would increase rapidly after 1900 when sharp changes occurred in the marketing of wheat products. Per capita wheat flour consumption in the United States experienced a decline of almost 20 percent between 1900 and 1920; foreign sales rose sharply during World War I and then collapsed after the war. Moreover, the rise of commercial bakeries and grocery chains altered the marketing patterns for flour products and interposed powerful business conglomerates between the miller and the ultimate consumer. The changing business structures in the milling and food-processing industries is confirmed by the observation that by 1970 Kellogg Company, General Mills Incorporated, General Foods Corporation, and Quaker Oats Company shared 91 percent of the market for ready-to-eat cereal products. As in many businesses, the food-processing industry experienced consolidation, diversification, and specialization.[24]

THE CATTLE KINGS

Lewis Atherton, historian and author of *The Cattle Kings*, finds the most significant feature of the American range-cattle industry to have been the cattleman, not the cowboy. Cattlemen were more significant as marketing specialists rather than producers. Texas and cattle became synonymous even before the Civil War. Texas longhorns were driven to Missouri, New Orleans, and even New York City before that time. Raising cattle in Texas, many believed, was a sure way to wealth, and entrepreneurs came from every walk of life, and from many foreign countries. Pennsylvania, Rhode Island, England, Scotland, Ireland, and Germany were just some of the places Texas ranchers once called home. Some did achieve wealth, but most did not. And if they did, many lost it again.

Charles Goodnight with his partner Oliver Loving blazed the famous Goodnight-Loving trail in 1866. From Texas through New Mexico territory into Colorado they survived Indians, stampedes, and water shortages to net in excess of $12,000 on that one drive. Goodnight quit herding in 1869 to turn to ranching near Pueblo, Colorado. He invested much of his wealth in real estate and banking, only to be wiped out in the financial panic of 1873.

Joseph G. McCoy was another Texas herder who was bankrupted in the 1873 panic. McCoy and most cattlemen operated heavily on borrowed money. Cattle prices were unusually high in 1872, and exceptionally large herds were accumulated by the cattlemen in anticipation of greater profits. These herds began moving north in the spring, only to find that the market at Abilene, Kansas, and other rail terminals was glutted. Cattle herds driven north in 1872 had been held over on local ranges in anticipation of the higher spring prices. Moreover, the corn crop in 1873 fell unusually short and buyers were hesitant to purchase cattle that could not be fattened. More cattle and fewer buyers brought collapsed cattle prices. Banks were forced to foreclose on their loans to cattlemen. McCoy estimated that Texas cattlemen lost over $2 million in that one market season. Scores of ranchers were bankrupted, including McCoy.

Money was a scarce commodity in the Southwest, and interest rates often ran from 2 to 3 percent per month. George Littlefield, for example, decided that banking was preferable to cattle marketing after having to pay 24 percent interest on his cattle investment in 1869. Littlefield subsequently made a habit of operating on a cash basis, and this led him by accident rather than by design into banking. In a word, the range-cattle industry was a highly speculative business that attracted a diverse group of entrepreneurs, and in which success hinged on the vagaries of weather, feed supplies, water, interest rates, railroad rates, and vigorous competition.

FOOD PROCESSING

The development of specialists in the processing and marketing of foods occurred over a long period of time and had a close association with improvements in transportation and urbanization and with changes in dietary habits. Until the 1830s most foods were preserved by salting, spicing, or pickling, smoking, and drying, and, indeed, throughout the nineteenth century these processes remained widely used. Ice was rarely employed as a refrigerant until a few decades before the Civil War, although George Washington and Thomas Jefferson constructed icehouses on their estates in the 1790s. Cellars, spring houses, and food "safes" provided temporary storage for meat and dairy products. Until the 1860s most meat, poultry, and fish arrived at the city markets alive, to be slaughtered and cleaned in the city. Dairy products and vegetables went from the farm to the market to the table in a matter of hours, or not at all. Until the advent of the railroad, the "garden district" of the city had to be within or in close proximity. The railroad immediately expanded the food-growing ring to a radius of several hundred miles. It became possible, and because of dietary changes increasingly desirable, to obtain fresh vegetables and dairy products.[25]

The more sedentary life of the urban dweller made the traditional consumption of high-calorie, high-fat diets—such as the southern rural diet of meal, molasses, and pork or the midwestern diet of hogmeat and hoecakes—less satisfactory. Dietary reforms stressing vegetarian diets swept the country after the 1830s. American diets were also strongly influenced by the French fashion for dairy products and vegetables, iced drinks, and ice cream.

The use of ice as a refrigerant expanded rapidly after 1830, largely because of improved techniques in harvesting and shipping natural ice. Nathaniel J. Wyeth invented a horse-drawn ice cutter, patented in 1829. Drawn like a plow over a field of ice, it greatly speeded the harvesting of evenly cut squares. Steam-driven endless elevators fed the blocks into large icehouses, which then shipped commercial quantities of ice by ship and rail to cities in the North, South, and even overseas. New Orleans's consumption of ice, for example, rose from 375 tons in 1827 to 24,000 tons by 1860, and in the latter year New York City consumed over 100,000 tons of ice. Ice boxes for preservation became prominent in urban homes by 1860.[26]

Until the Civil War refrigeration was limited to the shipment of seafood and dairy products, and even then for relatively short distances. Beef and pork still entered the city markets on the hoof—or salted, pickled, and dried. Cincinnati emerged as a major pork-packing center in the 1840s, to be eclipsed by Chicago in the early 1860s. Chicago opened the Union Stock Yards on Christmas Day 1865 and experienced a surge in beef packing and fattened live-beef shipments to the East. But midwestern slaughtered beef products did not begin to enter eastern markets in significant quantities until Gustavus F. Swift began commercial shipments of slaughtered beef to Boston markets in ice-refrigerated cars about 1877. Armour and Company, and other packers in Chicago, soon followed, and the day of mass marketing of processed meat products had arrived.[27]

The efficient processing of meat products, however, did not depend solely on the railroad, refrigeration, and the development of mass-consumer markets in the cities; it depended as well upon the growth of industries utilizing the by-products of the meat packers. In Chicago, for example, lard and tallow provided the raw materials for independent businesses manufacturing soap, lard, and illuminating oil. A brush manufacturer had utilized animal hair by 1860, glycerine and gelatine production occurred by 1867, and substantial fertilizer industries and glue factories had developed by 1871. Tanning, leatherworking, saddle and bridle, and boot and shoe manufacturers absorbed hides from the packing industries, creating successful businesses and in turn making the packing industry more profitable and efficient.[28]

The canning of perishables developed in Napoleonic France in the early 1800s. It was introduced to America about 1819 by William Underwood, who came to Boston from England and established a small cannery using glass or ceramic jars and specializing in seafoods. Thomas Kensett, also from England, established a similar cannery in New York, and in 1825 he patented a method employing tin cans instead of jars. In 1856 Gail Borden developed a process for condensed milk and during the Civil War obtained contracts to supply the Union army. In 1860 canners marketed some 5 million cans of commercially produced foods, but not until the twentieth century did canned-food products represent a major form of food processing.[29]

By the 1880s specialized marketing structures developed to handle the distribution of processed foods in national and international markets. The Great Atlantic and Pacific Tea Company (A&P), which incorporated before the Civil War, became a leading distributor of foods through retail outlets of chain stores after the war. Kroger (1882) and the National Tea Company (1899) were among those businesses that made possible the rapid and efficient distribution of foods to the burgeoning urban centers. Agribusiness—implying the specialization and commercialization of the production and distribution of foods and commodities—made possible an increase in per capita food and fiber consumption, despite large increases in population, and the even more dramatic shift in population from rural to urban areas.

NOTES

1. Gavin Wright, *The Political Economy of the Cotton South: Households, Markets and Wealth in the Nineteenth Century* (New York: W. W. Norton & Co., 1978), p. 3.

2. Herbert G. Gutman, *Slavery and the Numbers Game: A Critique of Time on the Cross* (Urbana: University of Illinois Press, 1975), p. 126; James H. Dorman and Robert R. Jones, *The Afro-American Experience: A Cultural History through Emancipation* (New York: John Wiley, 1974), pp. 71–82.

3. Lewis Cecil Gray, *History of Agriculture in the Southern United States to 1860*, vol. I (Washington, D.C.: Carnegie Institution, 1932; reprinted, Gloucester, Massachusetts: Peter Smith, 1958), p. 302.

4. Wright, *The Political Economy of the Cotton South*, p. 64.

5. Ibid., pp. 43–88.

6. Stuart W. Bruchey, ed., *Cotton and the Growth of the American Economy, 1790–1860* (New York: Harcourt, Brace & World, 1967), p. 64.

7. See Robert William Fogel and Stanley L. Engerman, *Time on the Cross: The Economics of American Negro Slavery* (Boston: Little, Brown, 1974); and Gutman, *Slavery and the Numbers Game*.

8. Bruchey, *Cotton and the Growth of the American Economy*, pp. 221–227.

9. Ibid., pp. 226–227; and Douglass C. North, *The Economic Growth of the United States, 1790–1860* (Englewood Cliffs, New Jersey: Prentice Hall, 1961), p. 113.

10. Charles P. Roland, *Louisiana Sugar Plantations during the American Civil War* (Leiden, Holland: E. J. Brill, 1957), p. 3.

11. Paul Wallace Gates, *The Farmer's Age: Agriculture, 1815–1860* (New York: Holt, Rinehart & Winston, 1960), pp. 100–107.

12. See Sam Bowers Hilliard, *Hog Meat and Hoecake: Food Supply in the Old South, 1840–1860* (Carbondale: Southern Illinois University Press, 1972); and Forrest McDonald and

Grady McWhiney, "The Antebellum Southern Herdsman: A Reinterpretation," *The Journal of Southern History* 41 (May 1975), pp. 147–66.

13. Percy Wells Bidwell and John I. Falconer, *History of Agriculture in the Northern United States, 1620–1860* (Washington, D.C.: Carnegie Institution, 1925; reprinted, Gloucester, Massachusetts: Peter Smith, 1941), pp. 171–183.

14. Clarence H. Danhof, *Change in Agriculture: The Northern United States, 1820–1870* (Cambridge: Harvard University Press, 1969), pp. 27–31.

15. Ibid., pp. 33–38.

16. Ibid., pp. 31–33.

17. Cyrus McCormick, *The Century of the Reaper* (Boston: Houghton Mifflin, 1931), pp. 1–26.

18. Ibid., pp. 26–51.

19. Ibid., pp. 89–127.

20. See Mark Alfred Carleton, "Hard Wheats Winning Their Way," in *Yearbook of the United States Department of Agriculture, 1914* (Washington, D.C.: United States Department of Agriculture, 1915), pp. 391–420.

21. Ibid., p. 522.

22. Herman Steen, *Flour Milling in America* (Westport, Connecticut: Greenwood Press, 1973), pp. 62–65.

23. Ibid.

24. Ibid., pp. 66–67; Brian F. Hanis, *Shared Monopoly and the Cereal Industry: An Empirical Investigation of the Effects of the FTC's Antitrust Proposals* (East Lansing, Michigan: Division of Research, Graduate School of Business Administration, Michigan State University, 1979), pp. 1–2; and for an excellent study of the rise of oligopoly, see Alfred S. Eichner, *The Emergence of Oligopoly: Sugar Refining as a Case Study* (Baltimore: Johns Hopkins University Press, 1969).

25. Oscar Edward Anderson, Jr., *Refrigeration in America: A History of a New Technology and Its Impact* (Princeton, New Jersey: Princeton University Press for the University of Cincinnati, 1953), pp. 3–11.

26. Ibid., pp. 11–30.

27. Ibid., pp. 59–62; and see Bessie Louise Pierce, *A History of Chicago*, vol. III (Chicago: University of Chicago Press, 1957), pp. 103–144.

28. Pierce, *Chicago*, vol. II, pp. 100–103.

29. John T. Schlebecker, *Whereby We Thrive: A History of American Farming, 1607–1972* (Ames: Iowa State University Press, 1975), pp. 127–128.

SUGGESTED READINGS

ANDERSON, OSCAR EDWARD, JR. *Refrigeration in America: A History of a New Technology and Its Impact.* Princeton, New Jersey: Princeton University Press for the University of Cincinnati, 1953.

BIDWELL, PERCY WELLS, and JOHN I. FALCONER. *History of Agriculture in the Northern United States, 1620–1860.* Washington, D.C.: Carnegie Institution, 1925; reprinted, Gloucester, Massachusetts: Peter Smith, 1941.

BROEHL, WAYNE C. JR. *John Deere's Company: A History of Deere and Company and Its Times.* New York: Doubleday, 1984.

BRUCHEY, STUART W., ed. *Cotton and the Growth of the American Economy, 1790–1860.* New York: Harcourt, Brace & World, 1967.

DANHOF, CLARENCE H. *Change in Agriculture: The Northern United States, 1820–1870.* Cambridge: Harvard University Press, 1969.

FOGEL, ROBERT WILLIAM, and STANLEY L. ENGERMAN. *Time on the Cross: The Economics of American Negro Slavery.* Boston: Little, Brown, 1974.

GATES, PAUL WALLACE. *The Farmer's Age: Agriculture, 1815–1860.* New York: Holt, Rinehart & Winston, 1960.

GRAY, LEWIS CECIL. *History of Agriculture in the Southern United States to 1860.* Washington, D.C.: Carnegie Institution, 1932; reprinted, Gloucester, Massachusetts: Peter Smith, 1958.

GUTMAN, HERBERT G. *Slavery and the Numbers Gaame: A Critique of Time on the Cross.* Urbana: University of Illinois Press, 1975.

HEITMANN, JOHN ALFRED. *The Modernization of the Louisiana Sugar Industry, 1830–1910.* Baton Rouge: Louisiana State University Press, 1987.

HILLIARD, SAM BOWERS. *Hog Meat and Hoecake: Food Supply in the Old South, 1840–1860.* Carbondale: Southern Illinois University Press, 1972.

LITTLEFIELD, DANIEL C. *Rice and Slaves: Ethnicity and the Slave Trade in Colonial South Carolina.* Baton Rouge: Louisiana State University Press, 1981.

MCCORMICK, CYRUS. *The Century of the Reaper.* Boston: Houghton Mifflin, 1931.

NORTH, DOUGLASS C. *The Economic Growth of the United States, 1790–1860.* Englewood Cliffs, New Jersey: Prentice Hall, 1961.

PIERCE, BESSIE LOUISE. *A History of Chicago.* Three volumes. Chicago: University of Chicago Press, 1957.

SCHLEBECKER, JOHN T. *Whereby We Thrive: A History of American Farming, 1607–1972.* Ames: Iowa State University Press, 1975.

SCHOB, DAVID E. *Hired Hands and Plowboys: Farm Labor in the Midwest, 1815–1860.* Urbana: University of Illinois Press, 1975.

SKAGGS, JIMMY M. *Prime Cut: Livestock Raising and Meat Packing in the United States, 1607–1983.* College Station: Texas A&M University Press, 1986.

WOODMAN, HAROLD D. *King Cotton & His Retainers: Financing & Marketing the Cotton Crop of the South, 1800–1925.* Lexington: University of Kentucky Press, 1968.

———, ed. *Slavery and the Southern Economy.* New York: Harcourt, Brace & World, 1966.

WRIGHT, GAVIN. *The Political Economy of the Cotton South: Households, Markets, and Wealth in the Nineteenth Century.* New York: W. W. Norton & Co., 1978.

6 | The Expansion of Commerce

Although the Constitution organized the American states into what was then the largest free-trade zone in the world, geographical constraints sorely inhibited trade and commerce. Enormous physical obstacles and great distances divided the republic. Henry Adams wrote, "No civilized country had yet been required to deal with physical difficulties so serious, nor did experience warrant conviction that such difficulties could be overcome."[1] From colonial times to the beginning of the nineteenth century, the movement of goods from the places of production to the points of sale continued to be a major problem for merchants and consumers alike. Throughout much of the nation goods were transported by water from coastal port to coastal port and along navigable rivers and streams. Some freight moved over primitive, rutted roads, but in many areas the absence of roads meant that commodities could be transported only by pack horse. The cost of shipping items in such fashion often exceeded their value. Conditions for travelers were equally as bad. A five-day trip north from Philadelphia would take a traveler only as far as Connecticut. The political and economic leaders of the country recognized the obstacles to commerce that distance and geographical barriers presented. Entrepreneurs and politicians proposed many internal development schemes to improve transportation. In most instances these involved local and state improvements, and the projects called invariably for the expenditure of substantial amounts of capital.

GOVERNMENT AID AND TRANSPORTATION

It became clear to many Americans that the transportation needs of the country were so large that more than private, state, and local government support was necessary—the aid of the federal government was essential. When Secretary of the Treasury Albert Gallatin issued his report on "Roads and Canals" in 1808, he emphasized the necessity of federal involvement in the transportation system.[2] Businessleaders and politicians knew that the nation had vast resources, but they were of modest value without transportation. Farms and factories could only be located near navigable waterways or the few improved roads.

Although by the time of the War of 1812 the frontier stretched beyond the Alleghenies, commerce remained dominated by the seaports along the Atlantic coast where the majority of America's over 8 million people lived. Large-scale economic development would be limited until the coming of more efficient and less expensive transportation and that could only be achieved when the issue of providing capital for internal improvements had been resolved. The marketing and distribution of goods depended upon an expanded transportation system.

The transportation revolution that occurred after 1800 was created by people of vision who seized the opportunities that the nation provided.[3] Business owners, whether they were natives or immigrants, prospered because the social structure allowed for their emergence, as did the open nature of the economic order. No less important was the aid of government.[4] The United States government from its beginnings promoted transportation, encouraged manufacturing, and protected commerce. While it had no central plan, there was, nevertheless, a deliberate effort to stimulate economic growth. The federal government did not engage directly in massive public enterprises, but political leaders believed in the importance of aiding transportation whether it be the building of roads, improving rivers, developing canals, or, later, promoting railroads. The federal role was still less important, however, than that of the state, county, and city governments. The federal government subsidized transportation through tariffs, engineering surveys, and land grants. Only to a limited extent did it provide cash loans and subsidies, but between 1816 and 1830 it completed the Cumberland or National Road and purchased securities in four canal companies.[5] Although it has been argued by some economists that economic growth in this period was the function of the marketplace, and that the price of goods and services and production factors generally explain the economic expansion and change, it is evident that government as an institution played a major role in the transportation sector.[6]

In the first half of the nineteenth century several competing forms of transportation emerged with technological change stimulated by private and public investment. As each new mode developed, it largely replaced the preceding system. The turnpike with its stagecoaches and wagons gave way to the canal with its packets and lineboats. The canal, in turn, would be supplemented by the steamboat and then replaced by the railways. Private investors and state and local governments promoted and developed the turnpikes and canals. Similarly, the federal government supported the expansion of foreign commerce and an American merchant marine. These transportation systems provided the base for an industrial economy that became firmly established by the time of the Civil War. The first major effort to improve transportation was the construction of roads and turnpikes.

ROADS AND TURNPIKES

The American colonists did not build roads. Their primary commercial arteries were the creeks, rivers, and bays along the coast. As they moved into the interior, they followed the Indian trails. The trails were narrow but direct, and with the removal of trees and underbrush it was possible for wagons to traverse some of the routes. The wagon traffic that developed was intermittent, and freight rates were extraordinarily high. Wagoners charged as much as $5 to transport a barrel of flour ten miles. In the 1790s state governments sponsored road-building programs to facilitate the movement of freight and people.

By 1815 a system of roads joined much of the settled area of the United States, but the roads were often simply cleared spaces between the trees. In swampy areas the roads became a series of mud holes, and in dry periods the surface turned to a deep layer of dust. The surface of some roads was covered with logs placed side by side to form what became known as a "corduroy road." There were few bridges; rivers were crossed at fords or on ferries. Country roads tied farms to nearby towns where produce could be taken to mills, gins, and stores. Usually the villages were located on navigable water allowing for commerce beyond the immediate locality. Bulky produce could not be moved far beyond the waterways, however.

Prior to the War of 1812, the New England states, and to some extent the mid-Atlantic states, became linked by turnpikes. The turnpikes charged tolls, and in most cases were built by private-stock companies chartered by the state governments. The turnpikes connected the most important cities, and some of the best "pikes" were built with stone foundations and a gravel surface. Drainage ditches on either side kept the roads dry, and some of the turnpikes reduced grades by cuts and fills.

From the time of the War of 1812 through the mid-1830s, the states chartered numerous turnpike companies. Pennsylvania alone issued 86 charters to firms that built more than 2,000 miles of road at an expenditure of almost $40 million. New York had 135 companies that constructed over 1,500 miles of roads. The turnpike developers formed corporations to build the roads. Most of the companies were small in terms of capitalization, but hundreds of thousands of dollars were invested in some of the larger schemes. Farmers, business leaders, storekeepers, manufacturers, and wealthy merchants bought the securities. State and local governments participated in the financing by purchasing securities, and occasionally they acquired complete ownership. In Pennsylvania the state owned almost one-third of the securities of the turnpikes. In Ohio the government purchased a similar share, and even Virginia, a state which did not normally engage in support of commerce, purchased $5 million in turnpike stocks and bonds.

The turnpikes often reduced the time necessary to ship commodities by as much as 50 percent, but still the movement of goods remained very slow. Wagoners averaged only 20 miles a day or 2 miles an hour. For example, it took almost a month to ship goods from Boston to Baltimore. The turnpikes also reduced shipping costs, but hauling remained a very expensive form of transportation. At fifteen cents a mile, flour could be profitably shipped no more than 150 miles. Turnpikes failed to provide cheap transportation for bulky goods.

The turnpike movement declined during the 1830s and 1840s. The toll roads were often crowded, but rarely did the traffic generate substantial financial rewards for the owners. Even the most profitable routes rarely paid dividends exceeding 5 percent. In Pennsylvania a few of the turnpikes provided revenue sufficient to pay for repairs and maintenance, but as business enterprises the turnpikes were poorly organized and managed. Financial difficulties became the rule rather than the exception, problems which led the states to acquire the pikes and turn them into free public roads. It became evident by the 1820s that any large-scale road system needed the support of the federal government.[7]

THE NATIONAL ROAD

Within the federal government, voices in both the Congress and the cabinet called for federal aid to construct a road network. The postmaster general pointed to the need for adequate transportation to move the mail, and the secretary of war noted the difficulties of moving troops in the absence of a road system. The only significant federal road-building project, however, was the Cumberland Road, or the National Road, extending from Cumberland, Maryland, west to Wheeling, Virginia, and on to Ohio, Indiana, and Illinois.

Construction of the National Road was underway by the time the War of 1812 ended. The federal government extended the road west across the Allegheny Mountains to Wheeling by 1818, but intermittent funding slowed construction. Only in 1833 did the National Road reach Columbus, Ohio; by 1850 the road extended into central Illinois. For more than half a century the National Road represented the largest federal internal improvement project. Conestoga wagons and stagecoaches followed the advance of the National Road into the Old Northwest, and by the 1840s traffic on the road boomed. In states like Ohio, Indiana, and Illinois, the public and politicians clamored for additional federal projects and improvement of the National Road, but this would not be done. Many citizens felt that those who used the roads should pay for their maintenance. Indeed in Indiana the Hoosiers chanted:

The roads are impassable—
Hardly jackassable;
I think those that travel 'em
Should turn out and gravel 'em.[8]

ROADS TO THE WEST

The Hoosiers were not alone in demanding federal aid for roads, and the government responded indirectly. With the admission of Ohio to the Union in 1803, Congress required that 5 percent of the money from the sale of public lands in that state be allocated for road construction. Two-fifths of these funds were appropriated by Congress and three-fifths disbursed by the Ohio legislature. It appears, however, that a substantial amount of the proceeds were used for political purposes.

While some presidents, including James Madison, urged the construction of roads under national authority, and numerous road bills were introduced in Congress, opposition by other politicians precluded such developments. Arguing that federally sponsored internal improvements were unconstitutional, Andrew Jackson vetoed an appropriation for the Maysville Road. Congress divided sharply when it attempted to allocate money for federal projects. Southerners wanted roads in their region, while westerners fought for roads in the Old Northwest. Some federal funds were appropriated for the construction of post roads, that is, roads designed to transport the mail, but the monies provided were always very small. In only one respect did the federal government provide important and continuous aid to road construction, and that was in engineering support for such projects.[9]

The United States Military Academy at West Point represented the primary source of engineers in the United States. The engineers who graduated from West Point surveyed routes for roads, canals, and railroads. Even river dredging and harbor improvements came under the direction of the Corps of Engineers. Their duties included not only supervising the construction of roads and canals but also the removal of snags from rivers, the deepening of harbors, and the drawing of maps and topographical surveys for road, and later railroad, builders. The government justified the use of the engineers on the grounds that these projects were "defense-related."[10]

Roads became the primary means of transportation first in the Old Northwest and then in the trans-Mississippi West. Throughout much of the nineteenth century, wagon freighting left a record of service to frontier development. Huge Conestoga wagons pulled by teams of oxen, mules, or horses moved goods from river ports and railroad terminals to the isolated settlements of the West. The wagoner represented an important link between the centers of trade in the East and the frontier merchants, farmers, and miners. The federal government recognized the importance of the roads, and in the 1840s and 1850s it dispatched the Corps of Engineers into the West to help in the selection of routes.[11]

The expansion of the nation's road system did not prove revolutionary in terms of freight rates. The transportation of heavy and bulky goods, particularly agricultural commodities, remained tedious and expensive. As late as 1850 the cost of moving freight by wagon averaged fifteen cents a ton mile. Skeptical farmers and merchants believed that water-borne commerce would be much cheaper and, in many instances, faster. But water-borne commerce remained limited until a better source of power could be found. And indeed, the coming of the steamboat and the canal era would, in many parts of the country, diminish the importance of the wagoner. By the 1830s the canals and steamboats ahd reduced freight rates and stimulated the growth of the nation's cities.

THE CANAL ERA

Even as Americans extended their road network, they also determined to improve water-borne transportation. It has been estimated that as early as 1818, two-thirds of all marketable crops in some regions had to be grown within five miles of a navigable stream. But river traffic was often limited; it was seasonal, there were floods, or alternatively, low water could halt the flatboats. The movement was nearly all downstream with little upstream traffic because of the enormous expenditure of time and effort required to fight the current. Many Americans eagerly sought to remove the natural restraints on waterborne commerce. Both Benjamin Franklin and George Washington had endorsed the improvement of rivers and the construction of canals even before the American Revolution. A few short canals had been built near Boston, Norfolk, and Charleston, but none were significant. Most Americans probably agreed with Thomas Jefferson when he wrote in 1808, concerning a proposal for a canal across upstate New York, "It is a splendid project and may be executed a century hence. . . . It is little short of madness to think of it at this day!"[12] To many Americans, however, the canal seemed the answer to their transportation needs, and they embraced it with extraordinary enthusiasm.

The great canal building era occurred between 1815 and 1860 and was supported by land grants and stock subscriptions from government at all levels. More than 4,200 miles of canals were built at a cost exceeding $200 million. But this transportation breakthrough occurred only after great effort. Canal construction in Great Britain had begun as early as the 1760s, but because of the heavy expenditure of capital required little had been done in the United States. The nation needed a successful example to show that capital investment could be raised and that a profit could be returned to the investors. The example the Americans needed was the Erie Canal.

Easily the largest internal improvement project in the nation's history until that time, the Erie Canal was built for many reasons, not the least of which was nationalism. Americans in the period after the War of 1812 subscribed to a nationalism that emphasized unity, and the Erie Canal was seen not only as an important economic development for the state of New York but also as an internal improvement that would help bring the country together. Designed to cut through the Mohawk gap in the Appalachian chain—thereby linking the Great Lakes near Buffalo with the Hudson River in upstate New York—the canal was a bold and dramatic scheme based on an optimistic view of the future. The population in the area along the route was quite small, the largest town having only 6,000 people in 1820. In 1816 the legislature passed an act allowing construction of the canal, and a subsequent law created a canal fund with state support. Those who promoted the project argued that it would not only develop the land, improve the economy, and enhance communications, but that it would also help to meet military threats directed from Canada. Construction began in 1817, and continued for eight years. Forty feet wide, 4 feet deep, and some 363 miles long, the canal overcame 565 feet of elevation by eighty-three locks and crossed numerous streams on eighteen aqueducts. The New York legislature appropriated $2 million for the canal, but this sum proved inadequate as the total cost exceeded $7 million. In October 1825 completion of the Erie Canal was celebrated with "the Wedding of the Waters" of Lake Erie and the Atlantic Ocean.

Completion of the canal led to the development of packet lines. The packet vessels, usually 80 feet long and 14 feet wide, carried forty to fifty passengers. By 1836 over 3,000 boats traveled the length of the canal. A vast freight business developed with wheat and flour being brought from the Great Lakes east along the canal and down the Hudson River to the port of New York. It also proved an important route west for immigrants from Europe. Reaching New York City, they then took river boats up the Hudson, and packetboats on to Buffalo. From there they journeyed into the Old Northwest. Traffic exceeded expectations, particularly coal shipments, and by the 1850s the canal had to be enlarged. At no point did the federal government provide aid for this project.[13]

DeWITT CLINTON

Political detractors in New York referred to the Erie Canal as "Clinton's Ditch," and some opponents wished to deny him credit as its primary promoter. But DeWitt Clinton, who combined careers as officeholder, lawyer, and businessman, became the most powerful politician in New York. Clinton belonged to that segment of American society which believed national development was dependent upon internal improvements; he spent much of his life urging the state of New York to build the Erie Canal. Born in New York in 1769, Clinton graduated from Columbia College, studied law, and was admitted to the bar. In 1797 he initiated his lengthy political career, being elected to the New York State Assembly. The leading Democratic Republican in New York, he won a United States Senate seat in 1802 but resigned the following year to become mayor of New York City, a position he would hold three times. As mayor he not only developed the city and its services, particularly public education, but also became the primary advocate of a water route connecting the Hudson River and Lake Erie. His advocacy of internal improvements gained him the support of northeastern Federalists in 1812 when he ran against James Madison for the presidency. Many fellow Democratic Republicans never forgave Clinton for his opposition to Madison.

After 1815 Clinton devoted himself to promoting the canal. Clinton proved inept at political intrigue; nevertheless, he developed a coalition in support of "Clinton's Ditch." As early as 1810 Clinton began service on a canal commission that sought unsuccessfully to obtain federal aid for the project.

DeWitt Clinton (1769–1828). Politician, promoter, commissioner of the Erie Canal. (Courtesy: *Dictionary of American Portraits.*)

Elected governor in 1817, he continued to fight for the canal because he believed that the project would not only aid the port of New York, but it would also help to develop the whole state.

In 1824 Clinton's political opponents removed him from the New York Canal Commission; however, an irate public reelected him governor, and when the Erie Canal was completed in 1825, Governor Clinton participated in the opening ceremony. Throughout his career Clinton emphasized that canals would bind the nation together, and his motivations were largely those of an American nationalist. In that respect he is not unlike Daniel Webster, Henry Clay, and other leading politicians of the pre–Civil War era who saw internal improvements not only as aiding the economic development of the United States but also as creating an American nation.

The Erie Canal had been built because a generation of New Yorkers determined to exploit the underdeveloped economic resources of their state. The New York government took on this vast project and its several branches because the huge capital expenditure proved too large for any individual or for a private corporation. As one student of the Erie Canal has written, "The canals marked a turning point in the tradition of state intervention in the economy."[14] Traffic on the canal expanded rapidly following reductions in tolls in the 1830s and 1840s. It became a cheap means of conveyance, and even after the completion of competing rail lines canal traffic continued to grow. Low-value tonnage shifted to the canal, particularly agricultural and forest products. By the time of the Civil War most of the canal traffic moved from west to east, some 80 percent, indicating the degree to which the Old Northwest had become settled and how its economy had matured.[15]

The economy of New York City boomed with the opening of the Erie Canal. The city's competitors—Boston, Philadelphia, Baltimore, and

Charleston—sought similar projects to reach their hinterlands. Despite their serious efforts, however, New York's predominance, financially and economically, could not be challenged by its rivals.[16]

The wave of enthusiasm for canals led to the construction of projects to improve transportation between the upcountry and tidewater in states along the Atlantic from Maine to Virginia. Other projects sought to link the Atlantic coast states with the Ohio River valley, and western canals connected the Ohio and Mississippi river systems with the Great Lakes. In Pennsylvania canals brought coal to Philadelphia. The anthracite canals, as they were called, were often built with private funds rather than with state money. Philadelphia sponsored the so-called Pennsylvania system, a 394-mile-long route extending from Philadelphia west to Pittsburgh. The Alleghenies proved too steep for a lock system, so incline planes were developed that pulled the barges up one side of the mountain and lowered them down the other side. Canal boats moved westward with cargoes of hardware, notions, calico, and manufactured goods, and they returned carrying timber, wheat, whiskey, furs, and livestock.

Sometimes enthusiasm for the canals led to projects of dubious economic viability. In several states millions of dollars were invested in canals. Following the models of Pennsylvania and New York, the states of Ohio and Indiana built elaborate systems. In Ohio canals interlaced the state, connecting its major cities and navigable rivers. State securities, marketed in England, paid for these projects. In 1836 the state of Indiana began a massive canal program, and within five years the state debt exceeded $13 million, of which $9 million had been spent on the canals.[17]

By 1840 over $125 million had been expended on the construction of more than 3,000 miles of canals in twenty states. Much of the financing came from the state and local governments, probably 70 percent of the total investment. The canals had often been conceived of as civic rather than business enterprises. Why had public rather than private enterprise been the vehicle for canal construction? It was clear that public investment was necessary because of the size of the projects. But the questionable private rate of return was outweighed by the larger benefits to society—the social rate of return.

Congress recognized the need for federal aid for internal improvements, and, despite denying funds to the Erie Canal, it subsequently made contributions toward the construction of other projects. The federal government by the time of the Civil War had granted approximately 4 million acres of the public domain to help finance construction of canals in the Old Northwest. In addition, it subscribed to over $3 million in the securities of canal companies. The states, however, were the major sources of capital for their construction. As a consequence, state debts became enormous, and the funding of these debts exceeded the ability of the states to pay. Indiana and Pennsylvania were virtually bankrupted by their canal bonds, and Ohio's credit was badly strained. Nevertheless, the canals made important contributions to the economic growth of the nation.

The canals drastically lowered freight rates. Where canals had been built, the rates fell from an average of 15 cents a ton mile by road to 2.3

cents by canal boat. These low rates spurred the development of the upper midwest and also reoriented trade routes from a north-south axis along the Mississippi River to an east-west traffic along the major canals. While most of the canals lost money, they provided benefits in the form of better transportation at lower rates. The completion of the canal systems was particularly important for the development of major cities. The anthracite coal brought to Philadelphia by the canal system helped to create heavy industry in that city; in turn, the growth of the coal and iron industries caused the merchants of Philadelphia to shift their investments from shipping to manufacturing.

The canals made contributions to the organization of American business. Because the canals operated over substantial distances, a complex organizational structure had to be created. The executives of the canal companies initially had little knowledge of managerial functions. Actual construction forced the development of a structure that organized the canal into divisions. Each division was the responsibility of an engineer who would survey the route and then inspect the progress of construction. A chief engineer at the canal headquarters supervised the work of the men in the field. A technical task rather than administrative, all they had to do was lay out the line and see that the contractors carried out the construction. A board of directors, either public or private, raised the funds and made the ultimate decisions on terminals and general locations. The operation of the canal called for a more complex administration than had its construction. In some cases the chief engineer in charge of planning became the general superintendent. He supervised the employees who operated the locks, collected the tolls, and maintained and repaired the canal. While essentially a simple organization, it was more complex than that of most businesses in the nation.[18]

THE CHESAPEAKE AND DELAWARE CANAL

Even before the Revolutionary War the cities of Philadelphia and Baltimore became intense rivals for the trade of the mid-Atlantic states. Philadelphia, located on the Delaware River above Delaware Bay, had access by water to western New Jersey and eastern Pennsylvania. Baltimore dominated Chesapeake Bay and the Susquehannah River valley that extended north and west into Pennsylvania. The merchants of Philadelphia looked askance as its rival drained away the wheat, flour, and lumber of a part of Pennsylvania that Philadelphia considered its own. The merchants of Baltimore sought to gain a more direct route to the Atlantic Ocean than that which extended south through Chesapeake Bay to its perilous entrance into the Atlantic. Therefore leaders of both cities saw an advantage in digging a canal across the narrow isthmus that separated the Delaware River from the upper reaches of Chesapeake Bay. At one point the isthmus was only about 14 miles wide, and the terrain extended only 100 feet in elevation above sea level. Boats from Philadelphia could use the canal to reach the Susquehannah, and ships from Baltimore could save many miles on trips to the Atlantic. By the 1790s considerable agitation had developed in Maryland and Pennsylvania for the construction of what became known as the Chesapeake and Delaware Canal.

The St. George's Bridge spans the Chesapeake and Delaware Canal, which follows the path of its nineteenth-century predecessor.   (Courtesy: Delaware Bureau of Travel Development.)

In 1804–1806 the famous engineer and architect Benjamin Latrobe surveyed the route for the Chesapeake and Delaware Canal Company. Subsequent efforts to obtain federal support for the canal were unsuccessful until 1823, when Secretary of War John C. Calhoun agreed to provide army engineers to consult with the canal company on the site and the excavation work. Recognizing the military and strategic value of such a canal, the federal government in 1825 purchased $300,000 in stock of the company. The company initiated construction in 1824, and during the next five years excavation work proceeded. In 1829 the canal opened, but not until the federal government had purchased an additional $150,000 in stock.

The Chesapeake and Delaware Canal symbolized the canal era, but while most of the canals would fall into disuse and disrepair during the railroad era, it remained operative. The Chesapeake and Delaware connected two of the most important waterways, and by the time of the Civil War it had become part of the national transportation network. Eventually, because of the need to deepen and widen the channel, the federal government took over the route, which became a part of the Intercoastal Waterway System. The Chesapeake and Delaware Canal is yet another example of the importance of federal and state aid to internal improvements before the Civil War.

The canal era ended because of a number of factors. The financial crisis of 1837 brought catastrophe to some of the states that had invested heavily in canals. Their costs often exceeded engineering estimates, and revenues fell far short of expectations. Poor management in many instances precluded the generation of profits. Canals in the Northeast and the upper Midwest were often closed in the winter because of ice. These factors contributed to their financial woes, which worsened with the coming of the railroads. Nevertheless, the canals served as effective links to the large river systems, particularly the Mississippi River and its tributaries. It would be on these rivers that another form of transportation would add a new dimension to the transportation revolution. On the rivers of the West, as well as in the East, the steamboat would provide a faster and more effective conveyance for water-borne commerce.

THE STEAMBOATS

While the canals eased the problems of large-scale commerce in the Northeast and the Old Northwest, the rivers in the central portion of the United States remained the primary means of transporting goods to the Gulf of Mexico. Agricultural products were floated downriver in flatboats on journeys of a thousand or more miles. Flatboats from western Pennsylvania, for example, reached New Orleans in a month to six weeks, but only a few keelboats or barges returned upriver. Moving a flatboat from New Orleans to Pittsburgh, a journey of almost 2,000 miles, could consume four months or longer. On a few expanses of the great rivers sails could be used, but generally to move upstream flatboatmen simply poled their vessel or sometimes rowed. On some tributaries, the swift currents, shallow water, or narrow, winding channels precluded the use of even a flatboat. In order to make maximum usage of the navigable waters, a new power source had to be found.

The solution was the application of steam power to water transportation. Several American inventors and engineers demonstrated that riverboats could be moved by steam engines, but the means to apply steam power was limited by the available technology. Finally, in 1807, Robert Fulton demonstrated the commercial feasibility of a steamboat on the Hudson River. The War of 1812 precluded further immediate developments, but after basic technical problems had been resolved and engineering concepts were devised for the construction of steam-powered vessels, Americans created a new business. Extensive steamboat service could soon be found in the northeastern, southern, and western portions of the United States. Numerous inland towns became great river ports—cities such as Louisville, St. Louis, and Memphis. While the steamboat had been first used in the East, it was the tremendous Mississippi River system that saw this form of transportation achieve its greatest success. Army engineers estimated that 16,000 miles of waterway were available to steam navigation, which by 1830 dominated river transportation. During the next four decades steamboats played an important part in the development of the United States.[19]

Steamboats drastically reduced the cost and time necessary to transport goods on the inland waterways. By 1850 trips along the Mississippi River, which had taken ninety days or more by flatboat, could be made in less than a week. Some flatboats and keelboats remained in service on the Mississippi and its tributaries, particularly in isolated areas or where the rivers were shallow, but even there small steamboats were built that drove these crude craft from the waterways. Indeed, vessels moved up the Missouri River as far as Fort Benton, Montana. Furs, timber, lead, grain, and other products flowed downriver to the port of New Orleans. Many of the larger vessels were 300 feet long and carried three to four hundred passengers on the decks besides those in the palatial cabins. The western steamboats looked like floating wooden castles as they glided along the river. Yet the average life span of a steamboat on the Mississippi was only five years. Snags, boiler explosions, collisions, and other catastrophes often destroyed these ornate vessels.[20]

Steam navigation also appeared on the Great Lakes. By the 1830s steam dominated the transportation of passengers on Lakes Huron and Michigan, and over 360 steam-driven ships could be found on the Great Lakes by 1860. Many of these lake steamships exceeded 1,000 tons, and a few, like the *City of Buffalo* of over 2,200 tons, were giants. In many ways the lake steamers resembled ocean rather than river craft because of their deep hulls and low superstructures. These were not mere modifications of ocean ships, however, but entirely different vessels. By mid-century the tonnage on the Mississippi River and on the Great Lakes exceeded that of all shipping from New York City by over 200 percent.

Shortly after Fulton demonstrated the economic viability of steam power, steamboat companies emerged. Little capital was required to enter the business: There was no construction or maintenance of a right-of-way, but simply the acquisition and operation of a vessel. A medium-sized steamboat cost from $20,000 to $60,000, and such a sum was not beyond the ability of one person or a small group to raise. Partnerships, corporations, and proprietorships operated the steamboats. Much of the original capital came from merchants, but soon other investors bought the securities of the steamboat companies. On the Mississippi River each steamship was often a separate venture owned by a small group. A disastrous accident could wipe out such firms, but profit levels remained relatively high even after the coming of the railroads. Ironically, while the steamboat helped to stimulate the economic growth of the nation's heartland, ocean steamers signaled a decline in American maritime activity.

THE MERCHANT MARINE

The rise of steam navigation in the American maritime service paralleled the development of the steamboats in the rivers. The sail-powered shipping industry of the United States peaked in the early 1800s and entered a decline by the 1830s. The great increase in shipping at the outset of the nineteenth century can largely be explained by the wars in Europe. The military adventures of Napoleon kept Europe in turmoil until 1815, and the United States, taking advantage of its position as a neutral, became an important factor in international commerce. Americans provided Europe with imports from the rest of the world by utilizing the superiority of their ships and their entrepreneurial abilities.

The federal government also played an important role. From the time of the Constitution the government strongly encouraged the maritime industry. Goods brought to the United States by American ships received a 10 percent reduction on tariffs. Another law gave United States shippers a virtual monopoly of the coastal trade. Yet another statute required that American ships pay the port tax only once a year if engaged in coastal shipping; foreign ships were required to pay the tax at each port. Likewise, state governments in the Northeast and the mid-Atlantic states, and the governments of the major port cities, attempted to stimulate international and coastal commerce.

Baltimore, Philadelphia, New York, and Boston labored mightily to promote their ports. Merchants in each of those cities often specialized in one commodity. Baltimore, for example, tended to be a major port for the export of wheat, while New York dominated the cotton trade. Indeed, by 1810 New York became the nation's major port of entry, and its lead increased markedly by 1820. No other city could rival New York's geographical setting, and none was more strategically located. Further, the citizens of New York engaged in an aggressive policy to attract foreign trade. The city established an auction system for disposing of imports; merchants organized regularly scheduled transatlantic packet services; investors created a coastal trade that brought the cotton traffic to the city; and finally, as has been seen, residents of New York promoted the Erie Canal. As a consequence, the city received an enormous flow of goods from the West. Although Philadelphia continued to remain important as an exporter of wheat, its future seemed to rest in finance rather than in trade. Baltimore's merchants developed the swift clipper schooners in the coastal trade, created markets in Latin America, and aggressively sought the produce of the Ohio valley. Charleston, South Carolina, once one of the nation's leading ports, declined and was stagnant by the 1830s. New Orleans, however, entered its greatest growth period after 1815 with products from the Ohio, Tennessee, Mississippi, and Missouri valleys flowing downriver to the Crescent City. With steam transportation firmly established, New Orleans became the nation's second major port. For a few years in the late 1830s and early 1840s, the exports from New Orleans actually exceeded in value those from New York.[21]

Those who dominated the seaports and the ships that plied the coastal waters were merchant capitalists, often the leading citizens of the cities in which they resided. They bought and sold goods, both at wholesale and retail, owned and sometimes built their own ships, and in many cases had commission agents or factors in other coastal cities performing functions that included banking. The commercial newspapers in the ports reported their activities, and these newspapers advertised the wide variety of services they offered. Their warehouses, wharves, and stores filled with commodities from all over the world. Casks, bales, barrels, and boxes contained the

Merchants and merchandise crowd the lower levee in Cincinnati lined with steamboats in the shadow of the new suspension bridge.   (Courtesy: The Ohio Historical Society.)

agricultural products and industrial goods from American farms and factories being exported for the world market. These merchant capitalists located credit or working capital both in this country and abroad, and in many cases they borrowed from local banks to cover their charges. As American trade expanded, specialization by merchants increased, and by the middle of the 1840s there were sixty different types of importers in New York City alone.[22]

One of the most profitable of the maritime ventures was the China trade. As early as 1784 a group of New York and Philadelphia merchants sent the vessel *The Empress of China* to the Far East. After a 15-month voyage, *The Empress* returned with a cargo of tea and silk. The profits proved extraordinary, and Philadelphia soon became the center for trade with China. Ships sailed to China carrying cargoes of turpentine, tar, wine, brandy, and hard cash, but perhaps their most important item was ginseng, a root which the Chinese believed slowed advancing years and acted as an aphrodisiac. The 25 percent profit returned by *The Empress of China* was not matched by all of the thirty to forty ships that sailed to China each year, but between 1804 and 1846 the trade made wealthy people of some residents of the City of Brotherly Love. Stephen Girard, a Philadelphia merchant, became a leader in this trade. Girard placed his profits in more ships, land speculation, banking, manufacturing, and other forms of transportation. The Philadelphia merchants became deeply involved in the opium traffic. The British had imported opium from India to China for many years, but after 1800 opium had been banned by the Chinese government. Philadelphia merchants purchased Turkish opium for resale in China, and many of the merchants had great difficulties with the Chinese government. During the Opium War (1839–1842), military forces sent by the United States intervened on behalf of the American merchants, but by 1846 the Chinese trade had ended.[23]

Between 1815 and 1860 world shipping witnessed almost revolutionary changes. Not only did the shipping companies alter their organizations, but the size, speed, construction, and propulsion of ocean-going vessels shifted dramatically. The United States developed regular transatlantic scheduled service, and by 1845 over fifty packets to Europe operated out of New York City alone. The ships increased in size, and the square-rigged vessels of 200 to 300 tons became the backbone of the American fleet. With the streamlining of the hull, the clipper ship emerged. By the 1840s the clippers dominated the seas. Ocean steamers did not enter the transatlantic trade until after the 1840s. Serious technological and economic problems had to be surmounted, primarily because of the crudity and bulkiness of the steam engine and its enormous fuel consumption. By the early 1840s new engine designs and safety features allowed for the profitable utilization of the steamships in the Atlantic. The technological evolution included the use of the iron hull and screw propulsion.

Again the United States government intervened in the economy when, in the late 1840s, it began to subsidize ship lines to Europe. But the subsidized lines proved unsuccessful, and federal financial support ended by 1858. European companies took over much of the transatlantic trade by the time of the Civil War as Americans turned inward; fortunes made in shipping were invested in other forms of transportation, in banking, and in industry. The nation began to produce more of the goods it needed; imports for consumption purposes fell from almost $10 per person in the 1800s to slightly over $5 per person in the 1840s. The supremacy of American shipping had rested on superior timber and able seamen. As iron ships replaced wood and steam replaced sail, America not only lost its advantages but also its incentive to continue to dominate the seas. The merchant capitalist declined in importance as the manufacturer became the dominant figure in the American economy. This change can be seen dramatically in the career of John Jacob Astor.

JOHN JACOB ASTOR

Astor, the richest man in America before the Civil War, lived in New York City, and his extensive interests in the fur trade and foreign commerce made him almost the perfect merchant capitalist. A seller, promoter, speculator, and trader, Astor had virtually a Midas touch. In addition, he pioneered in the creation of a premodern business structure. Born in southern Germany in 1763, Astor lived in London briefly before coming to the United States, where he found a job as a clerk in a fur-trading establishment. As a result of the demand for pelts in Europe, the fur trade was one of the most profitable industries in the country. Traders in the interior acquired furs from the Indian tribes, reselling them to the merchants in Albany and elsewhere. Astor determined to learn all aspects of the trade, and he journeyed west to visit the Indian villages. Marriage in 1785 brought not only a wife but also a dowry of $300, enabling him to open a general store. Astor quickly specialized in the trade of furs. He made commercial arrangements with trappers to cover the region between the Ohio River and the Great Lakes, but he realized that one of the most profitable aspects of the trade was the selling of pelts in China. The Chinese especially prized the fur of the sea otter, which could be obtained in the Pacific Northwest. American ships entered the mouth of the Columbia River, traded for a cargo of sea otter pelts, and sailed across the Pacific to China. The ships returned with holds filled with silks, tea, and Chinese art objects. The risks in this traffic were extraordinary indeed, whether it be a hurricane in mid-Pacific or the danger of pirates along the Chinese coast. Though vessels were often lost, John Jacob Astor had a motto to cope with such risks: His response to bad news was, "Make the best of things!"[24]

The Napoleonic Wars created a major market for American shipping, but they also increased losses. President Jefferson, afraid that intervention by European countries in American shipping and their frequent seizure of American ships would bring the United States into the war, enacted an embargo in 1807. The law terminated foreign trade and confined American ships to port. Astor, however, less concerned about the law than with the profits to be made, told customs officials that his ship *The Beaver* was sailing to China to return a Chinese governmental leader. In reality *The Beaver* carried 3,000 otter skins. It returned with a cargo estimated to be worth more than $200,000. Astor had learned his business methods in the notorious fur trade; he simply operated in the ethical milieu of his time.

Astor obtained a charter from the New York legislature in 1808 for the American Fur Company. Capitalized at $1 million, he was the only security holder. The American Fur Company operated trading posts on the Great Lakes and along the Missouri River above St. Louis. When rivals appeared, Astor bought them out and made them part of his company. Astor's American Fur Company obtained a virtual monopoly on fur trapping and trading in the West. He divided the growing company into major departments. Each department administered a number of outfits, which, in turn, were led by a trader who supervised the day-to-day work of the clerks in the posts and those who did the actual trapping. The men who served as department heads became partners in the company. Astor, as senior partner, found that his time was not wholly consumed by the American Fur Company, and he was able to engage in other profitable enterprises. Indeed, in 1834 he withdrew from the partnership. Nevertheless, Astor had discovered the necessity of organizing a more complex business structure in order to carry out his strategy of dominating the fur industry in the United States.[25]

Seventy-one years of age in 1834, Astor left the fur industry to engage in land speculation, one of the prime activities of American business leaders and merchants. More money could be made in land than in virtually any other activity. Small American towns were growing into cities, and the

John Jacob Astor (1763–1848). Fur trader, merchant, and financier. (Courtesy: *Dictionary of American Portraits*.)

phenomenal urban growth rates drove up the value of real estate. A speculator with a little money and more vision or foresight could make a huge profit. Astor bought his first lots in New York City as early as 1789. He did not believe in credit or in borrowing; he paid for his acquisitions in cash. The town that numbered 25,000 when he arrived there became the nation's largest city in 1810. He bought a Dutch farm in the middle of Manhattan in 1797, paying $25,000 for the property; the farm would sell for that much per square yard by the time of Astor's death.

Like many other merchants, Astor withdrew from shipping. Though much of Astor's reputation as a businessman centered on his famous China enterprises, by 1825 he had discontinued using his own ships, and three years later he withdrew from maritime activities entirely. The merchants saw that the development of banking, credit agencies, mortgage markets, and, in particular, inland transportation provided other areas for potential investments. The merchants became leaders in the organization of factories and other businesses. The national economy had grown, industries developed, and trading facilities expanded because of the clipper ship, the steamship, and the Erie Canal. That growth accelerated in the 1830s and the 1840s because of the arrival of yet another more efficient transportation form: the railroad.

NOTES

1. Henry Adams, *The United States in 1800* (Ithaca, New York: Cornell University Press, 1957), p. 11.

2. Albert Gallatin, "Roads and Canals," 10th Congress, 1st Sess., Document No. 250, April 4, 1808, *American State Papers, Miscellaneous*, vol. I, pp. 724–741.

3. George Rogers Taylor, *The Transportation Revolution, 1815–1860* (New York: Rinehart and Co., 1951), is still the best study of the transformation of the economy before the Civil War.

4. Thomas C. Cochran, *200 Years of American Business* (New York: Basic Books, 1977), pp. 23–24, 26–47.

5. Carter Goodrich, *The Government and the Economy, 1783–1861* (Indianapolis: Bobbs-Merrill, 1967), pp. vii, xvi, and xxii.

6. Carter Goodrich, *Government Promotion of American Canals and Railroads, 1800–1890* (New York: Columbia University Press, 1960), pp. 3–4; Douglass C. North, *Economic Growth of the United States, 1790–1860* (Englewood Cliffs, New Jersey: Prentice Hall, 1961), pp. 66–67, vii.

7. Taylor, *The Transportation Revolution,* pp. 15–18, 22–24.

8. Philip D. Jordan, *The National Road* (Indianapolis: Bobbs-Merrill, 1948), p. 136.

9. Taylor, *The Transportation Revolution,* pp. 19–22.

10. Forest G. Hill, *Roads, Rails & Waterways: The Army Engineers and Early Transportation* (Norman: University of Oklahoma Press, 1957).

11. W. Turrentine Jackson, *Wagon Roads West: A Study of Federal Road Surveys and Construction in the Trans-Mississippi West, 1846–1869* (New Haven, Connecticut: Yale University Press, 1965); this is the definitive study.

12. John Stover, *Transportation in American History* (Washington: The American Historical Association, 1970), pp. 9–10.

13. Ronald E. Shaw, *Erie Water West: A History of the Erie Canal, 1792–1854* (Lexington: University of Kentucky Press, 1966).

14. Nathan Miller, *The Enterprise of a Free People* (Ithaca, New York: Cornell University Press, 1962), p. xii.

15. Ronald W. Filante, "A Note on the Economic Viability of the Erie Canal, 1825–1860," *The Business History Review* 48 (Spring 1974), pp. 95–102.

16. Robert Greenhalgh Albion, *The Rise of New York Port [1815–1860]* (New York: Charles Scribner's Sons, 1939), p. 94.

17. Taylor, *The Transportation Revolution,* pp. 37, 49–50.

18. Cochran, *200 Years of American Business,* pp. 49 and 43–44; and Alfred D. Chandler, Jr., *Strategy and Structure: Chapters in the History of the American Industrial Enterprise* (Cambridge: MIT Press, 1962), p. 21.

19. Taylor, *The Transportation Revolution,* pp. 56–73.

20. Louis C. Hunter, *Steamboats on the Western Rivers: An Economic and Technological History* (Cambridge: Harvard University Press, 1949).

21. Taylor, *The Transportation Revolution,* pp. 7–9.

22. Cochran, *200 Years of American Business,* pp. 25–33.

23. Jonathan Goldstein, *Philadelphia and the China Trade, 1682–1846: Commercial, Cultural and Attitudinal Effects* (University Park: Pennsylvania State University Press, 1978).

24. Kenneth Wiggins Porter, *John Jacob Astor, Business Man* (Cambridge: Harvard University Press, 1931), p. 1073; this is the definitive study of America's first millionaire.

25. Chandler, *Strategy and Structure,* p. 20.

SUGGESTED READINGS

ALBION, ROBERT GREENHALGH. *The Rise of New York Port [1815–1860].* New York: Charles Scribner's Sons, 1939.

BALDWIN, LELAND D. *The Keelboat Age on Western Waters.* Pittsburgh: University of Pittsburgh Press, 1941.

GOODRICH, CARTER. *Government Promotion of American Canals and Railroads, 1800–1890.* New York: Columbia University Press, 1960.

GRAY, RALPH D. *The National Waterway: A History of the Chesapeake and Delaware Canal, 1769–1965.* Urbana: University of Illinois Press, 1967.

HAITES, ERIK F., JAMES MAK, AND GARY M. WALTON. *Western River Transportation: The Era of Early Internal Development, 1810–1860.* Baltimore: Johns Hopkins University Press, 1975.

HILL, FOREST G. *Roads, Rails & Waterways: The Army Engineers and Early Transportation.* Norman: University of Oklahoma Press, 1957.

HUNTER, LOUIS C. *Steamboats on the Western Rivers.* Cambridge: Harvard University Press, 1949.

HUTCHINS, JOHN G. B. *The American Maritime Industries and Public Policy, 1789–1914.* Cambridge: Harvard University Press, 1941.

JACKSON, W. TURRENTINE. *Wagon Roads West.* New Haven, Connecticut: Yale University Press, 1965.

JORDAN, PHILIP D. *The National Road.* Indianapolis: Bobbs-Merrill, 1948.

MILLER, NATHAN. *The Enterprise of a Free People: Aspects of Economic Development in New York State during the Canal Period, 1792–1838.* Ithaca, New York: Cornell University Press, 1962.

PORTER, KENNETH WIGGINS. *John Jacob Astor, Business Man.* Cambridge: Harvard University Press, 1931.

RUBIN, JULIUS. *Canal or Railroad? Imitation and Innovation in the Response to the Erie Canal in Philadelphia, Baltimore and Boston.* Philadelphia: American Philosophical Society, 1961.

SHAW, RONALD E. *Erie Water West: A History of the Erie Canal, 1792–1854.* Lexington: University of Kentucky Press, 1966.

TAYLOR, GEORGE ROGERS. *The Transportation Revolution, 1815–1860.* New York: Rinehart and Co., 1951.

7 | Railroads and Business Expansion

Before the coming of the railroad, virtually no basic changes in transportation had taken place for two thousand years. People and goods moved as they had during the Roman Empire, by packhorse, wagon, or boat. Beginning in the late 1820s the railroad revolutionized transportation in the United States and laid the basis for a modern industrial economy. The railroad was invented in western Europe, particularly in England, but by 1840 European countries had only 1,818 miles of track while the United States had almost 3,000 miles. The United States became the leader in the development of the railroad because of the vast distances to be overcome, and because it was not hampered by the entrenched vested interests and long-established customs that hindered European rail expansion. Although some opposition to railroads did exist—one Ohio school board held that the steam railroad was "a device of Satan to lead immortal souls down to Hell"—such sentiment was rare. The American people welcomed the railroad with unbounded enthusiasm and invested their savings and supported the promoters who built the lines across the virgin territories of the country. Their enthusiasm reflected the pioneering spirit of the people of the United States.[1]

PIONEER RAILROADS

The experience of three major commercial centers, Baltimore, Charleston, and Boston, illustrate America's fervor for railways. Each city sought to expand its hinterland to the west, and each pioneered in the construction of railroads. Baltimore built the Baltimore and Ohio Railroad, chartered in 1828, across the Alleghenies to tap markets in the Ohio River Valley. The people of Charleston constructed a railroad inland to the Savannah River, where they hoped to divert the cotton trade to their port, thereby defeating their archrival Savannah. Frightened by the sudden rise of New York after the completion of the Erie Canal, Bostonians sought to build a railroad westward to Albany on the Hudson River and take away traffic going to the port of New York. These three cities initiated the railroad era in their respective regions.

On July 4, 1828, Charles Carroll, one of the signers of the Declaration of Independence, turned the first earth to initiate the construction of the horse-drawn Baltimore and Ohio Railroad. Later that summer steam power came to the B&O when Peter Cooper, a part-time inventor from New York, brought the locomotive "Tom Thumb" to the line. The "Tom Thumb" was not a success, however, and lost a race with a horse-powered vehicle. Not until 1831 did steam locomotives replace horse-drawn wagons on the railroad. The successful utilization of steam power and construction to the west enhanced the profitability of the B&O, which soon had gross revenues of over a quarter of a million dollars per year. On Christmas Eve 1852, the B&O reached the Ohio River at Wheeling, Virginia, and traffic from the Ohio River Valley began to flow east to Baltimore.

Meanwhile, the South Carolina Canal and Rail-road Company constructed its line westward from Charleston. On Christmas Day 1830, the "Best Friend of Charleston," the first locomotive built for sale in the United States, carried over 140 passengers on the first scheduled steam railroad in this country. The 136-mile route to Hamburg, South Carolina, completed in 1833, was the longest continuous railroad in the world.

Railroad promoters in Boston soon had three fledgling lines extending from that city to Lowell, Providence, and Worcester. They formed the basis of a New England railway system. The success of these cities generated a wave of railway construction in the 1830s. Railroad enthusiasm became wild and boisterous railway *fever* as every town and city sought to emulate Baltimore, Charleston, and Boston.

From then on the rail system grew rapidly: Of the twenty-six states in the union in 1840, only four were without railroads. The lines largely served the cities along the Atlantic coast, and New England and the mid-Atlantic states had over 60 percent of the total mileage in the country. Only the Panic of 1837 and the subsequent depression slowed the expansion of the railroads. Some states, particularly those in the Old Northwest, suffered heavily because of their investments in railroad projects. Nevertheless, by the end of the decade the United States far outstripped European countries in the development of this new transportation artery.[2]

Throughout the 1830s and 1840s the railroads constantly improved

"The Best Friend of Charleston" began the first regular steam railroad service on December 25, 1830.   (Courtesy: Southern Railway System.)

their trackage and rolling equipment. The first railroads had been built on tracks of iron straps or bars fastened to wooden rails that, in turn, were attached to blocks of granite or other stones imbedded in the earth. The iron-strap rails, only 20 to 25 feet long, often broke loose and curled under the weight of passing trains to form "snake heads" that tore through the bottoms of the cars. The solution to the problem appeared in 1831 when Robert L. Stevens, an engineer and president of the Camden and Amboy Railroad of New Jersey, designed the T-rail. Supporting the T-rail were wooden sleepers or ties that replaced the heavy stones or granite blocks under the rails. A roadbed surfaced with crushed stone or gravel supported the track. American railroads did not have a uniform track gauge, or distance between the rails. In England the standard gauge was 4 feet 8½ inches. This became the usual track gauge in New England and portions of the North, but some railways, the Erie for example, were 6-foot gauge. Other railroads, particularly in the southern states, had 5-foot gauge. This necessitated transshipment of goods where lines of different gauges intersected. Locomotive design also improved. Originally most of the engines were imported from England, but Philadelphia jewelry manufacturer Matthias Baldwin began to build locomotives, and soon other locomotive builders emerged in the Northeast. Passenger cars, which were nothing more than stage coaches with railroad wheels, evolved into longer, more comfortable accommodations. The diminutive freight cars, usually with only four wheels, became longer and heavier with greater carrying capacity, and most were outfitted with eight wheels. Thus the railways spawned auxiliary enterprises in T-rail manufacturing, locomotive works, and car and wheel shops, and they gave impetus to the lumber industry, which furnished the wooden ties.[3]

Railroad construction, which had rapidly expanded in the 1840s, turned into a veritable explosion of new tracks and rail lines in the prosperous 1850s. In 1850 the nation's railway mileage was 8,879; by 1860 the total exceeded 30,000 miles. The 1850s also saw the consolidation of many short rail lines into large companies, particularly in the North and Northeast. While a few roads like the Erie and the Baltimore and Ohio had been built as single companies, most of the trunk lines were created through mergers. Yet the nation did not have a unified rail system. The railways north of the Ohio River and those in the south connected in only three places.[4] The proliferation of railways in the 1850s resulted from financial stimulation by private capital and by government.

FINANCING THE RAILROADS

The financing of the railroad boom in the 1850s was aided by the federal, state, and local governments. State governments granted liberal railroad charters, and in a few cases they actually built the lines. State and local governments supplied money and credit for many of the private railroads. The federal government also contributed by making surveys at government expense and by reducing the tariff on iron used by the railroads. Between 1845 and 1860 state governments borrowed more than $90 million, largely to finance railroad construction, and state and local governments often purchased securities in the railway corporations.

The federal government also supported the railways by providing almost 25 million acres of land for railroad construction before the Civil War. The debate over the use of federal lands to aid railroads deeply divided the Congress, with members from the Northeast generally opposed while those from the West and South strongly urged such help. On September 20, 1850, the government made its first significant railroad land grant: a railway to be built from northern Illinois to Mobile, Alabama. The grant included a 200-foot right-of-way and alternate even-numbered sections of land on each side of the track for a depth of 6 miles. If the granted lands were occupied, the railroad could have other sections within 15 miles of its track. The law provided that railroads constructed with the land grant should transport the property or troops of the United States free from any toll or charge and that Congress would determine the rate of the mails that the lines would carry. This initial rail grant created a precedent, and additional grants before the Civil War benefited forty-five railroads.[5]

The federal land grant program expanded rapidly after the Civil War. Many politicians believed that western settlement would take place on a large scale only if people were induced to go west where railroads already existed; tracks had to be laid ahead of demand. The national government subsidized the railroads because the existing populations were sparse and state, territorial, and local governments were unable to provide the level of support that had existed in the South and the East before 1860. Between 1850 and 1871, 175 million acres of land were granted to railroads by Congress, although 35 million acres were eventually forfeited and returned when contracts were not fulfilled. While seventy railroads received federal land grants, four (the Northern Pacific, Santa Fe, Southern Pacific, and Union Pacific) received over 70 percent of the total. Yet it must be kept in mind that the land grants covered only 20,000 miles of railroad, or only 8 percent of the nation's total.

The grants did give impetus to railroad construction, and they nourished the belief that the railroads would eventually pay interest and dividends: Land grants were often necessary to attract capital for construction. In all cases the government required that railroads built with land grants reduce charges for federal shipments, the general reduction being 50 percent from ordinary rates. A congressional report in 1945 estimated that the government had saved $900 million because of this clause. A long and heated debate has continued as to whether or not the land grants were justified or even if they were required. Clearly, the major contribution of grants was to furnish a basis for credit so that construction could begin. The belief that the land grants would provide instant profits proved an illusion, but they did encourage the construction of railroads in advance of settlement. Unfortunately, they also encouraged the lines to be built quickly and often poorly. The economic consequences of the land grants did not bring a halt to such aid; rather, revelations of corruption and bribery caused public opinion to demand that such assistance be ended. Direct federal aid terminated early in the 1870s, and most state and local support for railroads ceased during the next decade. But as will be seen, governmental aid was relatively small in comparison with investment by private capital.[6]

Private investors largely financed the construction of the railway system. Merchants, farmers, manufacturers, and professional men and women bought stocks and bonds in rail companies. In cities such as Boston, New York, and Philadelphia, investors purchased the securities of lines in the West and South. Boston, for example, became a major contributor the the construction of lines west of Chicago. Some railway bonds were sold in London before the Civil War, but most of the capital came from the United States. Investors were willing to purchase the securities because the railroad had triumphed over other forms of transportation. Turnpike and plank-road companies disappeared, and canals, even before the 1850s, were being abandoned. The railroads could transport goods cheaper than the turnpikes and more efficiently than the canals.

By 1860 the railways provided much of the nation with fast and economical transportation. Tonnage rates fell, and increased speeds reduced the financial burdens of other industries. Wagon rates for wheat had been as high as 30 cents per ton-mile in the Old Northwest. By the time of the Civil War, farmers could ship a bushel of wheat from Chicago to New York for only 1.2 cents per ton-mile. Only half of this reduction reflected the general price decline of the period. The consequences for domestic commerce were important indeed. The building of the railroads, more than any other factor, gave rise to industrialization. The building of the railroads, more than any other factor, gave rise to industrialization. Markets for manufacturers, miners, and commercial firms expanded with the rail network, and additional markets encouraged more complex machinery in manufacturing. In turn, machinery increased output even further, providing yet another impetus for expansion and continued growth. The railroads also proved to be important in war as well as peace.

THE IMPACT OF WAR

When the Civil War broke out in April of 1861, the rail systems of the Union and the Confederacy stood in sharp contrast. With only 9,000 miles of line the eleven Confederate states claimed only one-third of the nation's total rail mileage. The railways of the South were lightly constructed and less systematic in design and operation; rolling stock and locomotives were less numerous and had smaller capacities. The South had few facilities for the construction and maintenance of rolling stock, and the modest locomotive-building facilities were soon pressed into the production of ordnance. As the war expanded it became clear that the American Civil War would be the first in which railroads were vital tactically and strategically.

Shortages of basic commodities, such as lubricating oil and car wheels, soon made effective management of the railways in the South a virtual impossibility; but in the North the railroads prospered. The Illinois Central, for example, carried heavy trainloads of troops, animals, forage, and ammunition south to Kentucky and Tennessee, while the Baltimore and Ohio moved troops from Maryland into western Virginia and to Ohio. Some northern railway companies paid their first dividends in 1863–1864.

Neither the Confederate nor the Union governments took complete control of their railway systems. Both armies, however, recognized that successful campaigns often depended on possession of major railroad junctions, and both engaged in widespread railroad destruction in order to deny opponents use of the lines. The end of the war found the railway system of the South generally in ruins, and a massive rehabilitation program began almost immediately. The northern system, however, was in excellent condition. War demands resulted in greater cooperation among the railways, and the increased traffic led to the replacement of iron rails with steel and of wood with coal for fuel. The era of expansion in the 1850s—and of consolidated operations to meet the challenges of the war—placed the railroads on the threshold of even more rapid growth after 1865.[7]

THE TRANSCONTINENTALS

The post–Civil War era saw track mileage double in the first eight years after 1865, and double again in the next fourteen years. The construction of the transcontinental railroads dramatized this expansion. The Pacific Railway Act of 1862 authorized construction of the Union Pacific and Central Pacific railroads, which built toward each other from Omaha, Nebraska, and Sacramento, California. Completed in 1869, the Union Pacific–Central Pacific route proved to be the forerunner of additional transcontinentals. In 1883 the Northern Pacific extending west from Minneapolis and St. Paul reached Tacoma, Washington, and a few years later the Southern Pacific and the Santa Fe linked the west coast to New Orleans and Chicago.

While the transcontinentals were the work of many men, James J. Hill provided the leadership in the construction and operation of the Great Northern Railway. Born in 1838, Hill left Canada as a young man and settled in St. Paul, Minnesota, in 1856. He entered business, engaging in freighting, merchandising, and transportation. With a group of Canadian investors he took over the small St. Paul and Pacific Railroad and expanded the line north and west to Winnipeg to connect with the Canadian Pacific. He organized another railroad to build westward, reaching Great Falls,

Montana, in 1887. Hill constructed feeder lines only where he saw potential profitable traffic, and he encouraged immigrant farmers by providing cheap passage westward if they agreed to homestead near his line. His company, which had become the Great Northern Railway, reached Seattle in 1893. The panic of that year destroyed other transcontinentals, but not Hill's Great Northern. Indeed, the Great Northern paid dividends during the depression years. This resulted from his requirements that the construction be sound, that the financial operations be conservative, and that he control the management. Between 1891 and 1907 the Great Northern built one new mile of road every working day of the year. When Hill retired in 1907, he had won the name "Empire Builder" because of his encouragement of agricultural and industrial development in the Northwest. Few railroad leaders could rival Hill for the imaginative development of an entire region of the United States.[8]

Even as construction of the transcontinentals proceeded, the railroads improved and standardized operations. New giant bridges spanned the Ohio, Mississippi, and Missouri rivers. In 1871 over twenty different track gauges still were in use; by 1880, however, 80 percent of the mileage had been converted to standard gauge (4 feet 8½ inches), and during the next decade virtually the entire network was converted to standard gauge. The railroads recognized that interchange of traffic required other forms of cooperation and soon standardized coupling devices, car trucks, bills of lading, and classification of products. Larger locomotives and freight cars with increased carrying capacities required the replacement of iron rails

May 10, 1869, at Promontory, Utah, the first transcontinental railroad is completed.   (Courtesy: Union Pacific Railroad and The Association of American Railroads.)

with steel. Steel rails provided a smoother, safer, and faster track. More apparent to the public than any of the technical changes was division of the nation into four time zones to enhance the movement of trains.[9] Yet an even more significant contribution to the development of business enterprise in America was the creation by the larger railroads of complex, but highly efficient, managerial systems.

MANAGING THE RAILROADS

The railroads created the modern business structure. While management of canals, steamboats, and turnpikes had been relatively simple, distance, complexity, and size required a larger and more systematic business organization for the railroads. Before the 1840s businesses operated not unlike those of fifteenth-century Venice, but the railways needed system and order to move freight and passengers efficiently, quickly, and safely. The companies had to provide direct, scheduled, and reliable delivery of freight. Internal procedures had to be routinized and accounting, maintenance, and statistical controls devised.

The modern manager emerged to meet these needs. Many of the initial railway employees were civil engineers, a handful had military experience, and most had some knowledge of bureaucratic process. The railroad managers did not copy European models; rather, they designed rational responses to the problems they faced. They established divisions of responsibilities with specific functions throughout the corporation and developed ways to discover costs and methods to reduce them. This involved daily detailed reports from all segments of the railroad. They devised new accounting procedures and created billing systems. Many of the brightest and most promising young men in the country became part of these new railway enterprises, which offered many challenges and financial rewards. They formed structures to manage hundreds, and even thousands, of employees scattered across a number of states. As Alfred D. Chandler has written, "The railroad and the telegraph provided the fast, regular, and dependable transportation and communication so essential to high-volume production and distribution—the hallmark of large modern manufacturing or marketing enterprises. As important, the rail and telegraph companies were themselves the first modern business enterprises to appear in the United States."[10]

Because of the scope and intricacies of their operations, the railroads demand absolute discipline from employees. Technically skilled employees were placed on strict schedules, thus creating managerial problems. Detailed work rules were required in a society based on equalitarianism; individuals suffered a loss of rights. Workers often felt that the rules were arbitrary and against their interests. The railroads demanded minute controls over their employees, and as a consequence labor relations were extremely difficult and occasionally violent. In order to cope with management, some railroad workers joined one of the four large brotherhoods—the engineers, conductors, firemen, and enginemen, or trainmen—but relatively few were members of labor unions before 1890. Nevertheless, in times of strife the workers co-alesced in order to cope with their employers. In July of 1877, for example, in the midst of the depression following the Panic of 1873, the Baltimore and Ohio Railroad twice cut wages by 10 percent. It also increased the length of freight trains without expanding crews. After its firemen and brakemen struck, violence ensued. Mobs in Baltimore and in Pittsburgh attacked com-pany property, and in Pittsburgh damages exceeded $5 million. The vio-lence spread, and soon police, the militia, and regular army regiments were called out. The strike was broken, but the public knew that while the workers suffered wage cuts, dividends were still being paid on the B&O and other railroads. Considerable sympathy developed for the Pullman workers when they struck George M. Pullman's carworks in 1894—after he reduced wages but not the rents on company-owned housing. Railroad employees in the Chicago area attempted to aid the Pullman workers by refusing to haul the Pullman Palace sleepers on passenger trains. The federal government and local courts intervened on the side of Pullman, and the strike failed. The railway companies exacerbated the situation by creating blacklists of workers who were union members or who were sympathetic to the brotherhoods. Undoubtedly these events played a large part in creating a negative image of the corporations.[11]

The public also resented the scandals that surrounded the construc-tion and operation of some of the nation's major railways. During the building of the Union Pacific Railroad a construction company, the Credit Mobilier, distributed shares of stock to members of Congress and even the vice president of the United States. The Credit Mobilier received contracts to build the Union Pacific far in excess of the value of the track that the railroad acquired. It is estimated that those involved in the Credit Mobilier pocketed $23 million. The public was incensed at revelations that the Union Pacific had a capitalization of $110 million, but perhaps as much as half represented "watered stock." Railway companies often sold more secu-rities, or "watered stock," than the lines were actually worth. This was justified on the grounds that capital was extremely difficult to obtain—that investors would buy securities only if interest rates were high and if they received more in stocks and bonds than the cash they had actually paid. The result, of course, was overcapitalization, which made it extremely diffi-cult for those companies to pay interest on bonds and dividends on stocks. Some Americans believed that this corruption was primarily to be found in the South and in the far West, and yet a corruption of a different sort, the manipulation of the prices of securities, became a common practice in the money markets of the Northeast.

In 1867 Commodore Cornelius Vanderbilt attempted to add the Erie Railroad to his collection of lines in New York. Vanderbilt had created the New York Central and Hudson River Railroad, which largely replaced the Erie Canal in moving goods from Lake Erie to New York City. Competing with the Commodore's line was the Erie, controlled by Daniel Drew, who reduced rates, thereby causing Vanderbilt enormous difficulty. The Commo-dore proceeded to purchase Erie securities to rid himself of this competitor. Aided by Jim Fisk and Jay Gould, Drew provided Vanderbilt with securities to purchase, selling the Commodore 100,000 unauthorized shares of Erie stock. Vanderbilt obtained from a friendly judge a warrant to arrest Drew, Fisk, and Gould, but the trio fled across the Hudson River to safety in Jersey City, surrounded by $6 million in cash and a group of guards. Gould traveled secretly to Albany, where he spent half a million dollars bribing the legislature to legalize the issuance of the securities that the Commodore had purchased. Vanderbilt would say that fighting to gain control of the Erie and losing had "learned me it never pays to kick a skunk." Such scandals angered the public, which soon saw all railroad leaders typified by Vanderbilt, Drew, Fisk, and Gould.[12]

JAY GOULD

For decades, American historians have titillated undergraduates with stories of the "Robber Barons," and frequently the businessman used to illustrate the unrelieved rapaciousness of those Gilded Age vulgarians is Jay Gould, who is exhibit A for unrestrained capitalism. Journalistic accounts and "popular" historians such as Matthew Josephson and Burton Hendrick created a portrait of the "Mephistopheles of Wall Street" showing Gould to be a wizened, avaricious coward who helped form a legacy of unethical conduct that revealed the worst aspects of capitalism.

Jay Gould (1836–1892) "The Mephistopheles of Wall Street." (Courtesy: *Dictionary of American Portraits.*)

In 1986 historian Maury Klein published a lengthy, detailed biography of Gould that presented both an entirely different picture of the man and an analysis of the myths surrounding Gould. Born in rural Roxbury, New York, in 1836, the son of a farmer, Gould was not Jewish, as detractors later charged, and his given name was Jason, not Jay. A small, frail young man, he resisted farming and became successively a surveyor, tanner, and leather merchant. In the latter capacity he journeyed to New York and discovered the stock exchange. There his intensity and single-mindedness brought financial success.

Not until the 1860s did Gould enter the railroad security market, but in 1867 with Daniel Drew and Jim Fisk he formed the Erie Ring that became synonymous with fraud, manipulation, corruption, bribery, and ruthlessness. An effort to corner the Gold Market two years later led to a national financial collapse on "Black Friday." Certainly to this point Gould's behavior appeared to justify the legend.

Klein contends that once Gould had acquired a modest fortune, and rid himself of some unsavory associates, his renewed entry into the railway industry produced positive results. He argues that Gould was not a "raider" on the market and that after gaining control of the Union Pacific, Missouri Pacific, and Wabash railroads he committed himself to developing the properties. Klein shows Gould constantly touring the railroads, seeking new industries for their territories, demanding improvements in equipment and operations, and often providing cash to the carriers when they were hard pressed. Despite ill health, family problems, and fiscal crises in New York, Gould labored to create viable, profitable railways. He reinvested profits to improve the system and introduced new technological advances. Klein argues that Joseph Pulitzer's statement that Gould was "one of the most sinister figures that have ever flitted bat-like across the vision of the American people" is simply wrong.

The Gould who emerges from this revisionist study is a builder, not a raider. He attempted to form the nation's first communications conglomerate with Western Union, the *New York World,* and the Atlantic cables. Gould loved his family and tried to protect his financial interests so that at the time of his death (in 1892), they would be secure. This new interpretation of Jay Gould stands in sharp contrast with earlier views and forces scholars to take yet another look at this so-called Robber Baron.

Where intense competition existed between railroads, a reduction in railway rates often resulted. The railroads established the concept of charging on the basis of the value of the product carried, and the railroads classified freight for rate-making purposes. But when faced with competition of a cutthroat nature, rates plunged and the carriers suffered. Economies of scale did allow the railroads to reduce some rates drastically. Between 1866 and 1897 the rate for carrying wheat fell by 70 percent and the rate for dressed beef decreased 55 percent, but during that same period general prices declined by only 43 percent. The expansion of lines in the Great Plains brought further reductions. Between 1879 and 1889 the Santa Fe Railroad cut rates by 42 percent, the Chicago, Burlington and Quincy by almost 50 percent, and the Northern Pacific by 46 percent. These reductions were more substantial than the decline in agricultural prices. Farmers received 37 percent less for their wheat in this period, and 25 percent less for their corn. Nevertheless, farmers, small businesspersons, and shippers in general argued that the rates were still too high. The public believed that when the companies charged more for short hauls than for long hauls, it was discriminatory. And yet it was clear that such rates were necessary if the corporation were to have an equitable return on their investment. The railroads had higher rates for short hauls because their fixed charges had to be paid, and terminal charges were the same whether the haul was for 100 or 1,000 miles. It was also evident that large corporations had distinct advantages in dealing with the railways and, where multiple-line service was available, could threaten to move their traffic if the railroads did not reduce rates or give a rebate on part of the charges. The debilitating effect of rate wars led the railroads to seek solutions.

The railroads created pools that divided traffic and income between particular points along competing lines. For example, the three major railroads between Chicago and Omaha decided in 1870 to split the traffic by thirds. The Iowa Pool gave rise to the development of freight associations, or pools, in various regions of the country. The pools worked relatively well, but in the early 1880s a series of railroad wars broke out, and many of these gentlemen's agreements collapsed.[13]

Small shippers complained bitterly that the railroads granted rebates to larger customers. Standard Oil Company, for example, forced the railroads in its area to rebate over $10 million in only a year and a half. The railroads gave free passes to politicians, ministers, and community leaders to gain support. It became necessary for the railroads to seek such favor because of the rate-making philosophy they had adopted. Most railroad managers firmly believed that they should, and could, "charge all the traffic will bear." The railroads moved people and products at a fraction of the rates that had prevailed in 1860, but because of their heavy indebtedness, wildly fluctuating stock prices, short-haul–long-haul discrimination, rebating, and the granting of passes, the alienated public demanded regulation.

Farmers in the West, small-business persons in upstate New York, grain elevator owners in Iowa, and other groups sought regulation in response to what they perceived to be abuses of economic power by the railroads. In the 1870s several states in the upper Midwest passed statutes known as Granger Laws. Named after their sponsors, the National Grange of the Patrons of Husbandry, or the Grangers, these laws created state railway commissions to establish maximum rates and end discrimination. The railroads fought back in the courts; but in 1877, in *Munn v. Illinois*, the Supreme Court upheld such state regulation. Rate making by the states proved complex and difficult, and state legislatures and railroad commissions were often uninformed and disinterested in the plight of the companies being regulated. A series of appeals by the railways led to partial reversals of the earlier decision, and in 1886 the Supreme Court in the Wabash Case severely limited state regulation of railroads.[14]

FEDERAL REGULATION

In 1887 the federal government responded to cries for national railroad regulation with the passage of the Interstate Commerce Act. This act created the Interstate Commerce Commission (ICC) whose primary responsibility was, according to the law, the regulation of the rail system. But its vague language said only that rates should be "reasonable and just," that is, not so high as to destroy the traffic. The law prohibited rebates, pools, and higher rates for noncompetitive short hauls with the five-person ICC to administer and enforce the act. The ICC could hear shipper complaints and examine witnesses, but the commission did not specifically receive the power to set maximum railroad rates. The commission could enforce its decisions only through the federal courts. The first five commissioners proved to be qualified and capable people, but in the following decade the federal judiciary undermined their efforts to implement the law. Between 1887 and 1905 the Supreme Court ruled in favor of the railroads and against the government in fifteen of sixteen cases. The courts found that the ICC had no rate-making power and that it could not effectively prohibit discrimination. The Interstate Commerce Act did, however, create a regulatory precedent. Perhaps more important than regulation was the impact of the depression of 1893 on the nation's rail system, as well as the subsequent reorganization of the carriers by the investment bankers of Wall Street and State Street.

Companies operating one-third of the mileage of the American railroads entered bankruptcy between 1873 and 1897. A federal court decision in 1882 made it possible for the railroads to enter receivership with the management of the line acting as receivers. This decision allowed the railroads to recover financially and pay their creditors, but it also enabled the investment-banking houses to play highly influential roles in their reorganization. By the late 1880s J. P. Morgan and Company and other banking houses not only refinanced the railroads but also came to dominate their boards of directors. Morgan reorganized the Reading Railroad in 1886, the Chesapeake and Ohio two years later, and the Baltimore & Ohio in 1896. Following the Panic of 1893 many railroads declared bankruptcy, and in four years over 40,000 miles of line with a capitalization (stocks and bonds) of more than $2.5 billion entered receivership. Morgan then reorganized the Erie, Northern Pacific, and Richmond Terminal (Southern Railway) during the 1890s. Similar functions were provided by other banking houses such as Kuhn, Loeb, and J. and W. Seligman. The investment bankers reduced the debt structures and rationalized the distribution of routes; they also reduced competition.

Nearly two-thirds of the nation's rail mileage fell under the control of seven financial investment groups. These transportation "communities of interest" came under increasing criticism from the reform-minded Progressives. After 1903 state and federal investigations of the financial manipulations of the railroad companies were conducted, and charges of "loose, extravagant, and improvident" management were rife. Higher railroad operating costs led to increases in average freight rates after 1900, adding to general public hostility. As a consequence, pressure developed for further federal regulation of the industry. President Theodore Roosevelt and his attorney general sued under the Sherman Anti-Trust Act to dissolve Northern Securities Company, a giant holding corporation put together by E. H. Harriman and James J. Hill. Northern Securities controlled several of the major railways in the Pacific Northwest after 1902, but two years later the Supreme Court ordered Northern Securities dissolved. The year before, Congress passed the Elkins Act, which made both the giver and the receiver of a railroad rebate liable for prosecution.

THE ATCHISON, TOPEKA AND SANTA FE RAILWAY

On April 26, 1869, the management of the Atchison, Topeka, and Santa Fe Railroad hosted a picnic to celebrate the opening of the first seven miles of track from Topeka to Wakarusa Creek, Kansas. Cyrus K. Holliday, the company president, predicted that this short, jerkwater line would soon extend to the Rocky Mountains, across the deserts of the Southwest to California, and even to the Gulf of Mexico at Galveston. In a flight of fancy Colonel Holliday predicted that Santa Fe rails might one day reach Mexico City. His unbounded optimism was typical of the promoters of the American railroads in the three decades after 1865. Holliday, however, was far more accurate in his predictions than the promoters and managers of most lines. Indeed, the Santa Fe, as it was soon known, did ultimately reach the destinations forecast by the colonel, with the exception of Mexico City.

In the period from 1869 until 1892, the Santa Fe Railroad expanded rapidly. Its base was Kansas and the wheat traffic, but soon lines reached Colorado, and then south through New Mexico and Arizona to the California border. There Collis P. Huntington and the Southern Pacific Railroad blocked expansion to the Pacific coast. The Santa Fe then built a line into northern Mexico seeking a port on the Pacific. A series of battles with Huntington led the Santa Fe to construct lines to San Diego and Los Angeles. Kansas wheat farmers sought an outlet for their grain on the Gulf of Mexico, and the Santa Fe built a line south through Indian Territory to join the Gulf, Colorado and Santa Fe, which served Galveston, Houston, Fort Worth, and Dallas. Seeking an independent entry to the East, the Santa Fe built a line to Chicago. The expansion in the 1880s increased at a rapid rate as the company sought to prevent competitors from acquiring lines in its territory. The company purchased the Colorado Midland in the Rocky Mountains and acquired control of the Frisco Railroad in the late 1880s. This heedless overexpansion brought the railroad to fiscal disaster. Santa Fe stocks and bonds sold at heavy discount with the interest on the bonds at an excessive rate. The management concluded that it could no longer service these heavy debts, and on December 23, 1893, the railroad entered bankruptcy; a federal court appointed receivers.

In 1894–1895, investment bankers in New York and Boston reorganized the Santa Fe Railroad. Many of the acquisitions were simply lost, including the Colorado Midland and the Frisco. The new management was led by E. P. Ripley, who served as president of the Atchison, Topeka, and the Santa Fe *Railway* from 1896 until 1918. The Santa Fe before reorganization included

Tracklaying on the Texas plains in 1909.   (Courtesy: Santa Fe Railway.)

9,328 miles of track and was capitalized at $647 million. The new operation began with a much-reduced mileage and capitalization. By the turn of the century, however, Ripley was once again expanding the company, but at a much slower rate and only where potential traffic justified growth. A new line was built to San Francisco, for example, and short cuts were constructed from the Santa Fe's tracks in New Mexico to its main line in Texas. By 1906 the Santa Fe had 9,624 miles of track, but its capitalization was only $502 million. Indeed, Ripley not only expanded the company at a justifiable rate but also rehabilitated existing lines, purchased new locomotives and equipment, and rebuilt tracks laid before the reorganization. In two decades Ripley created a vital and profitable corporation in the transportation sector of the economy.

But leading political figures, such as William Jennings Bryan, advocated federal ownership of the railroads, not regulation, as a solution. President Roosevelt, who opposed nationalization of the rail network, finally agreed to federal legislation incorporated in the Hepburn Act of 1906. The Hepburn Act expanded the powers of the ICC to include express and sleeping-car companies and pipelines, abolished the granting of passes, and strengthened the law against rebating. More importantly, the Hepburn Act gave the ICC power to establish "just and reasonable" maximum freight rates, thereby becoming a landmark in the development of federal regulatory policy. During the administration of William Howard Taft, the Mann-Elkins Act of 1910 further expanded the jurisdiction of the ICC. The burden of proof as to the "reasonableness" of rates fell on the carriers. The Progressives capped their regulatory efforts with the Railroad Valuation Act of

1913. This legislation ordered the ICC to evaluate all railroad property. The law proposed to estimate the "true" worth of the lines for the basis of establishing freight rates. Senator Robert M. LaFollette argued that the railroads wished to base rates on inflated values, or "watered stock," rather than upon the actual value of their operating properties.[15]

Ironically, the Progressives limited the ability of the railroads to raise additional investment capital at the very time when hundreds of millions of dollars were needed to modernize the system. The railroads invested in larger, more powerful locomotives, freight-car fleets were expanded, and passenger cars became longer, heavier, and more luxurious as steel replaced wood construction. Some railroads built extensive new city terminals. The Pennsylvania Railroad dug tunnels under the Hudson River to reach its new midtown New York City station, and both the Pennsylvania and the New York Central began to electrify major urban trackage. Most companies replaced lightweight rails with steel rails of much heavier carrying capacity.

Even as major capital improvements were conducted, the railroads faced increasing demands for higher wages from railroad workers. Over a million rail employees in 1900 earned an average annual wage of $567. By 1916, 1.7 million workers were earning an average of more than $880 per year. The unionization of the workers contributed to their relatively high wages. Increased wages and greater capital expenditures brought the operating ratio (the ratio of operating expenses to operating revenue) of the railroads from an average of 66 percent in 1890 to almost 70 percent by the time of World War I. When the railroads requested rate increases from the ICC, however, the commission denied them under the authority granted by the Hepburn Act and the Mann-Elkins Act. The ICC simply inhibited the modernization efforts.

Railroad mileage in the United States peaked in 1917, a year in which the companies were called upon not only to meet domestic demands but also to make preparations for entering World War I. Despite the hindrances placed on the railroads by the Progressive legislation, modernized plants existed on some of the carriers. Between 1900 and 1915 general price levels in the country increased by 30 percent while average railroad wages rose by more than 50 percent. The taxes paid by the carriers tripled, yet gross earnings only doubled in that decade and a half and freight rates remained almost unchanged. As the carriers sought to cope with traffic conditions produced by the war, management found only public ill-will. When in 1916 the four operating brotherhoods demanded an eight-hour day instead of a ten-hour day, negotiations collapsed. President Woodrow Wilson attempted to serve as mediator, but his compromise proved unacceptable to management, and a general strike appeared imminent. When the negotiations between the president and the railroad companies broke down, Wilson complained bitterly, "I pray God to forgive you, I never can."[16] Threatened with a nationwide strike, Wilson asked Congress to approve legislation creating the eight-hour day, and the Adamson Act became law. The immediate issue had been resolved, but labor relations remained highly unsatisfactory in the spring of

1917, when Wilson requested a special session of Congress to hear his request for a declaration of war.

The outbreak of war in April found the railroads attempting to deal with a shortage of cars. Over 180,000 freight cars were blocked in America's ports with no place for their cargoes to be unloaded. The railroads attempted to meet the problem by forming the Railroads' War Board, which organized car pools and coordinated operations. The railroad executives on the board were hampered by the Sherman Anti-Trust Act, which limited cooperation by the carriers. By December the ICC recommended that President Wilson assume control of the nation's railroads, and on December 26 the president issued a proclamation for government operation to begin within forty-eight hours.

Wilson appointed William G. McAdoo director general of the railroads. McAdoo formed the United States Railroad Administration (USRA), and throughout the remainder of the war USRA brought the nation's railroads under one system. Duplicate trains were terminated, stations closed, unnecessary civilian traffic eliminated, and competing routes coordinated. McAdoo declared stringent controls on utilization of freight cars and purchased 100,000 new freight cars and almost 2,000 locomotives built to standardized USRA specifications. McAdoo also granted a series of wage increases for the workers, including one of almost 40 percent. The workers on the USRA saw average wages increase from $1,000 a year to $1,800 a year in 1920. Total labor costs rose from $1.8 billion in 1917 to $2.7 billion in 1918. Average railroad wages by 1920 stood more than a third higher than those in manufacturing; the proportion of each dollar the railroads earned going to labor costs rose from forty cents in 1917 to fifty-five cents in 1920. The cost of coal nearly doubled during the war years, although freight movements increased by only 11 percent in 1920. The average operating ratio of 65.5 percent in 1916 soared to 94.3 percent in 1920. Federal control of the nation's railroads cost the taxpayers over $1.1 billion before the government returned the companies to their owners on March 1, 1920. Some Americans proposed federal ownership of the railroads, and one labor leader, Glenn E. Plumb, urged the government to purchase the railroads and operate them with a fifteen-person board. This plan won little public support.

Congress, however, did pass the Transportation Act of 1920. This new legislation again increased the power and responsibilities of the ICC; however, the law provided that the carriers should receive fair rates of return on their investment. The original figure was 5.5 percent. The ICC finally granted freight rate increases ranging upward to 40 percent. The act also encouraged mergers to provide more efficient operations and gave the ICC greater control over new construction and abandonments. The latter power would be misused by the ICC to prevent elimination of superfluous mileage.

Ironically, the federal government expanded its regulatory authority at a time when the railroads faced increasing competition from other forms of transportation. Congress passed the Transportation Act of 1920 based on assumptions that had some validity in the 1890s. But Congress failed to perceive the major impact on the railroads of the automobile, pipelines, an expanding trucking industry, intercity buses, and the incipient airlines. The nation's rail industry had peaked in importance in 1920 as other transportation industries began to diminish the significance of the rail system.

NOTES

1. George Rogers Taylor, *The Transportation Revolution, 1815–1860* (New York: Rinehart and Co., 1951), pp. 74–75.

2. John F. Stover, *American Railroads* (Chicago: University of Chicago Press, 1961), pp. 13–21.

3. Taylor, *The Transportation Revolution*, pp. 80–84.

4. John F. Stover, *Iron Road to the West* (New York: Columbia University Press, 1978), *passim.*

5. Taylor, *The Transportation Revolution*, pp. 95–96.

6. Stover, *American Railroads*, pp. 87, 93.

7. George Edgar Turner, *Victory Rode the Rails* (Indianapolis: Bobbs-Merrill, 1953); and Robert C. Black, *The Railroads of the Confederacy* (Chapel Hill: University of North Carolina Press, 1952); these are the best studies on this subject.

8. Albro Martin, *James J. Hill and the Opening of the Northwest* (New York: Oxford University Press, 1976).

9. On the standardization of the American railroad system, see George Rogers Taylor and Irene Neu, *The American Railroad Network, 1861–1890* (Cambridge: Harvard University Press, 1956).

10. Alfred D. Chandler, Jr., *The Visible Hand: The Managerial Revolution in American Business* (Cambridge: Harvard University Press, 1977), p. 79.

11. The best accounts are Almont Lindsey, *The Pullman Strike* (Chicago: University of Chicago Press, 1942), and Stanley Buder, *Pullman* (New York: Oxford University Press, 1967).

12. Charles Francis Adams, Jr., and Henry Adams, *Chapters of Erie and Other Essays* (New York: Henry Holt and Co., 1886).

13. Julius Grodinsky, *The Iowa Pool* (Chicago: University of Chicago Press, 1950).

14. The following summarize the various interpretations of railroad regulation: Solon J. Buck, *The Granger Movement* (Cambridge: Harvard University Press, 1913); Lee Benson, *Merchants, Farmers and Railroads* (Cambridge: Harvard University Press, 1955); Gabriel Kolko, *Railroads and Regulation, 1877–1916* (Princeton, New Jersey: Princeton University Press, 1965); and Albro Martin, "The Troubled Subject of Railroad Regulation in the Gilded Age— A Reappraisal," *The Journal of American History* 61 (September 1974), pp. 339–371.

15. Stover, *American Railroads*, pp. 134–151.

16. Ibid., p. 183.

SUGGESTED READINGS

ATHEARN, ROBERT G. *Union Pacific Country.* Chicago: Rand McNally, 1971.
BRYANT, KEITH L., JR. *History of the Atchison, Topeka and Santa Fe Railway.* New York: Macmillan, 1974.
COCHRAN, THOMAS C. *Railroad Leaders, 1845–1890.* Cambridge: Harvard University Press, 1953.
FISHLOW, ALBERT. *American Railroads and the Transformation of the Ante-bellum Economy.* Cambridge: Harvard University Press, 1965.

FOGEL, ROBERT W. *Railroads and American Economic Growth.* Baltimore: Johns Hopkins University Press, 1964.

GRODINSKY, JULIUS. *Jay Gould: His Business Career, 1867–1892.* Philadelphia: University of Pennsylvania Press, 1957.

HOOGENBOOM, ARI, and OLIVE HOOGENBOOM. *A History of the Interstate Commerce Commission: From Panacea to Palliative.* New York: W. W. Norton & Co., 1976.

JOHNSON, ARTHUR M., and BARRY E. SUPPLE. *Boston Capitalists and Western Railroads: A Study in the Nineteenth-Century Railroad Investment Process.* Cambridge: Harvard University Press, 1967.

KLEIN, MAURY. *History of the Louisville & Nashville Railroad.* New York: Macmillan, 1972.

———. *The Life and Legend of Jay Gould.* Baltimore: Johns Hopkins University Press, 1986.

KOLKO, GABRIEL. *Railroads and Regulation, 1877–1916.* Princeton, New Jersey: Princeton University Press, 1965.

LICHT, WALTER. *Working for the Railroad: The Organization of Work in the Nineteenth Century.* Princeton, New Jersey: Princeton University Press, 1983.

MARTIN, ALBRO. *Enterprise Denied.* New York: Columbia University Press, 1971.

———. *James J. Hill and the Opening of the Northwest.* New York: Oxford University Press, 1976.

OVERTON, RICHARD C. *Burlington Route.* New York: Alfred A. Knopf, 1965.

STOVER, JOHN F. *History of the Illinois Central Railroad.* New York: Macmillan, 1975.

———. *Iron Road to the West.* New York: Columbia University Press, 1978.

———. *American Railroads.* Chicago: University of Chicago Press, 1961.

TAYLOR, GEORGE ROGERS, and IRENE D. NEU. *The American Railroad Network: 1861–1890.* Cambridge: Harvard University Press, 1956.

WARD, JAMES A. *Railroads and the Character of America.* Knoxville: University of Tennessee Press, 1986.

8 | Transportation and the Marketplace

The revolution in transportation which occurred during the six decades after 1920 exceeded in magnitude that which took place between 1820 and 1860. The internal-combustion engine, cheap gasoline, and mass production placed the automobile in the hands of virtually every family, and, as a result, the long-distance passenger train and mass transit almost died. Expansion of the federal and state highway systems provided intercity trucks with the means to compete with, and then largely surpass, freight trains as carriers for all but bulk commodities. By the 1950s airlines provided expensive but fast service between major cities, and by the 1970s they moved millions of travelers at relatively low fares. The nation's pipelines, barge operators, and intercoastal shipping companies carried larger and larger volumes of petroleum products, coal, and grain. The federal government subsidized the new transportation forms with improved highways and waterways and often with direct cash subsidies, yet it developed no plan for an integrated national transportation system. Ironically, large segments of the great rail network that had pioneered in big business fell into physical disarray and fiscal chaos.

THE RAILROADS AFTER 1920

The plight of portions of the rail network and the success of other carriers can be seen in the divergent histories of the Pennsylvania Railroad and the Union Pacific Railroad. In the 1890s a leading railway security analyst, S. F.

Van Oss, declared, "The Pennsylvania is in every respect the standard railway of America."[1] He praised its management, locomotives, cars, track, terminals, and operations. The Pennsylvania made large profits and came to control the Norfolk and Western, Wabash, Lehigh Valley, and other competitors in the East. The Pennsylvania prospered in the 1920s and during the Great Depression electrified its main lines from Washington and Harrisburg through Philadelphia to New York. World War II brought record traffic volume and greater prosperity, but after 1945 problems developed. The Pennsylvania paid high property taxes on its yards, terminals, and trackage; competing truck lines were taxed only on their trucks. The management spent hundreds of millions of dollars on new streamlined passenger trains even as the subsidized airlines took away passengers. The railroad remained labor intensive, and federally approved wage rates rose faster than freight rates. Expensive terminal operations, short hauls for freight, the cost of dieselization, huge losses from passenger and commuter services, and managerial laxity caused the Pennsylvania to fail rapidly. Industry fled the Northeast to the South and West, and traffic on the line declined drastically. By the 1960s the railroad was surviving only because of real estate holdings and dividends from the securities of other companies.

As railroads sought relief from these problems, they turned to mergers as a solution. The Pennsylvania divested itself of its holdings in other carriers so that it could merge with its long-time rival, the New York Central. The Penn-Central merger of 1966 proved disastrous. The old Pennsylvania management ("the Red Team") and the New York Central managers ("the Green Team") refused to cooperate, and even their computers were incompatible. Losses mounted and bankruptcy came in 1970. The federal government, moving to prevent the collapse of the nation's largest railway, created Conrail (the Consolidated Rail Corporation) in 1976 to salvage the Penn-Central and other bankrupt lines in the Northeast. Over $4 billion in federal loans kept Conrail operative.[2] Yet the vastly expanded Norfolk and Western and the Chesapeake and Ohio System operating in the same region remained strong, profitable railroads, as did the Union Pacific in the West. In 1987, a vastly reduced but profitable Conrail, rid of excess trackage and with new labor agreements, was sold by the government through an offering of securities to the public.

Even as S. F. Van Oss wrote about the Pennsylvania as the "standard" railroad in the 1890s, the Union Pacific needed rapid modernization. Debilitated financially, threatened competitively by the Southern Pacific, and blocked from reaching California, it appeared to some a hopeless wreck. Financier E. H. Harriman of the Illinois Central bought control of the Union Pacific after it entered bankruptcy in 1897 and rebuilt the property. New locomotives and cars moved over revamped tracks, and Harriman acquired a line to Los Angeles. Although Harriman's efforts to create a rail monopoly in the West failed, he made the Union Pacific a rail showcase. The company prospered in the 1920s, and World War II brought more prosperity. The postwar era saw dramatic changes in the corporation. Because of its land grant, the Union Pacific held substantial coal, petroleum, and timber reserves that the railway began to exploit. It purchased a large independent oil firm and created a holding company for both its rail and nonrail properties. The company ended most passenger service, took advantage of its long-haul freight lines, especially for piggy-back trailer traffic, and by 1980 earned 16 percent on its equity.

The success of the Union Pacific was repeated on the Santa Fe, Southern Pacific, Southern, Burlington Northern, and other railroads. The rail industry as a whole declined, however, and by 1980 some lines in the Midwest were following several northeastern carriers into the federal bankruptcy courts. The plight of the nation's railroads received considerable attention, but little was done. In 1945 the railroads had hauled 60 percent of freight ton miles; by 1980 they carried less than 30 percent. The federal government did create Amtrak (National Railroad Passenger Corporation) to operate a few long-distance passenger trains, thus relieving the carriers of that obligation. The moribund ICC stirred slowly and allowed more rapid freight rate increases, but the railroads' return on equity was still less than 1 percent; twenty-one of the seventy-one largest railroads in the United States lost money in 1970. Deregulation became another panacea, as did rapid abandonment of duplicate and unprofitable mileage. The newly created Department of Transportation sought to devise a national rail plan, but political interference, labor opposition to consolidation, and bureaucratic ineptitude precluded meaningful efforts to rescue the weak elements of the industry and strengthen the profitable carriers. The railroad industry responded with a series of megamergers that reduced the Class I systems to only fourteen by 1988. By the end of the 1970s the federal government had spent over $100 billion for highways and more than $15 billion for waterways, but the railroads could raise only $5 billion for private investment in the decade of the 1970s as capital became more difficult to obtain when profit levels fell. The Staggers Act of 1980 provided the railroads with relief from crippling regulations and allowed for flexible rate making. Ironically, the automobile industry, which had helped to create the railways' problems, also had to seek help from Washington in the 1980s.

THE AGE OF THE AUTOMOBILE

The automobile represents one of the most significant elements of the American culture and economy. President Warren G. Harding told Congress in 1921 that "the motor car has become an indispensable instrument in our political, social, and industrial life," and a resident of "Middletown" exclaimed to the inquiring sociologists Robert and Helen Lynd, "Why on earth do you need to study what's changing the country? I can tell you what's happening in just four letters: A-U-T-O."[3] Wags joked that the car had taken sex off the front-porch swing and into the rumble seat of the Model T, but Wall Street knew that the internal-combustion engine and mass production had vastly altered the economy and created an industry that, with its auxiliary enterprisies, employed millions of workers. In only a quarter of a century the transportation market witnessed a revolution of massive proportions.

The coming of the automobile set forces in motion that helped establish a consumer-goods economy. The car manufacturers introduced new production and marketing methods—the moving assembly line and installment buying, for examples—that changed the national economy. The automobile created demands for gasoline, lubricating oil, steel, glass, and rubber, and for better and expanded highway and street systems. Cars and buses made possible the consolidation of rural schools and the establishment of regional shopping centers. The suburb blossomed with expanded automobile ownership. Henry Ford put it this way: "We shall solve the city problem by leaving the city." As in so many other matters, Ford was dead wrong! But there can be no doubt that the automobile industry provided one of the basic ingredients for the creation of the American middle-class culture.[4]

Few visitors to Chicago's Columbian Exposition of 1893 could visualize the implications of the six cars displayed by their builders. The next decade saw the construction of a successful gasoline engine by the Duryea brothers and a demonstration of the auto's durability in a road test from Cleveland to New York in 1897. After 1900 the auto came of age as the number of builders reached the hundreds and output could be measured in the tens of thousands. By 1910 auto manufacturing had become the twenty-first largest enterprise in terms of product value, and 458,000 cars were registered in the United States. A mass market had been created.

The automobile industry developed under ideal circumstances. The United States had a higher per capita income than Europe and a broader

Vehicles move along Henry Ford's assembly line in the Dearborn plant.　(From the collections of Henry Ford Museum and Greenfield Village.)

distribution of income. Some industries that already served mass markets had established the concepts of mechanization and standardization to lower production costs. The demand for cars exceeded the supply for over a decade, and buyers paid cash before delivery, providing working capital for the manufacturers. Only a modest plant was needed to build the cars, and some models were assembled from parts furnished by suppliers. Ford Motor Company began with $28,000 in paid capital, and in 1909 Hudson Motor Car Company received deposits from its dealers equal to one-half of its annual production costs. Many of the early builders were well-trained engineers with extensive experience in related industries—bicycles, carriages and wagons, and locomotive building. Thus, as credit and capital came easily, the number of manufacturers rose rapidly. Profits reinvested in plants and new production lines enhanced output, thereby reducing per-unit costs and prices. As some of the companies increased in size, they began to manufacture components rather than make purchases from suppliers. Henry Ford's Highland Park plant, which opened in 1910, became the basic model for the industry. The smaller manufacturers often merged to form larger companies, and by 1912 over half of all cars were being built by only seven firms.[5]

Henry Ford did not originate the concept of mass-marketing cars; much credit can be given to Ransom E. Olds and the curved-dash Oldsmobile of 1901–1904. Sold for only $650, the Olds became America's first popular car. Two Oldsmobiles raced from New York to Portland, Oregon, in 1905—in only forty-four days—and the public recognized that an American car was as reliable as a European import.[6] Olds manufactured cars with a new technique of assembly, bringing materials to the workers rather than workers to the materials. By 1904 he was producing 5,000 cars and paying dividends of 105 percent in three years. Olds split with his financial backers, who wanted higher-priced products while he sought to lower prices and further develop a mass market.

What Olds sought, Ford achieved. Henry Ford introduced his Model T in 1908 and reshaped the industry. His first car was built in 1896, and seven years later he formed Ford Motor Company. When he introduced the Model N in 1906, Ford was deluged with orders and soon was building 100 cars per day. With the Highland Park plant in full production, he reduced the price of the Model T to $345 in 1916. By that year Ford had sold 734,811 Model Ts, almost half of all cars sold in the United States. Economies of scale could drive the small producers out of the market, but Ford did not attempt to create a monopoly; an oligopoly was much better, he said. The moving assembly line, added to Highland Park in 1913, represented Ford's genius at its best, but his creation was part of an ongoing evolution in mass production. He made a good product at a low price that allowed for large-scale distribution; standardization meant lower prices and any color the customer wanted—as long as it was black. Ford opposed the trend toward higher-priced cars and in the process helped transform America. In 1914 production of motor vehicles exceeded the production of wagons and carriages for the first time.[7]

The oligopolistic trend in automobile manufacturing accelerated with the formation of General Motors by William C. Durant in 1908. Billy Durant took over the failing Buick Motor Company in 1904 and soon made it the largest-selling car. The Buick was a high-quality, reliable auto and became the backbone of Durant's empire. Like Ford, he saw the need for large-scale capital for the mass production of nonluxury cars, but unlike Ford, who created a single corporation to build one product, Durant favored mergers of several companies to blanket the market with cars in all price ranges.[8] The "flamboyant" Durant had been in the carriage business for almost two decades, and like so many other carriage and wagon builders made the step from that enterprise to automobiles. Determined to build an integrated company with Buick as its basis, he began trying to consolidate his company with Ford, Maxwell, and Reo, but Durant could not raise the necessary cash. Instead, he brought together his own Buick with Cadillac, Oldsmobile, and Oakland in an enterprise he called General Motors Corporation. Capitalized at $10 million, General Motors (GM) almost failed when automobile sales declined in 1910. Durant was forced to borrow nearly $13 million from Wall Street bankers, and control of General Motors passed into a voting trust. In 1915, however, Durant came back to GM aided by the Du Pont family, with whose support he had also acquired control of Chevrolet Motor Company. The Du Pont family invested almost $50 million in GM, and Durant continued to acquire more and more units. As a result, GM again came close to bankruptcy when sales of automobiles collapsed at the end of World War I. Once more Durant was forced out, and the Du Pont family and the House of Morgan took over.[9]

One of Durant's acquisitions for GM was Hyatt Roller Bearing Company headed by Alfred P. Sloan. Sloan became an executive with General Motors, and he impressed the Du Ponts. Pierre Du Pont, who succeeded Durant as GM president, recognized that Durant's erratic managerial style and uncontrolled acquisition policy had created the fifth largest of all industrial enterprises in the United States, but he also realized that it had created an industrial empire without a structure. Many talented young GM executives, men like Charles W. Nash and Walter P. Chrysler, left GM because they were unable to determine what policies Billy Durant wanted them to carry out. Two days before the end of 1920, the board of directors of GM approved a plan proposed by Alfred Sloan that created the structure that became the corporation's essential organization.

Sloan's plan made GM a single coordinated enterprise by creating a general office to set broad corporate goals and policies for the many operating units. Sloan argued that the operating divisions had to retain some autonomy, and that a totally centralized structure would not work given the size of GM. He firmly believed that independence encouraged innovation and initiative. On the other hand, some activities had to be coordinated in the best interests of the entire corporation. Sloan established clear lines of authority, sought to determine actual costs and profits for each division, and created a procedure whereby performances of one unit could be measured against those of other units. The general office would be concerned, not with details in the divisions, but with a flow of general information that could be used to make decisions about unit efficiency in the allocation of

Alfred P. Sloan (1875–1966). Organizational genius and creative administrator.   (Courtesy:
General Motors Corporation.)

corporate resources. Each division would be placed in a logical relationship
with the others, and the overall administrative office would set the policies
for the multifunctioning autonomous operating divisions. The activities of
GM would be based on market forecasts of demand and estimated economic conditions. Finally, Sloan defined for the different divisions their
function in the marketplace. Chevrolet would compete directly with Ford;
Buick, a more expensive car, would be aimed at the middle of the market,
as would the Oldsmobile. The Cadillac division, while producing the most
expensive models and the fewest number of cars, often made good profits.
In the mid-1920s the Pontiac was introduced to fill the need for a quality
car priced between the Chevrolet and the Oldsmobile. General Motors
achieved the goal of including in its product line "a car for every purse and
purpose." Sloan provided a structure for GM that was designed to carry out
the market strategy required after 1920.[10]

One student of the automobile industry has argued that the supply of
entrepreneurs in the United States was so vast that the importance of any
individual contribution was negligible: "Individual entrepreneurs, whether
alone or as archetype, don't matter."[11] And yet the Sloan plan demonstrates
that business leadership is an essential, and in many cases the most meaningful, factor in the growth of the automobile industry.[12] General Motors, not
Ford, established the industry pattern, that is, annual model changes and
production by one firm of a full price range of vehicles through a wholly
decentralized organization. Ironically, this pattern would be adopted by
Ford Motor Company itself in the 1930s.

But in the 1920s Henry Ford refused to accept the changing strategy
adopted by GM. Angered by demands of Ford stockholders that a portion
of profits be returned to them, Ford went heavily into debt to repurchase
securities owned by non-Ford family members. The Dodge brothers, for
example, received $35 million for their shares of Ford, which represented
an original investment of $20,000. Ford acquired total control of his com-

pany, but the decline in sales and falling prices brought Ford to the brink of disaster in 1920. Refusing to produce new models or to alter the Model T, Ford faced catastrophe. With a $75 million bank loan due in 1921, Ford dealt with the problem by canceling all orders for materials and supplies, closing his factories, and shipping 125,000 cars to his dealers. The dealers were told that they must pay cash for the cars they had received or lose their franchises. Virtually all of the 17,000 Ford dealers responded, many at a significant loss to themselves, for their franchises were too valuable to be abandoned. When the inventory had been depleted, and as car sales began to rise, Ford reopened.

Prosperity returned after 1920. Over 2 million cars were marketed that year, and the automobile boom peaked in 1929 when 5,337,000 cars were sold. Automobiles used 20 percent of all American steel, 90 percent of the gasoline produced, and 80 percent of the rubber, but by 1925 overproduction of automobiles had become an increasing problem. Ford's Model T dominated the market until 1923, but it declined seriously after that, falling from 46 percent of sales in 1923 to 9 percent in 1927 before the introduction of the Model A. General Motors prospered throughout the 1920s, as did Chrysler, which became the third-largest producer. Walter Chrysler had worked on locomotives and become the manager of the American Locomotive Works in Pittsburgh before joining General Motors in 1911. A brilliant young executive, Chrysler eventually quarreled with Billy Durant and left. He saved the ailing Maxwell Motor Car Company and introduced his own make, the Chrysler. The Maxwell and the Chrysler were so successful that he soon acquired Dodge from the Dodge brothers, and before the end of the decade introduced the Plymouth and the De Soto, following the strategy of General Motors of having a car line in all price ranges. Throughout the 1920s many of the small automobile manufacturers either went out of business or were merged into the larger firms. Advanced advertising techniques, emphasis on automobile purchases with credit, and new models every year made automobile manufacturing the nation's number-one industry. With over 26 million cars clogging the highways and streets, America became a car culture in the 1920s.

THE RISE AND DECLINE OF STUDEBAKER

Henry and Clem Studebaker entered the wagon business in South Bend, Indiana, in 1852 with $68 in capital and two sets of tools. Their father John had built Conestoga wagons, and his sons soon prospered in the trade. By the 1860s they were worth $10,000, largely as a result of federal contracts for wagons during the Civil War. The Studebakers produced strong, well-constructed wagons, carriages, buggies, and delivery vehicles, and in the 1870s they were doing a million-dollar business yearly in the world's largest vehicle plant. Even as Studebaker wagons became part of America's export trade in the late 1890s, a second generation of Studebakers built an experimental automobile. In 1902 the company offered an electric car in five models, and it sold 20 units the first year; a gasoline version entered the market two years later. Sleds, wagons, and buggies still constituted the major source of sales in 1907, when the company achieved $7 million in revenue, but a commitment to the automobile led to a reorganization in 1911. The family purchased the E.M.F. Corporation, a major automaker, in 1909 and placed a new emphasis on car production. What had been a sideline became the central focus of the company. Studebaker soon exported 37 percent of all American cars sold abroad, and the coming of war brought vast orders for trucks, including one order for 5,000 military caterpillar trucks. Studebaker prospered, paid off all loans in 1917, and declared a 10 percent dividend. Two years later wagon building terminated, and a new car plant in South Bend made the company the nation's third-largest auto producer. One reason for the great increase in sales was Studebaker's decision to sell cars on credit. As early as 1911 it accepted car notes endorsed by its dealers, thus making high-priced automobiles available to more buyers.

Studebaker's postwar output peaked in 1923, with sales of 145,167 units. The company, seeking to cover the entire market, purchased luxury-car-builder Pierce-Arrow in 1928. Management of Studebaker, which had passed from the family, proved to be ineffective as sales plummeted after 1929. New models failed to attract buyers, yet a large cash dividend was paid from capital in 1931. Purchase of White Motor Company led to Studebaker's receivership two years later. Reorganization by a strong, young management team put Studebaker in the black by 1938. World War II demands aided the financial recovery. Studebaker built trucks and aviation motors, and it resumed dividends in 1943.

With $33 million in working capital Studebaker reentered the car market in 1946, and it soon produced "radical" new models. Sales reached 334,554 cars and trucks in 1950, but like all of the independents, market penetration declined. Desperate for survival, Studebaker merged with Packard Motor Car Company; the sales decline accelerated. Finally in 1964, the South Bend plant closed and small-scale production was transferred to Canada, but even that effort failed. Like Willys, Hudson, Packard, and Nash, Studebaker could not build models in all price ranges to compete with the Big Three (General Motors, Ford, and Chrysler). Short of capital and with its weak dealer system, Studebaker failed to survive in the postwar car market.

The most significant change to take place in the industry in the 1930s was the coming of unionization when Franklin Roosevelt's New Deal and the Depression drastically altered labor relations in the automobile industry. The National Industrial Recovery Act established the National Recovery Administration (NRA), which drafted industrial codes to get the nation's economy moving. Section 7A of the code required businesses participating in the NRA programs to allow their workers to bargain collectively. The automobile companies resisted strenuously, but the New Dealers forced the manufacturers to sign the agreements. Young labor activists in the American Federation of Labor (AFL) set out to organize the automobile industry with a broadly based industrial union. The leadership of the AFL, however, unwilling to accept any labor organization based on anything other than skills, forced those with such beliefs from the union. After the NRA had been emasculated by Supreme Court decisions, the Wagner Act, or National Labor Relations Act, again created a structure that allowed for the growth of industrial unions. The beleaguered employees joined the United Automobile Workers union (UAW), and through sit-down strikes and major work stoppages forced General Motors and Chrysler to bargain and recognize the union. Ford's resistance produced violence as the company hired a private army of detectives and thugs in an effort to thwart unionization. This brought intervention by the National Labor Relations Board (NLRB). An NLRB election led to an overwhelming prounion vote by Ford workers, much to the distress of the elder Ford. Thus, prior to World War II, the automobile industry was unionized.[13]

From 1940 to 1945, the automobile manufacturers shifted to wartime production. Their plants produced tanks, trucks, jeeps, and other military hardware. Each month saw increasing records of production, and in five years the automobile manufacturers would build more than 4 million engines, almost 6 million guns, and almost 3 million tanks and trucks in addition to thousands of aircraft, millions of rounds of ammunition, and a host of other military products. When the war ended in 1945, the companies moved quickly to convert to civilian production. Consumers with cash stood ready to buy the first cars off the production line, and automobile dealers were swamped with customers placing orders for new cars.

There were only nine automobile companies in the United States in 1945: General Motors, Ford, Chrysler, Studebaker, Hudson, Packard, Nash, Kaiser-Frazier, and Crosley. The companies rushed to fill the demand for automobiles created by the war, but strikes and the lack of materials prevented full-scale production until 1947. Studebaker and Kaiser-Frazier brought out new models, but not until 1949 did Ford drastically alter its line. The Korean War of 1950 again limited production, and only in 1953 did output reach pre-1940 levels. But that year strikes and failure to obtain transmissions grievously harmed the independents. Nash, Packard, Kaiser-Frazier, Hudson, and Studebaker saw sales plummet. The grossly undercapitalized Kaiser-Frazier withdrew from the automobile market in 1955. Hudson, which had won a good share of the market with its "stepped-down" design of 1948, failed to change its styling and merged with Nash, whose lumbering design had lost public favor. Packard, which had never recaptured the luxury market after the war, merged with Studebaker, whose "radical" designs had not been well received. The two new independents, American Motors (Hudson-Nash) and Studebaker-Packard, could not regain large shares of the market. The latter would leave the automobile business, and the former would continue as a marginal producer of compact cars.

General Motors dominated the domestic market after the war, with Ford a distant second. By 1945 Ford Motor Company was an administrative disaster. Henry Ford had fired or emasculated anyone who showed initiative within the firm. It was that year that young Henry Ford took control of the business and hired Ernest R. Breech, who brought the company back from the edge of catastrophe. The company's medieval structure was reorganized and its primitive accounting system replaced. Its product was poor, but it had over $600 million in cash in the bank. Breech saved Ford, challenged General Motors' lead, and only the disastrous Edsel marred the generally positive emergence of Ford after 1947.

Chrysler Corporation never regained its pre-1940 position, however. From a 25 percent share of the market in 1946, its sales fell to 9 percent by 1962. Stylistic rejection and a reputation for poor quality harmed the company. Efforts to develop a worldwide market led to huge losses outside the United States. Chrysler seemed unable to compete with General Motors and Ford at home or abroad.[14]

In the 1970s all three major car companies faced intensive competition from imports. The trickle of imported sports cars of the 1950s became a flood of compacts, trucks, and family cars. Imports represented only 7 percent of the market in 1960, but almost 30 percent by 1980. The imports captured larger shares of the market with models that were more economical and were reputedly of higher quality of construction. Reluctance of the domestic manufacturers to produce compact models with fuel-efficient motors created a vacuum that the imports filled. In 1979 Chrysler had to call on the federal government to guarantee loans to stay in the automobile business, and General Motors and Ford admitted that they had lost money in the domestic market. All three producers blamed federal regulations and high labor costs for declining sales. Yet foreign models had to meet the same pollution and safety requirements. Wage scales and fringe benefits in Japan were lower than those of American workers, but consumer preference based on qualitative judgments rather than price seemed to be the main reason for the boom in imports. The sickness of the American automobile industry began to have a sharp negative impact on the national economy. That impact could be seen not only in the industries that supplied materials to the builders but also in the service industries that had developed to meet the requirements of cars, trucks, and buses.

The economic difficulties of Chrysler Corporation in 1979–1982 pointed to the extreme risks in the industry. Vast shifts in taste and sales often occurred even as the companies planned to enter certain phases of the marketplace. The greatest example of such a disaster was Ford Motor Company's introduction of the Edsel, and yet that same firm could note the substantial achievement of the Mustang. When the manufacturers introduced compact cars in the early 1960s, a market was found, at least initially. The Ford Falcon sold 480,000 units in 1961, but only 110,000 six years later. General Motors' Corvair in 1965 sold over 200,000 units; in 1967 only 25,000 were sold. The Chrysler Corporation was able to market only 80,000 full-sized Chryslers in 1960, but six years later consumers purchased 230,000 Chryslers. Fluctuations of 75,000 to 100,000 units per year were not unusual. Thus, one reason multiple-model firms have survived is the flexibility that they have over the single-model car producers; shifts in public taste can more readily be dealt with by larger firms. More than technology is required to make a successful automobile producer: clearly, liquidity and management skills are significant.[15]

Intense competition from Japan in the 1980s led to a vast reduction in the size of the automobile industry in the United States. All three of the major domestic producers closed plants, consolidated functions, and laid off tens of thousands of blue-collar and white-collar workers. In Congress demands for a high tariff on Japanese cars or a tough quota system led the federal government to negotiate a voluntary reduction in exports from Japanese automakers. At the same time domestic firms began to purchase complete cars, motors, and parts from Japanese companies and entered into joint-production agreements with them. The Japanese builders then entered the domestic market by acquiring or building new plants in California, Tennessee, and Kentucky. Ironically, the first foreign car builder to produce automobiles in the United States, Volkswagen, was forced to close its plant in 1988 because of deteriorating sales. General Motors, Ford, and Chrysler, protected by the threat of reprisals against Japanese imports, and with far more efficient facilities and higher-quality products, returned to profitability by the end of the decade. Indeed, profit levels at Ford reached unprecedented levels.

Despite the ever-increasing costs of operating automobiles and constantly escalating purchase prices of new cars, the love affair of the American people with the automobile has not ended. It may be that the 1990s, will present a period of estrangement, but certainly the society requires widespread car ownership. Not even the introduction of an efficient mass transit system can cope with the hundreds of thousands, indeed millions, of Americans who live fifteen, twenty, or more miles from the places where they work and the stores where they shop. The 80 million cars on American roads will continue to need service and replacement through the next decade, and American automobile manufacturers continue to develop more efficient models and engines to meet the altered energy-source requirements.

The American "love affair" with the car produced federal and state programs to construct highways and streets for the auto. Federal legislation in 1916 began the program, which accelerated after 1945. And the modernization and expansion of highways provided additional arteries for the trucking industry. While the railroads maintained their dominance in ton miles of freight carried, the trucking industry surpassed the railroads in total tonnage in the postwar years. Seventy-five percent of the freight transported in the United States moved in trucks by the 1970s. The trucking lobby played an important role in securing passage of the Interstate Highway Act, and, thereby, the vast expansion of long-distance movement of freight by trucks.[16]

THE TRUCKING INDUSTRY AND INTERCITY BUSES

New York City department stores began to use steam-powered delivery trucks in 1901, and by 1906 the United States Postal Service was delivering mail with steam trucks built by the White Motor Company. The employment of trucks in cities expanded rapidly as did the size of the units. Mack trucks with a capacity of 7½ tons became available in 1911, and mass-produced trucks of 1½ tons or 2 tons became commonplace. Trailmobile introduced the first four-wheel trailer designed to be pulled by a Model-T

Ford in 1915. The coming of World War I led to the production of tens of thousands of trucks and trailers for military purposes, and truck convoys from Detroit to Baltimore in 1917 proved that long-distance truck transportation could be feasible economically in the Unitd States. Trailer production soared in the 1920s and by the end of the decade the Mack Truck Company produced high-speed, 6-cylinder truck engines for tractors with a capacity to pull 8 tons. Trucks provided a flexible, low-cost means of moving goods and could serve areas lacking rail transportation. Thus, the trucking industry helped to end rural isolation and provided door-to-door service for less-than-carload-lot shipments (LCL). The 3 million trucks of 1929 provided almost 4 percent of the total intercity freight ton mileage. Throughout the 1930s truck traffic grew, and by the time of World War II trucks carried one-sixth as much freight as the railroads. Military needs during the war stimulated the production of heavy-duty trucks and trailers, and transportation demands after 1945 hastened the expansion of truck systems—and of intercity bus systems.

The intercity bus replaced the interurban railways that had been constructed prior to World War I and in the early 1920s. Buses proved far more flexible in terms of routes and less expensive to operate. The bus companies initially operated short, nonintegrated segments from major cities to smaller, nearby localities. The improved highway system of the 1920s, and the construction of larger buses, made it possible for routes to be extended. Hundreds of competing small bus companies were consolidated, and in 1929 the Greyhound System emerged. The bus industry grew with the coming of the depression of the 1930s and expanded its services dramatically during World War II to meet heightened transportation needs. Mileage of highway bus routes tripled that of railroad passenger service by the 1960s, and communities that had never had rail passenger service often had at least once-a-day bus service. Although the bus systems had already largely supplemented rail passenger service, later in the 1960s, when the tremendous reduction of railway passenger trains took place, bus traffic expanded and filled the void. The intercity bus sytems of the 1970s replaced the railroad as a provider of economical transportation. Ironically, by the 1980s reduced air fares hit the intercity bus lines hard, and in 1988 the nation's two largest systems, Greyhound and Trailways, were merged in order to survive. The airlines, however, produced the most startling changes in post–World War II passenger and mail service.

THE AIRLINES

Commercial aviation in the United States did not "take wings and fly." Instead, the evolution of the industry proved long, painful, and costly. From the barnstormers of the post–World War I era to the jumbo jets, the financial risks taken by the airline companies and their investors have been massive, and losses have been significant. The absence of a consistent long-range federal policy for commercial aviation and the enormous capital requirements of the companies have taken a heavy toll. However, without substantial governmental expenditures for airports and navigational systems, and military purchases of civilian aircraft, the industry might have remained the toy of the rich and the adventuresome.

When World War I ended, the government and the infant aircraft companies flooded the market with surplus planes. Young veterans of the skies of France returned home to inaugurate mail runs between the nation's major cities, and transcontinental mail service opened on September 8, 1920. By the mid-1920s night flights expanded operations, but the fledgling industry was still dangerous: Thirty-one of the first forty pilots hired by the Post Office Department lost their lives. Federal airmail operations ended in 1925 when the Air Mail Act transferred the service to private operators. The government had decided to contract with commercial carriers and take the Post Office out of the aviation business.

Contracts for mail service provided the basis upon which the early airlines emerged. For example, airmail routes One and Two, Boston–New York and Chicago–St. Louis, later became portions of American Airlines; routes Five and Eight in the West became basic units of United Airlines. Initially, however, each short segment had a single operator; there were no "systems." Many of the carriers raised capital from automobile dealers and manufacturers, and Henry Ford owned the Detroit-Chicago-Cleveland franchise, which flew his own Ford trimotored aircraft.

The exploits of Charles Lindbergh in the 1920s made aviation history, but more importantly they gave the industry publicity and generated more investment interest. In Seattle young lumberman Bill Boeing acquired an airmail contract from Chicago to San Francisco. In a few months he had designed and built twenty-five large biplanes (B-40) to operate the route. A holding company, United Aircraft and Transport, soon included Boeing's aircraft plants and airmail line, enginemaker Pratt and Whitney, and Hamilton's Propeller Company. The parent corporation, the brainchild of New York's National City Bank, also acquired Sikorsky Airplane Company, leading builder of flying boats. The pattern established hy United would soon be followed by other aviation conglomerates.[17]

The industry entered a transition period in the late 1920s. As larger, enclosed aircraft became available, passenger traffic began to grow. Fares for air travel were very expensive, and few Americans could afford to fly. Without mail contracts as a form of subsidy, passenger service would have been virtually impossible because of the high costs of operating these new planes. Only 33,000 passengers traveled by air in 1930, and expansion of service was possible only with additional mail revenues.

The profit potential in air commerce attracted investments from bankers, automobile dealers and manufacturers, and even railroad leaders. It also led to intense competition for mail contracts and, as a result, federal intervention. Forty-four carriers bidding against each other could not meet the needs for a large-scale, coordinated service. The Air Mail Act of 1930 sought to build systems to replace the small, undercapitalized carriers. Contracts to the largest firms forced a series of mergers, with General Motors a large security holder of one of the winners, Transcontinental and Western

Air. Competitors cried foul, and the rush to gain advantage created chaos in aviation stocks even as the Great Depression began.

An investigation of the awarding of airmail contracts by Senator Hugo Black led to revelations of favoritism, if not fraud. In 1934, in a gross overreaction, the federal government resumed airmail operations with President Franklin Roosevelt ordering the Army Air Service to carry the mail. Within a week the service lost eighteen pilots: twelve dead and six injured. With poor planes, little experience, and seriously understaffed, the service struggled on, but the results were tragic. Costs of operation rose from 54¢ a mile by the airlines to $2.21 under federal operation. The Air Mail Act of 1934 separated the aircraft manufacturers from the airlines and returned airmail service to private operators. Under the New Deal, commercial aviation began anew. The Civil Aeronautics Act of 1938 established permanent routes for passenger service and provided generous subsidies for mail service. In effect, the government guaranteed a profitable return on the industry's investment. The technical advances provided by the new DC-3s from Douglas Aircraft and the Boeing 247 spurred further expansion of air service. The nation's cities often spent Works Progress Administration funds for runways and terminal buildings to handle enlarged passenger operations.

The rise of the airline industry in the United States was paralleled in Western Europe. Competition for markets in Latin America, Asia, Africa, and the Pacific reached a feverish pitch. The Dutch and French established lines to Africa and the Middle East by the mid-1920s, and Imperial Airways of Britain extended service to India. German companies established airlines in South America that by the 1930s represented a threat to the security of the United States, and particularly to the Panama Canal. To block the Germans, the United States government gave strong support to Juan T. Trippe and Pan American Airways.

Trippe built Pan American with a combination of foresight, diplomatic skill, and commitment to operating the best aircraft over the most economical routes. Throughout the 1920s Trippe invested in several airlines, none of which achieved success. In 1927 a mail contract to Cuba became the first leg of a soon-to-be awesome route system for Pan American. Trippe acquired multiengined planes and pioneered in the use of Sikorsky flying boats. He dispatched engineers to find the best landing sites, and Pan American devised new radio navigation systems for long-distance flights. The Department of the Navy encouraged the awarding of mail subsidies to Trippe, which furthered his expansion efforts in the Carribean and Latin America.

With additional support from the federal government, Trippe moved to expand Pan American service to Europe via the Azores, and across the Pacific to China. Constantly in search of larger aircraft capable of longer flights, Pan Am turned to Sikorsky, which designed the huge Clipper flying boats for the burgeoning international carrier. Trippe dispatched Charles Lindbergh to the Arctic and around the Pacific to find the most feasible routes, but the State Department insisted on a mid-Pacific flight, island-hopping from one United States possession to another. Using the Martin-built China Clippers, Pan American began operations from San Francisco to Hong Kong. The new Boeing Clippers allowed Pan American to fly from the United States directly to England in 1938. Trippe took advantage of the diplomatic requirements of the United States and the subsidies it brought to build his company. Pan Am, in turn, spurred the domestic aviation industry to higher levels of technological achievement.[18]

The coming of World War II halted the development of commercial aviation as the airlines lost planes, pilots, and crews to the war effort. But with the conflict over in 1945 the companies stood ready for rapid expansion in the domestic and international markets. The Douglas DC-3 had stimulated the industry prior to the war, and now hundreds of the military version of the plane were available at low surplus prices. In addition, larger four-motored DC-4s and Lockheed Constellations were available for longer flights. Every carrier wanted to acquire new routes and enter new markets, and the Civil Aeronautics Board (CAB) stood in a maelstrom of conflicting demands, intensified competition, and political pressures. In the three decades after 1945, the Board tried to strengthen the carriers, maintain competition, and expand services. It largely failed. Several major carriers— Capital and Northeast—had to be rescued by mergers before bankruptcy ended their existence. Some of the companies came near extinction as a result of unprofitable route awards and heavy purchases of aircraft at times of declining traffic. The federal, state, and municipal governments invested billions of dollars in runways, terminals, navigational systems, and safety programs that directly benefited the carriers in addition to massive federal subsidies through mail contracts. By 1963 the local service subsidy alone ran over $85 million yearly. Yet the costs of operation, and particularly the purchase of jet aircraft, made aviation a most unstable investment prospect.

Following the end of the war, numerous new regional carriers emerged to operate between small cities and even smaller towns. Other lines, the nonscheduled, carried freight and chartered passenger service. The intensive competition of the late 1940s led to the introduction of coach fares and further encouraged the airlines to seek larger aircraft to spread costs over greater seating capacity. The CAB tried to balance route awards, but political interference precluded the most prudent assignments and heightened the marginal economic situation of some carriers. The coming of the jet age heavily taxed the ability of the airlines to find needed capital. In 1952 the British began operating the jet-powered Comets, which immediately raised competitive levels on international flights. A series of tragic crashes caused by metal fatigue drove the Comets from the air and retarded the development of the jet airplane for commercial aviation. Nevertheless, the jet age had begun. Boeing built its prototype of the 707, but for some time the carriers stayed away fearing the consequences of the purchase price and operating costs. Juan Trippe broke the resistance with orders for twenty of the 707s and twenty-five Douglas DC-8s, which Pan Am put in service in 1958. Other carriers quickly placed orders, and the manufacturers soon could not meet demands. The aviation manufacturers that did not respond to the jet age immediately—Convair and Lockheed— were virtually driven from the commercial-plane market.

JUAN T. TRIPPE AND THE BOEING 747

Between December 1965 and January 1970 Pan American World Airways and the Boeing Company risked over $2 billion on the development of a revolutionary aircraft, the Boeing 747. Juan T. Trippe of Pan Am and President William M. Allen of Boeing had known each other for decades, and both were pioneers in aviation. The famous Clippers produced by Boeing in the 1930s played a significant role in establishing Pan Am as the nation's major international carrier. Now Trippe wanted a huge airplane with both passenger and freight capacity to handle traffic-growth projections for the next two decades. The plane had to be quiet, efficient, fly at altitudes greater than 33,000 feet, and have a range of at least 4,400 miles. Pan Am wanted an aircraft that would give it dominance in international traffic, and Boeing wanted to enter a new market ahead of Douglas Aircraft and Lockheed, its two major competitors.

Boeing agreed to develop the plane, but Pan Am had to invest $500 million in predelivery payments for the first twenty-five aircraft. The advance would be paid even before the Federal Aeronautics Administration tested the plane. Just over four years passed between the contract signing and the first flight. During that time both corporations came close to withdrawing from the project. Boeing engineers could not meet some of Trippe's demands on schedule, and the airline wanted positive answers as it made the huge advance payments. The design went through many modifications: The engine manufacturer, Pratt-Whitney, had to develop two new series of motors; and the wide-body concept had to be sold to other carriers if Boeing's investment was to prove profitable.

The great gamble paid off for Boeing and Pan Am. The manufacturer sold hundreds of planes, and Pan Am gained a more efficient aircraft and an advantage, albeit temporary, in the competition for international travelers.

Juan T. Trippe (1899–1981). Father of American overseas commercial aviation. (Courtesy: Pan American World Airways.)

Both corporations profited from their willingness to risk over $2 billion in private capital. Trippe's requirements created a new era in air travel and helped produce a significant reduction in fares on longer routes, particularly the transatlantic run.

The four major domestic airlines—United, American, Eastern, and TWA—came to dominate four-fifths of the market by the early 1960s. United and American received high marks from investors for their sound expansion and stable management. Eastern, however, under flying pioneer Eddie Rickenbacker, almost failed because of a declining reputation for service. TWA suffered from control by Howard Hughes and the huge orders for airplanes it could not use, which Hughes Tool Company had to finance. United acquired Capital Airlines in 1961 to become the largest domestic carrier, replacing American Airlines. C. R. Smith, president of American, who had determined that international operations would not be as profitable as domestic ones for his company, concentrated very successfully on the latter market. But by the 1970s, the major carriers were strongly challenged by several of the larger regional lines.[19]

Delta in the South, Braniff in the Southwest, Northwest Orient in the Northwest, Continental in the West, and National in the Southeast slowly gained additional routes during the decades of the 1960s and 1970s. The CAB allowed a constant expansion of markets for these lines, and with sound managements, which emerged simultaneously, they became competitive with the four largest airlines. The CAB expansionist policy gave travelers greater choices and often lowered fares, but it also imperiled some of the carriers financially; in 1982 Braniff declared bankruptcy because of overexpansion, and it emerged as a much smaller company. Continental expanded across the nation, overextending the carrier. It entered bankruptcy to break union contracts and became a low-cost, high volume airline. Its parent, Texas Air, absorbed other carriers and gained control of Eastern to become the nation's largest airline, but one that lost money every year because of the deeply discounted fares. The airlines replaced the railroads as the major transporters of long-distance passengers and mail, yet the industry lacked economic stability.

Intensified competition, conflicting CAB policies, and a fare system of nightmarelike confusion brought cries for deregulation of the industry. In 1978 the federal government embarked on a new policy to allow the marketplace to establish fares and rationalize the route structures. Many of the smaller regional carriers moved into markets abandoned by the majors, and commuter air services sprang up to fill voids in the system. Federal agencies, mainly the Federal Aeronautics Administration, continued to provide major subsidies in the form of safety and navigational services while city and county governments built larger and more architecturally impressive terminals and longer runways with federal funds. Yet the industry remained turbulent, without a consistent national policy to provide direction.

The annual cost of travel and freight, both commercial and private, represents approximately 20 percent of the GNP. The United States is unique as the only industrialized country in the world lacking a national transportation plan—which has contributed to both confusion and opportunities in the marketplace.

NOTES

1. S.F. Van Oss, *American Railroads As Investments* (New York: Putnam's, 1893), p. 235.

2. Richard Saunders, *The Railroad Mergers and the Coming of Conrail* (Westport, Connecticut: Greenwood Press, 1978); this is an outstanding study of the merger movement.

3. James J. Flink, *The Car Culture* (Cambridge: MIT Press, 1975), p. 140.

4. James J. Flink, *America Adopts the Automobile, 1895–1910* (Cambridge: MIT Press, 1970), pp. 1–3, 39.

5. Ibid., pp. 294–296.

6. Ibid., pp. 40–41.

7. Ibid., pp. 52–53, 57, 59; John B. Rae, *The Road and the Car in American Life* (Cambridge: MIT Press, 1971), p. 57.

8. John B. Rae, *American Automobile Manufacturers: The First Forty Years* (Philadelphia: Chilton, 1959), pp. 86–87.

9. Alfred D. Chandler, Jr., *Strategy and Structure: Chapters in the History of American Industrial Enterprise* (Cambridge: MIT Press, 1962), pp. 116, 297–298; Flink, *The Car Culture,* pp. 62–66.

10. Chandler, *Strategy and Structure,* pp. 114–115, 117–126, 143, 152, 158.

11. Robert Paul Thomas, "The Automobile Industry and Its Tycoon," *Explorations in Entrepreneurial History,* 2nd series, vol. 6 (Winter 1969), p. 141.

12. Rae, *American Automobile Manufacturers,* p. 2.

13. Sidney Fine, *The Automobile under the Blue Eagle* (Ann Arbor: University of Michigan Press, 1963); this is the definitive study.

14. Lawrence J. White, *The Automobile Industry since 1945* (Cambridge: Harvard University Press, 1971).

15. Ibid., pp. 44–53.

16. Mark H. Rose, *Interstate: Express Highway Politics, 1941–1956* (Lawrence: Regents Press of Kansas, 1979).

17. Charles J. Kelly, Jr., *The Sky's the Limit: The History of the Airlines* (New York: Coward-McCann, 1963), pp. 15–69.

18. Robert Daley, *An American Saga: Juan Trippe and His Pan American Empire* (New York: Random House, 1980); see also Wesley Phillips Newton, *The Perilous Sky: U.S. Aviation Diplomacy and Latin America, 1911–1931* (Coral Gables, Florida: University of Miami Press, 1978).

19. Kelly, *The Sky's the Limit,* pp. 199–283.

SUGGESTED READINGS

DALEY, ROBERT. *An American Saga: Juan Trippe and His Pan American Empire.* New York: Random House, 1980.

FLINK, JAMES J. *America Adopts the Automobile, 1895–1910.* Cambridge: MIT Press, 1970.

HOFSOMMER, DON L. *The Southern Pacific, 1901–1985.* College Station: Texas A&M University Press, 1986.

JARDIM, ANNE. *The First Henry Ford: A Study in Personality and Business Leadership.* Cambridge: MIT Press, 1970.

KELLY, CHARLES J., JR. *The Sky's the Limit: The History of the Airlines.* New York: Coward-McCann, 1963.

KUTER, LAURENCE S. *The Great Gamble: The Boeing 747*. University: University of Alabama Press, 1973.

LEWIS, W. DAVID, and WESLEY PHILLIPS NEWTON. *Delta: The History of an Airline*. Athens: University of Georgia Press, 1978.

NEVINS, ALLAN. *Ford: The Times, the Man, the Company*. New York: Charles Scribner's Sons, 1954.

———. *Ford: Expansion and Challenge, 1915–1933*. New York: Charles Scribner's Sons, 1958.

———, and Frank Ernest Hill. *Ford: Decline and Rebirth, 1933–1962*. New York: Charles Scribner's Sons, 1963.

NEWTON, WESLEY PHILLIPS. *The Perilous Sky: U.S. Aviation Diplomacy and Latin America, 1919–1931*. Coral Gables, Florida: University of Miami Press, 1978.

RAE, JOHN B. *The Road and the Car in American Life*. Cambridge: MIT Press, 1971.

———. *American Automobile Manufacturers: The First Forty Years*. Philadelphia: Chilton, 1959.

———. *The American Automobile: A Brief History*. Chicago: University of Chicago Press, 1965.

ROSE, MARK H. *Interstate: Express Highway Politics, 1941–1956*. Lawrence: Regents Press of Kansas, 1979.

SAUNDERS, RICHARD. *The Railroad Mergers and the Coming of Conrail*. Westport, Connecticut: Greenwood Press, 1978.

STOVER, JOHN F. *The Life and Decline of the American Railroad*. New York: Oxford University Press, 1970.

WHITE, LAWRENCE J. *The Automobile Industry since 1945*. Cambridge: Harvard University Press, 1971.

9 The Energy Industries

The use of cheap energy was fundamental to the rise of large-scale enterprise in modern America. With less than 7 percent of the world's people, the United States uses nearly one-third of the world's energy supply. Over 40 percent of all energy consumed in this country is absorbed by industry, and transportation takes another 20 percent, thus the industrial economy is energy based. Until the introduction of nuclear power the principal sources of energy were oil, natural gas, coal, and electricity, with petroleum the predominant source. Coal, which at the time of World War I contributed 75 percent of the nation's energy, provided less than 25 percent by 1960. The shift from coal to petroleum eventually made the United States an importer rather than an exporter of oil. Petroleum replaced coal even as coal had replaced wood after 1870; but in contrast with the case of petroleum, the United States never found it necessary to import either wood or coal for fuel. The utilization of fuels changed dramatically after the emergence of giant manufacturing enterprises that initially depended upon coal as a source of energy.

THE COAL INDUSTRY

Industry in America became significant only after the adoption of coal as its principal fuel. With the expansion of the rail network in the 1840s, anthracite (hard) coal could be brought cheaply to centers of population. The geographical location of the anthracite coal fields of northeastern Pennsylvania helped give rise to the iron and steel industries of that region and furthered the replacement of wood as fuel in New York, Philadelphia, and other nearby cities. Production of anthracite coal rose from 457,000 tons in 1834 to 3,724,000 in 1849, even as the average price per ton fell from $4.84 to $3.62. Cheap, clean-burning, high-quality coal helped change industry from its almost cottagelike basis to large-scale industrial production. Several industries, particularly iron and steel, were profoundly affected in terms of output, technology, organization, and location by this new source of energy.

Industries producing consumer goods turned to coal to fuel steam boilers that powered the machinery in their plants. Textile mills, for example, often converted from direct water power to steam in the 1840s. The rapid expansion of the American factory system in the next decade can be attributed to, in large part, the adoption of coal-fueled steam power. The increasing demand for coal, especially with the shift to coal-powered locomotives on the expanding railway network, placed a high premium on anthracite. Because of the growing demand, the price of anthracite coal rose, making it too costly for industrial use, and soon it was employed almost exclusively for home heating.[1] Other consumers then turned to bituminous (soft) coal, which lowered fuel costs but horribly polluted cities and towns.

The massive employment of bituminous coal as the basic fuel for industry came after 1870. In that year wood still constituted three-fourths of the total fuel supply, and direct water power remained a substantial source of energy. But yearly production of coal soared from 4,429,000 tons in 1870 to 269,684,000 tons three decades later. The railroads had been the primary consumers of bituminous coal, but with the introduction of the Bessemer process for steel making that industry became a major purchaser of the fuel. With a rapid increase in the rate of industrialization, and as the use of wood for domestic heat declined, the demand for coal grew enormously in the last three decades of the nineteenth century.

The bituminous coal industry expanded rapidly as it sought to meet increasing energy demands. Annual production rose 200 percent between 1894 and 1912, but the industry could best be described as wasteful, inefficient, and overly competitive. "Excessive competition" led to repeated failures to control output and prices. Coal poured from the mines of Pennsylvania and West Virginia to compete with coal from Kentucky, Illinois, and Ohio. Interregional competition grew as the railroad network and Great Lakes ships easily moved coal from one market to another at low freight rates. The result was an industry with high productivity but meager profits. Little capital was required to enter coal mining, and labor was plentiful and cheap; consequently, there were no firms with large shares of the national market. Coal mining was an industry made up almost entirely of highly competitive small operators. Efforts by the coal companies to bring stability to their industry failed.

The coal industry mechanized rapidly after 1900 to reduce production costs and discourage efforts to unionize the miners. The industry also

Consolidated Coal Company mine at Fairmont, West Virginia, near the turn of century.   (Courtesy: Consolidated Coal Company.)

attempted to export surplus production to maintain profitable price levels, but the export market grew very slowly. Railroads, which derived large revenues from hauling coal, supported the operators by stabilizing freight rates, but the ICC refused to allow the use of coal rates to balance interregional competition. Similar efforts by the companies to fix wages for miners and the price of coal also failed. A major movement to organize a national association of coal operators in 1912 met defeat. Only some small, regional marketing cooperatives proved successful, and they were terminated by federal antitrust suits for price fixing.[2]

Faced with what appeared to be insurmountable problems, the coal industry joined the merger movement of the progressive era. For example, the Pittsburgh Coal Company, the Consolidated Coal Company, and the Dering Company emerged as major firms in Pennsylvania, West Virginia, and Illinois respectively. The consolidations of coal companies were not attempts to create regional monopolies; they were instead aimed at stabilizing prices. The mergers failed in this regard because firms not part of the consolidations continued to reduce prices. Fear of antitrust activity precluded significant mergers beyond those affected. The Bituminous Coal Trade Association did publish production and sales figures to aid the marketing process. Overproduction continued to depress the coal industry, however, until the outbreak of World War I.

Although the war provided temporary relief, it failed to resolve basic issues, and the producers remained undisciplined. In the 1920s the industry divided sharply as the southern producers bitterly fought unionization efforts and attempts by Secretary of Commerce Herbert Hoover to build a meaningful trade association. Shortages, strikes, and "high prices," as judged by users, plagued the coal industry. The New Dealers in the 1930s worked with the United Mine Workers (UMW) and the mining companies to stabilize the industry, but not until 1940 did a minimum-price act become effective. The coal industry remained chaotic, generally unprofitable, and a tragic waste of a major resource.

Despite the relatively low cost of coal as fuel, producers saw their market decline drastically. Natural gas pipelines reached midwestern and northern cities after World War II, and homeowners replaced coal furnaces with gas heat. Industry shifted to oil or natural gas to reduce fuel costs, pollution, and dependency on a source that remained in chaos. The output of coal reached 658,265,000 tons in 1920, fell to 512,257,000 tons in 1940, rose again during World War II, but fell to only 419,834,000 tons in 1955. Dieselization of the nation's railways eliminated a major market as did the shift to oil in the maritime industry. Advanced technology allowed steel companies to produce a ton of steel with far less coal than in the pre-World War I period. The major market for coal remained utilities that used the fuel to produce electricity.[3]

Ironically, coal was the most plentiful fuel in the United States. But as long as oil and natural gas were cheap and readily available, coal would be a "sick" industry. Production of coal declined sharply in the 1950s, especially after the small independent coal operators closed mines that were no longer profitable. The consolidation effort of the early 1900s had failed, but the collapsing market led to extensive mergers in the 1950s and 1960s. Larger operators, such as Peabody Coal, purchased smaller holdings and invested heavily in huge machines for surface mining. When domestic petroleum production began to decline, and foreign supplies became problematical, several petroleum companies acquired coal lands or merged with coal producers to secure a place in another energy field. Output of coal revived slowly as petroleum prices rose in the early 1970s. With an energy shortage of massive complexity developing in that decade, coal again became a significant industry. Indeed, the United States became a major exporter of steam coal as well as metallurgical coal, and new mines were opened, particularly in the western part of the country. Production reached 770 million tons in 1979, although that was 100 million tons below total capacity. As petroleum reduced the nation's dependence on coal in the nineteenth century, coal became part of the answer to overdependence on imported petroleum and nuclear energy in the 1980s, especially for generating electricity. Production rose to 888 million short tons in 1986, and the United States became the second leading coal exporter in the world. The coal, petroleum, and electrical power industries emerged almost simultaneously, and they established an interdependency that continues to the present.

THE ELECTRIC INDUSTRY

At the same time that coal replaced wood as the basic fuel, the use of arc-lighting for streets gained widespread acceptance. In the 1880s incandescent lights appeared, and as a result, demands for electric power increased rapidly during the next decade. The simple arc-lights gave way to more complicated electric systems, and most cities developed central power stations for the generation and transmission of electricity. Electrical manufacturing firms expanded their product lines in the same pattern. Inventions and scientific advances laid the basis for the industry's rapid growth.

Key to this development was the engineer-entrepreneur who saw the commercial possibilities of the application of scientific discoveries. The entrepreneur used new knowledge to create new products and manufacturing techniques. Continuous technological advances altered the structure of the industry and its marketing methods, and the electric industry was among the first major enterprises to be built upon a constantly changing technology. Product improvement became the basis for competition between firms and was more important than price competition in the oligopolistic industry that electrical manufacturing became. In an oligopoly a small number of firms dominate a large market. This basic pattern in the industry was formed before 1900.

The first electrical manufacturers built and operated arc-lights for the illumination of streets. The arc-lights began to replace gas street lights in the late 1870s. The power for the arc-lights came from dynamos, or generators, located in small central power stations, and the electricity was transmitted to the lights by wires strung on poles. The Brush Electric Company, named after its founder and the inventor of the arc-light system Charles F. Brush, pioneered the electric power industry. Two Philadelphia high school science teachers, Elihu Thomson and E. J. Houston, improved on Brush's scheme and developed more powerful dynamos for larger systems. Their Thomson-Houston Electric Company, formed in 1883, became a leading electrical manufacturer. Soon other companies emerged to compete with the two pioneers. Thomson-Houston held title to many of the basic patents, but it came to dominate the industry by acquiring other manufacturers rather than by control through patents.

That policy continued after Thomson-Houston merged with Edison General Electric in 1892, and one of the former's most aggressive executives, Charles A. Coffin, became president of the new General Electric Company. General Electric sought to dominate the incandescent-light industry as Thomson-Houston had arc-lighting. Incandescent lighting offered an even larger market as home owners, storekeepers, and industrialists sought a cheap, smokeless, safe means to illuminate homes, shops, and factories. Thomas Alva Edison invented a successful incandescent lamp in 1879, but he needed at least $500,000 in risk capital to develop less expensive lamps and an efficient transmission system. Recognizing the economic implications of his work, Edison sought to enter the field of lighting homes, offices, and factories, which represented 80 percent of the gaslight business. An already famous inventor, Edison received the financial backing of Drexel, Morgan and Company, and in 1882 personally turned on the incandescent lighting system in the Morgan offices in New York City, his first commercial installation. A central power station with "jumbo" generators, underground transmission wires, and screw socket lamps gave Edison a better product and allowed him to undercut the cost of gas illumination. The Edison Lamp Company manufactured the incandescent lamps for the system, while the Edison Electric Light Company constructed the generating facilities. These two firms and several others had been merged to form a $12 million combine, Edison General Electric, in 1889. Edison then withdrew from the industry to return to his Menlo Park laboratory, his goal of creating an incandescent lighting system achieved. General Electric (GE) continued to improve his design and to develop larger electric systems.

The electrical manufacturing industry after 1890 grew at an unprecedented rate. After incandescent street lights proved to be cheaper and of higher quality than gas or arc-lighting, cities granted licenses for central generating stations, thus stimulating the development of larger dynamos. Rather than providing cheap, but poor-quality, electrical service, General Electric adopted a policy of high-price, high-quality equipment and lamps. Its principal competitor, Westinghouse Electric Company, used the same policy.[4]

Like Edison, George Westinghouse had little formal education, but the railroad braking system he had designed became the standard in that industry. After investigating the possibilities of gas illumination, he shifted his interest to electricity. Purchasing transformers and other equipment in Europe, Westinghouse conducted experiments in power transmission and devised a transformer network to transmit greater voltage over longer distances. The Westinghouse Electric Company, formed in 1886, manufactured the components of his system. Unlike General Electric, his firm sold lighting systems (generators, transformers, power lines, and related equipment) for cash only and did not accept stocks and bonds of central power station companies as payment. Westinghouse lamps sold at about the same price as Edison's, and the two companies became bitter rivals. Edison defended his direct-current (dc) concept, while Westinghouse pursued his alternating-current (ac) design. Allegations of unsafe products being sold and patent suits between the firms became a part of the competition of the industry through the 1880s. General Electric began to produce alternating-current systems after Edison withdrew as a participant in the company in the 1890s.

The application of small electric motors in industry created an even greater demand for power, leading to the construction of giant power stations with extensive transmission lines. Both GE and Westinghouse developed systems to meet this demand. They also built electric railway motors and equipment as urban transit lines expanded. The construction in 1896 of a giant power station at Niagara Falls, New York, pioneered large-scale electrical power generation and transmission and created another dimension for the industry.

Both General Electric and Westinghouse marketed ac industrial motors after 1894 and built high-speed generators that supplied the electrical needs until the late 1890s, when huge turbo generators with capacities of 5,000 kilowatt hours or more became available. The intense competition between GE and Westinghouse for these and other markets led them to establish a patent pool in 1896 to allow fuller development of electrical apparatus by both firms. It also strengthened the two giant companies at the expense of smaller competitors, several of which were purchased by the duopoly shortly thereafter. The larger firms also acquired smaller innovative companies to gain access to new technologies and products, and this pattern would continue into the twentieth century.[5]

After 1900 the electrical industry's major contribution was the expansion of services and the enlargement of generating equipment. Revenue from the operation of power systems leaped from $85 million in 1900 to over $500 million by 1920. With increased consumption of electricity by industry and homes, power generation became a $2 billion business by 1929. In that decade output of central power stations increased by over 250 percent, but electric rates fell drastically as a result of economies of scale. The central power stations, licensed, built, and sometimes financed by General Electric and Westinghouse, were both privately and publicly owned. Many cities and towns operated municipal power systems while other utilities were investor owned. Franchise elections proved very divisive as advocates of government or public power battled those supporting private systems. Conservationists during the Progressive era argued for public development of federally-owned hydroelectric sites, adding another dimension to the controversy. Little federal or state power-generating activity occurred before the New Deal, and the vast expansion of electric power generation in the 1920s was almost exclusively private. Indeed, the industry's image became synonymous with one individual during those years—Samuel Insull.

GERARD SWOPE OF GENERAL ELECTRIC

When Gerard Swope assumed the presidency of General Electric on May 16, 1922, he inaugurated a new era of expansion for this leading energy firm. Swope's prior experience included many years with Western Electric and its worldwide operations, as well as with the War Department during World War I. Born in St. Louis, Missouri, in 1872, he came from an upper middle class family. Educated at Massachusetts Institute of Technology (MIT) as an electrical engineer, he joined Western Electric in Chicago as a blue-collar employee. During the Chicago years he moved through the ranks of that firm and came to know progressive reformers Jane Addams, Julia Lathrop, and Dr. Alice Hamilton of Hull House. That association, and his acquaintance with Louis Brandeis at MIT, made Swope a unique corporate executive in the 1920s.

Swope not only restructured General Electric but also gave it new direction. Following his own motto—Analyze, Organize, Deputize, Supervise—he made two major corporate decisions. After analyzing the market for electrical goods, he decided to dispose of General Electric's holdings in power companies. Chairman of the Board Owen Young agreed that it was unethical for GE to "sell to itself," and they distributed the securities of subsidiary Electric Bond and Share Company to GE stockholders. His analysis not only led to a decision to remain a manufacturer of electrical generating and transmission equipment and high-quality light bulbs, but also to enter the market with electricity-using consumer goods bearing GE's trademark. Swope believed that millions of households represented an untapped market for refrigerators and small appliances, and they in turn would create an expanding market for more generators and transmission equipment. Much of GE's manufacturing

Gerard Swope (1872–1957). Mass-marketing innovator and pioneer in improving labor relations and company benefits for workers. (Courtesy: General Electric Company.)

facility was underutilized, and its skilled workers could be more efficiently employed. The firm then organized new divisions to manufacture the consumer products with young executives trained by Swope to supervise the plants and distribution of the appliances.

Under Swope GE developed a new labor relations program. He constantly toured the manufacturing facilities and held meetings with employees for frank, open discussions. Doctor Hamilton of Hull House was hired to inspect the facilities for health and safety problems. Swope proposed an unemployment insurance plan in 1925, but the employees rejected it; they welcomed it wholeheartedly after 1929. A lifelong Democrat, Swope supported the New Deal, suggested an economic recovery program in 1930 not unlike the National Industrial Recovery Act of 1933, and advised Franklin Roosevelt on the Wagner Act and the Social Security Act. Swope wanted his employees in an industrial union, but the American Federation of Labor with its craft structure said no. When the Electrical Workers Union did emerge, Swope worked closely with its leaders. Roosevelt's secretary of labor, Francis Perkins, praised Gerard Swope as an industrial statesman.

Samuel Insull entered the electric business in 1881 as Thomas Edison's private secretary. He helped to develop the concept of the central power station, organized Edison General Electric, and created a model for the national distribution of consumer products that was adopted by many industries. Insull developed the concept of load or usage to establish utility rates, and he applied rigorous cost accounting to electrical production. He urged effective public regulation of electric companies as "natural monopolies" and devised financial structures that allowed the formation of huge power combines. In the 1920s, with Chicago as his base, Insull put together a utility holding company empire that had 600,000 stockholders and 500,000 bondholders. At the end of the decade his companies were worth

$3 billion and provided power to 4 million customers in 5,000 towns and cities in thirty-two states. Insull created a large number of firms that simply owned minority, but controlling, shares of companies that actually produced and transmitted electric power. By manipulating these securities, Insull could dominate a substantial electrical network with a relatively small investment. Yet he could issue a vast array of securities of the non-power-generating firms and sell them to unwary investors. Insull's empire collapsed in 1932, and investors lost millions of dollars. The value of the holding company securities evaporated, and speculators "took a bath" as their investments washed away. The flight of Insull to Greece solidified the public's view of him as a corrupt security manipulator. He returned to the United States, was tried and acquitted, but the negative reaction against private, investor-owned electric utilities that Insull's debacle helped to generate gave support to cries for public power development during the New Deal.[6]

In the 1930s the federal government enacted the Public Utility Holding Company Act to prevent the formation of empires such as the one Insull had built. The Rural Electrification Act provided federal loans to cooperatives to extend power lines to farming areas. More importantly the government also created the Tennessee Valley Authority (TVA), a massive socialized power system. The TVA project incorporated many ideas, including an effort to use it as a "yardstick" to determine what electrical generation cost and what fair rates should be. Efforts to develop the 40,000-square-mile Tennessee River Valley began as early as 1916, when President Woodrow Wilson signed legislation to build a hydroelectric facility at Muscle Shoals, Alabama, to power a nitrate plant for the manufacture of munitions. Completed in 1925, the Wilson Dam supplied electricity for the immediate area and for a nitrate-fertilizer plant. Senator George W. Norris of Nebraska fought for the development of the entire valley. He wanted more dams to create cheap electricity for farmers there and inexpensive nitrate fertilizer for all farmers. The dams would end the devastating floods on the Tennessee and make the river navigable for hundreds of miles, thereby lowering transportation costs. President Franklin D. Roosevelt saw the project an an opportunity for a federally supervised regional planning experiment. Together, Roosevelt and Norris fought for TVA. Private power companies all over the United States attacked the scheme, but particularly those in the Tennessee River Valley. Wendell Willkie, president of Commonwealth and Southern Company, the major private utility in the area, fought bitterly against TVA, but he lost in Congress, in the federal courts, and at the polling place in 1940, when as the Republican presidential nominee he was defeated by Roosevelt. The Tennessee Valley Authority became a massive project that by the 1970s generated more electricity and burned more coal than any other agency in the nation, private or public. TVA purchased the Commonwealth and Southern interests and provided electricity to urban governments that formed municipally owned utilities. Although it never became either a meaningful "yardstick" or a true exercise in regional planning, TVA was successful in providing cheap electricity and thus transforming the economy of the valley. The TVA served as a model for the construction of more federal hydroelectric projects, particularly in the West. None, however, was of the scale of TVA.[7]

The entrance of the federal government into the production of electrical power was paralleled by increasing involvement in the regulation of the private sector and in forcing the industry to employ different fuels. While the Federal Power Commission, created by Congress in 1920 to license the construction and operation of power facilities on federal lands and navigable waterways, proved weak and ineffectual, other agencies played major roles in shaping national electrical policy. The REA (Rural Electrification Authority), for example, engaged in a vigorous campaign of expanding its cooperatives, not only in rural areas, but also into small towns and urban fringes. Through the Atomic Energy Commission (AEC) the government encouraged private utilities to develop nuclear power facilities during the 1950s and 1960s. As a result, billions of dollars of capital had to be raised to construct nuclear plants. Generally, electrical utilities need $3 in capital investment to produce $1 of revenue yearly. Profits in the industry are high in terms of earnings but low in terms of capital invested. After World War II the federal government also urged the utilities to end the use of coal to fuel steam-generating plants because of the tremendous pollution problem and because oil and natural gas were cheaper. After 1974, however, the federal government reversed its policy of three decades and demanded conversion back to coal to reduce America's dependence on imported foreign oil. The utilities then faced more capital expenditures for conversion to coal and for pollution abatement equipment. Public opposition to nuclear power plants, which developed simultaneously, and ever-rising construction costs of nuclear facilities, placed additional pressures on the utilities. Thus one energy industry, the electrical, had to make significant changes in production methods largely because of alterations in another energy industry, petroleum.

In short, because of government policy and directives, public fears about nuclear power, the traditional competition of the marketplace, and the drastic alterations within the interrelated petroleum industry, the electrical power industry has made significant changes in production methods and in its business structures. Coal, electricity, nuclear power, and petroleum are interdependent energy industries wherein the market and costs of one, and government policies and regulations, have an immediate impact on the others. But none of the other energy enterprises have been so visible, so controversial, and so central to modern society as petroleum.

THE PETROLEUM INDUSTRY

The oil deposits of western Pennsylvania supplied the Indians and early white settlers with "medicine," lubricants, and a smoky, foul-smelling source of light. Not until 1855 did Yale University chemistry professor Benjamin Silliman, Jr., demonstrate that a refining process could transform the crude oil into a quality lubricant and a much cheaper source of illumination than whale oil. The nation needed a new, inexpensive source of light because whale oil and "coal gas" were expensive and in diminishing supply. Silliman's Pennsylvania Rock Oil Company hired Edwin L. Drake to drill on its property near Titusville, and in 1859 the well produced petroleum at a rate of one thousand gallons per day. Within a year some two thousand wells were producing over one thousand barrels of oil daily, and an industry had been born. Problems of transportation, refining, distributing, and creating a mass market needed to be dealt with, but few new enterprises would see such complex matters so readily solved.

Only twenty years old when Drake produced oil from his well, John D. Rockefeller had already established himself as a businessman. His father, an itinerant medicine salesman, taught him thrift, and his high school in Cleveland, Ohio provided him with basic mathematical skills. As a book-keeper for a commission merchant firm, he learned that trade and opened his own business in 1859. A dedicated worker who believed that God rewarded the elect, Rockefeller prospered in the produce business. With his partner, Maurice B. Clark, Rockefeller decided to enter the petroleum business when he discovered that one gallon of refined kerosene exceeded in value a barrel of crude oil. Aided by a Cleveland chemist, they built a refinery in 1863 to produce naphtha and kerosene. Located near the Pennsylvania oil field, Cleveland offered several rail routes to the production area and access to eastern markets via Great Lakes shipping. Constantly reinvesting profits and keeping expenses and salaries to a minimum, Rockefeller expanded his operations.

Rockefeller created not only a corporate structure but also, and more importantly, an organization of outstanding young businessmen. Henry M. Flagler, S. V. Harkness, William Rockefeller, Oliver H. Payne, and John D. himself formed Standard Oil Company in 1870 based on the refineries that Rockefeller had built in Cleveland. With only $1 million in capital, Standard was the largest oil concern in the world. Rockefeller realized that control of the refining process would give him control of the industry. His main product, kerosene for illumination, had to be produced in the refineries, then sold in the retail market. Yet the ultimate strategy adopted was vertical integration, which meant Standard Oil ownership of not only refineries but also a barrel plant, warehouses, tank cars, and eventually pipelines, as well as crude oil production. Standard soon perfected the capital-intensive, high-volume concept that came to dominate American industry.

The petroleum business was chaotic until Standard arrived. Prices rose and fell as the market was alternatively glutted or suffered from an insufficient supply of crude oil. Rockefeller desired to stabilize the market by bringing all the major refineries into Standard Oil. In 1873 he bought 80 percent of the refining capacity in Cleveland, about one-third of the total in the United States. Standard refineries made the most efficient use of by-products, generated profits at each step of the refining process, and used a highly elaborate cost-accounting system. After the depression of 1873 a Rockefeller associate bought the independent refineries in New York, Philadelphia, and Baltimore and then placed them under Standard's control.

The Standard Oil Refinery No. 1 in 1889, the beginning of a petroleum empire.   (Courtesy: The Standard Oil Company, Ohio.)

Simultaneously, Flagler labored to gain Standard an advantage in transporting petroleum.

Henry Flagler contributed capital, business experience, and administrative talents to Standard Oil. He also obtained the lowest freight rates for Standard products from the railroads and, thereby, established a virtual monopoly. In 1870 Flagler and Rockefeller helped to create the South Improvement Company as a scheme to pool oil shipments on three railroads in return for rebates of up to 50 percent of the freight charges to those refiners who formed the company. Refiners who were not members, and therefore did not receive the rebates, would have been forced out of business. Flagler and Rockefeller even proposed that the South Improvement Company be given rebates on the freight bills of the remaining independent refiners. A public uproar, and an act of the Pennsylvania legislature, prevented the scheme from working, but Flagler did obtain the lowest rates and substantial rebates for Standard because of the extraordinary volume of its traffic. The smaller refiners, who could not compete, sold out to Standard, which generally paid them a fair price for their properties. Rockefeller and Flagler, moving aggressively, soon built a pipeline network that ended their dependence on the railroads for bringing the crude oil to the refineries.[8]

Standard controlled almost 100 percent of the nation's refineries, and in 1880 had a cash reserve of $40 million, but its huge empire lacked structure. The loose amalgamation of many Standard operations was ended in 1879 with the formation of Standard Oil Trust. Holders of all the securities of fourteen companies and blocks of securities in twenty-six others turned over their stocks and bonds to nine trustees, who issued them $70 million in trust certificates. The trustees controlled and coordinated the companies and paid dividends on the trust certificates they had issued. A brilliant attorney, Samuel C. Dodd, devised the new instrument for Standard. Although an Ohio court ordered the trust dissolved in 1892, for over a decade it gave Rockefeller and his associates the means to integrate the company's far-flung operations and further reduce the cost of its major products. The trust's executive committee made general policy for all the various Standard components.[9]

Efficiency, monopoly, and research and development allowed Standard to make huge profits—$11 million in 1883 alone—and pay immense dividends of $500 million between 1882 and 1906. Shortly after 1879 the trustees closed thirty-one of Standard's fifty-three refineries and concentrated production in three massive new refineries. Standard built ocean-going tankers to carry its products to Europe, where it initially dominated the market. The Ohio court order of 1892 led to the formation of Standard Oil Company of New Jersey, a state which allowed holding companies and did not slow the growth of the nation's first major trust. The trustees built an integrated enterprise, abandoning Rockefeller's first strategy of a horizontal monopoly of refineries. Standard, however, did not cut prices to drive out its remaining competition, but kept prices high enough to earn substantial profits. There were major competitors at home and abroad as other large integrated firms developed after oil discoveries were made in Russia, Mexico, the Dutch East Indies (Indonesia), and in the American Midwest and Southwest. The Russian oil fields soon produced 11 million barrels of petroleum a year, an output greater than that of the United States, giving Standard significant competition in Europe. The opening of the new oil fields created enormous price variations, with crude oil prices as low as ten cents per barrel before World War I, rising to $4 per barrel after 1917. By 1911 eight other large integrated oil firms operated in the United States, substantially reducing the dominance of Standard in many areas.

Standard's corporate headquarters at 26 Broadway in New York City continued, however, to represent to many Americans the most flagrant abuse of economic power in this country. Muckrakers assaulted Standard throughout the 1890s and early 1900s as the citadel of greed and rapaciousness run rampant. The twenty different "Standard Oil Companies" came under constant attack in the press, the halls of Congress, and the courts. Finally, the Supreme Court in 1911 ordered Standard Oil Trust dissolved and broken into competitive units.

The end of Standard Oil was only one aspect of the dramatic changes between 1900 and 1920. The coming of the automobile created a vast market for gasoline even as expansion of the electrical industry reduced the demand for kerosene for light. Gasoline had been an unwanted by-product in the refining process, and not until 1915 did gasoline production surpass kerosene as a marketable item. A new "cracking" process, developed by Standard Oil of Indiana in 1913, increased the proportion of gasoline produced from a barrel of oil from 15 to 45 percent. Marketing changed significantly also. Automobile owners initially filled their gasoline tanks from small cans using a funnel, but the service station appeared just before World War I and the roadside gas pump soon became commonplace. By 1929 motorists could find 120,000 stations owned or leased by the oil companies. The independent station owners assumed the financial risks in the retail sale of the industry's major product. In the 1920s, General Motors and Standard Oil spent $25 million developing "ethyl" as an additive to reduce cylinder knocking, thus creating a "premium" fuel for the service stations. Expanding markets, new oil fields, and the Standard Oil antitrust decision brought about substantial changes in the industry.[10]

The end of Standard Oil Trust led to the formation of a number of new, not wholly integrated, firms. Only Standard Oil of California could be considered an integrated oil company. Throughout the 1920s and 1930s the former "Standard" companies purchased independent refiners, crude-oil producers, pipeline companies, and transportation facilities in order to compete with non-Standard companies such as Pure, Texaco, and Gulf. All sought to assure a continuous flow of oil through their capital-intensive facilities to their retail dealers. By 1931 the twenty largest integrated companies provided the nation with over half its crude oil. Additional petroleum discoveries in Oklahoma, Texas, California, and Louisiana drove domestic crude oil prices to very low levels in the early 1930s, leading to serious efforts at conservation in those states. Many of the major firms also acquired crude production in Venezuela and the Middle East, thereby becoming international in scope.

MAGNOLIA PETROLEUM AND AN INTEGRATED INDUSTRY

The dissolution of Standard Oil Trust by the U.S. Supreme Court in 1911 led to the creation of a number of "independent" petroleum companies, including Standard Oil Company of New York, or Socony. Largely a marketing company in New York, New England, and abroad, Socony had no crude-oil production and only a small refinery capacity. The executives of Standard Oil of New York wanted to build an integrated firm, which meant additional refineries, access to petroleum at the wellhead, and ownership of pipelines and retail outlets, soon to be known as service stations. Socony thus embarked on an acquisition program that included the Magnolia Petroleum Company.

"The Magnolia," as its employees referred to it, was formed on April 24, 1911, in Texas, when the Sealy Company, Security Oil Company, and Navarro Refining Company were merged. Within a few years the firm had three refineries and 435 service stations in Oklahoma, Arkansas, and Texas. By 1917 Magnolia operated 1,245 producing oil wells, and within three years was the tenth-largest oil refiner in the country. The company built pipelines from Oklahoma to its Beaumont refinery and entered the new oil fields in southern Oklahoma and west Texas. This expansion program required substantial capital, which was raised largely after 1916 when Magnolia came under the control of the presidents of Standard Oil of New York and Standard Oil of New Jersey. The attorney general of Texas insisted that the

Magnolia Petroleum Company service station in Corpus Christi, Texas, 1918.   (Courtesy: Mobil Oil Corporation.)

securities of Magnolia be placed in a voting trusteeship in Texas; this was done, but the independent oil company disappeared, and Socony very shortly held 70 percent of Magnolia's stock.

During the next nine years Magnolia grew rapidly. It purchased the McMann Oil Company, a major crude producer in Oklahoma and Kansas, to become one of the largest crude-oil companies in the nation. Throughout the 1920s Magnolia drilled more wells, extended its pipelines, expanded refinery capacity, and opened additional service stations. In 1925 all pretense of independence ended when a new Magnolia Petroleum Company was formed in Texas with Standard of New York as the sole owner.

The acquisition of Magnolia by Socony represents the trend throughout the 1920s and 1930s of major oil firms acquiring minor companies in order to develop wholly integrated petroleum operations. The firms purchased were usually located geographically outside the major's territory to avoid antitrust action, but the effect was to reduce competition in the future. Socony merged with Vacuum Oil Company in 1931, and they would eventually become part of Mobil Corporation. Magnolia's crude production and refining capacity remained an important asset of Mobil Corporation in the 1980s.

Competition in the petroleum industry after 1920 was based on technology, advertising, service, and convenience, not price; the companies rarely resorted to "price wars" for a share of the market. Research laboratories maintained by the larger firms sought to reduce refining costs and create additional marketable by-products. Most oil companies concentrated their efforts in refining and marketing gasoline where the principal demand was, but they also produced heating oil, diesel fuel, and high-octane aviation gasoline. World War II brought the oil companies into petrochemicals, adding a major new dimension to the industry.

The coming of World War II put great pressure on the petroleum industry. The government curtailed domestic gasoline consumption through rationing to meet military needs for fuel, especially for aviation purposes. German submarines made Gulf to Atlantic petroleum shipments dangerous, with a great loss of vessels early in the war. In March 1942 industry leaders proposed that pipelines be built from Texas to New Jersey and Pennsylvania to carry millions of gallons of oil safely to the east coast. The federal government built the pipelines, opened by April 1943, at a cost of $140 million. After 1945 the government sold the pipelines to private corporations that converted them to natural gas transport, further undermining the sale of coal in the East.

Following the war petroleum became the preferred fuel for the world. The expansion of the ownership of automobiles and the production of more trucks, buses, and diesel locomotives created a worldwide demand for gasoline and diesel fuel. Like the United States, Great Britain and other western European countries shifted from the use of coal for heat to oil and natural gas. The demand for petroleum led to the discovery of more oil fields in Saudi Arabia, Iraq, Iran, Libya, Nigeria, and the feudal states in the Persian Gulf. Even as world oil production rose, however, domestic production in the United States failed to meet demands, so that in 1947 the nation became a net importer of petroleum for the first time. Federal tax policy had been designed to encourage exploration by allowing the companies to depreciate up to 27.5 percent of their gross incomes, though not to exceed 50 percent of the net income. The depletion allowance provided a substantial part of the profits of the industry; it also led to severe criticism. Pressure from consumers led Congress to reduce the oil-depletion allowance in 1976.[11]

Dependence on foreign petroleum grew throughout the three decades after 1947. As late as 1954 only 17 percent of the petroleum used in the United States was imported, but that figure would increase markedly as consumption grew and domestic production declined. Simultaneously, the federal government embarked on a program to develop nuclear power as an alternative energy source, and later it urged greater utilization of coal. As a result, the major oil companies began to acquire non-petroleum-related subsidiaries to protect the integrity of the firms. Some purchased coal producers and coal lands, while others acquired department stores, chemical companies, and vast real estate holdings. The wealth of the oil firms had reached such high levels that as early as 1955 eight of the nation's twenty-six largest corporations were petroleum companies. With the tremendous rise in crude-oil prices after the Arab oil embargo of 1973, the gross revenues of petroleum firms reached unprecedented levels. Exxon Corporation (formerly Standard Oil of New Jersey) had revenues of $84.8 billion in 1979, a sum equal to the GNP of Switzerland. Revenues of Mobil

Corporation were larger than the GNP of Austria, and those of Standard Oil of California's exceeded the GNP of Greece.

The size and economic power of the petroleum giants raised serious questions about legitimate profit levels and the growing interdependence of the energy industry as a whole. Many of the major petroleum firms had invested heavily in coal and uranium production as well as petroleum. After 1974, the Organization of Petroleum Exporting Countries (OPEC) established new and generally higher prices for crude oil, thereby creating havoc in the domestic petroleum price system. Artificially controlled ceiling prices on domestic oil and natural gas eased temporarily the problems of consumers, but they became subjects of criticism by domestic oil firms as well as by governments in western Europe and Japan. Ironically, the soaring price of crude oil led to a variety of conservation measures and shifts to other fuels, especially coal and natural gas. Consumption of petroleum around the globe declined sharply, and suddenly a world petroleum glut resulted. International and domestic oil prices fell precipitously, and OPEC could not halt the fall. Domestic firms moved quickly to replenish their reserves as cheaply as possible. The result was a series of mergers and hostile takeovers as companies with proven reserves were eagerly sought by those unwilling to spend precious capital on exploration. As a consequence Getty Oil became part of Texaco, British Petroleum swallowed up Standard Oil, Gulf became part of Chevron, and Mobil Corporation acquired Superior Oil. The energy crisis of the 1980s became inexorably linked to global inflation, America's foreign policy, and international trade, making it one of the nation's central political and economic issues.

NOTES

1. Alfred D. Chandler, Jr., "Anthracite Coal and the Beginnings of the Industrial Revolution in the United States," *Business History Review* 46 (Summer 1972), pp. 141–181.

2. William Graebner, "Great Expectations: The Search for Order in Bituminous Coal, 1890–1917," *Business History Review* 48 (Spring 1974), pp. 49–72.

3. Sam H. Schurr and Bruce C. Netschert, *Energy in the American Economy, 1850–1975* (Baltimore: Johns Hopkins University Press, 1960), p. 63.

4. Arthur A. Bright, Jr., *The Electric-Lamp Industry: Technological Change and Economic Development from 1800 to 1947* (New York: Macmillan, 1949).

5. Harold C. Passer, *The Electrical Manufacturers, 1875–1900* (Cambridge: Harvard University Press, 1953).

6. Forrest McDonald, *Insull* (Chicago: University of Chicago Press, 1962).

7. Thomas K. McCraw, *TVA and the Power Fight, 1933–1937* (Philadelphia: J.B. Lippincott, 1971).

8. Harold F. Williamson and Arnold R. Daum, *The American Petroleum Industry: The Age of Illumination, 1859–1899* (Evanston, Illinois: Northwestern University Press, 1959).

9. Alfred D. Chandler, Jr., *The Visible Hand: The Managerial Revolution in American Business* (Cambridge: Harvard University Press, 1977), pp. 321–326.

10. Thomas C. Cochran, *200 Years of American Business* (New York: Basic Books, 1977), p. 121.

11. J. Stanley Clark, *The Oil Century: From the Drake Well to the Conservation Era* (Norman: University of Oklahoma Press, 1958).

SUGGESTED READINGS

CHANDLER, ALFRED D., JR., "Anthracite Coal and the Beginnings of the Industrial Revolution in the United States." *Business History Review* 46 (Summer 1972): 141–181.

CLARK, J. STANLEY. *The Oil Century: From the Drake Well to the Conservation Era.* Norman: University of Oklahoma Press, 1958.

CLARK, JOHN G. *Energy and the Federal Government: Fossil Fuel Policies, 1900–1946.* Urbana: University of Illinois Press, 1987.

DE CHAZEAU, MELVIN G., AND ALFRED E. KAHN. *Integration and Competition in the Petroleum Industry.* New Haven, Connecticut: Yale University Press, 1959.

EAVENSON, HOWARD N. *The First Century and a Quarter of American Coal Industry.* Pittsburgh: privately printed, 1942.

HAMMOND, JOHN W. *Men and Volts: The Story of General Electric.* Philadelphia: J.B. Lippincott, 1941.

HIDY, RALPH, AND MURIEL HIDY. *Pioneering in Big Business, 1882–1911.* New York: Harper Brothers, 1955.

JOSEPHSON, MATTHEW. *Edison.* New York: McGraw-Hill, 1959.

LOTH, DAVID. *Swope of G.E.: The Story of Gerard Swope and General Electric in American Business.* New York: Simon & Schuster, 1958.

MCDONALD, FORREST. *Insull.* Chicago: University of Chicago Press, 1962.

NEVINS, ALLAN. *Study in Power: John D. Rockefeller, Industrialist and Philanthropist.* New York: Charles Scribner's Sons, 1953.

PASSER, HAROLD C. *The Electrical Manufacturers, 1875–1900.* Cambridge: Harvard University Press, 1953.

SCHURR, SAM H., AND BRUCE C. NETSCHERT. *Energy in the American Economy, 1850–1975.* Baltimore: Johns Hopkins University Press, 1960.

WHITTEN, DAVID O. *The Emergence of Giant Enterprise, 1860–1914: American Commercial Enterprise and Extractive Industries.* Westport, Connecticut: Greenwood Press, 1983.

WILLIAMSON, HAROLD F. AND ARNOLD R. DAUM. *The American Petroleum Industry, 1859–1959.* Two volumes. Evanston, Illinois: Northwestern University Press, 1959, 1963.

10 Giant Enterprise

In their classic study of the rise of large-scale business enterprises, Adolf Berle and Gardiner Means described what they called a "corporate revolution" that occurred in the dozen years from 1895 to 1907. During that time a major organizational upheaval took place in the national economy. Mergers increased to such levels that an average of 266 firms disappeared each year into the corporate shells of other companies. Soon single firms controlled, or at least dominated, significant shares of the market for major products. By 1904, of all manufacturing assets, 40 percent were held by only 318 firms. As late as 1955, of the 100 largest corporations in the nation, 20 had emerged during that era. Clearly, the giant corporation became the central economic institution in American capitalism. The rise of these firms had both immediate and long-range effects on the economy and the society, and initially it produced a negative response from the public and from the federal government.[1]

The public reaction to massive concentrations of economic power produced demands for "antitrust" enforcement and for new legislation and agencies to "bust" the growing trusts. The Progressive Era saw Presidents Theodore Roosevelt, William Howard Taft, and Woodrow Wilson respond with vigor to these fears. The termination of competition, first by monopoly and then by oligopoly, challenged the concepts of economic democracy, "free enterprise," and *laissez faire*, the philosophical staples of a growth-oriented society. No longer did firms appear, function, fade, and die with their entrepreneurs. Now huge, professional, bureaucratic managements perpetuated themselves in impregnable positions in the marketplace. To the conspiracy-oriented it appeared that even limits of economies of scale had been surpassed, and that total economic power would soon fall into the hands of a dozen "great bankers." Old views of market behavior evaporated, and demands for social control arose in response to the "corporate revolution."

The rise of the modern corporation and the vast expansion of capital markets allowed for the "corporate revolution" and gave impetus to the merger movement. The growth of the New York Stock Exchange symbolized the infusion of large-scale investments and the issuance of new securities by the industrial giants. Economies of scale also contributed to the trend toward mergers as firms sought financial advantages in the manufacturing process and the greatest distribution system possible for their products. But most firms saw consolidation as a means to end ruinous competition, to bring stability to production and marketing, and to maintain reasonable profit levels. The primary motivation for consolidation was to end price competition. Many factors, however, determined the extent of consolidation, its effectiveness, and long-range success. The number of competing firms, the barriers to entrance in the market, and the degree to which products differed were all significant factors.[2]

Industrial firms had previously expanded by entering into the supply and marketing function or through mergers. The former led to the concept of vertical integration, which sought to raise profit levels by reducing costs and increasing productivity. The latter aimed at horizontal integration by controlling all or most of the firms in a particular market and thereby establishing prices and production levels. The most successful firms soon abandoned the horizontal combination strategy, which allowed for only a broad, administrative effort to regulate the flow of goods. The corporate giants moved rapidly to acquire positions in all phases of production from ownership of sources of raw materials through the entire manufacturing process to the sale of finished products to other firms or directly to consumers in mass markets. Many of the horizontal combinations, or trusts, converted into legal structures and moved forward to form vertically integrated firms, often through mergers with other companies in the same industry. Many became dependent on manufacturing and marketing technologically complex products, often spending large sums on research and development. Thus, the trusts or monopolies were often metamorphosed as holding companies under the New Jersey general incorporation law passed in 1889. The holding companies owned the securities of the firms actually engaged in providing goods and services and coordinated their activities. Once the legal structure was altered, the holding companies moved quickly to centralize their administrative structures and integrate their operations.[3] The "corporate revolution" was underway.

The merger era sprang from the successes of some of the earlier trusts, with Standard Oil often the model. The passage of the Sherman Anti-Trust Act in 1890 called the trusts into legal question, leading to the seeking of a more acceptable corporate structure. The financial failure of the National Cordage Company and several other horizontal combinations also raised serious questions about trusts. The depression of 1893 demonstrated the advantages of vertical industrial consolidation, as did the Supreme Court's acceptance of such combinations in the E. C. Knight sugar case two years later. The return of prosperity, the rising market for securities, and federal court approval of large-scale combinations enhanced the changes taking place in industrial organization.

FROM MONOPOLY TO OLIGOPOLY

Initially the "corporate revolution" created firms with almost monopolistic powers in many markets. The response by the Progressives, as seen in Roosevelt's "trust busting," led to Supreme Court rulings against Standard Oil, American Tobacco, and others, and to the Clayton Anti-Trust Act and the establishing of the Federal Trade Commission (FTC). As the court dissolved the monopolies or near monopolies, the result was the creation of oligopolies in many industries. The oligopolies consisted of a few firms of enormous size controlling a large part of a particular market. Court orders, new technologies, and rising firms in other geographical areas produced a few rival companies that came to share market dominance of particular products. Even the Wilson administration's ardor for trust busting waned as the giant firms cooperated in the war effort after 1917. Noting a changing public attitude toward the corporations, particularly the oligopolies, the Supreme Court refused to dissolve United States Steel Corporation in March 1920. Judge Elbert Gary, president of U.S. Steel, had allowed its market share to fall from 80 percent when the firm was created to less than 50 percent at the time the decision was rendered. The court decided that mere size did not violate the Sherman and Clayton Anti-Trust Acts. Thereafter, the growth of the oligopolies accelerated, and their boards of directors came to dominate the firms and the marketplace. Separation of ownership from management had produced yet another phase in corporate reorganization.[4]

The dilemma the federal government faced in antitrust actions can be seen in the International Harvester (I-H) case. Organized in 1902 with capitalization of $120 million, International Harvester was one of the many consolidations put together by J. P. Morgan & Company. It merged five formerly competitive manufacturers of farm implements, which together sold 80 percent of the production in the United States. Central to the combination were the McCormick and Deering companies whose intense competition had driven prices of implements lower and lower. The merger eliminated that "unreasonable" competition. After the firm acquired a sixth manufacturer to increase its output to 85 percent of the market, it began forcing dealers to sign exclusive contracts to sell I-H products. President Taft ordered an antitrust suit brought against I-H, and in 1914 a lower federal court ordered the firm dissolved, though no unfair practices had been discovered. An appeal reached the Supreme Court just as the United States entered World War I, and the Wilson administration accepted a consent decree that forced I-H to sell three of its divisions. Ironically, I-H had never fully integrated its operations and still had various product lines sold by the same dealers. The firm admitted violations of the Sherman act, but the proposal for the drastic break-up of I-H was never carried out, largely because of the need to meet wartime production demands. International Harvester would proceed to integrate and reorganize in the 1920s in order to cope with the agricultural depression that followed the armistice. The changes made in structure and orientation in this firm reflected similar alterations among other giants.[5]

The industrial corporations included in the 100 largest firms in the United States changed markedly after the turn of the century. Only by the greatest effort and concern for competitive advantage did companies in that select list maintain their position. Between 1909 and 1948, for example, 205 firms moved in or out of the 100 largest industrials. Size alone did not enable firms to stay among the giants. Without constant attention to product and market development, economies of scale in manufacturing, and efficient allocation of capital, a firm could not remain on the list. For almost forty years the relative size distribution of the nation's largest firms remained nearly constant, while the composition of the group was in a perpetual state of flux. Changes in size resulted from differential rates of growth, mergers, and dismemberments. The rate of such changes declined after 1935, however, and entrance into the list became more difficult. There was a significant decline in "equality of opportunity" among the larger industrials, at least until the 1960s.[6]

The era of merger for monopolistic goals largely ended with the Northern Securities case in 1904, when the Supreme Court ordered that firm dissolved. Subsequently the industrial giants moved very slowly and with caution when seeking additional acquisitions. For example, when U.S. Steel wished to acquire the Tennessee Coal and Iron Company in 1907, it first sought the permission of President Theodore Roosevelt. The creation of new firms with capitalization of over $1 million through merger declined most abruptly. The enforcement of the Sherman Anti-Trust Act by Presidents Roosevelt, Taft, and Wilson ended the movement for monopolistic mergers; it did not end efforts to use mergers for oligopolistic motives.

After the Progressive Era, mergers created oligopolies in petroleum, automobiles, steel, cement, glass, and many basic industries. In the foods industry, for example, hundreds of small producers were swallowed up by Borden, General Foods, General Mills, National Dairy, and the large bakery chains. Yet it is not clear how much of a share of an industrial market a firm or group of firms must have to be a monopoly. Judge Learned Hand wrote that "it is doubtful whether sixty or sixty-four percent would be enough [to constitute monopoly]; and certainly thirty-three percent is not."[7] Therefore, the chief task of antimonopolistic legal action on the part of the government was to prevent oligopoly by mergers deemed harmful to the marketplace. In addition, the Anti-Trust Division of the Attorney General's Office had to be concerned with efforts of existing firms to close entry to new companies in their field. Since 1945, however, technological change has allowed new firms with new products to enter the 100 largest industrials, while some of the corporations previously included remained strong, viable economic units, but not of the highest rank. Innovation did not reduce oligopoly, but it did alter the composition of the nation's largest firms.

GENERAL FOODS CORPORATION

When C.W. Post invented Postum Cereal beverage in 1894, this hot breakfast coffee substitute laid the basis for one of the world's largest food conglomerates. By 1980 General Foods Corporation, which Postum Cereal Company became in 1929, employed almost 50,000 people worldwide in manufacturing and distributing food products. It was the largest producer of bubble gum, operated the Burger Chef fast-food restaurants, and owned W. Atlee Burpee garden products. Its Maxwell House coffee was sold in Europe as were its instant beverages and pudding products. C.W. Post pioneered in the advertising of consumer products, and the firm made its goods household words for decades: Jell-O, Sanka, Birds Eye, Swans Down, Minute Rice, Calumet, Log Cabin, Kool-Aid, and Post Toasties. By acquisition, merger, and technological advance, C.W. Post's firm became a food-centered conglomerate.

Following the introduction of the beverage Postum, its inventor found that his product sold primarily in the winter months, so he created Grape-Nuts cereal, a light, cold product, to be marketed primarily in the summer, thus balancing production. Post spent $400,000 for advertising in 1899, a time when few firms committed more than $150,000 to advertising budgets, and he wrote the copy himself. He expanded sales to Great Britain and continually introduced new products. When he died in 1914, he owned a $50 million firm.

Throughout the 1920s Postum Cereal Company acquired additional lines by purchasing Jell-O and chocolate, coconut, and baking-powder producers. Ironically, one acquisition included Maxwell House coffee, the very beverage "Postum" was designed to replace. The diverse nature of its acquisitions led to a new name: General Foods. General Foods pioneered in the frozen-food industry by acquiring Birds Eye in 1929. Clarence Birdseye's quick-frozen methods were not well received by the public, however, and not until 1941 did the line show a profit. Other products based on dehydrogenation won consumer confidence, especially beverages. General Foods' advertising emphasized that the astronauts took its orange-flavored drink to the moon.

In the post-1945 period General Foods expanded its line of pet foods, adapted the freeze-dried process to coffee, and improved an emulsification technique to create a nondairy whipped topping. High-volume sales came through massive advertising campaigns in several media. In the extremely competitive food industry, General Foods achieved sales of over $5.4 billion and net earnings of $232 million in 1979. By 1981 General Foods had 32 percent of the nation's coffee market, including 46 percent of the instant coffee segment. As the nation's consumption of coffee declined abruptly—per capita consumption fell by one-third after 1957—General Foods turned to other food groups and acquired Oscar Mayer & Company, the Wisconsin meat processor. In response to dietary trends, General Foods acquired

C. W. Post (1854–1914). Breakfast-food manufacturer and advertising specialist. (Courtesy: General Foods Corporation.)

Orowheat, Ronzoni, and the Entenmann bakery chain in the mid-1980s. By the end of the decade the firm was one of the largest food processors in the world, with more than sixty major brands. Its size and prosperity attracted the attention of the Philip Morris Companies, and in 1985 General Foods was acquired for $5.6 billion dollars. Just as General Foods diversified to counter changes in consumer purchasing, Philip Morris diversified in response to the declining market for tobacco products.

It is often assumed by critics that mergers always reduce competition and lead to higher prices for consumers. After 1945 that was not always the case. In the steel industry, for example, the pre–World War II giants of U.S. Steel, Bethlehem, Republic, and Jones & Laughlin did not acquire any additional size or capacity after the war ended. But some of the regional steel manufacturers and specialty firms made substantial gains through mergers. Inland Steel seized a large share of the market in the Midwest, and Colorado Fuel & Iron, after acquiring Wickwire Spencer Steel, became a major factor in the Rockies and the West. These mergers made the industry more competitive, not less so.[8]

CORPORATE MANAGEMENT AND CONTROL

One of the key issues in business history is who controls the corporate giants. The progressive reformers often charged that the well-established urban banking houses in New York City, Boston, Philadelphia, Pittsburgh, Chicago, and Cleveland dominated the major firms. Their power came from access to capital that the expanding businesses required. The restrictions placed in the Clayton Anti-Trust Act on acquisition of stock to reduce competition and on interlocking directorates among large banks and trust companies sought to diminish banker control of giant corporations. The clamor reached such a peak in 1914 that J. P. Morgan, Jr., who had succeeded his father as head of the firm, announced that he and his partners would resign from the boards of twenty-seven corporations. However, they retained thirty-three directorships in the corporations they controlled or could influence. The investment banking houses made substantial profits from underwriting the mergers of industrial corporations, and they often retained securities acquired during the underwriting and sale of stock. The power that bankers exerted waned somewhat in the 1930s and 1940s, only to reappear in the last three decades.

Control in the larger corporation is on two levels, broad policy decisions and day-to-day management. The board of directors establishes the policies that guide the firms, and thus the bankers on the board can have a major impact. Because trust departments of banks manage billions of dollars of securities for personal trust funds and corporate pension funds, they exert great influence on businesses. Similarly, when corporations borrow huge sums in the form of bond issues, the bankers are able to place restrictions on the policies of the firms to ensure that the borrower repays the loan. Or, some bankers provide loans in exchange for blocs of securities. This was the technique used by the Mellon National Bank of Pittsburgh to gain control of Gulf Oil Company and the Aluminum Company of America (Alcoa). While the growth in the sources of capital in the 1920s diminished the power of bankers, and the Great Depression drastically reduced the holdings in industrial firms by banks, it continued as a major aspect of the corporate scene.

The Banking Act of 1933 (The Glass-Steagall Act) and the Securities Act of 1933 separated commercial and investment banking and restricted public offerings of securities, further reducing the power of the banking houses over nonfinancial corporations. The resurgence of the American economy after World War II again created an opportunity for the banking houses to engage in greater involvement in business. Much of the external finance necessary for economic expansion came from the bankers. In the period 1966–1974, commercial bank loans provided 22 percent of the funds used by nonfinancial corporations. In the latter year bank trust departments held $171 billion in corporate stock, or 26.9 percent of all such securities outstanding. The ten largest banks held 32.2 percent of all trust department assets. Financial institutions became the managers of savings belonging to all income groups. Owner and managerial control over the industrial giants declined as financial control in an institutionalized form accelerated.[9]

The role of bankers became a major factor in the rise of the great conglomerates after 1960. The banks provided short-term loans to firms merging with or taking over another corporation. For example, after 1964 the Chase Manhattan Bank supplied a line of credit to Gulf and Western to enable the latter to make further acquisitions. By 1970 Gulf and Western

Birthplace of the Bank of Italy, October 17, 1904, in San Francisco; now the Bank of America. (Courtesy: The Bank of America.)

was the thirty-third largest firm, in terms of assets, in the United States. The bank received interest on its loans, new depositors, new checking accounts, and information about Gulf and Western's acquisition policies that proved invaluable to the Chase trust department. Thus, the "merger mania" of the 1960s received a sharp nudge from the great banking houses that was not unlike those delivered from 1895 until 1917. And yet it did not appear that the problem of concentration had worsened.

American industry is highly concentrated and the major industries are dominated by the largest businesses. Yet the degree of concentration has not altered substantially in recent years. Concentration occurred in some industries, but not in others, and some vertically integrated companies have developed into multi-industry enterprises. Indeed, only a minority of American manufacturing firms are part of a highly concentrated structure; they include, however, the most crucial industries in our modern, technologically sophisticated economy. By the 1960s these firms had become the leaders in diversification, especially those in food, metals, chemicals, rubber, electrical products, and, more recently, petroleum. Ironically, when these companies entered other concentrated industries, they often increased competition in that market.

DIVERSIFICATION AND DECENTRALIZATION

The leaders in diversification have been companies with the technological, engineering, and research skills to create new products and with the administrative apparatus and experience to produce and market the products. Size and managerial skills enabled these firms to manufacture their basic product and simultaneously enter new markets. When sales and profits in their original product line fell, diversification allowed reallocation of plant and management into more profitable endeavors. In the depression of the 1930s when automobile sales slumped, General Motors entered markets in diesels, appliances, and airplanes. Primary copper producers turned to consumer products such as kitchenware. Rubber companies saw tire sales decline, so they developed new rubber-related chemical products. The diversification movement accelerated with the coming of World War II when defense needs brought new markets to old firms.

Science has been the handmaiden of diversification and the rise of the industrial conglomerate since 1945. Firms in chemistry and those dependent on modern physics have been most prone to diversity. Those firms with the greatest number of personnel in research and development—electrical, chemical, metals, machinery, aircraft, instruments, and electronics—not only produced new products but also developed the administrative structures to manage widely diversified operations. Autonomous operating divisions reported to a general office that planned grand strategy; the general office allocated resources on the basis of performance evaluations—thus, the decentralized structure institutionalized diversification. By 1963 the 200 largest companies accounted for 41 percent of value added by manufacturing. They were largely responsible for developing new products in new markets, especially in the science-based industries. They also generated most of the research and development capital for the nation. As Alfred Chandler has written, "The modern diversified enterprise represents a calculated, rational response of technically trained professional managers to the needs and opportunities of changing technologies and markets."[10]

The individuals who have carried out the diversification of American industry have been the anonymous business bureaucrats with the administrative skills to create the required structures. When large industries failed to invest in research and development, the end result was often a declining market share or perhaps the loss of marketability. For example, steel executives in the 1960s spent only 60 cents of each $100 in sales on development when the average among all manufacturers was $1.90. Because they failed to develop new furnace and casting procedures, the industry fell far behind technologically and lost its markets first to German and Japanese steel mills and then to new plants in Korea, Brazil and even India.

The constantly changing nature of large-scale enterprises from the 1890s to the present can be seen in the tobacco industry. Before the Civil War tobacco was a widely used product in the form of cigars, chewing tobacco, snuff, and pipe tobacco. It was a highly diffuse industry based on small producers of the raw material and thousands of scattered small manufacturers. Competition existed only in local markets. After 1880 the industry became concentrated as new products, technology, mass marketing, and advertising and managerial skills came together to produce one of the nation's greatest monopolies, the American Tobacco Trust. Although the trust existed for only a brief period before the Supreme Court ordered it dissolved, it attained such a dominant position that its break-up produced a highly successful oligopoly. The oligopoly expanded its markets through advertising, and it reached ever higher levels of profitability until the 1960s. At that point fears raised over the health implications of smoking caused the major tobacco firms to diversify, change their names, and emerge as conglomerates. The tobacco industry represents an excellent case study of the major transitions among the corporate giants.

THE AMERICAN TOBACCO COMPANY

Washington Duke and his sons owned and operated a small tobacco farm near Durham, North Carolina. As the Civil War ended, they sold their chewing and pipe tobaccos to the soldiers passing through the area. Their product was of high quality, and soon a large market existed and the Dukes expanded their production. By 1881 young James B. "Buck" Duke, the youngest son, had entered the cigarette business by obtaining use of patented cigarette-rolling machines. His machine-made cigarettes sold for half the price of handmade cigarettes and were far more convenient than "rolling your own." Where four major firms shared the cigarette business in the 1880s, Buck Duke had 38 percent of the market by 1889; and after forming the American Tobacco Company the next year, he soon captured 89 percent of the trade. With $25 million in capital, and emphasis on price cutting and quality control, he purchased or merged with his major competitors. American Tobacco "mechanized, organized, and merchandised" throughout the 1890s to capture over 60 percent of the entire tobacco industry by 1900. Even "independent" companies such as R. J. Reynolds and P. Lorillard were controlled by American.

In 1904 Duke consolidated a vast array of tobacco-related firms into a new American Tobacco Company established in New Jersey with $235 million in capital. Duke controlled 88 percent of cigarette production, 75 percent of the smoking tobacco market, and 90 percent of the snuff business. His one weak area was cigar sales—the major tobacco product at that time—of which he controlled only 14 percent of the market. Of each dollar spent for tobacco, only five cents was for cigarettes and thirty-three cents for chewing tobacco, while consumers purchased sixty cents worth of ci-

James B. Duke (1856–1925). Industrialist, trust builder, and philanthropist. (Courtesy: *Dictionary of American Portraits*.)

gars. Duke then entered the Cuban cigar industry and acquired United Cigar Stores to enhance his total operation. Because licorice constituted one of the major flavorings for tobacco products, Duke gained a monopoly on licorice paste, which proved very harmful to his competitors. He also spent enormous sums to advertise cigarettes, and between 1904 and 1910 the average consumption of cigarettes increased by 138 percent!

The power of American Tobacco and its profits, as well as its questionable marketing methods, led to an antitrust suit, and on November 6, 1911, the Supreme Court ordered the trust dissolved. The government divided the trust into thirteen new companies and made units such as R. J. Reynolds truly independent. Together with Reynolds, the major cigarette producers were American Tobacco with 33 percent of the market, Liggett & Myers with 28 percent, and P. Lorillard with 15 percent. Theoretically, the "Big Four" were now competitive, and consumers would benefit. In actuality an oligopoly had been created, and little price competition resulted. The major cigarette companies concentrated on advertising competition, and they were soon spending millions on radio, magazine, and newspaper advertising. They stressed volume sales and mass marketing, and as it became permissible and fashionable for women to smoke, their potential market doubled in the 1920s. By the end of the following decade, the firms of American, Reynolds, and Liggett and Myers each had about 20 percent of the cigarette market, with Lorillard and newcomer Phillip Morris each holding about 6 or 7 percent of national sales. Public taste had changed mainly as a result of the intensive advertising campaigns so that other tobacco products had greatly diminished in importance. Despite the Great Depression and World War II, sales held up strongly and the industry continued to be highly profitable.

Cigarette consumption grew after 1945, but the industry fell on hard times in the 1960s. Research relating cigarette smoking to cancer and warnings by the surgeon general led to banning cigarette advertising from television and radio as well as a requirement that a warning be placed on packages and allowed advertising. The major tobacco firms moved quickly to protect their positions. Management began substantial efforts at diversification. American Tobacco in 1969 became American Brands to recognize its acquisition of Sunshine Biscuits, James Beam, Andrew Jurgens, Master Lock, and Franklin Life Insurance. The next year Reynolds Industries, with sales of $2 billion yearly, replaced R. J. Reynolds to encompass Sea Land container ships, American Independent Oil, Burmah Oil in the United States, Patio Foods, Chun King, Morton Foods, and Del Monte. P. Lorillard became part of the Loews conglomerate of theaters, hotels, and insurance firms, while the Liggett Group included Liggett and Myers, Izmira Vodka, Alpo dog food, and Pepsi Cola franchises. Phillip Morris, which had led the way in diversification as early as 1957, now included major paper and packaging processors, real estate, Miller Brewing, and Seven Up. Interestingly, nearly all the firms simultaneously expanded tobacco operations overseas; they used the same marketing techniques, especially in the Third World, that they had used for four decades previously in the United States. The conglomerates emphasized research and development, mass marketing, and efficient management of their properties. These new conglomerates were part of a much broader movement across American industry.

THE CONGLOMERATES

The most significant changes among the major firms of the nation after 1960 came with the rise of the conglomerates. These merger-oriented giants acquired firms that had no direct relation to any other division of the parent. The conglomerates faced little or no opposition from the Federal Trade Commission or the Anti-Trust Division of the Attorney General's Office, at least initially, as they seemed to have little effect on competition. Many of the conglomerates had large military procurement divisions, with "seasonal" operations that needed to be balanced in "peace time." Also, the executives in the burgeoning conglomerates believed that moribund corporations could be "turned around" by strong, efficient leadership and made far more profitable. Some firms, such as American Home Products, were essentially conglomerates in the 1940s, but most would emerge two decades later. Their leaders shared the view of Tex Thornton, head of Litton Industries, who when asked what business he was in responded, "We are in the business of opportunity."

Litton Industries began as a small electronics firm, Electro-Dynamics Corporation. When it acquired a small company of a similar type in 1954, it assumed the name Litton. Three more firms were acquired the next year, and in 1958 the much larger Monroe Calculator became a division. That year Litton did $83 million in business; in 1966 Litton grossed $1 billion. The great source of strength for Litton was a spectacularly successful management team led by Thornton and a major line of credit from Lehman

Brothers. Acquisitions through stock transfers preserved capital, and because Litton stock sold for thirty or forty times its book value such exchanges were very advantageous to Litton. New divisions came into Litton at a rate of one every three or four months, with areas of concentration in office machines and equipment and military procurement. The Litton management reflected the backgrounds of its team of business school graduates and scientists who believed in efficiency, lean organizations, and dependence on new technologies.[11]

The conglomerates often built on old firms, such as Textron, a major textile producer, but they would then grow far beyond that base. While some conglomerates acquired other firms to solve specific problems, such as fluctuation in demand, others sought diversification to reduce dependence on declining markets. For example, as Textron grew, it liquidated its textile holdings, retaining only its name as a reminder of its origins. Unlike Litton, the Textron acquisitions had no general relationship. Royal Little, Textron's chief executive, sought only stagnant businesses that could be made profitable with new management.

Other old businesses became conglomerates and then abandoned their original markets. Studebaker left automobiles and merged with Worthington Corporation. W. R. Grace entered the chemical business and sold its airline operations. Philadelphia & Reading abandoned and Glenn Alden moved away from anthracite coal to become producers of clothing, toys, and leather goods, and owners of motion-picture theaters. Stock transfers produced giants such as Tenneco, Transamerica Corporation, and Ling-Temco-Vought out of a wide range of smaller, dissimilar corporations. The conglomerate movement peaked in the late 1960s only to revive again in the early 1980s as the national economy went through a series of massive changes.

JAMES LING AND L-T-V

A high school dropout who started a small electrical contracting business in Dallas, Texas, in 1946, James Ling built a conglomerate which by 1968 was the nation's fourteenth-largest industrial corporation with sales of $2.8 billion. Ling developed his electric company in the expanding Dallas market and by 1955, with sales reaching $1.5 million yearly, sold securities to the public. Seeing the potential for growth in electronics, Ling purchased a firm in that field and discovered that the rising price of stock in his company paid the indebtedness created by the acquisition. He then formed Ling Industries and by issuing stocks and bonds acquired more small electronics firms. With sales passing $48 million in 1959, he raised his sights, borrowed large sums from a local insurance company, and purchased aircraft builder Chance Vought. A new firm, Ling-Temco-Vought (L-T-V), resulted from the merger, and Ling proceeded to sell for cash various components of L-T-V. The parts proved more valuable than the whole, giving Ling cash to make more acquisitions. Total sales of L-T-V enterprises reached $325 million by 1962.

Ling drove the executives in L-T-V and its subsidiaries to produce the highest profit levels. Following the acquisition of Chance Vought he reduced its management from 700 people to 166. "Don't tell me how hard you work,"

Ling told his managers, "tell me how much you get done." A strong national economy and fortuitous mergers made L-T-V one of the major "growth" firms in the "go-go Sixties." In 1965, for example, L-T-V acquired Okonite from Kennecott Copper just as the $20 million Kennecott had invested in Okonite began to pay off.

In 1964 Ling "redeployed" L-T-V into three operating divisions. With L-T-V retaining 75 to 90 percent ownership, Ling then sold securities in the operating divisions. As these securities increased in value, L-T-V made substantial profits that provided capital for further acquisitions. In 1967 L-T-V purchased Wilson and Company, a meat-packing firm with sports equipment and chemical divisions. Ling then divded Wilson into three operating firms, "meatball, softball, and goofball" Wall Street analysts called them, and exchanged them for L-T-V stock, thus getting back the original purchase price for Wilson and Company!

A huge acquisition soon followed, Greatamerica Corporation, which controlled banking and insurance firms, Braniff Airways, National Car Rental, and other companies. Ling then began to sell parts of Greatamerica, which soon returned much of the original purchase proce of $500 million. When Ling then bought a substantial share of Jones and Laughlin Steel Company, the attorney general filed an antitrust suit to block total acquisition. This delayed additional security issues, forcing Ling to turn to the money market for cash. High interest rates made L-T-V debts difficult to service, and in 1970 Ling was ousted as head of the company. The new management renewed the acquisition program with additional purchases in aerospace, petroleum, and steel. In 1978 they acquired Lykes Corporation and with it Youngstown Sheet and Tube Company. In 1981 they merged Jones and Laughlin with Republic Steel and in the process took on huge debt burdens. Acquisitions in steel and petroleum, two "sick industries," brought L-T-V to Chapter 11 bankruptcy in 1986.

The conglomerate Ling built was not modeled after the trusts of the late nineteenth century. He did not create a monopoly in any area of the economy. Rather L-T-V, like most conglomerates, became a multimarket firm with subsidiaries in a wide variety of fields. The concentration of economic power resided not in controlling a single market, but in amassing vast capital to manipulate many firms in as many markets. A rising national economy had made the conglomerate movement temporarily successful.

THE GIANTS IN FLUX

Among the many misconceptions held by the public are the beliefs that all large firms grow continuously, are nearly always highly profitable, and that management, technology, and markets play small roles in the viability of the industrial giants. A comparison of the *Fortune* list of 500 major industries in 1955 with the list published in 1980 serves to undermine such hypotheses. Of the 500 firms in 1955, only 262 were still on the 1980 list; 185 had been absorbed by mergers, 29 had become too small to make the list, 14 were no longer industrial, 6 were privately held, 4 had gone out of business. Or, to look at the 1980 list in terms of where those companies were in 1955, the same 262 were in the 500, but 147 had been too small to be included twenty-five years earlier, 35 had been privately held, 26 were not industrial, and 30 had not been in existence. In the period from 1955 to 1980, some 932 companies had been on the lists at various times. To be in the *Fortune* 500 in 1955, a firm needed only $49.7 million in sales; to be included in 1980, sales of $410 million were required. Obviously, in the era of the giants there had been significant changes.[12]

Further analysis of the 500 shows that only 5 of the top 10 remained in that select group from 1955 to 1980—General Motors, Exxon, Gulf Oil, General Electric, and Mobil Corporation. Three of the top 10 in 1955 had fallen into the top 20—U.S. Steel, Chrysler, and DuPont—and Swift (as Esmark) resided in forty-second place and Armour had been absorbed by Greyhound. The 30 companies that had not existed in 1955, but that had joined the list in 1980, included many computer and electronics firms—Control Data, Digital Equipment, Memorex, National Semiconductor—and some entertainment giants—Warner Communications and Music Corporation of America (MCA). While old-line meatpackers such as Armour and Swift had declined in status, Iowa Beef Processors and Idle Wild Foods had joined the list with sales generated by new, modern plants and vast distribution systems. A comparison of the two lists showed great slippage in the textile and rubber industries, but enormous growth in high-technology areas represented by International Business Machines, Xerox, Polaroid, Hewlett-Packard, and Texas Instruments. Cosmetic and pharmaceutical houses such as Avon, Revlon, and Warner-Lambert also had vastly expanded. In most cases, the new giants were firms that had invested heavily in research and development to produce new technologies and products.

The *Fortune* 500 lists demonstrated not only a high rate of turnover among its membership but also the rapid alteration of business structures created by mergers. The 500 in 1980 had absorbed almost 4,500 other firms in the previous twenty-five years. Ling-Temco-Vought alone had acquired 5 of the original 500 to rank thirty-first in 1980. Change, growth, and mergers, abetted by science and technology, altered the landscape of American business.

The compilation of data by *Fortune* also revealed that the public's conception of business profits was also quite unrealistic. The average profit of the 500 in 1979 was 5.4 percent; the petroleum companies, which had gained newspaper headlines and extensive media coverage because of their "excess" profits, earned a return of 6.6 percent. The latter represented a decline from 9.2 percent in 1954. The giants remained generally profitable, but not to the extent many believed.

The mergers of the late 1970s and early 1980s differed from those of the conglomerate-oriented 1960s. The peak year of mergers, 1969, saw 6,107 corporate "weddings" as some companies seemed willing to buy anything. The more recent era has seen a slower rate and greater concern for acquiring firms with similar products or services. While some firms such as International Telephone and Telegraph could sell consumers Wonder Bread, rent a room in Sheraton Hotels, or insure families with the Hartford Insurance Group, other conglomerates attempted to put together more compatible businesses. Food processors Dart and Kraft merged, General Foods acquired Burger Chef, and toy maker Mattel purchased the Ringling Brothers, Barnum & Bailey Circus. By the end of the 1980s many of the conglomerates found themselves overextended: They had acquired indiscriminately and without purpose. Their companies were not compatible, and thus they engaged in wholesale restructuring. RCA acquired, then sold, Random House, Hertz car rental, and Banquet Foods; General Foods sold Burger Chef; and Mobil Corporation rid itself of Montgomery Ward. Yet the era of megamergers continued with RCA swallowed up by General Electric and Revlon becoming part of Pantry Pride. Many of the takeovers were funded by the sale of "junk bonds" with high interest rates. Corporate raiders often gambled that they could sell portions of the firms and use the proceeds to retire the debts. Bankers, brokerage houses, speculators, and major financiers helped to arrange "leveraged buyouts." As a result corporate debt in America rose to over $1.4 *trillion* by 1985. No wonder individual investors retreated from the security markets to the safety of federal bonds or insured accounts at banks.

NOTES

1. Alfred S. Eichner, *The Emergence of Oligopoly: Sugar Refining as a Case Study* (Baltimore: Johns Hopkins University Press, 1969), pp. 1–5. This is an excellent introduction to the larger issues of trusts, monopolies, and oligopolies.

2. Alfred D. Chandler, Jr., *The Visible Hand: The Managerial Revolution in American Business* (Cambridge: Harvard University Press, 1977), pp. 331–333.

3. Ibid., pp. 315–320.

4. Eichner, *The Emergence of Oligopoly,* pp. 7–25.

5. Ibid., pp. 317–319.

6. Norman R. Collins and Lee E. Preston, "The Size Structure of the Largest Industrial Firms, 1909–1958," *The American Economic Review* 51 (December 1961), pp. 986–1011.

7. George J. Stigler, "Monopoly and Oligopoly by Merger," *The American Economic Review* 40 (May 1950), p. 32.

8. Robert Sobel, *The Age of Giant Corporations* (Westport, Connecticut: Greenwood Press, 1972), p. 191.

9. David M. Kotz, *Bank Control of Large Corporations in the United States* (Berkeley: University of California Press, 1978), pp. 63, 68–69.

10. Alfred D. Chandler, Jr., "The Structure of American Industry in the Twentieth Century: A Historical Overview," *Business History Review* 43 (Autumn 1969), p. 279.

11. Sobel, *Age of Giant Corporations,* pp. 195–197.

12. Linda Snyder Hayes, "Twenty-Five Years of Change in the Fortune 500," *Fortune* (May 5, 1980), pp. 88–96.

SUGGESTED READINGS

ALASCO, JOHANNES. *Intellectual Capitalism: A Study of Changing Ownership and Control in Modern American Society.* New York: World University Press, 1950.

BERLE, ADOLF A., AND GARDINER C. MEANS. *The Modern Corporation and Private Property.* New York: Macmillan, 1932.

CHANDLER, ALFRED D., JR. *The Visible Hand: The Managerial Revolution in American Business.* Cambridge: Harvard University Press, 1977.

———. "The Structure of American Industry in the Twentieth Century: A Historical Overview." *Business History Review* 43 (Autumn 1969): 255–298.

———. "The Emergence of Managerial Capitalism." *Business History Review* 58 (Winter 1984): 473–503.

COLLINS, NORMAN R., AND LEE E. PRESTON. "The Size Structure of the Largest Industrial Firms, 1909–1958." *The American Economic Review 51* (December 1961): 986–1011.

DIDRICHSEN, JON. "The Development of Diversified and Conglomerate Firms in the United States, 1920–1970." *Business History Review* 46 (Summer 1972): 202–219.

EICHNER, ALFRED S. *The Emergence of Oligopoly: Sugar Refining as a Case Study.* Baltimore: Johns Hopkins University Press, 1969.

GALBRAITH, JOHN KENNETH. *American Capitalism: The Concept of Countervailing Power.* Sentry Edition. Boston: Houghton Mifflin, 1962.

KOTZ, DAVID M. *Bank Control of Large Corporations in the United States.* Berkeley: University of California Press, 1978.

LAMOREAUX, NAOMI R. *The Great Merger Movement in American Business, 1895–1904.* New York: Cambridge University Press, 1985.

NELSON, RALPH L. *Merger Movements in American Industry, 1895–1956.* Princeton, New Jersey: Princeton University Press, 1959.

NUTTER, G. WARREN, AND HENRY ADLER EINHORN. *Enterprise Monopoly in the United States: 1899–1958.* New York: Columbia University Press, 1969.

SKLAR, MARTIN J. *The Corporate Reconstruction of American Capitalism, 1890–1916.* Cambridge, England: Cambridge University Press, 1988.

SOBEL, ROBERT. *The Age of Giant Corporations.* Westport, Connecticut: Greenwood Press, 1972.

STIGLER, GEORGE. "Monopoly and Oligopoly by Merger." *The American Economic Review* 40 (May 1950):23–34.

TIFFANY, PAUL A. *The Decline of American Steel: How Management, Labor and Government Went Wrong.* New York: Oxford University Press, 1988.

11 Advertising and the Mass Media

Advertising and the mass media are innovations of the modern business world and together they have shaped popular standards. They are essential ingredients of the marketing structures that oversee the transfer of goods and services from producers to consumers. The technology of the high-speed printing press, radio, film, and cathode tube revolutionized an industry that only began to develop in the mid to late nineteenth century. Alfred D. Chandler attributes the emergence of the modern, mass-consumer market to the railroad and telegraph, which greatly enlarged the geographical limits of the marketplace. Standardization of products and packaging were concomitants of the expanded market, and rapid urbanization permitted specialization by merchants.[1] Facilitated by the telegraph, telephone, and typewriter, mass marketing reached a plateau at the turn of the century, became reinvigorated by the radio and the automobile between World Wars I and II, and then lurched forward with the advent of television and computers in the last two decades. Advertising reoriented national magazines, transformed the modern newspaper, and created the radio and television broadcasting systems.

According to David Potter, advertising compares with institutional religion and the school system in the magnitude of its social influence.[2] It developed from a modest $10 million business in 1865 to a hefty $95 million industry by 1900. In the 1890s advertisements by local retailers and

A 1935 Pierce Arrow ad stresses the "finer things of life." (*The New Yorker,* April 13, 1935, p. 13.)

wholesalers declined as major national campaigns were launched by manufacturers. The sales "pitch" in this era also changed from a simple factual statement of goods or services available at a stated price to the inspirational motif that usually promised, either specifically or by lyrical appeals, a better or a more romantic life for the purchaser of the goods or services advertised. Manufacturers no longer sought to sell a supply of goods, but rather to create a demand for their products.

In more mundane terms, advertising ceased being "news" and became salesmanship in print. Advertising had become, according to one of its earliest prophets, Phineas T. Barnum, "The Science of Money-Making and the Philosophy of Humbug." Certainly that is what Barnum made it out to be. Barnum scored his first advertising triumph by exhibiting Joice Heth, alleged to be George Washington's 161-year-old nurse, in New York City in

August 1835. He printed her life story in a pamphlet and plastered the streets with handbills and posters. When the 80-year-old woman died during the showing, Barnum publicized her as a hoax and himself as having been duped by hucksters. He then discovered "General Tom Thumb," and, following a successful European tour, brought the Swedish singer Jenny Lind to America and had another triumph through a vast advertising campaign. Patent medicine hucksters, merchants, the general public, and finally newspapers and magazines got the point: It paid to advertise.[3]

By the close of the Civil War even the staid and genteel *Harper's New Monthly Magazine* could advise thus:

I. To Merchants:
    (1) Advertise.
    (2) Advertise liberally.
    (3) Advertise conspicuously.
II. To the People at Large:
    (1) Read the Advertisements.
    (2) Study them, and verily they shall be for your profit.[4]

An example of early newspaper and journal "block" ads, 1866. (*Harper's Weekly*, February 3, 1866, p. 78.)

The high-speed press and automatic typesetters helped revolutionize publishing, and thereby advertising and marketing, but equally important were changing social norms. Although by the 1870s most newspapers, albeit reluctantly, had accepted a larger and bolder advertising format with a modern look—changing from the one-inch column blocks and small agate print to a sometimes full-page, illustrated, bold-type composition—magazines generally remained conservative. American literary magazines, such as *The Southern Literary Messenger* and *The North American Review*, followed the traditions of the English literary quarterlies and often declined any form of advertising. Circulation increases generated by Civil War reports, as well as modern photography and etching procedures, enabled "new" magazines such as *Harper's* and *Atlantic Monthly* to accept and then flourish because of commercial advertising. By 1868 both *Harper's* and *Atlantic Monthly* were filled with patent medicine, hair dressing, and cosmetic advertisments. More specialized business journals and weeklies provided advertisements for and information to particular industries. Journals devoted to the railroads, merchants, bankers, and manufacturers also proliferated in the 1870s and 1880s.[5]

The postal act of March 3, 1879, gave second-class franking privileges to magazines, and the growth of the railroad network made possible their rapid national distribution. A host of new journals appealing to popular taste and competing for the merchant's business appeared in the decades of the 1870s and 1880s. These journals included *McCall's* (1870), *Popular Science* (1872), *Woman's Home Companion* (1873), *Leslie's Monthly* (1876), *Good Housekeeping* (1885), *Cosmopolitan* (1886), *Collier's* (1888), and *National Geographic* (1888). By 1900 the *Ladies Home Journal*, founded by Cyrus H. K. Curtis in 1883, passed one million in circulation.[6]

The introduction of new magazines, a substantial growth in mass circulation, and rising advertising revenues led to the founding of *Printers' Ink: A Journal for Advertisers*. On July 15, 1888, George P. Rowell, "acknowledged in a later day as the main figure in advertising in the nineteenth century," mailed 5,200 copies of the new magazine to firms with large advertising needs.[7] There is no better historical and technical source on the development of modern advertising than the pages of *Printers' Ink*, which clearly demonstrate how "machine distribution came to replace the old hand methods of selling."[8] It is the story of how time, distance, and costs, standing between the factory and the marketplace, were reduced, and, so the editors claimed, it is also the story of the advertiser as "an integral and important part of the advance of civilization in the nation."[9]

From the days of Phineas T. Barnum until the twentieth century, advertising gave old products new forms, shapes, and significance. Goods lost their generic quality and became brand names. Beans became Anne Page, Campbell's, or Hormel. Chewing tobacco, under the aegis of James B. Duke, became "Battle Ax" and "Horseshoe." Duke conducted "plug wars" with his "fighting brands," which he often distributed as free samples to prospective customers. He gave away so many samples over so long a period that many competitors were forced out of business. Brands made it possible to sell on the basis of quality, style, taste, status, or sex appeal, and by 1926 over 25,000 trademarks and brand names had been registered. Brand advertising sought to create an emotional involvement between the customer and the product, be it automobiles, beer, cigarettes, or soap. Efforts to persuade potential buyers to select a particular brand enhanced the art of advertising.[10]

Advertising became increasingly important after the 1890s as manufacturers reduced price competition and stressed product differentiation. As manufacturing capacity came to exceed demand, firms used advertising to create additional markets. Profit levels provided for ever-expanding advertising budgets and for the hiring of experts in advertising techniques as well as in sales. There was little need for advertising in an economy of scarcity where manufacturers could sell all that they produced. In an economy of excess, advertising became the means to dispose of an oversupply.[11] The effect, in the long run, was the development of a consumer society with advertising as one of its major institutions. The advertising industry would come to exert great influence, with few responsibilities, while it stimulated materialism and sanctioned the drives and anxieties it created as national social values.

As the volume of advertising increased, agencies that specialized in placing ads and developing national campaigns became more important

By 1915, modern full-page illustrated ads were prominent in many, but not all, magazines. (*Printer's Ink*, October 28, 1915.)

aspects of the field. A few advertising agencies appeared in the 1850s, but the founding of N.W. Ayer & Son in 1869 saw the emergence of this new business on a large scale. N.W. Ayer took advertisements for newspapers in the Philadelphia area for several years, but in the late 1870s, his son, Francis W. Ayer, began to charge clients to place advertisements rather than being paid by newspapers for selling space. He charged advertisers a fee of 10 to 15 percent for buying space and placing ads. His innovations created a major advertising agency whose clients included Montgomery Ward, Proctor and Gamble, Burpee Seeds, and other large firms. The concept of a national ad campaign with a single agency in charge became the norm of the industry.[12]

The agencies became increasingly sophisticated in their techniques after the turn of the century. They hired psychologists and other social scientists, as well as artists and lithographers, to create advertisements that persuaded or cajoled consumers to purchase their client's products. By 1910 advertising costs reached 4 percent of the national income. The propaganda efforts of World War I provided additional insights into the mass marketing of goods and ideas. Simultaneously the advertising agencies, newspapers, and magazines began to establish "codes" and "rules" within their industry. Independent trade associations, such as the Audit Bureau of Circulation established in 1913, reported certified circulation figures of newspapers and journals to stabilize rates and space charges. The advertising agencies also found an expanding market in the early 1920s as industrial firms began to sell themselves as well as their products.

BATTEN, BARTON, DURSTINE AND OSBORN

In the 1950s the initials BBD&O came to symbolize the pinnacle of success among Madison Avenue advertising agencies. As early as the 1920s Bruce Barton, a partner of one of the firms that was to become part of BBD&O, achieved notoriety when he depicted Jesus Christ as a great businessman and the first advertiser in a book called *The Man Nobody Knows*. A best seller in 1925–1926, the book contended that Christ had been the founder of modern business. Despite his questionable theology, Barton was a successful advertising executive. After his firm merged with the George Batten Company in 1928 to form BBD&O, it acquired clients such as DuPont and United States Steel. When the investigations of the Nye Committee in 1935 seemed to lay considerable blame for America's entry into World War I on DuPont and the "munitions trust," BBD&O moved quickly to strengthen its client's image. It produced the "Cavalcade of America" radio program in which war was never mentioned. The programs emphasized humanitarianism, achievement, and the progress of women. No shots were heard and no explosions caused tremors on the airwaves. DuPont, as the sponsor, was linked to an entirely different image than that suggested by Senator Gerald P. Nye. It also softened public perceptions with the new slogan "Better things for better living through chemistry."

Advertising campaigns and image building helped to make BBD&O a leader in its field. It entered political campaigns where the same tactics used to sell soap and cigarettes were employed to market politicians. The large industrial-oriented agencies such as BBD&O came to depend heavily on market research based on techniques developed in the social sciences. They utilized consumer panels, questionnaires, psychological studies, and other devices to test advertising programs prior to purchasing magazine space and radio and television time. As the agency became increasingly involved in mass marketing of consumer goods, it created a merchandising department to aid clients opening such campaigns. Indeed, the firm used the same techniques in selling its own services to businesses. BBD&O purchased full-page ads in business papers to describe work being done for its clients. The advertisements briefly and imaginatively outlined several campaigns and used illustrations to display packaging or media programs. Researchers at BBD&O employed computer technology in designing advertising campaigns as early as 1961. Using a model developed by a division of Control Data, the agency could allocate an entire advertising budget in such a way as to deliver the largest possible number of exposures for the dollar.

Innovation, research, and aggressive campaigns made BBD&O the sixth largest advertising agency in the nation by 1986. It had annual billings to clients in excess of $1 billion that year. Its billings were divided among television (44 percent), magazines (24 percent), newspapers (22 percent), and radio (6 percent). Its many large industrial clients included the faithful DuPont, and its operations spanned the globe with offices located in many foreign countries. Advertising agencies followed American investment abroad and applied their marketing techniques for mass merchandising of consumer goods around the world. Indeed, in 1986 BBD&O merged with Doyle Dane Bernbach Group (now Omnicom Group, Inc.) to form a worldwide advertising agency with $5 billion in yearly billings.

PUBLIC RELATIONS

Institutional or image advertising emerged during the progressive era as reformers assaulted big business with charges of excess profits, poor commodities, dangerous workplaces, and unethical practices. A press agent named Ivy L. Lee, working for the Pennsylvania Railroad, developed a campaign to "sell" the company rather than its services. Lee became a "public relations" counselor to other companies and to the Rockefeller family, and soon spawned a new but related field, public relations. Many advertising agencies entered this area and developed simultaneous campaigns to sell products and the firms that made them. Some businesses then created divisions within their managements that were responsible for advertising and public relations and that worked directly with the ad agencies hired by the firm. The allocation of the advertising budget became a major management tool in the 1920s. The rapid growth of institutional advertising and new consumer products in that decade helped to raise annual advertising expenditures from $2.3 billion in 1919 to $3.4 billion ten years later. Even the most conservative companies abandoned the notion that advertising was "hucksterism" and began to employ the agencies of Madison Avenue.[13]

In the 1920s the advertising agencies created a view of American life that included a happy family at home drinking milk from Carnation's "contented cows." Romantic love in ad copy urged women to use Woodbury soap for "a skin you love to touch." Americans were told to expand upon their leisure hours, and that they should "walk a mile for a Camel." Material success had to be demonstrated to the community by ownership of an expensive automobile, and potential Packard buyers were told to "ask the man who owns one." The old mores which said that consumption with abandon was sinful, and that thrift and frugality were true values, were pushed aside deliberately and replaced with values of consuming, acquisition of material goods, and expanded leisure hours. In a society of seeming abundance, advertising became a guide to social success and achievement. The trends of the 1920s would become firmly institutionalized in American society by the 1950s.[14]

THE COMING OF RADIO

The development of the commercial radio networks enhanced the institutionalization of advertising. World War I demonstrated the importance of radio as a means of communication, and several firms transformed radio from an experimental toy into a major source of entertainment and a significant advertising medium. Broadcasts across the Atlantic were made by Guglielmo Marconi as early as 1901, but not until the perfection of the vacuum tube by Lee De Forest in 1906 had broadcasting begun to move beyond the experimental stage. The federal government seized the Marconi Wireless Telegraph Company of America during the war, and the Radio Corporation of America (RCA) was organized to take over its assets when the war ended. General Electric, American Telephone and Telegraph (AT&T), Westinghouse, and RCA established a patent pool and cross-licensing agreements to manufacture radio sets, broadcasting equipment, and parts. In 1920 pioneer station KDKA in Pittsburgh broadcast the presidential election returns and soon began regularly scheduled programming of music, news, and public service notices.[15]

The radio-equipment manufacturers encouraged the development of stations, and the number of licensed stations increased to 30 in 1922 and to 500 by 1924. The price of a crystal radio set fell to $27.50 in 1922, and soon millions of American homes had access to local radio programs. Simultaneously, hesitation ended on the part of station owners and managers to accept advertising, and that became their primary source of revenue. When AT&T decided to rent wire connections from station to station in 1926, it became possible to form radio networks.[16] That year David Sarnoff created the National Broadcasting Company as a subsidiary of RCA, and within three years there were three major networks. Soon advertising agencies began to place radio ads on a nationwide basis, and the volume of such ads grew quickly.

WILLIAM S. PALEY AND THE COLUMBIA BROADCASTING SYSTEM

In 1964 William S. Paley, founder of the Columbia Broadcasting System (CBS), and Frank Stanton, the president of CBS, restructured the network to reflect its broad holdings in the field of entertainment. At that time CBS owned radio and television stations, production facilities, record and book clubs, toy and musical instrument companies, and two publishers, as well as the New York Yankees baseball franchise. The conglomerate grossed over a billion dollars yearly. In thirty-five years Paley had built one of the nation's most successful entertainment giants, and he had become one of the major figures in the industry.

A recent graduate of the University of Pennsylvania, Paley joined his father's cigar company in the early 1920s. A radio advertisement for their La Palina cigars doubled sales, and young Paley saw greater potential for radio than for cigar manufacturing. He invested $450,000 in the Columbia Phonograph Broadcasting System in 1929 and became president of the firm, which he renamed Columbia Broadcasting System. The twenty-eight-year-old Paley expanded the system from sixteen stations to ninety-seven affiliates by 1935. He also purchased stations in key markets, and in 1931 profits reached over $3 million.

Paley built CBS by developing radio stars, or personalities. Following a model not unlike that used by the motion picture producers, he created new talent and hired "names" from the competing National Broadcasting Company or from the vaudeville circuits. Soon Bing Crosby, Jack Benny, and Kate Smith were but three of the household names at CBS. The affiliates guaranteed they would carry Paley's popular programs at prime times, providing him with a national market for advertisers. Thus CBS gained control over time schedules—a brilliant coup in the industry. He brought a young educator named Edward R. Murrow to CBS, and Murrow helped develop a European radio news service that strengthened the network against its competitors in the late 1930s. The news broadcasters were a part of Paley's strategy of providing programs for his radio station affiliates rather than depending on independent producers who sold packaged programs to the networks.

CBS flourished and after 1945 entered television, which produced large profits by the late 1950s. Paley promoted Frank Stanton to president of CBS in 1946, and together they expanded the firm's operations. Holder of a doctorate in sociology, Stanton had been a researcher for CBS and had become the operations chief for the network. Together they introduced live drama to television, expanded the network's news presentations to include a series of programs featuring Edward R. Murrow, and produced documentaries that addressed serious social and economic problems. The network also popularized the "sitcom," or situation comedy program, which helped to make CBS a highly profitable enterprise. Paley and Stanton then converted the company into a conglomerate by acquiring other firms. Broadcasting remained the conglomerate's centerpiece, but only one of four large divsions in an entertainment empire.

The diversification of CBS proved less than a total success. Ideal Toy was bought, then soon sold. Several magazines were clear losses. There was a constant change in leadership in the 1980s as few executives seemed to meet Paley's expectations. When independent media magnate Ted Turner launched an "unfriendly" takeover effort, CBS found a "white knight," Laurence Tisch, who acquired 25 percent of the company and became president with Paley as chairman. Tisch inaugurated a cost-cutting program, laying off 700 people in the broadcasting division alone. Wall Street observers speculated that Tisch would eventually sell off much of the nonbroadcasting assemblage as the parts had greater value than the whole.

As the sale of radio advertising reached more than $10 million in 1928, both advertisers and listeners demanded that the stations do more than simply play phonograph records and present the news and sports events. While the station managers and network executives began to raise the quality of programs, the advertising agencies produced louder and more persistent jingles and singing commercials for the sponsors. Live broadcasts of musical performances, dramas, and comedy programs added millions of radio listeners, who were urged to purchase soaps, cereals, soft drinks, toothpaste, cigarettes, canned foods, and a vast range of other consumer products. Manufacturers of durable goods, such as automobiles and home appliances, also purchased radio time. While the main source of revenue for the stations and the networks was advertising, there was no federal regulation of the content or the frequency of the ads.

The federal government required operators and stations to be licensed as early as 1912 and did respond to requests by the broadcasters for further regulation. The Federal Radio Commission, established in 1927, assigned frequencies, established limits on power output, and tried to equalize geographical access to radio facilities. With the proliferation of stations, networks, and programming, the role of the government expanded with the creation of the Federal Communications Commission (FCC) in 1934, which absorbed the duties of the Federal Radio Commission. Still, the FCC regulated broadcasting largely through controlling entry into the industry and approving transfers of ownership of stations. In the absence of federal restrictions, the networks grew rapidly each year as a higher percentage of homes had radios and as the number of listeners increased.

The depression of the 1930s enhanced the broadcasting systems as declining family incomes made the radio the chief form of inexpensive entertainment. Throughout the decade the networks expanded programs and added not only more musical and comedy shows but also mysteries, adventure stories, children's programs, and, of course, the soap opera. Of the 660 radio stations in the United States in 1941, NBC had 160 affiliates and CBS had 107. The network stations, representing 40 percent of the total number of outlets, had 86 percent of the licensed nighttime power and were located in the key market territories. That year the federal government did force RCA to dispose of one of the two networks that operated as the NBC "Red" and NBC "Blue" systems. NBC "Blue" emerged as the American Broadcasting System and became a "new" competitor to NBC and CBS. World War II created even larger markets for the three networks, and the postwar era saw radio reach a peak as the national entertainment and advertising medium. The virtually unrivaled success of radio ended after 1948, however, with the coming of television.

TELEVISION AND ADVERTISING

In the late 1930s basic technological advances led to the experimental operation of a few television stations and the sale of small television receivers. Allen DuMont built sets in a converted pickle factory in New Jersey and developed a small network. Led by David Sarnoff, Radio Corporation of America spent large sums of money on the research and development of television and created a patent pool that gave RCA a technological advantage in the field. World War II delayed the emergence of television, but in the immediate postwar years NBC linked stations in New York, Philadelphia, and Washington by coaxial cable and formed a network. Within a brief time over $1 billion worth of sets had been sold, and ABC and CBS joined NBC and DuMont with network programming. The FCC continued to license television stations even though the first outlets lost large sums each year. However, as advertising began to shift from radio to television, the former soon lost 70 percent of its evening audience and network sales plummeted. By the mid-1950s half the homes in the nation had television sets, and the networks expanded programming from a few hours in the evening to eight, ten, and even twenty-four hours a day. The television boom was further enhanced by the introduction of color transmission and programs.

While CBS had taken the lead in the marketing of color television and obtained FCC approval of its design, the technology was not compatible with existing black-and-white sets, which could not receive the CBS color programs. Manufacturers refused to add the expensive converters that the CBS color system required. Meanwhile, RCA introduced a color system that was compatible and, after it was licensed by the FCC, was adopted by the industry. Color broadcasts expanded from a few hours in the evening to virtually all programs. The early color "spectaculars" attracted millions of viewers, led to the sale of large numbers of color television sets, and expanded the advertising revenues of the networks and the stations.[17] Madison Avenue adapted quickly to the new medium, and profits soared.

Advertising and broadcasting revenues grew as the price of television sets declined because of economy of scale in manufacturing and as the average hours of viewing by individuals increased. Mass marketers saw millions of viewers, and their children, as potential purchasers of their products. The fortunes of the motion picture industry, newspapers, and national magazines sagged as major advertisers and the public interest shifted to television. The leading advertisers in 1967 and in 1981 and their annual expenditures suggest the growing impact of television advertising:

1967		1981	
Procter and Gamble	$192,052,300	Procter and Gamble	$521,116,400
General Foods	93,812,000	General Foods	328,312,700
Bristol-Myers	74,278,800	American Home	
Colgate-Palmolive	71,087,800	Products	171,765,500
American Home		General Mills	169,324,700
Products	57,834,400	General Motors	160,808,100
R. J. Reynolds	57,230,300	Pepsico	139,272,200
Lever Brothers	55,969,400	Lever Brothers	137,992,100
American Tobacco	49,869,700	Ford	136,345,000
Gillette	43,068,600	AT&T	129,798,800
General Mills	42,571,400	McDonald's	129,379,300

The absence of tobacco firms in the 1981 list reflects the ban on cigarette advertising by the federal government and suggests the growing impact of federal involvement in advertising in general and in broadcasting in particular.[18]

The growth in advertising in the 1930s and the presence of only limited internal regulation of the industry led to piecemeal federal regulation. The advertising industry had created agencies to report accurate circulation figures of newspapers and magazines to assure advertisers reliable distribution of their ads. Further, the industry adopted codes in the 1920s concerning claims by advertisers. *Printers Ink* and the National Association of Broadcasters (NAB) established programs of self-regulation within their respective fields. *Printers' Ink* drafted a model state statute for truth in advertising, and the NAB created review committees for advertising copy. Nevertheless, federal regulation grew with the Wheeler-Lea amendment to the Federal Trade Commission Act in 1938, which gave the FTC authority to regulate unfair and deceptive advertising as well as jurisdiction over false advertising of foods, drugs, and therapeutic devices. The FTC gained "cease and desist" authority and the right to issue injunctions to stop deceptive advertising. The Pure Food, Drug and Cosmetics Act of 1938 strengthened federal regulation of advertising of those products.[19] In the 1960s additional authority was given to the FCC in requiring higher standards of programming by holders of radio and television station licenses. Consumer organizations and other groups contended, however, that not enough had been done to control the content, frequency, and pervasiveness of advertising in the society.

Since World War II, advertising expenditures have made quantum leaps in terms of dollars allocated. As early as 1968 the United States was spending $87.86 per capita annually on advertising while the amount spent in other industrialized countries was much smaller. Per capita expenditures ranged from $31.05 in West Germany to $28.11 in Great Britain, and $12.90 in Japan. More than half of the world's expenditures on advertising were made in this country.[20] The volume of advertising continued to accelerate into the 1980s, paralleling the rise of discretionary spending power of American families. Per capita advertising expenditures rose to nearly $100 in 1970, but that number more than doubled over the next decade and continued to increase throughout the 1980s. The results of this tremendous outlay of expenditures included the further "standardization" of American culture and the solidification of consumerism as a major factor in the national economy.

Advertising is itself the product of a vast infrastructure of newspaper, radio, magazine, and television industries that seeks to market the economy's goods and services. Despite sometimes cynical, and certainly materialistic, implications of modern advertising, it has become an essential industry in sustaining a free market in an increasingly complex economic order. Just as advertising has become the vital ingredient in the distribution of goods and services, insurance has become an essential element in protecting values accumulated as represented by one's life and property.

NOTES

1. Glenn Porter, "Marketing," in *Encyclopedia of American Economic History*, vol. 1 (New York: Charles Scribner's Sons, 1980), pp. 386–396.

2. David M. Potter, *People of Plenty* (Chicago: University of Chicago Press, 1954), pp. 166–188.

3. James P. Wood, *The Story of Advertising* (New York: Ronald Press, 1958), pp. 148–157.

4. Ibid., p. 182, citing "Newspaper Advertisements" *Harper's New Monthly Magazine* (November 1866), p. 789.

5. Ibid., pp. 193–199.

6. James P. Wood, *Magazines in the United States: Their Social and Economic Influence* (New York: Ronald Press, 1949), pp. 93–96.

7. *Printers' Ink, A Journal for Advertisers: Fifty Years, 1888–1938* (New York: Printers' Ink Publishing Company, 1938).

8. Ibid., p. 4.

9. Ibid.

10. Wood, *The Story of Advertising*, pp. 260–272.

11. Potter, *People of Plenty*, pp. 172–176.

12. Ralph M. Hower, *The History of an Advertising Agency: N.W. Ayer & Son at Work, 1869–1949* (Cambridge: Harvard University Press, 1949).

13. Otis Pease, *The Responsibilities of American Advertising* (New Haven, Connecticut: Yale University Press, 1958), pp. 5–43.

14. See Potter, *People of Plenty*, pp. 166–188; and David Riesman, *The Lonely Crowd* (New Haven, Connecticut: Yale University Press, 1950), pp. 159–160.

15. Erik Barnouw, *A Tower in Babel: A History of Broadcasting in the United States*, vol. I, to *1933* (New York: Oxford University Press, 1966), pp. 10–74.

16. Ibid., pp. 184–234.

17. For the development of television see Erik Barnouw, *The Golden Web: A History of Broadcasting in the United States, vol. II, 1933–1953* (New York: Oxford University Press, 1968), pp. 243–303.

18. S. Watson Dunn, *Advertising: Its Role in Modern Marketing* (New York: Holt, Rinehart & Winston, 1969), p. 488; and the annual reports of the Television Bureau of Advertising.

19. Wood, *The Story of Advertising,* pp. 426–431.

20. Dunn *Advertising,* p. 14.

SUGGESTED READINGS

BARITZ, LOREN *The Servants of Power: A History of the Use of Social Science in American Industry.* Middletown, Connecticut: Wesleyan University Press, 1960.

BARNOUW, ERIK. *A Tower in Babel: A History of Broadcasting in the United States, vol. I, to 1933.* New York: Oxford University Press, 1966.

———. *The Golden Web: A History of Broadcasting in the United States, vol. II, 1933–1953.* New York: Oxford University Press, 1968.

———. *The Image Empire: A History of Broadcasting in the United States, vol. III, from 1953.* New York: Oxford University Press, 1970.

BERNAYS, EDWARD L. *Public Relations.* Norman: University of Oklahoma Press, 1952.

CURTI, MERLE. "The Changing Concept of 'Human Nature' in the Literature of American Advertising," *Business History Review,* 41 (Winter, 1967), 335–357.

HOWER, RALPH M. *The History of an Advertising Agency: N.W. Ayer & Son at Work, 1869–1949.* Cambridge: Harvard University Press, 1949.

LAZARSFELD, PAUL F. *Radio Listening in America: The People Look at Radio Again.* Englewood Cliffs, New Jersey: Prentice Hall, 1948.

MOTT, FRANK LUTHER. *A History of American Magazines.* Five volumes. Cambridge: Harvard University Press, 1938–1968.

PEASE, OTIS. *The Responsibilities of American Advertising.* New Haven, Connecticut: Yale University Press, 1958.

POPE, DANIEL. *The Making of Modern Advertising.* New York: Basic Books, 1983.

POTTER, DAVID. *People of Plenty.* Chicago: University of Chicago Press, 1954.

PRESBREY, FRANK S. *The History and Development of Advertising.* Garden City, New York: Doubleday, Doran, & Co., 1929.

RAUCHER, ALAN R. *Public Relations and Business, 1900–1929.* Baltimore: Johns Hopkins University Press, 1968.

STEINBERG, CHARLES S. *The Mass Communicators.* New York: Harper & Brothers, 1958.

———. (ed.). *Mass Media and Communication.* New York: Hastings House, 1972.

WOOD, JAMES P. *Magazines in the United States: Their Social and Economic Influence.* New York: Ronald Press, 1949.

———. *The Story of Advertising.* New York: Ronald Press, 1958.

12 The American Insurance Industry

The accumulation of capital and the development of financial intermediaries were intrinsic to the rise of big business. Insurance companies, savings and loan institutions, and banks provided the capital that helped make possible giant enterprise. Author John Bainbridge has supplied a simple picture of how insurance works. Insurance involves the contribution of small sums of money by many individuals to form a pool. The contributors agree to compensate the members of the pool for specified losses. When losses occur, as from fire, theft, or accident, sums are withdrawn from the pool and paid to the policyholder as stipulated by the agreement or policy adopted by the contributors. "The machinery used to administer the pool is known as an insurance company."[1]

Insurance companies are of two kinds, *stock* and *mutual*. In a mutual company the contributors are both policyholders and stockholders. They own the company and receive the company's dividends or profits in cash or "kind," that is, as rebates on insurance premiums. A stock company, on the other hand, sells a policy at cost plus a profit that is returned as dividends to stockholders who may or may not be policyholders.

Insurance companies basically provide four principal types of insurance: fire, casualty, marine, and life. The first three, fire, casualty, and marine, are similar in that insurance is against losses to property. Life insurance provides, in part, protection against loss of a valuable asset—

human life and labor. With an estimated $2 trillion of coverage in force in the United States, life insurance is a primary vehicle for savings and investment, ranking third behind commercial banks and savings and loan associations in the volume of assets held by financial intermediaries.[2] Property insurance generally functions in the "pure" role of providing protection against loss. The accumulation and management of life and property insurance funds are the functions of the insurance company. Property protection, specifically marine and fire, developed earlier than life insurance, emerging in Europe during the era of mercantile expansion.

COLONIAL ORIGINS OF THE INSURANCE INDUSTRY

The modern American fire, casualty, and marine insurance industry was originally conceived in mid-seventeenth-century London and indirectly in Amsterdam and Antwerp. The businessmen of London who gathered at Edward Lloyd's coffee house, and who took upon themselves individually and collectively to insure the cargoes of British vessels bound to overseas destinations, were doing what merchants of maritime nations had done for centuries. Forms of commercial insurance existed in the time of Hammurabi (2,000 B.C.), thrived in ancient Athens and Rome, and became widespread in fourteenth-century and fifteenth-century Italian cities.[3] The British, and perhaps even more so the Dutch, who were the main commercial carriers of the seventeenth century, became the primary insurers of the modern world.

The insurance concept received a direct and unusual stimulus from the great fire of London that destroyed much of that city in 1666. The fire gave rise to the first organized stock insurance company, the Fire Office, created by London builder, speculator, and entrepreneur "Damned" Nicholas Barbon. Barbon's company sold insurance on brick buildings at 2.5 percent of their annual rental value, and at 5 percent of annual rental value of frame structures. In the first three years of business, 1680–1683, he insured 4,000 houses for which he received $90,000 in premiums and paid out $35,000 in losses. For the record, Barbon's policy for paying losses might best be described as "reluctant," a practice which bedeviled the modern as well as the more ancient insurance industry. Barbon faced competition from a City of London–sponsored insurance operation, but it was abandoned under court order in 1683. Subsequently insurance remained a private business. New companies, such as the Friendly Society, were organized in London, and in 1696 the first mutual company, the Hand-in-Hand, appeared. The Hand-in-Hand survived until 1905, when it was absorbed by the Commercial Union Assurance Company, Ltd., of London.[4]

The Hand-in-Hand served as Benjamin Franklin's model for the organization in March 1752 of the Philadelphia Contributionship for the Insurance of Houses from Loss by Fire. Policy No. 1, for $2,500 coverage, was issued to John Smith, the company treasurer, on July 4, 1752. In 1763 the directors agreed that only the interest on the deposit money (premiums) could be spent. Thus, the Philadelphia Contributionship established the first insurance company reserve account. In 1781 the Contributionship refused to write policies on structures with trees near or over the building. Subsequently, a protree group split from the Contributionship and organized a new insurance society called the Green Tree. By December 31, 1949, the Green Tree had returned $1.3 million in dividends to policyholders, and the Contributionship had returned $3.6 million.[5] The Friendly Society of Charleston, South Carolina, organized in 1735, actually preceded the Philadelphia Contributionship. A disastrous fire in 1741 wiped out the assets of the company and it ceased to exist. Also, the Mutual Assurance Society of Virginia, organized in 1749 by William F. Ast, who, according to one writer, "looked as if he were the descendant of the mother of vinegar," appeared a few years before Franklin organized the Contributionship. Irrespective of Ast's appearance, the society flourished and included among its counselors national figures such as Edmund Randolph and John Marshall. It survived the Civil War, but little beyond.[6]

Unlike fire and marine coverage, no life insurance companies were organized in America during the colonial or confederation periods. Parliament had organized two life companies in England in 1719, the Royal Exchange and the London Assurance, and these companies obtained a monopoly that was officially extended to America in 1741. An American life insurance prototype appeared in the colonies in 1759, when the Presbyterian church organized "The Corporation for the Relief of Poor and Distressed Presbyterian Ministers" and "The Poor and Distressed Widows and Children of Presbyterian Ministers Fund," but it was not true insurance because it depended upon outside contributions. Between 1787 and 1799, however, five companies came into being which did write life insurance, including the Insurance Company of North America (INA).[7]

INA: A STOCK INSURANCE COMPANY

The INA was and is the first stock company in America. It evolved from an aborted "tontine" insurance scheme that appeared in America in the late 1700s. Originating with Lorenzo Tonti in seventeenth-century France, the tontine was a lottery life insurance scheme that swept Europe for over a century. The winners were those contributors who survived a stated term of years and who then divided the pool among themselves. A Boston tontine came into being under the direction of one Samuel Blodgett, Jr., a merchant who dabbled successfully in the China trade. But the tontine failed to attract many takers, and at the invitation of a Philadelphia merchant, Ebenezer Hazard, Blodgett moved his tontine to that city and restyled it the Universal Tontine Association. They planned to sell 50,000 shares in Boston and 50,000 in Philadelphia with the distribution of all assets to the remaining survivors after twenty-one years. The day of the tontine, however, had passed, and participants were few. In 1792 subscribers met in Independence Hall and appointed a committee to study the situation. The committee recommended conversion of the tontine into a general insurance company. The committee report, creating the Insurance Company of North America, was approved by the tontine subscribers on November 12, 1792.[8]

First office of the Insurance Company of North America, 1792–1794, Philadelphia. (Courtesy: INA Corporation Archives.)

The shareholders agreed to sell 60,000 shares of stock at $10 per share, elected John M. Nesbitt president, and Ebenezer Hazard secretary. A building was rented for $100 per year, a clerk hired for $500 per year, and a porter engaged for $100 per year. The company concentrated on marine insurance, reflecting America's primary business concern, but offered life insurance as well. Policy Number 1 insured a $5,333.33 share of the *America* bound from Philadelphia to Londonderry for a premium of $120, and Policy Number 2 covered the cargo at a value of $3,200 for a premium of $72.50. In the first six months of business INA received premiums of $62,114.33, and paid losses of $4,515.74. Premiums rose to $151,350 in the second six months of operation and losses totaled $19,474.[9] The Articles of Incorporation for INA received approval on April 14, 1794.

The character of insurance coverage shifted radically in the decades after the organization of the INA. As has been noted earlier, foreign trade declined precipitously between 1793 and 1815 because of the Napoleonic Wars and the entry of the United States into war with England in 1812. Financial uncertainties made such investments hazardous. The necessity of marketing on a national scale, rather than relying primarily on the port of Philadelphia, led the INA to appoint special agents to sell its policies, thus beginning the independent agency system. The company also elected to set rates and accept risks at the home office on the basis of reports by agents rather than having the agent make that determination. The company dropped its life insurance coverage in 1817 and effectively made the transition from insuring ships and cargoes engaged in foreign trade to insuring steamships and cargoes on inland waters.[10] Changes in the property insurance business in the expansionist antebellum era were eclipsed, however, by the growth and development of the life insurance industry.

THE LIFE INSURANCE INDUSTRY

Historians of the life insurance industry have puzzled over the apparent "take off" of life insurance sales in America in the 1840s. Prior to that time businessmen regarded life insurance with indifference, while farmers—and most Americans were associated with the farm—believed life insurance to be downright useless and probably immoral, since it put a price on death. The remarkable surge in life insurance after 1843 has been attributed to general economic growth and particularly to the rise of the city. As mentioned previously, between 1840 and 1860 the urban population grew by almost 800 percent. Lower mortality rates, that is, a lower frequency of death in an age group, and improved actuarial knowledge, or the statistical compilation of death rates and risks, contributed to the increasing popularity of life insurance. The appearance of aggressive mutual insurance companies (seven major and still existing mutuals were founded between 1843 and 1847) helps to explain the subsequent marketing explosion in the life industry. The institutionalization of the insurance agent is also believed to have been a catalyst in the development of the modern insurance industry. But business also seems to have been equally good for those companies that did not embrace the agent system. An improved political and banking climate, internal improvements in the structures of companies, better quality and prices of policies, and an increase in the general knowledge about life insurance all contributed to the enlargement of the industry.[11]

None of these things, reports Viviana A. R. Zelizer, who conducted a sociological study of the life insurance industry, really explains why Americans became insurance conscious in the mid-nineteenth century. Rather, she argues that life insurance became swept up in the new age of science and humanism. It became an instrument to facilitate human control over death and a ritual in the preparation for death if not for salvation. What Christian would leave a defenseless family to the cruel mercy of charity? Life insurance provided a form of economic immorality: "It redefined death as an economic episode and life as an economic asset."[12] Thus, changing social values, rather than energetic salespeople, Zelizer concludes, were responsible for the take-off in insurance sales in the mid-nineteenth century. All these things undoubtedly contributed to the remarkable growth of the industry, but it is also evident that urbanization and the commercial revolution were fundamental to expanded property and life insurance sales.

The first company organized exclusively to handle life insurance, the Pennsylvania Company for Insurance on Lives and Granting Annuities, organized in Philadelphia in 1809, depended upon a hodge-podge of life-expectancy tables that estimated the rate of deaths within an age group.[13] There is little question but that the absence of reliable mortality tables adversely affected the development of the life insurance industry. By the mid-nineteenth century this deficiency was alleviated, however, and contributed to the substantial growth of the insurance industry after the Civil War.

Many of the firms organized in the 1830s achieved their greatest success after 1865. The New York Life and Trust Company and the Baltimore Life Insurance Company both received charters in 1830. New York Life broke new ground by adopting the agency system for marketing and by its use of advertising. Other firms specialized in one risk group. For example, the Traveler's Mutual Accident Association was founded in 1833 to provide accident coverage for traveling salesmen. Simultaneously, a number of mutual life insurance companies emerged to support the expansion of commerce and industry. The major commercial centers and ports witnessed the creation of large insurance firms from Boston to New Orleans.[14] By the 1840s the mutuals transcended the stock companies by creating new marketing techniques. Lower premiums, rigorous salesmanship, and the fraternal qualities associated with the mutuals made the public receptive to mutual insurance.

Most mutuals followed the conservative investment policies of Morris Robinson, organizer and president of Mutual Life Insurance Company of New York, who made investments only in mortgages on New York real estate, in United States bonds, and in New York City and state bonds. New England Mutual Life, thanks to the work of Sheppard Homans, initiated a revolution in rate making with the development of a new mortality table. Homans discovered that American life expectancy differed markedly from the British in that mortality rates were much higher for younger and older Americans, but much lower for Americans in their middle years.[15] The creation of accurate American mortality tables, and thus lower premiums, helped fuel the boom in the life insurance sales that began in mid-century and continued unabated for fifty years.

Some of the real prosperity of the Gilded Age came in the form of life insurance policies. By 1892 more life insurance was being sold annually in the United States than existed in the whole world in 1850; half of the estimated $11 billion in insurance in force had been subscribed to by American policyholders. Between 1880 and 1890 life coverage in the United States rose from $1.5 billion to $4 billion, and three of the largest New York insurance companies—Metropolitan, Equitable, and New York Life—held over one-half of that total. By 1890 over fifty "legal reserve life" insurance companies were operating—that is, those that, like banks, were required by legislative mandate to maintain a certain level of cash reserves. In the next decade another fifty companies entered into business.[16]

The explosion in the marketing of life insurance policies can be attributed in part to greater sales incentives for the agents as commissions for insurance agents became increasingly liberal. In the 1840s the agents received 5 to 10 percent of the first year's premium and 5 percent on renewals. In the 1850s and 1860s this figure rose to 14 to 20 percent on new business, to 80 percent in the 1870s, and as much as 100 percent in 1900. The companies also provided an assortment of prizes and bonuses to stimulate sales.

In order to meet competition, raise agents' fees, and lower premiums, both the stock and mutual companies began to defer dividends. This resulted, however, in a reduction in the value of the life policy. By 1885, 18 percent of Northwestern Mutual Insurance policies were of a semitontine type. Intense competition also led some firms to engage in unethical or even illegal sales efforts. One popular sales technique was to offer a "board-contract" to the first five hundred prominent citizens in a city or community who purchased a policy. The five hundred subsequently received a very nominal commission on all insurance written by the company in their community. A more disreputable practice was to sell insurance in states where the company was not licensed to do business, and then contest any claims on the grounds the contract was invalid. Other practices involved pay-offs to local and state officials, participation in speculative financial and investment syndicates, and irresponsible, if not fraudulent, investment policies. As was true with other industries, the economic power of the insurance corporations far outgrew the capacities of the states to control them. Unlike the cases of manufacturing and transportation, however, the federal government failed to assume regulatory authority over the insurance industry.[17]

REFORM AND REGULATION

Speculation and illegal or questionable practices among insurance firms after the Civil War led to efforts by the industry to reform itself: specifically, to impose operational standards, to institute a degree of self-regulation, and to encourage state governments to develop legislative guidelines. The National Board of Fire Underwriters, organized in 1866, established industry-wide premium standards. The stabilization of rate structures encouraged greater public trust and confidence in the industry and led to the sale of many new policies. The credibility and growth of the insurance industry depended, however, upon how well insurance companies honored their contractual and ethical obligations.

The Chicago fire of 1871 offered a serious challenge to the industry. The fire bankrupted sixty-eight insurance companies, but overall industry performance reaffirmed public confidence and certainly impressed urban dwellers with the necessity of fire insurance. Most companies such as INA, which paid out $658,000 to policyholders, fully met their obligations. In short, the Chicago fire demonstrated some weaknesses but, more importantly, the basic integrity of the property insurance industry, and it resulted in the sale of millions of dollars of new policies.

Additional signs of maturity began to appear. State insurance commissioners, whose primary function had to do with the licensing and taxing of insurance companies operating within their states, met in a national conference in New York in May 1871. This and subsequent conventions led to the adoption of the American Experience Table, which established uniform national risk statistics, and the preparation of the American Table, which provided accurate demographic data. The tables contributed a measure of uniformity in life insurance policies and encouraged reciprocity in state laws affecting insurance. In 1889 actuaries, who analyze vital statistics,

The actuarial office of New York Life Insurance Company creates and maintains mortality tables, 1909. (Courtesy: New York Life Insurance Company Archives.)

organized the Actuarial Society of America to enhance their professional status in the industry. To present a solid rank to the companies in order to obtain larger and more equitable fees, agents organized the National Association of Life Underwriters. This organization ultimately approximated the services of a consumer's protection agency by establishing codes of professional ethics.[18] It was not until the public exposure of insurance scandals in New York in 1905, however, that significant reform of the life insurance industry occurred.

Turn-of-the-century muckraking journalists, busy exposing corruption in railroading, meatpacking, government, and elsewhere, did not overlook the multimillion dollar insurance industry. Some progressives in both political parties pressed for federal regulation of big business and the destruction of trusts. A Supreme Court ruling in 1869 had held, however, that "issuing a policy of insurance is not a transaction of commerce," thus exempting the industry from such subsequent legislation as the Sherman Anti-Trust Act of 1890. Yet that act and the Progressive Era stimulated a new wave of efforts to reform in other areas, particularly in the railroad, banking, and insurance industries. Attacks on abuses by insurance companies began in the New York legislature in 1905.

The Armstrong Investigations

The Armstrong Investigations, led by New York Senator William W. Armstrong, sprang out of an internal feud in the Equitable Insurance Company over the investment of company funds in competing banks. A company-directed investigation, initiated by Andrew Carnegie's partner,

Henry Clay Frick, charged management with improper accounting and investment procedures. The company's board of directors rejected the report's conclusions, and several of the prominent directors, including Frick and Edward H. Harriman, president of the Union Pacific Railroad, resigned. A New York insurance commissioner picked up the scent of scandal and conducted his own investigation charging Equitable with irregular, if not illegal, activities. Finally, under intense pressure from the newspapers, the governor called a special session of the legislature, which formed an investigating committee headed by Armstrong. From September through December 1905, the nation was stunned, and occasionally amused, by the testimony from the chief executives of some great investment and insurance companies.[19]

Charles Evans Hughes, soon to be elected governor of New York, served as chief counsel for the committee, and his probing questions brought to public view many shocking disclosures. Most companies who furnished witnesses had their reputations tarnished, or at least they found themselves embarrassed. But not all companies were called. Aetna Life Insurance Company, for example, provided records and exhibits with a brief written statement which essentially declared that the Connecticut company did not do business "in the New York way."[20] Northwestern Mutual also sent reports, only to face, as did other companies, a new round of legislative investigations conducted by states such as Kentucky, Minnesota, Tennessee, and Wisconsin, the latter Northwestern Mutual's home.[21]

The 450-page Armstrong report recommended significant changes in actuarial and marketing practices. The committee, for example, urged prohibition of the investment by insurance companies in common stocks and their participation in syndicates underwriting corporate securities. Standardized policy forms that included a provision for automatic extension were recommended. Commissions to agents were to be limited, and prizes and bonuses prohibited. The acquisition cost of new business could not exceed the first-year loading charges (that is, the cost of agents' commissions and policy preparation fees). Both stock and mutual companies would be required to make annual distribution of dividends. The committee advocated imposing uniform values on surrendered policies, legal liability for misrepresenting the terms of insurance contracts, the elimination of permanent voting proxies, a ban on political contributions, the registration of insurance company lobbyists, and uniform accounting procedures. The Armstrong Committee distinctly favored mutual companies over the stock companies, and it advised the passing of new laws making it easier to convert stock companies into mutuals. Despite the unrestrained opposition of the life companies to the Armstrong recommendations, the New York legislature approved most of them. S. S. McClure, muckraking editor of *McClure's* magazine, believed that the New York investigations had a "tonic effect." Other states followed the New York example, to a greater or lesser degree, often after completing their own legislative inquiries.[22] The investigations did not produce either a federal inquiry or federal legislation, as Congress deferred to the authority of the states. The Armstrong report did result, however, in internal reforms and additional self-regulation by the insurance industry.

The American Life Conference

The Armstrong investigation stimulated the development of a new trade association within the industry. Southern and western life insurance companies, already distrustful of the apparent hegemony of northeastern insurance companies and investment-banking interests, met in a preliminary organizational meeting at Chicago in 1905. These companies used and endorsed the preliminary term valuation system, which meant that the first year's premium did not go into any accounting for a reserve fund but was used entirely for the promotion of new business such as agents' fees. The conference adopted a set of resolutions that (1) favored uniform state laws for the protection of policyholders; (2) opposed federal supervision and control of life insurance companies; (3) opposed state laws requiring payments to the state for the privilege of doing business, which the companies said were designed to extort money from insurance firms; and (4) opposed oppressive taxation and licensing of insurance companies. The conference led to the formation of the American Life Convention, which held its first annual meeting at Lookout Mountain, Tennessee, in September 1906.[23] Also in that year the Life Insurance Association of America, which had a northeastern orientation, was organized in New York. At first these organizations endorsed similar policies. For example, both actively promoted the passage of state laws regulating the insurance industry.

JOHN GARFIELD DRYDEN AND PRUDENTIAL LIFE

John Dryden's life (1839–1911) spanned those years when the American life insurance industry emerged from the chrysalis into a full-blown butterfly. Born in Temple, Maine, Dryden moved, with his family, to Massachusetts, where his father worked in a machine shop. Dryden attended Yale for a time, dropped out, eloped, and moved to Bedford, Ohio, now a Cleveland suburb. He went to work as a salesman for a local insurance agent handling policies for Niagara Fire Insurance Company and Aetna Life. He and a partner started their own agency in 1865 but dissolved their partnership two years later. Dryden then moved back East, relocated frequently, and faced a number of very difficult years. In 1870 he organized what was to be an industrial insurance company, but the governor of New York vetoed the charter. Next, at the age of thirty-four, John Dryden, having faced failure more often than success, went to work for the Widows and Orphans Friendly Society, an insurance company established by Allen L. Bassett. In 1873 Dryden and Bassett began to organize an industrial insurance company with a capital of $30,000. Finally, on February 18, 1875, the Widows and Orphans Friendly Society became the Prudential Friendly Society. It aims were

> to enable people of small means to provide: first, for relief in sickness or accidents; second, for a pension in old age; third, for an adult burial fund; fourth, for an infant burial fund.

Within ten years Prudential Insurance Company had assets in excess of $1 million, and in 1896 *Leslie's Weekly* carried the first instance of what is today a familiar advertisement: "Prudential Has the Strength of Gibraltar," or in more modern parlance, "Own a Piece of the Rock." John Dryden directed Prudential through its momentous growth period and presided over its organizational restructuring at the turn of the century. This reorganization, however, resulted in the removal of voting rights from policyholders and in confrontations with stockholders and legislators. The New Jersey legislature elected him to the U.S. Senate in 1901. He left the Senate in 1907 following a Democratic upset and died in 1911. What he had started as a humble widows and orphans insurance program, in which an agent sold a policy and collected the premium of "three cents a week," ended as one of the largest life insurance firms in the United States.

The San Francisco Earthquake and Fire

Even as the repercussions from the Armstrong investigations continued to threaten the industry, one of the nation's greatest peacetime disasters occurred. The San Francisco earthquake and fire of 1906 eclipsed the damage and losses of the Chicago fire. Total property losses were estimated at over $400 million. The earthquake and fire brought the property insurance industry to the brink of both psychological and financial disaster. As the reports of enormous destruction began to flood home offices in the East, insurance companies desperately sought to cut their losses by disavowing claims or offering only partial restitution. Most insurance companies agreed among themselves that earthquake damages should be deducted before fire losses were paid. Since fire policies paid no restitution for earthquake damages, and because the companies claimed that most of the losses in San Francisco were caused by the earthquake before the fire broke out, they held that their liability to policyholders was minimal.[24]

Responding to unverified newspaper reports, to the insistence of special INA agent Sheldon Catlin, and to accounts written by Jack London contending that only 10 percent of the damage in San Francisco could be attributed to the earthquake, INA and a small group of companies elected to make full restitution for property losses to policyholders under the fire clauses. INA paid claims of over $3.2 million to policyholders while a subsidiary paid another $1 million. Only 27 companies out of 113 that carried policies on San Francisco property paid their claims in full.[25] With public confidence already undermined by the Armstrong investigations, the insurance industry suffered a distinct loss of trust as a result of the San Francisco tragedy. The failure to honor claims led to a resurgence of interest in regulating insurance activities by the states.

Wisconsin

In Wisconsin, home of the Senate's then-leading Progressive, Robert M. LaFollette, and the headquarters of the nation's largest mutual insurance company, Northwestern Mutual, the legislature considered seventy-

The San Francisco earthquake and fire devastated the city and many insurance companies.　(Courtesy: California State Library.)

two bills to regulate the insurance industry during its 1907 session. Most of the laws that were passed followed the pattern set in New York. The most controversial proposal to pass required companies licensed to sell insurance in Wisconsin to deposit securities with the secretary of state "equal in value to the total liabilities on their outstanding Wisconsin policies."[26] The state also approved an act placing a ceiling on premiums. Major out-of-state insurance companies threatened to withdraw from Wisconsin if the governor signed the bills. He did, and they did. In 1915 portions of the controversial legislation were modified or repealed, but not until fifteen companies left the state.[27] The Wisconsin "deposit" requirement sought to guarantee that insurance companies would meet the obligations they had contracted with their policyholders. The demands for reform set in motion in New York and Wisconsin spread across the nation.

Texas

The state of Texas approved legislation in 1907 that paralleled the Wisconsin acts. The Robertson Law required that 75 percent of the reserves on Texas policies should be invested in the state, where the securities would be subject to ad valorem taxes. Fourteen insurance companies quickly ceased doing business in Texas. In 1915 the legislature considered repealing the legislation, but local insurance interests rallied and prevented such action in order to preserve the state market for Texas insurance companies. Governor James E. Ferguson, who favored repeal, argued that the issue was not the protection of Texas insurance companies against "outside" interests. Fewer than 7 percent of Texans owned life insurance company stock. Rather, the exclusion of large insurance companies from the state would deny farmers and businessmen access to loans, he said.[28]

Ferguson had touched upon a critical but generally unrecognized role of the life insurance industry, that is, as financial institutions to provide capital for borrowers. In Texas, for example, the conflict over the Robertson Law brought into sharp relief the importance of insurance company investments in the economic progress of Texas and the Southwest. This investment function was clearly recognized by Charles Fleetwood, the regional manager of Prudential Insurance Company, in Houston:

> For the good of our economy, it is essential that private capital be available for investment purposes in areas like Houston where rapid growth and development are taking place. Frequently these areas do not generate adequate investment capital for their needs, and a transfer of funds from the older, more mature regions of the country should be made to meet their legitimate needs.[29]

Fleetwood noted that in low-growth regions, such as the mid-Atlantic states, insurance companies invested sixty-nine cents for every dollar of policy reserve liability, while in the south-central states of Texas, Louisiana, Oklahoma, and Arkansas, investments averaged $3 for every dollar of policy reserve.[30] Thus, as Governor Ferguson intimated in 1915, a major role of insurance companies was not simply to sell insurance but to accumulate personal savings and to transfer those savings as investment capital to areas where they are needed.

Just as the insurance industry had developed large-scale capital for investment purposes, it also sought new business to generate additional profits. Some firms became carriers for employee benefit packages to include health, accident, and retirement programs. Other companies provided a variety of industrial policies to cover new business activities. But in no other area did the insurance companies find such rapid growth as they did in the coverage of automobiles.

THE AUTO AGE: THE KEMPER GROUP AND STATE FARM MUTUAL

Insurance certainly would not be what it is today without the automobile. When most Americans think of insurance, they think of their automobile policies that cover losses from collision and liability for damages to life and property. Even as the Armstrong Committee concluded its investigations, and Wisconsin and Texas approved initial packages of insurance legislation, the United States was on the brink of the automobile age. The first auto liability policy was probably written in 1912 by James S. Kemper, who eventually headed one of the largest insurance conglomerates in America.

Kemper founded Lumbermen's Mutual Casualty Company in 1912 to provide workmen's compensation coverage and manufacturers' public liability insurance. Innovations of the Lumbermen's Mutual included salaried company sales agents, low rates achieved by large dividend returns (25 percent return in the first four years of operation), and one of the early, if not the first, auto liability insurance policies. Kemper, who sold his first automobile policy to Frank J. Heitman in 1912, estimated premiums at a rate twice that of premiums for horse-team liability insurance. In doing so Kemper pioneered in developing a new dimension in casualty insurance. Automobile insurance now accounts for well over half of Lumbermen's premium income. Kemper ultimately developed a "fleet" of insurance companies, the Kemper Group, including Lumbermen's, National Retailers Mutual, Federal Mutual Fire Insurance, and American Farmers Mutual, among others.[31]

Kemper's automobile insurance business was soon eclipsed, however, by State Farm Mutual. Founded in 1922 by George Jacob Mecherle, who had retired to Florida after a successful farming career in Illinois, State Farm Mutual soon became the largest automobile insurance company in the world. Mecherle began selling insurance in Florida for a small local company and decided that the farm automobile insurance market was being completely ignored by insurance companies. He came out of retirement, returned to Illinois, and founded State Farm Mutual Auto Insurance Company, which specialized in insurance coverage for farm vehicles.

For five years State Farm was a one-man operation. Mecherle tailored his policies and his marketing techniques to the rural customer. He offered six-month term policies to lower the premium cost to the customer, arranged for the payment of premiums by mail to a central office, and when he began to acquire agents, allowed them to be full-time salespeople rather than salespeople and collection agents combined, as was customary with the agency system. Another innovation reduced claims by insuring a certain percentage of a loss rather than using the more traditional cash-deduction provision in policies. A $100-deductible policy cost State Farm more claims than a 20 percent deductible policy. By these mechanisms State Farm offered lower rates, outmarketed competitors, and retained a favorable earnings ratio. Mecherle sold 1,300 policies in his first six months of operation, and the assets of State Farm doubled every year for the next seven years. By the time of Mecherle's death in 1951 at the age of seventy-four, State Farm's premiums approached $100 million per year.[32]

Following World War II both automobile sales and insurance coverage escalated rapidly. The percentage of American families owning automobiles rose from about 50 percent to 82 percent by 1970, with one-third of the households owning two or more cars. Automobile insurance premiums climbed from $1.25 billion in 1946 to $14.6 billion in 1970. The percentage of losses in premium dollars also began to rise rapidly, particularly in the 1970s, as a result of more generous jury awards and consumer-oriented state and federal liability laws, but also because of larger vehicles, an expanded highway system, higher speeds, and more traffic miles per driver. In the post–World War II period the insurance industry became one of America's biggest big businesses and an integral part of economic expansion.

THE MODERN ERA

Between 1950 and 1974 life insurance capital financed a considerable part of the nation's economic growth. The distribution of assets held by life insurance companies in 1974 was heavily weighted toward investment in corporations with holdings of $35.2 billion in bonds and $32.8 billion in home and commercial mortgages. Policy loans ($8.7 billion) and common stocks ($8.3 billion) followed in size and greatly exceeded investments in federal, state, and local bonds, which totaled somewhat over $3 billion. The rate of growth in insurance assets declined after 1950, but it continued at a level that assured the industry its place as one of the top three financial intermediaries, with assets in excess of $430 billion by 1980.[33]

CONTINENTAL CASUALTY COMPANY

A rapidly expanding business volume does not mean rising profits. On the contrary, underwriting losses for capital-stock liability insurance companies, such as Continental Casualty Company (CCC), rose more rapidly than premium income between 1955 and 1970. Underwriting losses in these years totaled $1.5 billion. The liability-property insurance business had the lowest profit level of fifty-five leading industries in the United States. Much of this loss can be attributed to the automobile.

Costs associated with automobile accidents rose geometrically in the 1960s and 1970s. A comparable car selling for $3,000 in 1960 cost $6,000 in 1970 and $9,000 or more by 1980. Premiums generally lagged one or several years behind rising property costs, and state insurance commissions generally sought to protect consumer interests by allowing nominal and infrequent rate changes. Meanwhile, settlements in jury trials for bodily injury and property damage rose astronomically, and medical costs rose far more rapidly than property costs. Rising inflation rates added to the woes of the insurance companies as surety accounts and the value of investments eroded under the declining value of the dollar. The American casualty industry, and CCC, has had difficult times during the "prosperous" post–World War II years.

Continental Casualty Company confronted the fact that its liability-property division lost $34 million in 1965 alone. The company could not long survive this kind of attrition. President John A. Henry, then only one year away from retirement, met with his division managers in the autumn of 1967 to decide on a course of action. Should the division be scrapped? It would mean a general retrenchment of the company across the board, and as a multiline insurance company the reduction of services in one area would necessarily adversely affect business volume in other areas. The decision was made to retain the division but to streamline it and improve efficiency.

Continental Casualty Company embarked on a three-year crash program to do this. The company began to concentrate on commercial business rather than personal insurance. It trimmed its agency force to include agents who provided a more efficient volume business and who were alert to changing insurance needs and could detect new and profitable business. Management personnel were sent to school and to seminars. Stringent expense controls were instituted. Some of the changes and controls hurt, but, by the end of 1970 CCC had achieved the break-even point in casualty losses, and income and was moving the division into the profit column—a feat few other companies were able to achieve under the prevailing adverse environment.

The 1970s and 1980s brought new problems for the life insurance companies as inflation created a disincentive to place capital in relatively low interest and stable investments. Fixed-value insurance policies eroded rapidly under the onslaught of rampant inflation. Moreover, capital invested in policies bearing 4 to 6 percent interest was withdrawn by policyholders for investment in money market funds or bonds bearing interest rates as high as 15 to 17 percent. But while inflation created havoc with the industry, insurance companies became the financial administrators for millions of dollars in new investment capital channeled through retirement programs. The federal Keogh plan offered a tax incentive for investment in personal or group retirement programs, and the Employee Retirement Income Security Act of 1974 established standards for the collection, investment, and administration of private savings and retirement plans.[34] Tax and investment rulings made separate accounts and variable annuity retirement programs administered by insurance companies one of the most rapidly growing sources of investment capital. These programs supplemented the more traditional fixed-income insurance programs and reinvigorated the savings and investment function of the life insurance industry.

Nevertheless, the industry experienced pressures that altered the traditional "whole life" approach. The idea of safe long-term investments appeared doomed; reported one prominent investment official: "Insurance companies have no choice but to become multipurpose financial entities."[35] Through variable-annuity investment programs, participation in holding companies, and the development of banking and loan affiliates, insurance industries have joined banks in becoming diversified financial intermediaries.

From its beginnings the insurance industry has been a bulwark of trade, commerce, and property. It is a cooperative effort to protect the interests of the individual—both life and property. Insurance companies that manage the pool of money are either mutual or stock companies, but their external appearance, sales practices, policies, premiums, and public acceptance have become quite similar. The insurance industry has gone through three distinct phases of development and seems to be entering a fourth. The first, lasting until the mid-nineteenth century, can best be described as the pioneering and experimental phase. The two corporate structures, stock and mutual, and the types of insurance coverage became clearly defined then. During the second stage of development, lasting until about 1905–1906, there was rapid, but unregulated growth. The Chicago fire, the Armstrong investigations, and the San Francisco catastrophe left the consuming public convinced of the need for insurance but dubious about the integrity of the industry. During the next period, lasting to the 1950s, trade associations, self-regulation, and standardization, which had begun after the Civil War, welded the insurance firms into a cohesive and responsible national industry, but one where state rules and regulations created regional and local variations. Industry guidelines and state requirements meshed to provide a broad legal and ethical framework that maintained a remarkable uniformity and consistency in insurance operations across the nation. Most recently the scope of the insurance industry broadened to that of a multipurpose financial intermediary where federal regulation, as opposed to state or industry, played an increasingly greater role.

As hundreds of billions of dollars of investment capital accumulated by American insurance firms poured into land, buildings, and stocks and bonds, that industry increasingly became a competitor with other financial institutions such as banks and savings and loan associations. Under the theory that competition promoted both efficiency and equity, Congress began to deregulate the financial services industries in the 1970s and 1980s. For example, the Depository Institutions Deregulation and Monetary Control Act of 1980 eliminated interest ceilings on deposits and constraints on investments. The Garn–St. Germain Depository Institutions Act authorized savings and loan associations to offer interest rates and investment opportunities competitive with money market funds that had attracted capital to the banks and insurance companies. Thus, the lines of demarcation between insurance, banking, savings, and investment institutions became almost indistinguishable.

Banks, savings and loan associations, insurance funds, and indeed brokerage firms, have become increasingly competitive and alike. One product of this competition and deregulation was declining interest rates, and markedly lower inflation. Another, coupled with the drastic price collapse in petroleum and other factors, was the destabilization of the investment-banking industry, which resulted in serious banking and savings and loan association failures in the 1980s. This, in turn, contributed to a collapse in the stock market in 1987. The financial, insurance, and investment community thus experienced significant restructuring and revitalization.

NOTES

1. John Bainbridge, *Biography of an Idea: The Story of Mutual Fire and Casualty Insurance* (Garden City, New York: Doubleday, 1952), p. 19; and Viviana A. Rotman Zelizer, *Morals and Markets: The Development of Life Insurance in the United States* (New York: Columbia University Press, 1979), p. 150.

2. George A. Bishop, *Capital Formation through Life Insurance: A Study in the Growth of Life Insurance Services and Investment Activities* (Homewood, Illinois: Richard D. Irwin, 1976), pp. ix, 10, 23.

3. William H. A. Carr, *From Three Cents a Week . . . The Story of the Prudential Insurance Company of America* (Englewood Cliffs, New Jersey: Prentice Hall, 1975), pp. 33–35.

4. Ibid., pp. 34–35; Bainbridge, *Biography of an Idea*, pp. 22–28.

5. Bainbridge, *Biography of an Idea*, pp. 22–28.

6. Ibid., pp. 20, 41, 68.

7. R. Carlyle Buley, *The American Life Convention, 1906–1952: A Study in the History of Life Insurance*, vol. I (New York: Appleton-Century-Crofts, 1953), pp. 27–30.

8. Carr, *From Three Cents a Week . . .* , pp. 40–41.

9. Ibid., pp. 41–50.

10. Ibid., pp. 51–65.

11. Zelizer, *Morals and Markets,* pp. 9–18; Buley, *The American Life Convention,* pp. 18–19, 29–31, 42–44.

12. Zelizer, *Morals and Markets,* pp. 48–65.

13. Buley, *The American Life Convention,* p. 32.

14. Ibid., pp. 33–43.

15. Ibid.

16. Ibid., pp. 165–208; Zelizer, *Morals and Markets,* pp. 125–141.

17. Harold F. Williamson and Orange A. Smalley, *Northwestern Mutual Life: A Century of Trusteeship* (Evanston, Illinois: Northwestern University Press, 1957), pp. 100–114; Zelizer, *Morals and Markets,* pp. 17–19; Buley, *The American Life Convention,* pp. 165–208.

18. Buley, *The American Life Convention,* pp. 84–90, 179.

19. Ibid., pp. 199–240; Carr, *From Three Cents a Week . . .* , pp. 44–55; Williamson and Smalley, *Northwestern Mutual,* pp. 133–136.

20. Richard Hooker, *Aetna Life Insurance Company: Its First Hundred Years* (Hartford, Connecticut: Aetna Life Insurance Company, 1956), pp. 134–135.

21. Williamson and Smalley, *Northwestern Mutual,* pp. 136–146.

22. Ibid., pp. 136–137, 143–146; Buley, *The American Life Convention,* pp. 268–301.

23. Buley, *The American Life Convention,* pp. 247–284.

24. Ibid., pp. 68–81.

25. Carr, *From Three Cents a Week . . .* , pp. 38, 68–81.

26. Williamson and Smalley, *Northwestern Mutual,* p. 144.

27. Ibid., pp. 143–146; H. Roger Grant, *Insurance Reform: Consumer Action in the Progressive Era* (Ames: Iowa State University Press, 1979), pp. 46–49, 60–64.

28. Grant, *Insurance Reform,* pp. 49–53, 64–67; Buley, *The American Life Convention,* pp. 324–327.

29. Carr, *From Three Cents a Week . . .* , pp. 159–160.

30. Ibid.

31. Bainbridge, *Biography of an Idea,* pp. 286–302.

32. Ibid., pp. 320–327.

33. Bishop, *Capital Formation through Life Insurance,* pp. 14, 23.

34. Ibid., pp. 62–87, 141, 169.

35. Christopher Byron, "Shake-up in a Staid Industry," *Time* (May 25, 1981), p. 68.

SUGGESTED READINGS

BAINBRIDGE, JOHN. *Biography of an Idea: The Story of Mutual Fire and Casualty Insurance.* Garden City, New York: Doubleday, 1952.

BISHOP, GEORGE A. *Capital Formation through Life Insurance: A Study in the Growth of Life Insurance Services and Investment Activities.* Homewood, Illinois: Richard D. Irwin, 1976.

BULEY, R. CARLYLE. *The American Life Convention, 1906–1952: A Study in the History of Life Insurance.* New York: Appleton-Century-Crofts, 1953.

CADDY, DOUGLAS. *Understanding Texas Insurance.* College Station: Texas A&M University Press, 1984.

CARR, WILLIAM H. A. *From Three Cents a Week . . . The Story of the Prudential Insurance Company of America.* Englewood Cliffs, New Jersey: Prentice Hall, 1975.

CLARK, SYDNEY A. *The First Hundred Years of the New England Mutual Life Insurance Company, 1835–1935.* Concord, New Hampshire: Rumford Press, 1935.

COLTON, JOHN W. *The First Century of the Connecticut Mutual Life Insurance Company, 1846–1946.* Hartford, Connecticut: The Connecticut Mutual Life Insurance Company, 1946.

GRANT, H. ROGER. *Insurance Reform: Consumer Action in the Progressive Era.* Ames: Iowa State University Press, 1979.

HAWTHORNE, DANIEL. *The Hartford of Hartford: An Insurance Company's Part in a Century and a Half of American History.* New York: McClure, Random House, 1960.

HENDRICK, BURTON J. *The Story of Life Insurance.* New York: McClure, Phillips & Co., 1907.

HOOKER, RICHARD. *Aetna Life Insurance Company: Its First Hundred years.* Hartford, Connecticut: Aetna Life Insurance Company, 1956.

JAMES, MARQUIS. *The Metropolitan Life.* New York: Viking Press, 1947.

STAMPER, POWELL. *The National Life Story: A History of the National Life and Accident Insurance Company of Nashville, Tennessee.* New York: Appleton-Century-Crofts, 1968.

WILLIAMSON, HAROLD F., AND ORANGE A. SMALLEY. *Northwestern Mutual Life: A Century of Trusteeship.* Evanston, Illinois: Northwestern University Press, 1957.

ZELIZER, VIVIANA A. ROTMAN. *Morals and Markets: The Development of Life Insurance in the United States.* New York: Columbia University Press, 1979.

13 Banking and Finance

Banking is a business that provides financial services to other businesses and to individuals. The bank's business is to accumulate money, invest money, lend money, and transfer money. In return for these services banks receive interest, fees, service charges, and rentals that constitute income. Because of its intrinsic relation to the welfare of individuals and firms, banking is subject to more government regulation than most businesses. For example, all commercial banks are incorporated by either state or national governmental authority. Most banks today are national banks; but state banks, which operate exclusively under state authority, once exceeded national banks in number and in the volume of business. Indeed, private banks—that is, those owned by individuals operating without a specific legislative charter—once rivaled the state banks in number and capital. Banking structures and practices, and the laws affecting banking, have changed substantially over the past two hundred years, with rapid changes in the last decade.

Banks and bankers have enjoyed wide and largely unquestioned public acceptance in all but a few critical periods in the nation's history—the Revolutionary years, the Jacksonian Era, the Progressive Era, and the Great Depression. The debate in those times centered upon the issue of creating a central or national bank. Central banking, that is the creation of a single national bank or federal authority that would regulate banking and fiscal policy for the entire country, has had a checkered and controversial career.

No central bank, or any bank for that matter, existed in the colonies before the Revolution. Not that they were disapproved of; rather, banks simply seemed unnecessary. "The economy was in an early stage of development," writes one historian, "and until late in the period it was progressing through various stages of poverty."[1] Commercial banks finally appeared in the United States in the decade of the 1780s with the founding in Philadelphia of the Bank of North America in 1781. A central bank, the Bank of the United States, was created by Congress in 1790. By that year each of the four major cities—Baltimore, Philadelphia, Boston, and New York—had banks, and by 1800 all but four states had chartered state banks. Conflicts over money and banking policies, and which level of government had authority to regulate banking, contributed to the rise of political parties in the new nation.

The chartering of the Bank of the United States triggered a conflict between Alexander Hamilton and Thomas Jefferson that led to Jefferson's resignation as secretary of state and the eventual emergence of a two-party system. Banks, Alexander Hamilton remarked two hundred years ago, "are of great importance, not only in relation to the administration of the finances, but in the general system of the political economy."[2] Thomas Jefferson charged that the proposed national bank was both unconstitutional and unnecessary:

> It may be said that a bank whose bills have currency all over the states, would be more convenient than one whose currency is limited to a single state. So it would still be more convenient that there should be a bank, whose bills have currency all over the world. But it does not follow from this superior conveniency, that there exists anywhere a power to establish such a bank; or that the world may not go very well without it.[3]

Despite Jefferson's argument, the Bank of the United States became, for a time, a reality, and in the twentieth century even a world bank emerged. Nevertheless, banking has remained a politicized and controversial business activity.

THE FIRST AND SECOND BANKS
OF THE UNITED STATES

The first Bank of the United States was chartered by Congress for twenty years with a capital stock of $10 million, $8 million of which was subscribed by private investors and $2 million by the federal government. As an incentive to investors, the bank was to be the sole depository of federal funds and the sole lending agency for the national government. In other words, investors received a monopoly on federal banking business. Moreover, the bank received authority to issue bank notes equal in value to the amount of stock, such notes to be legal tender and redeemable in gold or silver. During its life, the bank loaned the federal government some $13.5 million, and several millions to private interests. The Jeffersonian Democrats, however, reflecting their leader's distaste for central banking, chose not to renew the bank's charter in 1811. Stephen Girard subsequently converted the bank into a private bank with $1.5 million capital and operated successfully on the premises of the first national bank.[4]

The United States entered the War of 1812 without a national bank and with few state or private banks. Girard, John Jacob Astor, and others organized a financial syndicate which, in the absence of a national bank, loaned the United States Treasury $16 million for conducting the war. The experiences of the war convinced even the Jeffersonian Democrats of the value of a national bank, and in 1816 Congress chartered the Second Bank of the United States.[5]

The second Bank of the United States "was a central bank in every respect but name," thanks largely to Nicholas Biddle, who "in addition to creating new concepts and new policies as a bankers' banker . . . led investment banking out of its infancy into the stage of adolescence."[6] President James Madison signed the bank's charter on April 10, 1816, providing for a $35 million capital stock subscription of which $7 million was to be purchased by the federal government. Of the twenty-five directors, five were federal appointees. Supporters intended that the bank would curb the radical inflation that had accompanied the war, but in this the bank and its first director, William Jones, failed. Indeed, the bank itself very nearly failed. Jones persisted in redeeming the bank notes with specie while failing to require state banks to do likewise. Thus, the bank paid off in gold but received sometimes worthless bank notes in return. Langdon Cheves followed Jones as director, and Cheves fashioned a policy of deflation through the withdrawal of both credit and currency. He was soon forced to resign, but only after numerous individuals and businesses entered bankruptcy, thus "the Bank was saved and the people ruined."[7]

BROWN BROTHERS COMPANY: BIOGRAPHY OF A BANK

Brown Brothers & Company thrived as a firm of merchant bankers for well over one hundred years. A brief review of the history of the firm illustrates the important family and personal connections that made private banking successful. While the Brown family clearly dominated the firm throughout its history, a healthy injection of in-laws and nonrelatives maintained the firm's vigor.

The founder, Alexander Brown, left Ireland in 1800 for Baltimore after a successful career as an auctioneer. He opened a merchandising firm with his oldest son William, and was soon joined by his other three sons, George, John, and James, who had been left behind in Ireland. Alexander's specialty was the linen trade. He imported linen, most of which was sold to southern customers, and exported cotton, tobacco, rice, or whatever consignments had an attractive market. The firm became Alexander Brown & Sons in 1805, and with the partnership of George (1808), John (1810), and James (1811), the firm became Brown & Sons. William returned to England in 1809 and opened his own firm in Liverpool, but he resumed his partnership with the Baltimore firm in 1815. The Liverpool connection became crucial to the banking enterprises of Brown & Sons.

Brown's own wide acquaintances in England, and the advantage of having a son in business in Liverpool, made his firm popular for the exchange of pounds sterling for dollars or other currencies. Brown began to extend bills of credit to merchants who shipped goods on their account from America to England or vice versa. Next, Brown began to receive goods and ship them to England in exchange for a sight draft of 4- to 6-months duration drawn on the Liverpool office or another bank in England. The drafts were discounted, the discount covering the interest charges, service fees, or other expenses. Having knowledge of merchants in England and America, Brown was able to buy and sell their drafts for sterling or dollars, and to serve as a clearinghouse or bank for merchants on both sides of the Atlantic.

The Browns opened a Charleston agency in 1806, a Savannah agency about 1810, a Philadelphia branch in 1818, a New York office in 1825, a Boston agency in 1844, and had correspondents in New Orleans, Mobile, and other points. Alexander Brown died in 1834, and George, who headed the Baltimore office, withdrew from the partnership. George Brown and his successors maintained their association with other offices, and particularly with the London office (the Liverpool office having closed in 1889) well into the twentieth century. Although private banking in the United States has ceased to exist but for a few isolated instances, family associations in banking have been remarkably characteristic of the industry.

Nicholas Biddle directed the bank with more finesse and delicacy until he was forced into a "bank war" with President Andrew Jackson. Biddle lost. He saw the role of the Bank of the United States as a true central bank whose primary function was to regulate the economy. The bank soon became a bankers' bank, lending money to state banks that pledged specie, currency, or mortgages as collateral. The bank could require repayment of loans in specie, U.S. bank notes, or state-issued currency, or in any proportion, and thereby controlled currency volumes and loan activity. If the national bank, for example, demanded a loan payment or the redemption of state bank notes in specie, the state bank might conceivably be forced to contract its loans outstanding in order to generate the required specie. Although it exercised great influence over state commercial banks, and therefore over economic development, the bank under Biddle was generally expansionist as was the economy. Silver from Mexico and new capital investments from England and France added to specie reserves and the proliferation of paper money. Biddle increased note issues from $3.5 to $19 million, and domestic bills of exchange from $9 to $49 million.[8]

State banks chafed under the financial controls imposed by the national bank, and states protested the immunity of branches of the bank from state taxation, which implied impairment of their sovereignty. Some "hard money" credit interests believed that only gold should circulate as a medium of exchange, while "soft money" people wanted "cheap" or paper money and abundant and easy credit. Whigs and anti-Jackson people sought to use the bank as a vehicle to dethrone "King Andrew." Congress passed a bill in 1832 rechartering the second Bank of the United States

Nicholas Biddle (1766–1844). Banker, financier, president of the Second Bank of the United States. (Courtesy: *Dictionary of American Portraits*.)

for twenty years, but President Jackson vetoed it. Nicholas Biddle responded to the veto by drastically reducing the supply of currency and credit. Jackson countered by refusing to deposit federal money in the bank while withdrawing existing deposits. When Biddle's recession failed to force approval of a new charter, he altered his strategy by flooding the country with paper money and easy credit. A speculative boom followed that Jackson defused with the "Specie Circular" which required payment for public lands in specie. A severe depression followed, and the bank, which was rechartered by the state of Pennsylvania in 1836, was forced into bankruptcy in 1841.[9]

Despite the political storms that surrounded the national banks, they contributed significantly to economic expansion between 1790 and 1840. They facilitated the accumulation of private and public capital, helped attract an estimated $500 million in foreign investments, and established a stable currency that did much to facilitate domestic and foreign trade. National banking ceased from 1836 to 1863, when a National Bank Act provided some uniformity in financial and monetary policies. Subsequently the Federal Reserve Act of 1913 established a central banking facility, but one not so powerful as the two Banks of the United States.[10] State banks with widely ranging charters and disparate regulations dominated the financial scene between 1840 and 1860, when railroad construction, steamboat building, westward expansion, and industrialization all fueled the demand for easier credit and conflicted with the desire of merchants and international traders for sound money. Louisiana, whose banks ranked third behind New York and Massachusetts in banking capital in 1840, provides an excellent example of the character and problems of banking in the expansive antebellum era.

STATE BANKING IN LOUISIANA

New Orlean's position as the nation's second-largest port and as a hub of interregional and international trade made banking particularly vital to its economy. Louisiana banking was atypically conservative in that it was the most subsidized and closely regulated of all pre–Civil War state banking systems. Louisiana's banks, like those of most states, served three distinctive banking functions: (1) They provided a mechanism for accumulating and investing savings, (2) they attempted to maintain an adequate money supply, and (3) they provided for domestic and foreign exchange. Louisiana's state banks fell into three legal categories: *chartered banks* created by separate, special acts of the legislature; *free banks* which, while incorporated, were created by blanket authorization of the legislature in 1853; and *private banks*, which were unincorporated ventures of a single proprietor or partnership and were subject to the general laws governing financial transactions but could not issue bank notes. Until the 1840s Louisiana banks were further differentiated by their function or purpose. *Property banks*, for example, made loans on real property. *Improvement banks* were designed to finance construction projects such as railroads and canals. *Commercial banks* essentially financed trade and commerce, but by the 1840s they had assumed all the banking activities of the property and improvement banks, which were liquidated under authority of the state.[11]

The Louisiana Bank, established in 1804 by the territorial legislature with a capital of $300,000, was the first bank established in Louisiana. It was joined almost immediately by the New Orleans Branch of the Bank of the United States. When the first Bank of the United States expired in 1811, the territorial legislature chartered the Bank of Orleans and the Planters' Bank. The Planters' Bank barely survived the War of 1812, while the Bank of Orleans operated until 1847. A branch of the second Bank of the United States opened in New Orleans in 1817, and the state legislature chartered the Louisiana State Bank in 1818. The latter issued $2 million in capital stock and the state purchased $500,000 of the securities. Five branches were established outside of New Orleans with each branch capitalized at $100,000. A few years later the state created the Bank of Louisiana capitalized at $14 million, with one half of the stock to be acquired by the state. Again, in deference to rural legislators, the bank established five branches and was required to devote two-thirds of its capital to mortgage loans.[12] While rural-urban conflicts permeated banking legislation in the state throughout the nineteenth century, cooperative government-private ownership of banking was widely accepted in Louisiana as well as on the federal level.

The Consolidated Association of Planters of Louisiana provides an interesting study of Louisiana's first property bank and of a mechanism by which states could provide financing for state banks. Chartered in 1827, the bank received $2.5 million in mortgages in exchange for $2 million in capital stock. The mortgages were then used as collateral for the issue of $2 million in bonds that were to be sold abroad. Unfortunately, the bonds did not sell. The state then stepped in and tendered $2.5 million in state bonds

The Bank of Louisiana in New Orleans was built in 1826 under a state charter. (Courtesy: Louisiana Office of Tourism.)

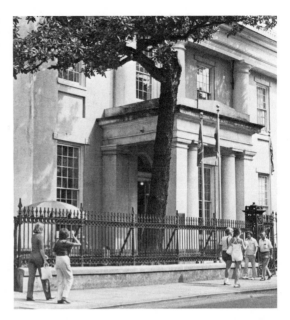

in exchange for $3 million in bond mortgages. The state bonds did sell and the bank began operation.[13]

Improvement banks—such as the Canal Bank established in 1831 to build a canal from the city to Lake Pontchartrain, and the Gas Light and Banking Company, which operated a $550,000 lighting system—were designed for specific projects but had incidental banking powers. Most improvement banks ceased to exist after the completion of the project, whereas others, such as the Canal Bank and Trust Company, survived into the twentieth century.[14] The Louisiana Constitution of 1845 prohibited deficit financing of public improvement projects and marked the end of improvement banks. The constitution also contributed to a contraction in the banking industry, which, in turn, imposed constraints on trade and commerce at a time when money and credit should have expanded.

This financial retrenchment after 1840 reflected national "antibank" sentiment that came on the heels of the Jackson-Biddle "bank war" and, with the depression of 1845, retarded economic development until 1853, when a new constitution and more liberal banking laws were adopted. Louisiana's financial institutions became increasingly committed to financing cotton, regional commerce, and slaves rather than supporting public improvements and industrial projects. Banks preferred short-term obligations, such as financing the production of a cotton crop for the New Orleans market, while leaving longer-term shipping and international trade business to northern banks. Most historians now reject the proposition that planter political dominance thwarted the creation of effective financial institutions that could promote industrial expansion. Rather, Louisiana's banks served the primary businesses of the region—cotton, sugar, commerce, and slavery—and earned greater returns than could have been achieved by investment in industrial plants and equipment.[15]

State and federal banking policies tended to extremes. Banking policies were often too loose or too conservative, and the legislative pendulum often swung between the two in a relatively brief time. Changes in state and federal banking policies such as occurred when the national banks were abolished or when Louisiana prohibited the deficit financing of public improvement projects contributed to the cyclical swings of the national and regional economies.

THE NATIONAL BANKS

The number of banks in the United States rose sharply in the decade of the 1830s, reaching a total of 901 in 1840 with combined assets of $658 million. The number of banks and the size of their assets declined rapidly in the early 1840s to 700 banks with assets of $434 million. This substantial reduction cannot be attributed simply to either antibank sentiment or to Andrew Jackson's Specie Circular of 1836. Historian Peter Temin argues rather that the Bank of England raised its discount rates and otherwise constricted credit, which resulted over the long term in international trade constraints, lower cotton prices, and, as a consequence, more commercial bankruptcies.[16]

In contrast to the 1840s the decade before the Civil War witnessed a boom in banking activities stimulated no doubt by the influx of gold from California and expanding exports of cotton and wheat. The number of banks rose from 824 in 1850 to 1,562 with $1 billion in assets by 1860.[17] Although the Civil War brought ruin to most banks in the southern states, the number and total assets of banks elsewhere actually grew. The National Bank Act of 1863 created a new central banking authority and established a structure for American banking that continued until passage of the Federal Reserve Act in 1913.

The National Bank Act provided for voluntary membership in an association created under the auspices of the Treasury Department. Specifically, the comptroller of the currency would approve national bank charters. Member banks were required to purchase federal bonds of up to one-third of their capital depending upon the size of the community in which the bank was located. Until 1933 banks were liable for losses up to double the par value of their stock, and after 1933 liability was limited to par. Member banks could issue a standard bank note acceptable by all others in exchange, but the total issue of such notes could not exceed $300 million. The notes issued by each bank had to be secured by an equal amount of government bonds. Banks were limited in the size of loans that could be made to a single borrower and in the value of loans secured only by real estate.[18] The system involved no real central banking authority, but it did promote the credibility of banks.

The system attracted few customers during the war years. But in 1865 Congress amended the act to exempt member banks from a 10 percent tax it had levied on state bank note issues in March 1865. It now became unprofitable for state banks to issue their own notes and profitable for them to join the national bank system. Member banks jumped from 467 in 1864 to 1,294 in 1865.[19] The 1865 act produced other consequences. It forced the retirement of large quantities of private and state bank notes, thus reducing the money supply in a time of rapidly expanding business activity; between 1865 and 1869 money in circulation was reduced by 30 percent. Credit costs soared, particularly for farmers in the West and South, and what capital was available tended to be concentrated in the industrial and financial centers of the Northeast. Paper-money deflation was paralleled by the elimination of silver coins as a medium of exchange. In 1873 Congress "demonitized," or removed silver from the currency system, an act later called the Crime of '73, thus further contracting the money supply.[20]

The Civil War left the country in a state of financial and monetary chaos. Inflation became rampant and the "good faith and credit" of the federal government was questioned. The nation had accumulated a massive per capita debt and had issued over $400 million in "greenbacks" or unsecured paper money. The prevailing wisdom, which would later be strongly challenged by "greenbackers" and "free-silver" advocates, held that the only resolution of the financial problem was to reestablish the gold standard and pay off the war debt. Congress passed legislation that proceeded to do just that. In 1869 and 1870 Congress refunded the war debt, ultimately providing for the repayment of bonds in gold that had most often been bought with "cheap" paper money. On July 2, 1879, Congress made "greenbacks" (that is, paper dollars), national bank notes, and Treasury-issued gold certificates redeemable in gold, thus putting the country on the gold standard. American monetary values became "hard" and fixed at about $4.86 to the British pound sterling.[21] The post–Civil War years became characterized by rapid deflation.

Wholesale prices fell almost 50 percent between 1875 and 1879, the total money supply increased at about 1 percent a year, and the value of goods and services rose at an annual rate of 3 to 5 percent. Additional deflationary pressures were being created. The national debt fell from $61 per capita in 1868 to about $12 in 1918. Much of that debt resulted from the sale of government bonds in exchange for greenbacks. The greenbacks that had circulated at a gold premium of 50 to 100 (that is, it required $150 to $200 in greenbacks to buy $100 in gold) were retired in gold.[22] Bondholders conceivably could receive three times their original investment. In eliminating wide variations in currency values, Reconstruction Era fiscal policies created a favorable climate for international trade and for the financial community, yet they also contributed to economic and social inequities and to farmer and labor unrest. New tax policies, particularly the elimination of the wartime income tax and manufacturers' tax and the imposition of high protective tariffs, generated a downward shift in real wages.[23] These policies also created new problems for the banking community.

Currency for ordinary business transactions became increasingly scarce, and credit, both for banks and their customers, became dear. The currency problem led to an innovation in banking that has continued to develop in interesting ways to the present day. Demand deposits, that is, "checkbook money," began to replace cash. Additional relief for the currency crisis came with cheaper and more efficient metallurgical processes, which resulted in greater gold production and new discoveries of that precious metal. A very modest amount of silver was reintroduced into the coinage system with the passage of the Bland-Allison Act of 1878, which authorized the Treasury to issue between $2 and $4 million of silver at prevailing market prices per month. The silver was to be coined into dollars of 412.5 grains each and to be circulated only if the federal government achieved an annual surplus of less that $24 million per year.[24] Farm and silver-mining interests continued to press for additional government purchases of silver, and thus in 1890 Congress approved the Sherman Silver Purchase Act, which authorized the Treasury to buy 4.5 million ounces of silver per month, with payment to be made in treasury notes. The treasury notes, however, were never redeemed in silver but always in gold, and the act did not increase the price of silver or stimulate farm prices as farmers anticipated.

As the value of silver dropped because of new production in the West, debtors, farmers, and silver miners began to flock to the banner of the People's (Populist) Party of America, which advocated, among other things, free and unlimited coinage of silver at a ratio of 16 units of silver to 1 of gold, a ratio which by 1893 would have allowed debtors to pay their debts with distinctively "cheaper" money. Demands for legal tender paper money and the free and unlimited coinage of silver rose sharply with the severe depression that struck in 1893. Credit and currency became even more scarce, and farm prices reached new lows. By 1896 the Democratic party had endorsed free silver and selected William Jennings Bryan to head the ticket. Currency issues, credit constraints, and cyclical fluctuations in the money supply accompanied by recurring financial panics produced the politically potent stirrings of the farmer and labor movements, which led to the Progressive Era and the substantive banking reforms of 1913.

THE FEDERAL RESERVE SYSTEM

The Aldrich-Vreeland Act of 1908, which paved the way for the Federal Reserve Act, derived partly from the preponderant distribution of treasury balances in the eastern and principally New York banks, and partly from the very real shortages of cash to finance the movement of crops from southern and western farms to market. The act established an association of banks to serve as a clearinghouse for checks. Members could issue bank notes secured by approved city, county, and state bonds—notes that eastern bankers promptly opposed and labeled emergency currency and funny money. The act recognized the need for central banking and made some movement back in that direction, but its real significance lay in the creation of the National Monetary Commission cochaired by Senator Nelson Aldrich and Congressman Edward Vreeland.[25]

The recommendations of the Monetary Commission resulted in a bill to create a National Reserve Association comprised of fifteen regional associations or branches. Member banks would own stock in the association, a bankers' bank governed by an advisory bureau and a board of forty-six directors among whom were specified government officials and presidential appointees. Although the bill received the support of President William Howard Taft and the American Bankers Association, it disappeared in the political upheavals of 1912 that brought Woodrow Wilson and the Democratic party to power.

The Democrats continued to pursue the central bank idea, and Congress passed the Federal Reserve Act, which created a system more public but less centralized than that envisioned under the National Reserve Association. The act created twelve largely independent regional reserve banks with a central bank holding advisory power. Each Federal Reserve Bank was required to maintain certain reserves and could issue notes and set a rediscount rate (the rate of interest on loans to member banks). All national banks were required to be members of the Federal Reserve System, and state banks could join if they desired. The system facilitated the more rapid and efficient payment of checks by allowing member banks to clear through their respective Federal Reserve regional bank. That is, a check sent to a business in New York and drawn on the Citizen's Bank in Valdosta, Georgia, would be presented to the New York Federal Reserve Bank, which would forward the check to the Atlanta Federal Reserve Bank, where the amount would be deducted from the Citizen's Bank account. Formerly such a check might have entered the accounts of a dozen banks and physically traveled thousands of miles. The system made currency and credit more flexible and attainable.

A member bank could obtain additional Federal Reserve notes by borrowing from the Federal Reserve on commercial paper (that is, on notes or

The Federal Reserve Board with secretary of the treasury William G. McAdoo as its first president, 1914. (Courtesy: Board of Governors of the Federal Reserve System.)

promises to pay by businesses), by selling government bonds for cash, and by simply borrowing on its own credit. The Federal Reserve, in turn, regulated the volume of currency and credit by varying the rediscount rate. Thus, if a business decided to borrow $100,000 from a local bank, it might expect to pay the prevailing prime rate, say 17 percent, or for one year $17,000 in interest charges, usually discounted at the bank. That is, the customer would receive $83,000 and pay back $100,000. If the rediscount rate is 12 percent, the bank might very well take the note to the Federal Reserve System and receive credit for $88,000, which could then be loaned again at 17 percent. If the rediscount rate is raised, a bank will be less inclined to discount a note at the Federal Reserve Bank and to lend money to a customer unless the bank can charge a higher prime rate, at which point the customer is likely to balk. Thus, higher rediscount rates ultimately result in fewer financial transactions and slow business expansion, while lower rates presumably, but not invariably, create a larger volume of business.

Banks also control business activity through open-market operations. The sale of government securities by reserve banks reduces currency in circulation, that is, cash is received by the bank in exchange for noncirculating bonds. The purchase of government securities by the bank, on the other hand, increases the supply of currency in that cash replaces noncirculating securities. The new banking system by no means solved the nation's banking and fiscal problems. The Federal Reserve System possessed little real central authority until much later. It did, however, make currency and credit more flexible and available and established a reasonably efficient clearinghouse for the transfer of checks from one bank to another. The number of commercial banks and their assets rose rapidly between 1913 and 1930, due primarily to World War I and the postwar economic boom. In 1920 the United States boasted over 30,000 commercial banks with assets nearing $47 billion. Assets continued to grow during the 1920s, although consolidation, suspensions, and bankruptcies reduced the number of banks to 23,000 with assets of $64 billion by 1930.[26] Subsequently, banks and bankers faced their worst crisis, the Great Depression.

THE DEPRESSION

Within a four-year period the number of banks in the United States declined from 25,568, with assets in excess of $72 billion, to 14,771, with assets of $51 billion. Perhaps no figures more dramatically tell the story of the depression. Certainly the depression cannot be attributed solely to banking practices, yet they were intrinsic to its coming. Banks enthusiastically committed themselves to the stock market and investment booms of the 1920s, but of course they were not alone. The Federal Reserve Board, for example, lowered the rediscount rate to 3.5 percent by 1927. As a result, borrowing by member banks and business rose markedly. Tax cuts and the Soldiers Bonus, as well as the very real increases in productivity and corporate profits, fed the expansive and increasingly speculative market. Stock prices soared. Too fast, some thought. In 1928 Benjamin Strong, chairman of the Federal Reserve Bank of New York, raised the rediscount rate from 3.5 to 5 percent, but the flow of money into brokers accounts to be loaned to buyers who purchased stock on credit continued unabated. Corporations found that using their surplus funds to finance stock purchases, or even buying their own or other corporate stock, was more profitable than investing in new plants and equipment. Although there were many causes for the Great Depression, the Federal Reserve Board and the large commercial banks contributed to both the stock market boom and its ultimate crash.[27]

Despite tremors in the stock market in 1928 and early 1929, bankers such as Charles Mitchell of the National City Bank and Treasury Secretary Andrew W. Mellon voiced continued optimism. Historian John Kenneth Galbraith has argued that the Federal Reserve failed to slow the boom of 1928 and 1929, and that it was helpless "only because it wanted to be." He believes that bankers should have obtained special Congressional permission to raise margin requirements, or at least publicly advised caution and retrenchment.[28] More recent analyses hold that, on the contrary, the Federal Reserve Board failed to increase the money supply adequately during the 1928–1929 "boomlet," and pursued a policy of disastrous retrenchment until 1933, which helped precipitate, and then aggravate, the depression.

The consensus of Franklin Roosevelt's New Dealers was that the Federal Reserve needed strengthening, and certainly that the faith of the American people in the banking system needed to be rekindled. In Febru-

A "run" on the People's Trust and Savings, Chicago, in June 1932. (Courtesy: Franklin D. Roosevelt Library.)

ary and March 1933 bank panics swept the nation. Herbert Hoover termed it the Great Fear, which he attributed to the uncertainties and the presumed irresponsibility of the incoming Democratic administration. Almost 4,000 state and national banks failed in 1933 alone. President Roosevelt declared a bank holiday on March 6, two days after assuming office, and closed all of the nation's banks. Three days later Congress passed the Emergency Banking Act, which provided for the appointment of examiners to inspect all banks and certify those that were sound, authorized the secretary of treasury to issue larger quantities of Federal Reserve notes, and called in gold and gold certificates. Loans were made to banks with liquidity problems, and most banks reopened for business in a matter of weeks—but some never did. The panic stopped, and public confidence in the banks was slowly restored.

In other actions the New Deal removed the United States from the gold standard, immediately making currency and credit more flexible and also subject to greater political management. In June 1933 Congress voided all obligations to pay debts in gold; in October the Reconstruction Finance Corporation began to purchase gold on the domestic market; and in November the New York Federal Reserve Bank began international purchases, continually but erratically increasing the number of dollars paid for an ounce of gold. These open-market operations inflated the dollar to a level equal to 59.06 percent of its 1900 value. Congress fixed the value of gold at that level ($35 per ounce), where it remained until the 1970s. Currency inflation provided some immediate relief for the financial crisis and offered longer-term relief for debtors who could pay debts contracted when gold was worth $20 per ounce with dollars based on gold valued at $35 an ounce.

The Glass-Steagall Banking Act, approved by Congress in June 1933, created the Federal Deposit Insurance Corporation (FDIC), which insured personal and business bank deposits up to certain levels with fees paid by banks according to the size of their deposits. Regulation Q enabled the Board of Governors to establish limits on interest rates banks could pay for time and savings deposits and prohibited the payment of interest on demand deposits. The act also separated commercial and investment banking. Commercial banks could no longer sell securities, and investment banks could not accept deposits and had to confine their activities to underwriting and marketing securities.

Two years later an amendment to the 1933 act created a board of governors for the Federal Reserve System whose seven members were all appointed by the president. The board was also authorized to appoint the heads of district banks and to set reserve requirements and approve discount rates. An open-market committee created by the 1933 act was reorganized to include the board of governors and five representatives of the district reserve banks. Since the 1930s the central banking authority of the Federal Reserve System has generally increased. Modern banking is increasingly characterized by consolidation of banks within holding companies, diversification in functions and services, and sophistication in the simple mechanics of banking. The relatively clear line of demarcation between the activities of commercial banks, mutual-savings banks, investment banks, and even insurance companies is beginning to fade. These changes reflect, in part, the efforts of commercial banks to circumvent the restrictive credit policies of the Federal Reserve Board. There are some historical parallels between events of the Jacksonian Era and contemporary affairs in that banks have recently tried to reassert a greater degree of autonomy and independence from the central authority.

BANKING IN THE MODERN ERA

The number of banks in the United States has remained relatively stable since 1945, but their assets have increased fourfold. The national economy and the population have grown so rapidly that financial institutions have been forced to become more flexible, to offer a greater diversity of services, and to be more competitive. Competition has been somewhat stymied by federal and state laws often designed to meet situations long past. Nevertheless, financial institutions have been quite innovative in offering new services and in circumventing state and federal banking restrictions.

For example, state and federal laws generally require commercial banks to engage in banking only; they are precluded from certain investment, trust, and savings activities. But by the 1950s bankers began to organize holding companies, which, not being chartered banks, could engage in nonbank activities that the associated banks could not. Congress subsequently enacted the Bank Holding Company Act of 1956, which halted the intrusion of holding companies into the business of regular investment banks by prohibiting the bank holding companies from acquiring shares of any company that was not a bank. The act did leave a loophole in specifying that holding companies could engage in activities "closely related to banking." In 1966 Congress amended the act to exempt holding companies that held stock in only one bank. Shortly thereafter "one-bank holding companies exceeded the assets of those covered by the Bank Holding Company Act."[29] In 1970 Congress brought the one-bank holding companies back under the authority of Federal Reserve regulations; this contributed to a decline in membership in the Federal Reserve System as banks concluded that the only way to evade Federal Reserve restraints was to withdraw from the Federal Reserve System. Assets of Federal Reserve member banks declined from 79 to 72 percent of total bank assets between 1974 and 1978.[30]

Withdrawal from the Federal Reserve System was a symptom of competition for deposits. The Federal Reserve System imposed limits on interest payments to bank customers with savings and time deposits, and it prohibited the payment of interest on demand deposits. Savings and loan associations generally had the right to pay slightly higher rates of interest on their savings accounts, and they attracted new customers and possible bank deposits by offering depositors limited checking and withdrawal rights on their accounts. They began to offer, in effect, bank checking services. Commercial banks then entered into the savings and loan field in 1960 by offering certificates of deposit (CDs) or long-term savings instruments with higher interest rates than conventional bank savings accounts. The volume of CDs rose from $1 billion to $20 billion in the first seven years they were offered.[31] Savings and loan deposits, however, began to decline.

C&S NATIONAL BANK

In the post–World War II era, few banks have rivaled the growth of the Citizens and Southern National Bank of Atlanta, Georgia. Founded well after the fall of Atlanta and the collapse of the Confederacy in 1865, C&S National Bank began as a sleepy, conservative, small-town bank, only to become one of the largest, most progressive, and competitive regional banks in the United States. This bank captured the spirit of modern banking more than any other by stressing its role as a *consumer's* bank rather than merely a commercial bank. It has been a leader in banking innovation and improvisation, which has not always won it accolades in the industry.

The bank had five branches outside of Atlanta when Georgia approved legislation severely restricting the expansion of branch banking. Under the direction of Mills B. Lane, Jr., who served as president of the bank for over thirty years, C&S found ingenious ways to expand. C&S organized its own registered bank holding company that, by 1970, had bought interests in or controlled over forty affiliated banks, some as far away as New Haven, Connecticut, and San Juan, Puerto Rico.

C&S introduced its own bank credit card in 1959, pioneering in a consumer credit device that did not sweep the nation until the late 1960s. Special "high interest" (4.5 percent) certificates of deposit, then almost unknown in banks, attracted unusually large deposits and enabled C&S not only to weather a business slump in 1965–1966 but also to provide expanded credit for burgeoning Atlanta businesses. In the 1960s, when civil rights movements and marches were having political and economic repercussions throughout Georgia and the South, C&S's newly organized Consumer Development Corporation provided financing for low-income housing and small-business loans aimed at aiding black business. For the suburbs and smaller towns, C&S branches were outfitted in Gay Nineties or frontier decor, and checks were delivered by helicopter. Banking, Mills Lane believed, should be fun as well as profitable. Banking had become a media and public relations event, a business that consciously competed for the mass consumer.

Beginning in June 1978 commercial banks as well as savings and loan associations began offering investors money market certificates (MMCs)—instruments similar to the certificate of deposit, but with two distinctive characteristics. The money market certificate offered a short, six-month maturity and a variable rate of interest. In a period when interest rates seemed to be constantly rising, the MMCs offered a particularly attractive investment opportunity in preference to the long-term CDs, and even to government bonds. By January 1979 over $32 billion had been invested in money market certificates.[32] Another innovation that allowed banks to evade the Federal Reserve requirement prohibiting the payment of interest on demand deposits was the NOW account. Introduced about 1980, deposits technically remain in a regular savings account until a check is drawn, whereon equivalent funds are automatically transferred to a checking or demand account.

The most popular and massive innovation of modern banking has been "plastic money." Credit cards such as VISA and Master Card have greatly expanded the range of consumer loans and have brought banks into competition with older credit card and marketing firms such as Diner's Club and American Express. In addition, branch banking has been an innovation of the post–World War II era in many areas where it is not prohibited by state statute.

Banks also moved quickly to reduce administrative costs through computer technology. Electronic fund-transfer systems that link computerized accounts slowly replaced the use of checks. Point-of-sale systems allowed clerical transfer of funds from a customer's account to a merchant's account in order to make a purchase. Payroll, retirement, and social security payments have also been handled by electronic transfer. These devices accelerated the clearance of funds, and in times of 18 to 24 percent interest, time was indeed money.

Banking is intrinsic to the general economic welfare. It has variously been both a private and a public business, and the country has operated both with and without a central bank. There are those who believe that banking should be completely divorced from the political system; similarly, there is a trend toward "deregulation," but it is more a product of innovative marketing than a political mandate. Concurrently, the traditional distinctions between the commercial banks, savings and loans, investment banks, and other financial intermediaries are beginning to fade. Modern banking is experiencing more radical changes in style and technique than perhaps any other area of American enterprise—the better, presumably, to serve business and the public.

NOTES

1. Herman E. Krooss and Martin R. Blyn, *A History of Financial Intermediaries* (New York: Random House, 1971), p. 12.

2. Alexander Hamilton, "Report on Financing" (December 5, 1791), in *The Reports of Alexander Hamilton,* Jacob E. Cooke, ed. (New York: Harper & Row, 1964), p. 60.

3. *The Writings of Thomas Jefferson,* vol. 6, Andrew A. Lipscomb, ed. (Washington, D.C.: Thomas Jefferson Memorial Association, 1903), p. 153.

4. See Bray Hammond, *Banks and Politics in America from the Revolution to the Civil War* (Princeton, New Jersey: Princeton University Press, 1957).

5. Ibid.; and see Krooss and Blyn, *A History of Financial Intermediaries,* p. 34.

6. Ibid., pp. 41, 44.

7. Ibid., p. 45.

8. See Robert V. Remini, *Andrew Jackson* (New York: Twayne Publishers, 1966; reprinted, New York: Harper & Row, 1969), pp. 141–168.

9. Ibid.

10. See Rendigs Fels, "American Business Cycles, 1865–79," *The American Economic Review* 41 (June 1951), pp. 325–349.

11. George D. Green, *Finance and Economic Development in the Old South: Louisiana Banking, 1804–1861* (Stanford, California: Stanford University Press, 1972), pp. 5–17.

12. Ibid., pp. 18–24.

13. Ibid., p. 21.

14. Ibid., pp. 33–35.

15. Ibid., pp. 177–181.

16. Richard H. Timberlake, Jr., *The Origins of Central Banking in the United States* (Cambridge: Harvard University Press, 1978), p. 62; also *Historical Statistics of the United States, Colonial Times to 1970*, Series X580–587, p. 1020.

17. *Historical Statistics*, Series X580–587, p. 1020.

18. See Rendigs Fels, "American Business Cycles, 1865–79," pp. 325–49; Timberlake, *The Origins of Central Banking*, pp. 87–88; Krooss and Blyn, *A History of Financial Intermediaries*, pp. 96–97; and Walter T.K. Nugent, *The Money Question during Reconstruction* (New York: W.W. Norton & Co., 1967), pp. 1–92.

19. *Historical Statistics*, Series X645–655, p. 1027.

20. Nugent, *The Money Question during Reconstruction*, pp. 69–92.

21. Ibid.

22. Ibid.

23. See Harry N. Scheiber, "Economic Change in the Civil War Era: An Analysis of Recent Studies," *Civil War History* 11 (December 1965), pp. 396–411.

24. Timberlake, *The Origins of Central Banking*, pp. 120–153.

25. Ibid., pp. 186–191.

26. *Historical Statistics*, Series X588–609, p. 1020, and Series X741–755, p. 1038.

27. Robert Sobel, *The Great Bull Market: Wall Street in the 1920s* (New York: W.W. Norton & Co., 1968), pp. 21, 92–93, 104–118.

28. John Kenneth Galbraith, *The Great Crash, 1929* (Boston: Houghton Mifflin, 1954), pp. 37–116; and see Peter Temin, *Did Monetary Forces Cause the Great Depression?* (New York: W.W. Norton & Co., 1976).

29. Herbert E. Dougall and Jack E. Gaumnitz, *Capital Markets and Institutions* (Englewood Cliffs, New Jersey: Prentice Hall, 1975), pp. 27–44.

30. Ibid., p. 45.

31. Kroos and Blyn, *A History of Financial Intermediaries*, pp. 226–227.

32. Dougall and Gaumnitz, *Capital Markets and Institutions*, p. 48; over $140 billion was invested by 1982.

SUGGESTED READINGS

ADAMS, DONALD R. *Finance and Enterprise in Early America: A Study of Stephen Girard's Bank, 1812–1831*. Philadelphia: University of Pennsylvania Press, 1978.

BUENGER, WALTER L., AND JOSEPH A. PRATT. *But Also Good Business: Texas Commerce Banks and the Financing of Houston and Texas, 1886–1986*. College Station: Texas A&M University Press, 1986.

CAROSSO, VINCENT P. *The Morgans: Private International Bankers, 1854–1913*. Cambridge: Harvard University Press, 1987.

CLEVELAND, HAROLD VAN B., AND THOMAS F. HUERTAS. *Citibank, 1812–1970*. Cambridge: Harvard University Press, 1985.

COOPER, S. KERRY, AND DONALD FRASER. *Banking Deregulation and the New Competition in Financial Services*. Cambridge, Massachusetts: Ballinger, 1984.

DOUGALL, HERBERT E., and JACK E. GAUMNITZ. *Capital Markets and Institutions.* Englewood Cliffs, New Jersey: Prentice Hall, 1975.

GALBRAITH, JOHN KENNETH. *The Great Crash, 1929.* Boston: Houghton Mifflin, 1954.

GREEN, GEORGE D. *Finance and Economic Development in the Old South: Louisiana Banking, 1804–1861.* Stanford, California: Stanford University Press, 1972.

HAMMOND, BRAY. *Banks and Politics in America from the Revolution to the Civil War.* Princeton, New Jersey: Princeton University Press, 1957.

———. *Sovereignty and an Empty Purse: Banks and Politics in the Civil War.* Princeton, New Jersey: Princeton University Press, 1970.

KROOSS, HERMAN E., and MARTIN R. BLYN. *A History of Financial Intermediaries.* New York: Random House, 1971.

KROOSS, HERMAN E., ed., and "Introduction" by Paul A. Samuelson. Four volumes. *Documentary History of Banking and Currency in the United States.* New York: Chelsea House, 1969.

LIVINGSTON, JAMES. *Origin of the Federal Reserve System: Money, Class, and Corporate Capitalism, 1890–1913.* Ithaca, New York: Cornell University Press, 1986.

NUGENT, WALTER T. K. *The Money Question during Reconstruction.* New York: W. W. Norton & Co., 1967.

OLMSTEAD, ALAN L. *New York City Mutual Savings Banks, 1819–1861.* Chapel Hill: University of North Carolina Press, 1976.

SCHWEIKART, LARRY. *Banking in the American South from the Age of Jackson to Reconstruction.* Baton Rouge: Louisiana State University Press, 1988.

SOBEL, ROBERT. *The Great Bull Market: Wall Street in the 1920s.* New York: W. W. Norton & Co., 1968.

TEMIN, PETER. *Did Monetary Forces Cause the Great Depression?* New York: W. W. Norton & Co., 1976.

TIMBERLAKE, RICHARD H., JR., *The Origins of Central Banking in the United States.* Cambridge: Harvard University Press, 1978.

14 | Foreign Trade

Foreign trade has been a major component of business activity throughout the nation's history. While American thought about business has been generally insular, business activity has always had a strong international dimension. The American colonists acquired capital and finished goods only by exchanging their crude products with English and Dutch traders. The modern multinational corporation is, as will be seen later, a logical extension of transatlantic merchant partnerships of colonial times. Between 1800 and 1980 the total volume of international transactions between the United States and foreign countries has grown from about $200 million annually to $200 billion.[1] The growth in foreign trade required the rebuilding of important structures and institutions that were lost after the United States declared its independence from the British Empire in 1776. Capital, credit, military forces, consulates and diplomatic missions, foreign-exchange facilities, and of course transportation, are all active ingredients of effective international trade. Foreign trade is basic to the welfare of a modern industrial nation. It is a complex business that must transcend language barriers, differing monetary systems, political and governmental impediments, as well as physical obstacles and vast distances.

Three major structures or institutional groupings make foreign trade possible: The business or corporation effects the actual trade of goods or services; the "money changer," or banker, transfers funds and exchanges currencies; the governments on both sides may impose regulations and taxes on the transaction or, to stimulate trade, may remove such constraints. For example, if Texas Instruments wishes to sell computer chips to Deutsch Industrie of West Germany, the initial contact may be made by a trade representative. The contact could be facilitated by a government-sponsored trade fair, an institution which is itself about as old as foreign trade. Once the sale is made, deutsch marks must be exchanged for dollars and transferred to the United States. The international banking transaction may involve a variety of currencies, all affected by governmental policies. The goods must then be shipped, cleared for export by a governmental authority, and received and taxed by yet another government. The exchange is, of course, greatly simplified when both Texas Instruments and Deutsch Industrie have corporate offices and bank accounts in each country.

Although this example is simplistic, the point is that foreign trade necessarily involves businesses, banks, and governments. This was true when Christopher Columbus established the first trading post in the New World, when Admiral Perry opened Japan to the West, when during the era of Dollar Diplomacy Minor Keith built railroads and developed United Fruit in Central America and Daniel Guggenheim opened copper mines in Mexico, as well as in the post–World War II era of international capitalism. This chapter attempts to capture a little of the flavor and illustrate some of the mechanics of foreign trade insofar as it relates to the direct exchange of goods and services. The story of the multinational corporations, which have direct investments abroad, is reserved for a later chapter.

DOLLAR DIPLOMACY

The idea that the federal government should actively promote and assist American bankers, businesspeople, and manufacturers in developing opportunities for profit in international trade did not originate with the Dollar Diplomacy of William Howard Taft's administration. Throughout the nineteenth century the government ordinarily responded positively to the needs of business interests overseas; and conversely, American investments abroad advanced United States foreign policy. American experiences with the China trade offer an example of government's active support of foreign trade.

As we have seen, following the close of the American Revolution the *Empress of China* left New York harbor with a cargo of trade goods and returned a year later, its hold filled with exotic herbs and artifacts from the Orient. Other merchant vessels followed, and in 1801 four American merchantmen reached Canton. By 1850 the China trade had become the prize of the stately and swift clipper ships, serviced along the way by American settlements scattered across the Pacific. In the early decades of this transpacific trade, the ships and seamen survived, if they did, in a precarious world. Official Chinese policy viewed Americans as barbarians and "foreign devils" with no rights, and certainly no privileges. China suffered Americans to land only in the open port of Canton, where they could engage in their "sordid" business. Crews were often imprisoned and merchants suffered indignities, yet the United States government established no official contacts with any far eastern government.

In 1832 the government did send Edmund Roberts as a special agent with instructions to conclude commercial treaties or trade agreements with Cochin China, Siam, Muscat, and Japan. His refusal to bow to the Chinese emperor led to the failure of his mission there, and very nearly cost him his life, but he did succeed in obtaining agreements with Siam and Muscat that the Senate soon ratified. He later made overtures to Japan but died before any real negotiations began. Subsequently, a war between England and China, the Opium War of 1839–1842, resulted in the occupation of Hong Kong by the British and the opening of five new "treaty" ports in China to western trade. In 1843 Commodore Lawrence Kearney obtained a most-favored-nation agreement with China allowing the United States the same trade privileges extended to other western nations. That same year Caleb Cushing was appointed the first American commissioner to China. Cushing went to China with four warships, gifts, samples of the scientific wonders of the West, and full authority to make a treaty with the Son of Heaven. The Treaty of Wanghia confirmed American commercial interests in China, formally granted the United States most-favored-nation status, and established the right to have Americans accused of crimes tried by American officials. The American government had clearly assumed an active role in promoting international trade in the Orient.

By the 1850s American whaling vessels ranged far out into the northern Pacific and, inevitably, shipwrecked sailors turned up on the coast of Japan, where they were treated as criminals. Japan absolutely excluded all westerners other than the admission of a few Dutch settlers at Nagasaki. The needs of the whalers, the advent of steam navigation, and the prospects of a lucrative Japanese trade—estimated by *De Bow's Review* to be a $200-million-a-year market—brought Commodore Matthew C. Perry and his great black ships to Tokyo in July 1853. The following year Perry returned to sign a treaty of friendship that opened two Japanese ports to American ships, and in 1856 the first American consul, Townsend Harris, set up office in Shimoda, one of the treaty ports. Perry and Harris introduced the Japanese to modern technology, railroads, and mass production. Ironically, a little over one hundred years later Japan had become the major trading partner of the United States and a leading supplier of modern technology, including automobiles, television sets, and computer components.[2]

After the Civil War American business interests were actively expanded throughout the world by energetic State Department personnel rather than by entrepreneurs. Industrial leaders seemed indifferent to foreign markets, and when business representatives did go abroad they often proved to be terribly uninformed, inefficient, and lacking in understanding foreign cultures. One of the pervasive problems was their seeming inability to master foreign languages in which they had to do business. Moreover, the spirit of individualism and competitiveness in America prevented cooperation among businesspeople abroad. Merchants sent American cheese, furniture, and stoves to Holland, only to find that the Dutch produced them better and more cheaply. American leather goods were banned in Germany because the hemlock dye used to color them was poisonous. American-made fur coats would reach the Canadian market in Quebec in July.[3] Despite such inefficiencies and errors, American exports climbed rapidly between 1865 and 1900, from $234 million to $1.5 billion. The bulk of exports continued to be farm products such as cotton and tobacco, joined by wheat, cattle, and pork; but the overseas sale of machine products, such as railroad equipment and guns, also rose rapidly.

American manufacturers and merchants offered 356 displays at the Paris Exposition of 1867, and in 1873, they sent a 654-person commission to the Vienna trade exposition funded by a $200,000 Congressional appropriation. Americans were well represented at the trade fair in Paris in 1878, at exhibitions in Sydney and Melbourne, Australia, in 1879 and 1880, at the International Fishery exhibition in Berlin in 1880, and the International Exposition of Electricity in Paris in 1881, where Thomas A. Edison's electric light system was the central attraction.[4] The flag both led and followed American businesspersons wherever they might go.

In 1868 Congress extended the protection of the president and the Department of State to American citizens abroad, and by the 1880s tourism had become an important business.[5] In that decade the State Department championed naval preparedness in support of the Department of the Navy, leading to a major ship construction program. The naval building program in turn led to the acquisition of naval bases and coaling stations around the world to service the burgeoning fleet. Government support of foreign trade led to the expansion of the diplomatic and consular services. Private interests, typified by the National Association of Manufacturers, began to send industrial agents abroad to search for markets and raw materials.[6] The Department of Agriculture sent "plant explorers," such as Seaman A. Knapp, overseas to search for new and more productive plant varieties. This late-nineteenth-century awakening focused on Latin America.

Trade with Latin America and capital investments there reached large proportions by the turn of the century, and in turn it prompted changes in American foreign policies and attitudes. Although the chronicles of American ventures into South America are too lengthy for elaboration, United States interest in Latin America as reflected by the Ostend Manifesto, which proposed the purchase or conquest of Cuba in 1853, and the filibustering expeditions of men such as William Walker in Nicaragua in 1853, increased rapidly after the Civil War. On the eve of the Spanish-American War American investments in Cuba alone exceeded $50 million. Americans owned and operated plantations in Cuba, Mexico, Argentina, and Brazil, among other places. Americans—particularly the Guggenheim, Hearst, and Anaconda interests—mined most of the world's copper in Latin American operations. Between 1890 and 1895 American sales to Cuba, Brazil, and Mexico averaged $45 million annually. Exports to the Western Hemisphere totaled $143 million in 1895; sales to Europe reached $628 million, with $18 million in exports sent to Asian countries.[7] American overseas expansion reached a critical level in 1898 when disagreement with Spain over the treatment of

Cuba triggered the Spanish-American War. There were broad, underlying causes for that war that had to do primarily with expanding American trade.

Throughout the 1880s and 1890s the United States moved tentatively into the world arena and began to create an overseas empire. Private interests in America aided Cuban revolutionaries in the 1870s, and when Spain seized an American ship, the *Virginius,* and executed fifty-three of the crewmen for piracy, the United States almost went to war. In the 1880s the United States came perilously close to war with both Germany and England over coaling privileges in the Samoan islands. Resolution of the conflict gave the United States yet another Pacific island possession, American Samoa. In 1893 Queen Liliuokalani led the Hawaiians in a movement that sought to eliminate American influence, but the American settlers launched a counter-revolution that brought down the queen's government. They rushed a treaty of annexation to the United States Senate, but the incoming administration of President Grover Cleveland withdrew the treaty, although the queen's government was not reinstated. Also in 1893 the United States nearly got drawn into a war with England over a boundary dispute between Venezuela and British Guiana. Venezuela alleged British aggressions and a violation of the Monroe Doctrine, which theoretically precluded any occupation or interference in the Americas by European powers. England answered Secretary of State Richard Oleny's protest with the observation that the Monroe Doctrine was not recognized as international law. The problem was finally settled, although not with the approval of the Venezuelans, by arbitration. The United States, however, could not successfully arbitrate its disagreements with Spain over the treatment of Cuba, and so the Spanish-American War ensued in 1898.[8]

What began as a crusade to free Cuba ended as a war for an American overseas empire. The United States acquired Guam, Puerto Rico, and the Philippine Islands from Spain and annexed Hawaii. Subsequently Panama was "liberated" from Colombia in order to build a canal from the Atlantic to the Pacific. In 1901 the United States concluded an agreement with England that abrogated the old Clayton-Bulwer Treaty of 1850 and gave the United States unrestricted rights (so far as England was concerned) to build a canal through the Isthmus of Panama. By virtue of a revolution the Republic of Panama became independent of Colombia, and the United States acquired the canal rights and properties that had previously belonged to French interests. Construction began almost immediately.[9]

Over the next decades the American presence in South and Central America became substantial. Under the Roosevelt Corollary to the Monroe Doctrine, the United States announced that it could, and would, intervene in the internal affairs of Latin American republics in order to forestall European involvement. At various times American troops operated the customs houses in the Dominican Republic, settled a disputed debt owed by Venezuela, collected payments due in Nicaragua, and provided assistance and supervision to other nations. Trade between the United States and these countries, especially Venezuela, grew with intervention and expanding petroleum production. The Panama Canal opened for business in August 1914, just at the outbreak of war in Europe.[10]

Although the American dollar had clearly penetrated much of Latin America and parts of Asia, in 1914 world trade was still between European countries and their empires and was largely conducted by Europeans. The standard of exchange was the pound sterling, not the dollar. World War I marked a decisive change in America's trade relations with the rest of the world, and particularly with Europe. American business leaders emerged from the war convinced of the economic and moral leadership of the United States in the world. They anticipated continuing prosperity, a new spirit of international cooperation, and important improvements in human welfare and political and economic relationships.[11] In most of these things they were to be disappointed. They were not to be disappointed, however, by the extension and magnification of American international trade between 1914 and 1930.

THE ADVENT OF INTERNATIONAL CAPITALISM

World War I brought significant changes in the relationship of the United States to other major nations as the American economy emerged as the strongest in the world. The United States became for the first time a creditor rather than a debtor nation and finally enjoyed a favorable balance of trade, selling more than it bought. Exports of manufactured products finally exceeded the export of agricultural goods, and the volume and value of all sales abroad increased enormously. The value of American exports multiplied fourfold between 1914 and 1920, from $2 billion to over $8

Dredges remove a slide from the Gaillard Cut in the Panama Canal in 1915.   (Courtesy: National Archives.)

billion. While the dollar had not replaced the pound sterling, or even the franc, in international exchange, it had become a coequal currency. By 1920 American business expectations and appetites had also matured.

Business rather than government led in discovering and expanding overseas markets. Dollar Diplomacy meant that the overseas interests of business and American foreign policy became synonymous. Government and business continued to cooperate in promoting trade, as they had before, but now business distinctly became the senior partner. Exporters and importers, bankers, and increasingly companies such as Armour, Swift, United Fruit, Goodyear, and others with investments in foreign enterprises consciously supported government policies in return for help in negotiating contracts and the protection of American lives and property overseas. Businesspersons came to regard the protection of the laws of the United States in foreign countries as an absolute right of American citizens and of their private interests. One of the derivatives of this policy in the 1920s, and again in the 1950s, was the basic opposition of the United States to social upheavals, revolution, and property confiscation by foreign governments. Stability and the status quo became cardinal rules of successful international trade and, subsequently, the manifestation of American foreign policy.[12] The great revolutionary force emanating from the United States with the "Spirit of '76" had now become counterrevolutionary.

Opposition to political upheaval, and the diplomatic pursuit of economic stability, complemented the American extension of *laissez faire* in international trade. In a sense the United States government had no foreign policy other than to assure an "open door" in international trade, which meant simply that American business interests should have the right to compete on an equal basis in any foreign nation doing business with another. If Brazil bought German-made radios, then Americans should have an equal opportunity to sell American-made radios in Brazil. Inasmuch as the American government did not establish such policies, and did not presume to control or possess foreign territories or nations (other than those already obtained), then it could not be charged with economic or political imperialism. Incongruously, Americans continued to champion the basic revolutionary ideals of individualism, *laissez faire*, and private property while opposing instability and revolution abroad. When military or political intervention by American authorities did occur, as happened intermittently in Latin America and occasionally in Asia, that intervention was justified as necessary for the protection of national independence, life, and property against the conspiracies of European governments. The 1920s brought a sense among businesspersons and the general public of both the benevolence and the inevitability of American economic expansion.[13]

JEFFERSON CAFFERY: A DIPLOMATIC MISSION TO JAPAN

The role of the American diplomatic service in foreign trade and commerce may be glimpsed by a view of the activities of Jefferson Caffery, who was appointed counselor of the embassy to Tokyo under Ambassador Cyrus E. Woods in September 1923, shortly after the near destruction of Yokohama

Jefferson Caffery, American ambassador to Egypt (1950–1955), takes tea with Egyptian business leaders. (Courtesy: Jefferson Caffery Papers, University of Southwestern Louisiana.)

by a disastrous earthquake. Even by 1923 Caffery's career was distinguished. He began his service in Caracas, Venezuela, in 1911, and served in Stockholm and Teheran during World War I. He served as protocol chief for the American delegation at Versailles before going to Japan. He left Japan in 1925 for assignments first in Spain and then Cuba, and next as assistant secretary of state. His first post as ambassador was to Brazil, 1937–1944, and then to France, 1944–1949, and Egypt, 1950 until his retirement in 1955.

In his unpublished memoirs, Caffery referred to the role of entertaining in foreign affairs. "Embassy entertaining is done for a purpose," he said, "we don't have parties for fun." A diplomat should know everyone who counts in a political, intellectual, and social way in the country of his residence. Knowing people, he believed, was the key to getting things done, to carrying out Washington's instructions and protecting Americans—and American business interests and American dollars. The diplomat, he said, conducts much of his business at parties.

Through the intercession of Countess Watanabe, the daughter of Marshal Iwao Oyama, a hero of the Russo-Japanese War, Caffery became a visitor to the inner circles of Japanese society. He attended banquets at the Imperial Palace presided over by then Prince Regent Hirohito. The America-Japan Society of Tokyo provided useful contacts between diplomatic officials, American business leaders, and influential Japanese. The Pan-Pacific Club, which Caffery attended and occasionally addressed, served as another focus for developing Japanese-American business contacts. Caffery frequently used the English language edition of the Tokyo *Nichi-Nichi* to provide stronger Japanese-American business relations. One article he wrote, for example, pointed out that in 1922 the United States absorbed 44.7 percent of Japan's total exports. Most of that was raw silk. Caffery similarly encouraged the Japanese to reciprocate by purchasing American products.

Unfortunately, trade opportunities declined rather than improved during the next decade. Although Jefferson Caffery and other American officials distributed almost $20 million in relief funds following the Yokohama disaster, American anti-Asian actions created tremendous distrust of Americans by the Japanese. The Gentleman's Agreement of 1907 had reduced Japanese immigration to the United States to a trickle. In 1922 the U.S. Supreme Court found the Japanese, like other Asians, to be "ineligible for citizenship," and section 13c of the new Immigration Act of 1924 excluded all aliens ineligible for citizenship, including the Japanese. Anti-American parades, demonstrations, an act of hara-kiri in front of the embassy followed by a nationally reported "heroes" funeral, and an episode involving the disappearance of the American flag from embassy grounds marked the beginning of stormy Japanese-American relations that ended with World War II. Curiously reminiscent of the strong Japan-America trade ties of the 1920s is the fact that Americans in the 1980s continued to absorb many of Japan's exports, which were no longer silks but automobiles and electronic components. In this trade relationship the work of the American diplomat has become increasingly significant.

This largely unquestioned economic intervention into the affairs of many smaller or weaker states was to reap a negative harvest in the years to come, as historian Joan Hoff Wilson has pointed out: "As the result of unchecked private activity more intense perhaps than could have been achieved through centralized, governmental planning, American economic expansion . . . achieved an imperialist posture which must now be continually promoted and guarded by the government."[14] Such a position became, even by the late 1920s, untenable. Herbert Hoover, and subsequently Franklin D. Roosevelt, began to disengage the government from what were essentially blind commitments. The Good Neighbor Policy was substituted for the Roosevelt Corollary to the Monroe Doctrine in Latin America. American railroad builders and mining engineers, including Herbert Hoover, returned from Asia when wars of revolution and conflicts between nations threatened to swallow American investments, policy and all. The public, too, withdrew its commitment to international capitalism when the Great Depression seemed to undermine all of the bright hopes and expectations of capitalism and business both at home and abroad. Depression and war checked economic expansion overseas, but that expansion would resume with renewed vitality after World War II.

IMPACT OF DEPRESSION AND WAR

Foreign trade suffered drastic reverses as the United States gradually entered the Great Depression. By 1931 European companies were wracked by similar economic and financial disasters, and even the Bank of England came close to defaulting on its obligations. Although there were many causes for the Great Depression, foreign trade, or rather the severe imbalance in that trade which had prevailed since World War I, was a contributing factor. Some American business interests, and Congress, had persisted in supporting protectionist tariff policies designed to discourage or to halt the sale of competing foreign products in American markets. For example, in 1909, when Taft called a special session of Congress ostensibly to lower tariff duties, Congress responded by approving the Payne-Aldrich Tariff, which carried 847 Senate amendments to restore tariff levels to previous highs. Throughout the 1920s protectionist tariffs sought to alleviate domestic marketing problems. After World War I, when prices immediately collapsed with the restoration of peace, Congress responded by approving the Emergency Tariff Act of 1921, which placed higher duties on farm products and other commodities with depressed prices. The next year Congress approved the Fordney-McCumber Act, which raised tariffs to their highest levels. The law did authorize the president to lower or raise rates upon recommendation of the Tariff Commission, but rates were only infrequently lowered. In 1931 the Smoot-Hawley Tariff effected a sweeping increase in duties on both agricultural and industrial commodities, and a disastrous decline in foreign trade followed.[15] High protective tariffs were counterproductive to expanding American sales abroad; the higher the tariff, the smaller sales by foreign producers in American markets. And the less our trading partners sold, the lower their incomes and subsequently their purchases from American producers. Before 1929 foreign sales had been supported by American loans and investments overseas, but when these disappeared as a result of the financial crash, export sales declined.

The total value of U.S. exports declined from $5.1 billion in 1929 to a low of $1.5 billion in 1932. A slow recovery followed until 1939, when the outbreak of World War II greatly stimulated sales abroad despite the threats of German U-boats. Exports reached a high of $14 billion in 1944 as World War II moved toward its conclusion. Imports, which stood at $1.5 billion in 1929, followed a similar pattern, recovering to former levels only with the return of peace.[16] By 1945 the wealth of the Western world was largely in American hands. The war left the United States in the role of global banker, with most of the world's money in its bank.[17] Conversely, America's old trading partners were financially impoverished, their factories often in ruins, their fields laid waste. Said Secretary of State George C. Marshall in June 1947:

> The truth of the matter is that Europe's requirements for the next 3 or 4 years of foreign food and other essential products—principally from America—are so much greater than her present ability to pay that she must have substantial additional help, or face economic, social and political deterioration of a very grave character.[18]

Congress approved the Marshall Plan devised by the secretary and provided $17 billion for European recovery between April 1, 1948, and June 30, 1952. The United States actually expended $15.7 billion, with

Flour exported to Europe under the Marshall Plan is unloaded at Trieste in 1948. (Courtesy: National Archives.)

another $7.7 billion allotted under the Truman Doctrine for military aid to foreign governments threatened by internal or external subversion. By 1960 the United States had provided various foreign aid programs at a cost of almost $73 billion.[19] These dollars allowed other countries to purchase American agricultural products, capital equipment, consumer goods, and arms. National security requirements merged with the traditional obligation of government to promote foreign trade.

THE DEPARTMENT OF STATE

The Department of State is the primary instrument of the United States government in foreign affairs, but it also has a major responsibility in economic and business matters. The secretary of state is a member of the President's Council on Economic Policy, which was created in 1971 to achieve consistency between domestic and foreign economic policies. A deputy under-secretary for economic affairs is the fourth-ranking officer in the State Department and is responsible for the coordination of foreign economic policies and programs. An assistant legal advisor for economic affairs within the legal advisor's office provides support, and deputy assistant secretaries for geographic regions and functions provide additional expertise. Field representatives include the ambassadors, consuls, attachés, envoys, and ministers. The United States maintains over 100 foreign embassies, 9 missions, 120 consulates, and an assortment of other special offices and agencies overseas. The consul, who may or not be attached to an embassy but who is located in major trading and metropolitan centers, is the key official in servicing American business interests abroad.

The consul is responsible for the protection of the extraterritorial rights and properties of American citizens. The consul also issues visas, both authorizing the travel of Americans to other countries and of foreigners to the United States. Consuls are specifically entrusted with maintaining an accounting and record of American merchant ships and seamen. Every ship of American registry calling at a port in which a consul resides must report to the consul within twenty-four hours of its arrival. Consuls frequently serve as the intermediary between American firms and businesses in the country of residence. State Department personnel are responsible for the vital task of gathering information and preparing detailed reports on all matters affecting American interests. Political changes, new laws (especially tariffs), trade agreements, currency policies, and domestic-production statistics have an immediate impact upon aspects of foreign trade or exchange between the United States and another country. This flow of information is one of the most significant activities provided by the foreign service for American business interests.

These duties in the postwar world were primarily confined to the principal trading partners of the United States, that is, the Western European, Asian, Latin American, and Mediterranean countries. After 1945 foreign service offices were opened in African, Pacific, and Southeast Asian nations that previously had few American business contacts, and that in many cases, had not existed as independent political entities. As former European colonies became new nations, American commercial interests in those areas intensified.

In 1961 Congress authorized the creation of the Agency for International Development (AID) under the direction of the Department of State. Its specific purpose was to carry out programs of economic aid and technical assistance to less-developed countries in order to bring them to a level of self-sufficiency. The agency offered host governments cooperative programs in diverse fields. Typically, a country with food or protein shortages might contract with AID for a poultry-growing and -processing industry. In turn, AID, would then contract with a university or business firm to provide a team of specialists to establish the hatcheries, feed-processing plants, poultry farms, and other facilities and train a local labor force to operate the industry. It would also provide loan assistance on favorable terms repayable in United States dollars, which the host country could use to purchase supplies, equipment, and services from American firms. Special commodity-assistance loans and some outright grants were also available under AID auspices that could be used to purchase grains. An AID poultry contract, in other words, can have a very positive impact on American poultry, feed, and farm-supply industries.

Information provided by the State Department and its agencies, as well as bodies such as the Food and Agriculture Organization (FAO) operating under United Nations auspices, have stimulated American exports, particularly of agricultural commodities. The Peace Corps also provided personnel and technical assistance to underdeveloped countries. Both AID and the Peace Corps supplemented the ordinary channels of information upon which the sale and exchange of goods and services abroad are dependent.

WORLD AGRICULTURAL TRADE

One of the anomalies of recent American trade patterns has been the rise in the value and volume of agricultural exports as compared to manufactured goods. Although agricultural products dominated American exports in the nineteenth century, by the 1920s the sale of manufactured goods surpassed agricultural products. But after World War II the volume of foreign agricultural sales began to rise again relative to the other trade sector, with both prices and quantities increasing rapidly. By the mid-1970s agricultural products again rivaled manufactured goods in foreign sales. Agricultural exports averaged about $28 billion annually by 1980, accounting for 20 percent of total American farm receipts.

The expansion of agricultural sales abroad in the 1970s can be attributed to a variety of factors, not the least of which was the rapid rate of population growth in many areas of the world. The declining value of the dollar also made the purchase of agricultural products and foodstuffs increasingly attractive to foreign buyers. Larger output in America was a necessary factor, but new types of production also opened up additional markets. The traditional mix of commodities and patterns of trade changed as grains and oil seeds replaced cotton and tobacco. The United States supplied 75 percent of the world's soybean exports, a crop virtually unknown in international trade before 1945. Fifty percent of the feed grains and 40 percent of the wheat entering international markets were supplied by the United States. Enormous bulk contract sales were made to Russia, and because of government-sponsored international programs sales to the developing nations increased.

RICE, AND SOME RAMIFICATIONS OF INTERNATIONAL TRADE

International trade can be a convoluted and curious business. In 1980 most American export dollars were accounted for by agricultural products, with cotton, wheat, tobacco, and soybeans being the largest export items. Some, however, would be surprised to find another commodity, rice, high on the international trade lists. The United States provides over half of the world's exports of rice, although it produces only a small percentage of the total output. Most of what the United States produces is for sale abroad.

International affairs have affected the domestic rice market since the days of the colonial trade in the Carolinas. Thus, the opening of the Cuban market to American rice in 1931, accomplished partly through the intercessions of the American consular force in Cuba, led to a new era of profitability for the industry. Similarly, the loss of the market with the severance of diplomatic relations upon Fidel Castro's coming to power brought ruin to American millers and growers. New Asian consumers, such as South Korea and then Vietnam, and government aid programs provided relief, sometimes prosperity, but always uncertainty for the international rice market.

Attempts to solve international marketing problems resulted in the General Agreement on Tariffs and Trade concluded in 1979 by American and other signatories, including Japan. The United States subsequently concluded a separate agreement with Japan in April 1980, essentially apportioning the South Korean rice market among United States and Japanese suppliers, except for certain "emergency" clauses that allowed Japan to sell beyond the approved quota. Since June 1980 the "emergency" sale of Japanese rice to South Korea has exceeded the approved quotas by over 1 million metric tons while purchase agreements between Korea and the United States have not been exercised. Exchanges of correspondence by representative government agencies have reconciled, but not satisfied, American rice exporters.

On the other hand, diplomatic crises in the Mideast have had a curiously favorable impact upon the American rice industry. The United States has for some time provided approximately one-half of all rice imported into the Mideast, and for the period 1975–1978 sold 80 percent of Iran's rice imports. After the OPEC embargo, American rice exports to the Mideast rose rapidly. Two circumstances affected the market. First, political troubles in Pakistan and Thailand, traditional Mideast rice suppliers, reduced the availability of supplies; and second, thanks to the oil embargo, the OPEC nations now had more money to buy rice—or anything else for that matter. American rice sales to the Mideast exceeded 2 million tons in 1980, despite the loss of the Iranian market following the overthrow of the Shah. Since 1977 rice sales to Saudi Arabia alone have risen from about 90,000 tons to over 250,000 tons, while the value has increased from about $40 million to over $150 million. But as American rice producers are aware, international trade is a precarious and curious business that is affected by war, diplomacy, drought, international rivalry, and international banking and fiscal policies, as well as by the economists' traditional laws of supply and demand.

In 1954 Congress passed the Agricultural Trade Development and Assistance Act, better known as PL-480. The law was designed to provide food for the hungry, create greater stability in developing areas of the world, and reduce growing American farm surpluses. Title I of the program provided for the sale of farm products to other countries in their currencies and required that such funds be spent or invested by Americans in that nation. Titles II and III provided for gifts of food and commodities for disaster or emergency relief. Title IV, authorized in 1961, created the Food for Peace program, which made available low-interest federal loans to nations that would use the money to purchase American food products. Domestic pricing and production programs, such as the Agriculture and Consumer Protection Act of 1973 (substituting "target" pricing for parity payments) and the Food and Agriculture Act of 1977 that specified minimum prices for the liquidation of government-stored commodities, also affected foreign sales. As exemplified in the case of agriculture, government stimulated international trade by direct subsidies, foreign loans, domestic price supports, and nonpecuniary assistance—that is, by providing market information, trade missions, and contract services.[20]

PATTERNS OF FOREIGN TRADE

American business has always had a strong international component. Beginning in the late nineteenth century with only occasional relapses, as in the 1930s, exports and imports have risen steadily. American business has become more and more international, and even those businesses not directly engaged in foreign trade are increasingly affected by international markets and conditions, as evidenced by the OPEC oil embargo and petroleum price increases in the mid-1970s and the subsequent price collapses of the 1980s.

The sale of agricultural products and raw materials dominated American exports in the colonial era and the nineteenth century. Although agricultural marketing to foreign countries expanded throughout the twentieth century, by 1920 the sale of manufactured goods surpassed the sale of farm goods. Exports of railroad equipment, farm machinery, guns, sewing machines, and iron and steel manufactures rose steadily, and then they were elipsed by the export of automobiles after 1920. America's share of the world auto market was shrinking steadily in the 1970's, first from competition with German and later from Japanese auto manufacturers. By 1980 imported cars had captured almost one-third of the domestic automobile market. American electronic components, aircraft, computers, and high-technology equipment, military hardware, and especially foodstuffs, both processed and unprocessed, began to displace the more traditional automotive, machine-tool, and fiber exports. The total dollar value of American exports increased in the 1970s, while imports, especially petroleum, rose at a more rapid rate. Concurrently, foreign investments in American business rose sharply. One aspect of the new international capitalism has been heavy overseas investment in plant and equipment by American firms, and similar investments in America by foreign firms. The multinational corporation, discussed in a later chapter, is a logical, but somewhat controversial sequel to the story of foreign trade.

NOTES

1. International balance of payments reflects exchanges of goods and services and gold and capital claims between the United States and the rest of the world. See *Historical Statistics of the United States, Colonial Times to 1970*, Series U1–25, pp. 864–867.

2. See Thomas Bailey, *A Diplomatic History of the American People* (New York: Appleton-Century-Crofts, 1950), pp. 32–339; William H. Goetzmann, *When the Eagle Screamed: The Romantic Horizon in American Diplomacy, 1800–1860* (New York: John Wiley, 1966), pp. 92–103; and Foster Rhea Dulles, *Yankees and Samurai: America's Role in the Emergence of Modern Japan: 1791–1900* (New York: Harper & Row, 1965).

3. Milton Plesur, *America's Outward Thrust: Approaches to Foreign Affairs, 1865–1890*, (DeKalb: Northern Illinois University Press, 1971), pp. 16–17.

4. Ibid., pp. 46–47.

5. Ibid., pp. 104–112.

6. See Thomas G. Paterson, J. Garry Clifford, Kenneth J. Hagan, *American Foreign Policy: A History* (Lexington, Massachusetts: Heath, 1977), pp. 162–163.

7. *Historical Statistics, Colonial Times to 1970*, Series U317–334, p. 904.

8. See H. Wayne Morgan, *America's Road to Empire: The War with Spain and Overseas Expansion* (New York: John Wiley, 1965); and Harold U. Faulkner, *Reform and Expansion, 1890–1900* (New York: Harper & Row, 1959).

9. See David G. McCullough, *The Path between the Seas: The Creation of the Panama Canal, 1870–1914* (New York: Simon and Schuster, 1977).

10. Ibid.

11. Joan Hoff Wilson, *American Business & Foreign Policy, 1920–1933* (Lexington: University Press of Kentucky, 1971), pp. 1–30.

12. Ibid., p. 157–159.

13. Ibid., p. 159–160.

14. Ibid., p. 160.

15. See Sidney Ratner, *The Tariff in American History* (New York: Van Nostrand, 1972); and Frank William Taussig, *The Tariff History of the United States* (New York: Augustus M. Kelley, 1967).

16. *Historical Statistics, Colonial Times to 1970*, Series U213–224, p. 889.

17. Eliot Janeway, *The Economics of Crisis: War, Politics, and the Dollar* (New York: Weybright & Talley, 1968), p. 236.

18. Remarks of Secretary of State George C. Marshall at Harvard University, June 5, 1947; reprinted in *The Congressional Record*, June 30, 1947, p. A3248.

19. See Harold G. Vatter, *The U.S. Economy in the 1950s: An Economic History* (New York: W.W. Norton Co., 1963), pp. 17–21, 258–281.

20. See John T. Schlebecker, *Whereby We Thrive: A History of American Farming, 1607–1972* (Ames, Iowa: Iowa State University Press, 1975), pp. 284–289; and Bruce L. Gardner and James W. Richardson, eds., *Consensus and Conflict in U.S. Agriculture: Perspectives from the National Farm Summit* (College Station: Texas A&M University Press, 1979), pp. 118–151.

SUGGESTED READINGS

BALDWIN, ROBERT E. *The Political Economy of Postwar U.S. Trade Policy.* New York: New York University Graduate School of Business Administration, 1976.

BECKER, WILLIAM H. *The Dynamics of Business-Government Relations: Industry and Exports, 1893–1921.* Chicago: University of Chicago Press, 1982.

DULLES, FOSTER RHEA *Yankees and Samurai: America's Role in the Emergence of Modern Japan: 1791–1900.* New York: Harper & Row, 1965.

FAULKNER, HAROLD U. *Politics, Reform and Expansion, 1890–1900.* New York: Harper & Row, 1959.

GOETZMANN, WILLIAM H. *When the Eagle Screamed: The Romantic Horizon in American Diplomacy, 1800–1860.* New York: John Wiley, 1966.

GORDON, WENDELL C. *International Trade: Goods, People and Ideas.* New York: Alfred A. Knopf, 1958.

HARRIS, SEYMOUR E. *The European Recovery Program.* Cambridge: Harvard University Press, 1948.

HEYWOOD, JOHN. *Foreign Exchange and the Corporate Treasurer.* London: A&C Black, 1979.

JANEWAY, ELIOT. *The Economics of Crisis: War, Politics and the Dollar.* New York: Weybright & Talley, 1968.

MORGAN, H. WAYNE. *America's Road to Empire: The War with Spain and Overseas Expansion.* New York: John Wiley, 1965.

PIQUET, HOWARD S. *Aid, Trade, and the Tariff.* New York: Crowell, 1953.

PLESUR, MILTON. *America's Outward Thrust: Approaches to Foreign Affairs, 1865–1900*. De Kalb: Northern Illinois Press, 1971.

POOL, JOHN CHARLES, AND STEVEN STAMOS. *The ABCs of International Finance*. Lexington, Massachusetts: Heath, 1987.

SWIDROWSKI, JOZEF. *Exchange and Trade Controls: Principles and Procedures of International Economic Transactions and Settlements*. Epping, Essex, England: Gower Press, 1975.

WILSON, JOAN HOFF. *American Business & Foreign Policy, 1920–1933*. Lexington: University Press of Kentucky, 1971.

15 | The Modern Corporate Image

The public perception of giant, complex corporations, and of their managers, has evolved slowly but steadily through both prosperous times and depression. Institutional religion, the political structure, and the media have helped formulate images of business leaders and their creations. Fear of size alone—for example, as in the Jacksonian Era when the Bank of the United States seemed so threatening—declined by the mid-twentieth century. The conception of the business executive in heroic terms, as an Andrew Carnegie, disappeared, and in its place arose the nameless, faceless corporate bureaucrat dressed in gray flannel. Concentrated wealth, feared by the Populists and some Progressives at the turn of the century, seemed of less concern to Americans fearful of "big government" in the 1980s. Thus conflicting and changing attitudes have emerged.[1]

For almost a century business leaders have dominated a corporate culture, but the monolithic industrial giant itself simply failed to exist except in the minds of critics. The generally favorable material progress of America, in contrast with much of the rest of the world, maintained public faith in capitalism. Neither severe depressions nor major wars could shake the commitment to the existing economic order. The system withstood shocks from without and within, to a great degree, because of the image of big business, its managers, and a social and economic order that seemed to keep open an entrance into that world. The roots of that faith were planted early and deep during the rise of corporate America and the emergence of the "self-made man."

MYTH OF THE SELF-MADE MAN

An enduring aspect of American mythology is the self-made man. With roots in the aphorisms of Benjamin Franklin, propagated by Andrew Carnegie, and cultivated by politicians, ministers, and businesspersons, the myth has grown to full flower in the post–World War II decades. The cult of success, of which the myth is only a part, explained or rationalized the rise of the business elite in this country. Those who promulgated the myth used the doctrine of stewardship to justify the acquisition of material wealth, and the Bible became a constant source of comfort and quotations. In reality, the boasts of the self-made man were largely untrue as well as ungenerous. Ironically, the phrase came from a speech made by Henry Clay in 1832 as he sought federal aid for business. But the myth endures and finds constant embellishment.

The self-made-man mythology made heroes of a handful of the most successful industrialists of the nineteenth century and captured the imagination of ambitious young men. Ralph Waldo Emerson's essay on self-reliance reinforced the Puritan work ethic as part of that myth, which emphasized the opportunities America offered to one who would work hard, lead a moral life, save money, invest, and persevere. Poverty was an advantage, according to the myth, and only served to encourage those who had pulled themselves up the economic and social ladders. Ministers preached the myth and praised the business leader as a public benefactor. The morality factor in the myth served institutional religion well, as did the donations by the successful. The pursuit of wealth became a religious duty, and poverty and sin became synonymous: God and Mammon became one.

The American culture supported and sustained the myth. Beyond grammar school, it was self-education, not college, that prepared the businessperson; university years simply slowed the ambitious and undermined their rugged qualities. The *McGuffey Readers* praised the virtues of the self-made man, and popular literature, particularly the Horatio Alger books, fictionalized the young business heroes. Books, pamphlets, and magazine articles glorified material progress and inspired those who sought to become "self-made." Well into the 1920s the myth endured, but its focus became the managerial elite. The secret of success remained the individual, not the society. The Great Depression temporarily brought the myth into question, but into the 1950s it would still be the source of inspiration for many Americans.

There were, scholars would note, very few successful businesspersons who had risen from poverty, and national economic conditions, such as depressions, could destroy a firm with a highly skilled management. By the turn of the century the so-called self-made man was being supplanted, if not replaced, by the industrial bureaucrat. The agrarians particularly faulted the myth, being distrustful of all urbanites whom they believed were motivated solely by greed. The upper class looked down on the uncultured, uneducated *nouveau riche* businessperson as William Dean Howells so skillfully noted in his classic novel *The Rise of Silas Lapham.* The emerging social sciences of the twentieth century emphasized environmental factors in determining success, not the individual, and they demonstrated that poverty was not solely a function of indolence or "sin." Still the myth endured.[2]

SOCIAL DARWINISM AND THE GOSPEL OF WEALTH

Science and religion came together to buttress and sanctify the image of businessleaders and their corporations. Scientific theories are often applied to nonscientific situations, and Darwinian science became the basis for an analysis of society called Social Darwinism. While Charles Darwin's scientific concept of evolution dealt only with physical transformation of animals and plants over a vast period of time, Herbert Spencer and William Graham Sumner took the language of Darwin and misapplied it to society. They described society as an arena in which individuals struggled and where the fittest survived. Sumner preached the predestination of the social order and the salvation of the economically successful. He declared that out of the terrible struggles of society the businessman had emerged as the fittest.

Spencer and Sumner developed a wide-ranging philosophy in support of Social Darwinism. They contended that any intervention in the arena by government would allow the less fit to survive. Therefore, government's policy must be one of *laissez faire.* There could be no laws to aid the poor because that would interfere with their evolution in society. Federal and state laws regulating business were not acceptable, for they created artificial barriers to natural selection of the strongest firms. Competition would regulate industry. Sumner strongly opposed tariffs as interference in free trade, a position not generally shared by his business supporters. The sociological application of this biological theory provided justification for the success of the few and a rationale against government interference. Ministers could, and did, use the concept in conjunction with another prominent belief, the Gospel of Wealth.

Andrew Carnegie promulgated the Gospel of Wealth even as he promoted tours of the United States by Herbert Spencer. The gospel emphasized the stewardship of the successful and the responsibility of the "fittest." Carnegie extolled hard work and material acquisition, but also the obligations of the wealthy. Thrift and investment produced profits that were to be used in philanthropic endeavors. As God's stewards, the successful should use their wealth to benefit society. For Carnegie this meant constructing libraries, working for world peace, and aiding higher education. For John D. Rockefeller it meant building the University of Chicago, endowing colleges for blacks, and aiding medical research. Money was the power to do good and the gospel made that obligation clear. Thus, Social

Darwinism justified the capitalist's existence, and the Gospel of wealth bestowed on them the blessings of God and the need for stewardship.[3] But, if these were the images cultivated, who were the businessleaders they presumably reflected?

BACKGROUND OF THE BUSINESS ELITE

According to the popular image of businesspeople in the Gilded Age, the typical entrepreneur was a poor, hard-working, honest, moral young man who had pulled himself up by diligence and perseverance. However romantic this view, it was, and is, essentially wrong. Those who correctly employed this image referred to Andrew Carnegie, John D. Rockefeller, Collis P. Huntington, Jay Gould, J. P. Morgan, and a few others who achieved massive wealth and power despite humble origins. But corporate executives rarely were only one generation away from poverty. Neither Carnegie nor Rockefeller could stand as models of later entrepreneurial mobility. A number of studies of the industrial leaders of nineteenth-century and twentieth-century America have found the popular "rags to riches" view far from reality.

Most industrial leaders came from middle-class and upper-class families, not from the poor; they were recruited from the families of professionals and other businesspeople. Few came from rural America; the majority were city born and bred. While the popular image portrayed the businessperson with only an elementary education, in reality many business leaders had high school educations or the equivalent, and some had attended college. Very few were immigrants or even the sons of immigrants; they were in fact native-born of native families. That is, they were white, Anglo-Saxon, and Protestant. In terms of religious faith they belonged to mainstream Protestant churches—Episcopal, Presbyterian, Congregational, Methodist, and Baptist; and relatively rare were Catholics or Jews. The New England states produced most of the business elite before 1900, with the Great Lakes states providing a larger share in each succeeding decade.[4]

The sources of the business elite in the twentieth century did not differ greatly from the earlier period. An increasingly large number of executives had law or engineering degrees, had inherited wealth or prominence, and some had inherited the business positions that they occupied. Few launched companies of their own; they were, not entrepreneurs, but bureaucrats in middle and upper management. The new executives manifested little loyalty to their companies and migrated from employer to employer in an effort to enhance position and income. Thus, the corporations had to find incentives in order to retain their managers. The white-collar executive replaced the independent entrepreneur by the first decade of this century. During the next fifty years the business elite remained white, male, Protestant, urban, upper class or upper-middle class, and college educated. Their dreams, hopes, and values reflected their backgrounds.

DREAMS AND IDEALS OF THE BUSINESS ELITE

The business elite of the Gilded Age did not always reflect their public image, whether it be that created by Horatio Alger or that portrayed by the agrarians. Yet they were far better known by the public than the industrial leaders of recent times, and their comments were duly recorded by the press and widely disseminated to readers. Their rhetoric sometimes contained references to Social Darwinism, the Gospel of Wealth, God and country, but what did they think about privately? And what were their dreams, goals, and ambitions?

Clearly most wished to live in luxurious surroundings and be free from want. Did that mean a twenty-room house, or a forty-room house, or several houses in as many locations? Mark Hopkins, the railroad tycoon, built a huge mansion on the top of Nob Hill in San Francisco, and Andrew Carnegie bought a castle in Scotland. William H. Vanderbilt's home stretched a block long on Fifth Avenue from 51st Street to 52nd across from Central Park in New York. Some also had country homes, or "cottages," in Newport, Rhode Island. The houses symbolized personal prestige and demonstrated financial success, especially for the *nouveau riche.* But many of the occupants of these ornate architectural extravagances worried that such ostentatiousness bred criticism, and even anger, among the poor and perhaps the middle class. Dreams of erecting a Venetian palazzo in Cleveland or Chicago or Denver could also produce nightmares starring rebellious steelworkers, meatpackers, and goldminers.

"The Breakers," the Vanderbilt family's "summer cottage" in Newport, Rhode Island, built in 1895.   (Courtesy: The Rhode Island Department of Economic Development.)

Contrary to their image, the business elite favored free, tax-supported schools. Many of these men were products of public elementary education and saw its value in terms of personal experience. More than that, they realized that educated workers were more productive. Less training and greater efficiency in the factory resulted when employees could read and write, at least at the elementary level. Some moved beyond espousing the public school to extolling the technical school or institute, and schools of commerce and business. They urged "practical" subjects in the schools and found much to laud in John Dewey's ideas on curriculum if not his views on discipline. As business and industry became more complex, and the needs for a white-collar bureaucracy grew, the businessman found much greater value in university degrees, and colleges found them sources of moral support as well as endowments. While some publicly praised their own education in the "school of hard knocks," they quietly sent their sons to the university.[5]

In terms of their lifestyles, the business elite often ignored the conventional wisdom about their attitudes, thoughts, and motivations. Sometimes they simply contradicted themselves. Their ambivalence about themselves as a class reflected the growing ambivalence of society toward them and their role in the economy.

ROBBER BARONS OR CAPTAINS OF INDUSTRY?

The image of the businessman and his corporation suffered from attacks by farm organizations, journalists, and some politicians in the last two decades of the nineteenth century and the first two decades of the twentieth. Populists, muckrakers, and some Progressives accused the businesses of abusing the powers of corporate wealth, of buying politicians and their votes, and of reducing competition in order to take advantage of consumers, laborers, and the society in general. The picture of corporate greed, poor-quality products, and political chicanery they painted tarnished the reputations of many business leaders, but ironically it only slightly altered the ardor of those who sought to enter business life.

A term popularized by Matthew Josephson in the late 1930s, the *Robber Barons,* could have been used just as effectively by the business critics of pre-1900 America. The artistocratic Charles Francis Adams laid bare the sordid story of the manipulation of the Erie Railroad by Jay Gould, Jim Fisk, and Daniel Drew. The Farmers Alliance and its political arm, the People's or Populist party, assaulted the railroads for high rates in the tradition of the Patrons of Husbandry (Grange). William Jennings Bryan joined the Alliance's call for nationalization of the railroads. The young journalists whom Theodore Roosevelt called the muckrakers used the pages of the new, cheap, illustrated magazines to expose the evils of big business. Ida Tarbell, daughter of an independent oilman, lambasted John D. Rockefeller and the tactics of Standard Oil Trust. Lincoln Steffins demonstrated the corrupt ties that linked municipal governments to electric, water, and traction companies. Robert LaFollette used the state of Wisconsin as a laboratory for reform to curb abuses by railroads, insurance companies, and public utilities. Novelists adopted these themes as Frank Norris attacked the transportation monopoly of California's Southern Pacific Railroad in *The Octopus,* and Upton Sinclair revealed the filth of the packing plants of Chicago and the desperate conditions of the immigrant workers who labored there in *The Jungle.* Newspapers, magazines, novels, and political speeches produced a searing assault on the Robber Barons and helped create an era of reform called progressivism.

The businessmen did not lack for defenders, and later efforts to rehabilitate their reputations would produce the phrase "Captains of Industry." But clearly the issue was never good versus evil, and such interpretations failed to clarify the basic issues. All businessleaders were not Captains of Industry, and few were Robber Barons. Such views were usually the products of studies of one businessman or a small group of corporate leaders. More recent analysis suggests that corporate executives, for a variety of motives, actually participated in the reform efforts of the Progressive Era.

By 1900 many prominent business leaders came to deplore cutthroat competition and the abuses it produced. Companies that manufactured goods in states with effectively enforced child labor laws sought a federal labor statute to prevent their competitors in other states from using children. Some railroad executives favored weak federal regulation rather than stringent state control of rates and services. Business leaders realized that public health services would protect their workers as well as the maid, cook, and driver who lived in their households. While some executives complained about state taxes used for workmen's compensation insurance, others saw such reforms as economically and socially beneficial. That some entrepreneurs supported some progressive reforms should not be surprising; after all, progressivism was largely a middle-class reform effort, and many of the corporate leaders came from middle-class America.

The commitment of business to Social Darwinism and the Gospel of Wealth softened markedly before World War I. Verbal support for *laissez faire* dwindled as business leaders accepted, albeit with reluctance, a greater role for government in the economy. While some embraced moral progressivism, stated simply as the pledge to industrialize society "without commercializing souls,"[6] others took a more hardheaded approach: Government regulation often enhanced profits. The image of monolithic corporate America standing solidly against change and reform simply was not accurate. Small businesses feared U.S. Steel as much as many consumers, perhaps more. Entrepreneurs trying to enter an established market fought trusts as readily as did the farmers. One of the key issues of the Progressive Era, the tariff, saw sharp divisions among businesspersons, trade associations, chambers of commerce, and manufacturers' organizations. There were high-tariff proponents, low-tariff advocates, and even a few free traders. Similarly, corporate leaders and executives could be found in both major political parties, and some became Roosevelt Progressives in 1912. The image of corporate America changed in the Progressive Era, but the 1920s would witness a return of the emphasis on the self-made man, individualism, *laissez faire,* and "normalcy."

Despite Sinclair Lewis's searing assault on the business mentality in *Babbitt*, the 1920s saw further entrenchment of the business leader as a heroic figure. The rising stock market, prosperity—even if superficial for some—and the proliferation of consumer goods enhanced the image of the corporations and their managers. It was the Crash of '29 and later the Great Depression that called into question the wisdom of the economic system and its leaders. Once again cries of "Robber Baron" arose as some prominent speculators went to prison or committed suicide. Yet much of the New Deal was deliberately designed to save capitalism despite the rhetoric of Roosevelt and the response by the American Liberty League. Finally, World War II gave business another opportunity to prove its worth, and once more a tarnished countenance was cleansed by productivity coupled with patriotism.[7]

THE AMERICAN BUSINESS CREED

In the years after 1945 the majority of the American people continued to believe in a body of ideas often described as the American business creed. This ideology permeated the society and came to represent a major source of unity in the country. The principal components of the creed included the belief that the American economic system was "coherent, unique and consciously designed." This belief "explained" American progress since 1776. The key institution in the creed was business enterprise, which had given the nation vast material goods. The high and rising standard of living in the United States resulted from its economic system. The output of goods and services, and the transformation of yesterday's luxuries to today's necessities, demonstrated the viability of the creed. Success was judged as it had been in the 1880s—the acquisition of a greater number of possessions by more people.

The creed had many corollaries: One argued that sheer productivity and efficiency underlay the economy. Little concern was expressed for nonmaterial achievements. The creed taught that equal opportunity and freedom of choice in vocations existed and that individuals rose in the economy on the basis of their ability and willingness to work. The success of the system could be explained by the terms *free enterprise* and *limited government*. That is, most nations with fewer material goods also had controlled economies and governments with enormous bureaucracies, be they socialist or Marxist—thus wealth was linked to democratic freedom.

The creed emphasized that American society deliberately chose free enterprise and capitalism. The founding fathers, according to the creed, planned the economic system, and there had been no change, no evolution since the eighteenth century. The economy worked because of healthy competition, managerial skills, reasonable wages, and legitimate profits. Capitalism succeeded because of the growth of savings and reinvestment in plants and processes. Thrift, invention, and research played important roles too, but no emphasis was placed on geography, natural resources, military security, the absence of feudalism, the size of the free-trade area, immigration of people and technology, or government stimulation of the private sector.

According to the creed, all businesses, large and small, were the heart of the system. A business sold goods or services based on a capital investment owned by one or more private individuals. The business was a business only if it sought to make profit. A subsistence farm was not a business; a commercial farmer was a businessperson. Most businesses were small, they had humble origins and were good neighbors. Investors from all across the nation participated in business enterprises; they represented a cross-section of America. Business managers functioned as a team to protect the property of these investors.

A basic tenet of the creed was the need to limit government and its activities. The Constitution, it held, provided for restraint of government which was viewed as inherently evil. Local and state governments were less malevolent, but these still represented a threat to free enterprise. The level of taxation and the tax structure also threatened capital accumulation and economic growth. Since government expanded inexorably, businesses had to be vigilant to block new programs or the creation of new agencies.

The creed accepted business fluctuations and the business cycle as normal. There would be good times and bad, and during the latter individuals and businesses accepted responsibility for their own circumstances. The best way to deal with economic adversity was greater productivity—hard work. Most believers rejected Keynesian economics and unbalanced federal budgets, but some felt that severe depressions meant a temporary need for large-scale federal expenditures.

The American business creed has never been without challengers, as has been seen earlier, but at no time did they reach the levels of the 1960s. Questions arose on issues of moral responsibility and of unrestricted corporate freedoms. Voices cried out against materialism and questioned whether productivity increases could alone solve depressions or ease inflation. Progress no longer could be defined solely in terms of the acquisition of goods. The all-pervasive optimism of the creed declined, and issues of social responsibility increased. This fundamental change altered the public view of corporations and the business elite, and it brought about greater criticism of the institutions and those who led them. The questioners could be heard as early as the 1950s.[8]

THE ORGANIZATION MAN IN THE GRAY FLANNEL SUIT

The Great Depression did not drastically alter American faith in business and the business leaders. Despite 15 million unemployed and Franklin Roosevelt's attack on "economic royalists," most Americans retained their conviction that capitalism worked and that they materially benefited from it. And the patriotism of the 1940s often gave more than a passing nod to the importance of industry in defeating fascism. But the 1950s brought serious doubts about the impact of business upon society and individuals, as well as suspicions of the motives of the managers of giant enterprises.

Not that the dream of success suddenly ceased to dominate the aspirations of most people. Children continued to hear the story of "The Little Engine That Could," with its recurring phrase, "I think I can, I think I can," from parents who were reading Norman Vincent Peale's *The Power of Positive Thinking*. Popular magazines contained articles praising successful business leaders and the "open" society that allowed their upward economic mobility. The articles celebrated material success and the acquisition of goods as the centerpieces of happiness and economic prosperity. Competition was healthy, there was equal opportunity for all, and the self-made man was alive and well according to the journals. In reality, class background, family ties, and inherited position continued to be more significant in business careers than hard work, thrift, and perseverance. The paradoxes that became more apparent in the 1950s between the image of the businessperson and the reality led to fictional and sociological studies such as *The Man in the Gray Flannel Suit* and *The Organization Man*.

Sloan Wilson's best-selling novel of 1955, *The Man in the Gray Flannel Suit*, depicted a young hero of World War II trying to adjust to the monolithic corporation mentality that most Americans felt existed in the business world. The struggles of Tom Rath and his wife Betsy seemed to mirror the problems of many junior executives of the postwar decades. They wanted a new house, car, and furniture, and the ability to send their children to college. Tom and Betsy sought money and security, but they found some of the demands of Tom's employer, "United Broadcasting Company," unacceptable. The president of this fictional corporation worked fourteen- to sixteen-hour days, often seven days a week. The executive had no home life, often went for a month without seeing his wife, and yet continually sought more activities, more projects for himself and the firm. He offered Tom two positions in United Broadcasting that would require the same devotion to work, but Tom refused saying, "I don't think I have the willingness to make sacrifices. I don't want to give up the time. I'm trying to be honest about this. I want the money. . . . [But] I can't get myself convinced that my work is the most important thing in the world."[9] Instead, he accepts the directorship of a mental health foundation that is located near his home at a lower salary, but with much less pressure.

THE IBM IMAGE

Few industrial giants can claim the degree of market penetration which International Business Machines (IBM) exercises in computers and data processing. With approximately 70 percent of the computers sold bearing the IBM trademark, the company's position is much stronger than General Motors in automobiles. Its position solidified as huge profits led large-scale research and development efforts, which in turn led to new technologies, equipment, and programming. As a result, the cost of data processing has declined sharply in the last two decades. With over 300,000 employees in seventeen plants in the United States alone, IBM wholly dominates the industry. One reason for this success, according to the company, has been its ability to attract and retain outstanding engineers, scientists, sales personnel, technicians, and managers. Yet in American business generally, the perception of IBM closely approximates the view of William Whyte in *The Organization Man* because of the corporate rules established by company president Thomas J. Watson, Sr., and elaborated upon by his son and successor Thomas J. Watson, Jr.

The roots of IBM extend back to 1911 when a predecessor company entered the tabulating business. Gradually the crude electric tabulating machines attained higher levels of sophistication, and the company began to produce recorders, scales, and other office machines. Thomas J. Watson joined the firm in 1914, and ten years later the name International Business Machines Corporation was adopted. Watson served as president until 1956.

Punched data cards, electric typewriters, accounting machines, computers, and data processors poured from the IBM plants—produced, sold, and serviced by IBM employees. All personnel were required to attend courses that dealt with sales, engineering, and manufacturing, but much more than that. The Watsons established a "set of beliefs" for the company to which all were expected to give allegiance. These ranged from the cosmetic to the significant. For decades all male employees who met the public wore white shirts and plain ties with suits of a neutral color: no blue shirts, no sports coats. Company employee benefits were good to those who gave total effort to the product. Pay was based on individual performance, which was evaluated annually. The Watsons believed that the success of the firm resulted from how well the organization brought out the talents and energies of the employees, but some critics argued that the firm's employees traded individuality for job security, and that internal criticisms of management decisions simply did not occur. Long and highly detailed training programs emphasized the reward package that was available to those who met higher levels of performance within the company. The employees were told to "aim for perfection." Junior executives attended "schools" that taught IBM's "outlook and its beliefs." One of the major "beliefs" was that profits were the measure of performance. The company also transferred employees to new areas at a rapid rate: IBM came to stand for "I've Been Moved." Internal and external criticisms of these policies led to significant changes in personnel management.

In the mid- to late 1950s, IBM decentralized its organization, ended hourly wages, put all employees on salaries, and reduced the number of transfers annually. The "gray flannel" image began to change, and some male IBM employees not only sported colored dress shirts, but also beards. The emphasis on perfection and performance remained, but the requirements for conformity in personal dress, beliefs, and lifestyles declined markedly. Productivity and creativity improved with the elimination of artificial barriers, and the corporation's public image changed as well.

Wilson's fictional hero and his company represented a growing image of business persons and their employers, the white-collar workers without convictions or beliefs, who shuffled papers, attended conferences, and wrote noncommittal reports on insignificant subjects. Other novels and films made the same case against the occupants of the executive suites themselves. A different perspective began to emerge in the popular mind.

The publication of William H. Whyte's widely acclaimed book *The Organization Man* (1956) provided an in-depth account of the lives of men not unlike Wilson's fictional characters. The middle managers depicted by Whyte dominated the society; they were a recognizable elite, but they were not always happy in their work. The corporate managers believed that the organization provided harmony, order, and stability in their lives but required absolute loyalty to behavioral norms established by the company. Individualism within the organization was not tolerated; conformity was the price paid for mobility up the corporate ladder. Whyte did not attack organization, only the worship of the structure.

According to Whyte the old values of thrift, hard work, self-reliance, and rugged individualism were no longer prized. Consumerism replaced thrift; leisure was more important than work; committees, not individuals, made decisions; and bureaucrats always preferred safety to adventure. The managers "belonged" to the organization, and they wished to belong together. Group work replaced individual effort within the organization, and decisions were compromises often achieved by conferences or committees. Ideas came from groups, they believed, not from individuals. Group expediters rather than leaders moved to positions of authority. The expediter was not the source of ideas; he hired staff people to provide ideas. Those who joined the organization had been trained in "practical" subjects at universities and colleges that offered undergraduates opportunities to learn organizational behavior patterns.

The young men, and occasionally women, who joined the organization accepted the goals of the company as personal goals. They also accepted the problems the loss of individuality created. Most discovered they labored very hard and often in the midst of tension and conflict. Fifty to sixty hours per week with several nights at the office were normal. The

Employee lunch and recreation center at the Hewlett-Packard facility in Cupertino, California.   (Courtesy: Hewlett-Packard Company.)

telephone at home proved to be an extension of the office. Their homes in suburbia looked like all the other houses; their wives appeared and sounded like all the other corporate wives; their children went to the same schools and churches as the children of other executives; and their poodles were cut at the same shop as all the other organization poodles. The organization moved its personnel frequently from one look-alike, classless suburb to another, eliminating the concept of geographical roots; the family's roots were corporate.[10]

While Whyte may have exaggerated the totality of the organization's impact on the executives and their families, his argument became of great concern to many corporations. Nevertheless, the upper reaches of corporate America remained essentially as Whyte described until the early 1970s. The impact of federal legislation on the hiring of women and minorities had an effect, as did the generally antibusiness tone of a younger generation that rejected the qualities the corporations required—while sometimes accepting allowances from fathers who managed these same firms. To counter the increasingly negative image, most firms began to emphasize or reemphasize larger corporate responsibilities.

THE IMAGE OF CORPORATE RESPONSIBILITY

That corporations had some public responsibilities emerged as a concept almost simultaneously with the creation of the legal device itself. A stable economy and healthy social conditions meant that the corporation had a greater opportunity for financial success, and, therefore, some attention had to be given to external forces. Self-interest, which took the form of paternalism, such as George M. Pullman's model town, usually proved effective only in the very short run. A broader concept of self-interest, often based on moral and humanitarian motives as well as profits, made far better sense in the long run. Beginning before the Civil War, companies assumed some responsibilities for their employees in the communities in which their facilities were located.

As the first substantial businesses with thousands of employees, the railroads had to deal with broader obligations of service. Their employees were often dispatched to cities and towns away from home where decent food and accommodations were lacking. And the saloons tempted workers whose discipline and skills needed total commitment. As a result, the railroads established their own Young Men's Christian Association (YMCA) program. They built "Y's," donated funds for buildings that contained bedrooms and dining facilities, and added their own reading rooms and even swimming pools. The companies established death and disability insurance programs, and hospitals and clinics for their workers in this hazardous occupation. The YMCAs and other facilities and benefits probably helped reduce demands for unionization, but they cannot be dismissed simply as an antiunion tactic. Healthy, happy workers were good business and good public relations.

MARY KAY AND HER COSMETICS

Few businesses are so totally dominated by their corporate leaders that the images of firm and executive become one. But there are exceptions, and an example is the personality of Mary Kay Ash and the image of Mary Kay Cosmetics. Formed in 1963 by Mrs. Ash with $5,000 in capital, the firm in 1979 had sales exceeding $90 million and a net income of over $9 million. The company produced a line of cosmetics that was sold by sales representatives referred to as beauty consultants. The original 10 consultants had become 70,000 by 1980. The firm sold only five basic pink-packaged cosmetic products, unlike larger direct-sale businesses in the same market, such as Avon, which had a wide variety of goods in their catalogues. The beauty consultants operated independently with no territories and no franchises. Expansion of the firm and its image became synonymous because of the evangelistic and "female emancipation" techniques used by Mary Kay Ash to motivate the army of beauty consultants, some of whom earned more than $100,000 yearly.

Almost a cult figure to many women, Mrs. Ash had several years experience selling consumer products in homes through direct sales before starting her company. She created the "beauty show" for her products in which no more than six potential customers were given a two-hour beauty-care program and personalized makeup instruction. The consultants receive the highest commissions in the direct-sales industry and are provided substantial inducements for recruiting other consultants. An annual convention, or seminar, for the sales force often attracted more than 8,000 people. The Seminar recognized sales leaders as "queens" who received pink automobiles, vacation trips, mink coats, jewelry, and other prizes. At the seminars the salespersons sang and applauded to the song "Mary Kay Enthusiasm." Mrs. Ash personally conducted seminars

Mary Kay Ash, marketing innovator and direct-sales specialist. (Courtesy: Mary Kay Cosmetics.)

for sales directors and individuals identified as "future sales directors" on how to conduct the "shows" and on her sales theories.

The firm is oriented toward a female sales force. The absence of territories has eased problems of mobility created by spouses being transferred. The consultants pay for products in advance so there are no accounts receivable or payable. Mary Kay manufactures most of its products and has a very limited advertising budget. It depends on the enthusiasm of the sales force, which is motivated by the prizes given, public recognition, and by the profit potential. The sales people are taught goal setting, self-motivation, and customer service. The concept of consumer-service marketing that Mrs. Ash designed has become part of the image of the firm as much as the pink cars given away at the annual sales meeting. Mary Kay Cosmetics took advantage of the changing role of women in the 1970s and an untapped labor pool to develop a unique and successful marketing approach. In turn, the approach created the firm's external image.

In the 1920s the professionalization of public relations gave added impetus to the effort to establish an image of corporate responsibility. The men and women hired to direct public relations of major companies tried to instill a sense of corporate service in the minds of the public. Executives gave speeches on broad, public issues and took the lead in charitable and fund-raising drives. The Community Chest movement became a major vehicle to demonstrate corporate responsibility. Using a structure not unlike a corporation, the Community Chest systematically raised funds for many agencies. In most cities and towns business leaders served as volunteers in the Chest drive. Other areas of public service included memberships and trusteeships on college and university boards, and as public officials in school districts and in local government. The companies also contributed large sums to these institutions as well as "volunteering" their employees. The Bell System, for example, spent almost $5 million between 1925 and 1934 on memberships in civic, charitable, and social organizations. The federal tax law enacted in 1935 permitted corporations to donate up to 5 percent of taxable income for charitable purposes. Such activities and donations accelerated through the Great Depression and during World War II, when the National War Fund coordinated fund raising and in three years collected and distributed $321 million.

After 1945 the concept of corporate responsibility expanded, and businesses entered new aspects of public activity. One of the areas of greater corporate involvement was education, particularly higher education. Businesses took a far more active interest in college and university fund drives, and they became inexorably linked with university-operated research and development programs. Gifts for buildings became commonplace, as did corporate promotion of bond issues for state universities and public schools. Similarly, business leaders took more active roles in agencies and institutions that sought to establish better race relations. After 1954 companies tried to reduce racial tensions in their plants and offices, particularly in cities where racial violence had occurred. At the same time, more companies offered support to the arts. Corporate gifts to museums, symphony orchestras, ballet and theatrical companies, and public television increased dramatically. Obviously, these new interests often reflected efforts to reduce, or at least mitigate, growing criticism of corporate economic behavior. But this did not mean that the viewer who enjoyed Masterpiece Theater productions on educational television made possible by the Mobil Corporation would be less vigorous in objecting to the price of gasoline at Mobil service stations. Even if the new responsibilities did not halt the flood tide of criticism, the corporations felt required to accept broader social responsibilities because the public expected them to do so. For example, a survey taken in 1970 showed that 60 percent of the adults in the country believed business was obligated to fight pollution. It was part of a postwar image that had to be maintained.

Company foundations became mechanisms to distribute more widely corporate largesse, and matching employee donations to colleges and universities became commonplace. Corporate giving increased from $30 million in 1936 to $482 million by 1960; the latter sum represented over 1 percent of pretax profits. When some stockholders objected that their assets were being given away, and in some cases went to court to protest, management responded that the donations were, not charity, but part of the company's greater community responsibility. Profits remained the goal, but the best interests of the firm and its owners could be served by cultivating an image of good citizenship. A growing sense of managerial trusteeship helped solidify this position. Practicality and idealism merged to produce increasing commitments to concerns other than profits.[11]

NOTES

1. For a quantitative analysis of the changing image see Louis Galambos, *The Public Image of Big Business in America, 1880–1940* (Baltimore: Johns Hopkins University Press, 1975).

2. Irvin G. Wyllie's *The Self-Made Man in America: The Myth of Rags to Riches* (New Brunswick, New Jersey: Rutgers University Press, 1954) is still the best study, but *Apostles of the Self-Made Man* (Chicago: University of Chicago Press, 1965) by John G. Cawelti is also most informative.

3. Richard Hofstadter's *Social Darwinism in American Thought*—revised edition (Boston: The Beacon Press, 1955)—overstates the impact of Darwinian science and Social Darwinism on businesspeople, but it is the standard work.

4. William Miller, ed., *Men in Business: Essays on the Historical Role of the Entrepreneur* (New York: Harper & Row, 1962) contains three major essays analyzing the origins of business leaders. For a critical review of Miller's methods and conclusions, see the chapter by Ralph Andreano in Louis P. Cain and Paul J. Uselding, eds., *Business Enterprise and Economic Change* (Kent, Ohio: Kent State University Press, 1973).

5. Edward Chase Kirkland, *Dream & Thought in the Business Community, 1860–1900* (Ithaca, New York: Cornell University Press, 1956).

6. Robert H. Wiebe, *Businessmen and Reform: A Study of the Progressive Movement* (Cambridge: Harvard University Press, 1962; reprinted, Chicago: Quadrangle Books, 1968), p. 9.

7. Galambos, *The Public Image of Big Business*, pp. 74–78, 112–114, 152, 156, 216–221.

8. Francis X. Sutton, Seymour E. Harris, Carl Kaysen, and James Tobin, *The American Business Creed* (Cambridge: Harvard University Press, 1956).

9. Sloan Wilson, *The Man in the Gray Flannel Suit* (New York: Simon & Schuster, 1955), p. 277.

10. William H. Whyte, Jr., *The Organization Man* (New York: Simon & Schuster, 1956).

11. Morrell Heald, *The Social Responsibilities of Business, Company and Community, 1900–1960* (Cleveland: Case Western Reserve University Press, 1970).

SUGGESTED READINGS

CAWELTI, JOHN G. *Apostles of the Self-Made Man.* Chicago: University of Chicago Press, 1965.

CHENOWETH, LAWRENCE. *The American Dream of Success.* North Scituate, Massachusetts: Duxbury Press, 1974.

DIAMOND, SIGMUND. *The Reputation of the American Business Man.* Cambridge: Harvard University Press, 1955.

GALAMBOS, LOUIS. *The Public Image of Big Business in America, 1880–1940.* Baltimore: Johns Hopkins University Press, 1975.

HOFSTADTER, RICHARD. *Social Darwinism in American Thought.* Revised edition. Boston: The Beacon Press, 1955.

KIRKLAND, EDWARD CHASE. *Dream & Thought in the Business Community, 1860–1900.* Ithaca, New York: Cornell University Press, 1956.

MILLER, WILLIAM, ED. *Men in Business: Essays on the Historical Role of the Entrepreneur* New York: Harper & Row, 1962.

PRIMER, BEN. *Protestants and American Business Methods.* Ann Arbor, Michigan: UMI Research Press, 1979.

SUTTON, FRANCIS X., SEYMOUR E. HARRIS, CARL KAYSEN, AND JAMES TOBIN. *The American Business Creed.* Cambridge: Harvard University Press, 1956.

TEDLOW, RICHARD S. *Keeping the Corporate Image: Public Relations and American Business, 1900–1950.* Greenwood, Connecticut: JAI Press, 1979.

WHYTE, WILLIAM H., JR. *The Organization Man.* New York: Simon & Schuster, 1956.

WIEBE, ROBERT H. *Businessmen and Reform: A Study of the Progressive Movement.* Cambridge: Harvard University Press, 1962.

WILSON, SLOAN. *The Man in the Gray Flannel Suit.* New York: Simon & Schuster, 1955.

WYLLIE, IRVIN G. *The Self-Man in America: The Myth of Rags to Riches.* New Brunswick, New Jersey: Rutgers University Press, 1954.

16 | Government and the Economy

The role of government in the economy has changed considerably over the past two hundred years, yet those changes have largely been consistent with precedent and previous experience. Alexander Hamilton and his Federalists believed that government had a very positive function in promoting business opportunities through management of tariffs, taxes, and banking, and by the active encouragement and subvention of business and manufacturing. Thomas Jefferson and his Democratic Republicans believed that the best government was that which governed least. They were more concerned about what government could do *to* an individual, rather than what government could do *for* an individual. The *laissez faire* view, that government should stay out of business affairs generally, prevailed in the nineteenth century. In the era before the Civil War the states rather than the federal government most often affected business development through the authorization of corporate charters, taxes, and banking laws. Federal intervention, largely through the rulings of the Supreme Court, upheld federal authority over that of the states in questions involving interstate commerce, contracts, and taxing authority. Not until after the Civil War, however, when business had clearly spilled over the boundaries of the states, did the issue of state-versus-federal regulatory authority come into clear focus.[1] By that time, the Civil War and business expansion had made regulation, if it existed, a federal affair. Business leaders requested federal regulation in order to free commerce from the shackles of localism, and critics of business sought to control veritable monsters that had outgrown the regulatory capacity of the state governments.

The first serious federal efforts to impose governmental controls and regulations over business derived in part from the farmer and labor movements of the late nineteenth century and from the vast expansion of the national economy. Between 1870 and 1910 the GNP rose from $7.4 to $35.3 billion, while per capita income doubled, as did the total population. Farm output quadrupled, and for industrial labor the output per worker doubled. Yet real wages for industrial labor increased only 50 percent, and real per capita farm income remained basically stable.[2] Farmers and laborers came to believe that the just profits of their labor were being denied them and that employers, corporations, bankers, and trusts, especially the railroads, conspired against them. Farmers organized unions and alliances that advocated federal regulation of the railroads, graduated income taxes, lower tariffs and, if necessary, government ownership and operation of the railroads and telegraph companies. Charles W. Macune, head of the Southern Farmers' Alliance, advocated a subtreasury system that would establish cooperative commodity banks in every region of the United States financed by low-interest government loans. The systems would store crops, facilitate orderly marketing, advance credit, and issue paper money. Labor unions, such as the National Labor Union and the Knights of Labor, supported a government mandated eight-hour day, equal pay for women, a graduated income tax, producer and consumer cooperatives, and laws that would restrict immigration and abolish the use of convict labor. The American labor movement demanded the right to collective bargaining. Few of these objectives became realities in the nineteenth century; but the agitation, the violence, and the very real inequities triggered a twentieth-century effort to bring about such reforms.

THE PROGRESSIVE IDEAL

The problem for American reformers was how to divide the growing abundance more equitably and yet retain a capitalistic economy. It was an abundance, most agreed, attributable to the industrial and technological revolutions, which concurrently imposed new evils and hardships upon individuals. Henry Demarest Lloyd protested the destruction of individual rights and liberties by the concentrated economic power of big business interests in his *Wealth Against Commonwealth.* Henry George attributed wealth to chance, accident, and monopoly, circumstances that robbed the individual of rightful earnings. Conversely, poverty came to be regarded as a social evil rather than the product of an individual's indolence or incompetence. The urban poor, Jacob Riis explained in *How the Other Half Lives,* were wretched examples of the impact of industrial society on some individuals. The industrial environment had simply overwhelmed the American people. Muckraking journalists as well as competitive pressures in certain industries contributed to the demand for legislation seeking to remove inequities and restore individual opportunities.

Progressivism, the vehicle for early twentieth-century reform, sought to preserve the capitalist system, to restore equality of economic opportunity, and to preserve for individuals their just rewards. Progressives presumed that corporations, trusts, and wealth created certain social problems, which they sought to resolve without destroying the structure of American business enterprise.

President Theodore Roosevelt, for example, informed Congress in 1902 that "our aim is not to do away with corporations. . . . We draw the line against misconduct, not against wealth." Woodrow Wilson expressed a similar view:

> Our life contains every great thing, and contains it in rich abundance.
> But the evil has come with the good. . . . We have been proud of our industrial achievements, but we have not hitherto stopped thoughtfully enough to count the human cost, the cost of lives snuffed out, of energies overtaxed and broken. . . .
> Our duty is to cleanse, to reconsider, to restore, to correct the evil without impairing the good.[3]

Although the historical literature on progressivism tends to discount the influence of business leaders in that reform effort, Robert H. Wiebe—while, conceding that the business community opposed labor legislation, social insurance, and welfare programs—argues that in the area of economic regulation business leaders "exercised their greatest influence on reform and laid their claim as progressives." Businesspeople led the fight for tariff reform, and midwestern business leaders and bankers supported the Federal Reserve Act against Wall Street critics. The FTC generally received the support of both large and small businesspeople throughout the country. Wiebe concludes that a great government bureaucracy was created by the progressives that, while ostensibly hostile or competitive with the national infrastructure of business leadership, was in fact not competitive at all. The "government" that regulated the economy and the individuals who headed the nation's businesses were intermixed and highly compatible.[4]

The Progressive Era initiated a new role for government in the national economy. Government encouragement and support of certain kinds of economic activity was an established tradition, but the question of whether or not government should regulate some economic activities in the interests of the general welfare remained unsettled. Did the government have a responsibility to protect individuals from social disabilities such as industrial accidents, slum environments, or illness? Should the government promote competition through the regulation of big business and by "busting" the trusts? Or did government intervention itself threaten personal liberties and impair rather than promote free private enterprise? These issues, of course, still have not been resolved. Government policy has tread a varied way, pursuing individualism and free enterprise while intervening with regulations and financial assistance or other support of business activities.[5] Railroad regulation, trust prosecution, and the tax policies of the Progressive Era illustrate the expanding role of government and provide precedents for the vastly expanded governmental control characteristic of the New Deal and post–World War II eras.

Businesses also obtained benefits from government regulations. Federal regulatory policies were not antibusiness but were in fact usually supportive. Moreover, with the passage of time, a clear affinity of interest developed between the regulatory agencies and the businesses being regulated. Examples of progressive legislation distinctly beneficial to industry include the Meat Inspection Act and the Pure Food and Drug Act of 1906. These acts required the inspection and certification of meat, food, and drug products by government agents and the accurate labeling of drugs and medicines. British consumers, for example, had discovered corruption in American meat products, and the industry came perilously close to being forced out of the British market. Government-inspected meat and government-approved drugs facilitated the marketing of those products at home and abroad. Progressives also wrestled with the problem of monopoly, which they believed prevented fair competition and equal economic opportunity.

"BUSTING" THE TRUSTS

"Monopoly is business at the end of its journey," wrote Henry Demarest Lloyd in 1894. Trusts, he argued, were antidemocratic and destructive of personal liberty. For the business leader, such as John D. Rockefeller of Standard Oil, the trust was an essential instrument for managing diverse properties scattered over many states.[6] Rockefeller formed the Standard Oil Trust Agreement in 1882, which was approved by the stockholders of Standard Oil of Ohio and the trustees who exercised control over stock in forty companies associated with Standard. A new board of nine trustees administered the $70 million firm. Stockholders of Standard Oil received prorated trust certificates reflecting their holdings. The trust created a policy-control committee while allowing for decentralized plant management. The directors of the trust further operated on the advice of special task committees, thus providing Standard with a sophisticated management structure.[7]

Trusts, and Standard Oil in particular, received increasing public attention and criticism. As we have seen, by 1890 Congress had passed the Sherman Anti-Trust Act, which forbade monopolistic practices in industries engaged in interstate commerce. Until as late as 1900, however, the courts still concluded that since trusts did not engage in production or business, they did not meet the test of the commerce clause of the Constitution and therefore did not fall under the jurisdiction of the federal law. Ohio, however, obtained a dissolution of the trust in a state court action, and subsequently control of the affiliates and subsidiaries of Standard Oil of Ohio was shifted to Standard Oil of New Jersey as a holding company.[8] But in 1911 the Supreme Court forced Standard Oil of New Jersey to divest its holdings under the antitrust law. The issue of how to control trusts dominated the election of 1912, and even stronger antitrust legislation was enacted by Woodrow Wilson's administration, which came into office in 1913.

The Clayton Anti-Trust Act of 1914 prohibited interlocking director-ates through which one or several company representatives controlled or influenced the policy of nonaffiliated companies. It forbade price discrimi-nation (that is, favoring one customer over another with lower prices), the granting of exclusive contracts to one firm without competing bids, and combinations of competing companies against one another. One section of the act exempted labor unions from antitrust prosecution and thus in theory created the right to collective bargaining. Despite the vigorous anti-trust activities of the Progressive Era, it became increasingly evident that a relatively few giant corporations held the "great bulk of the financial re-sources of American manufacturing."[9] The progressives were deeply di-vided over what constituted monopoly and whether size alone was an evil. While Roosevelt and Taft saw the need for "natural" monopolies, Wilson, and especially his adviser Louis Brandeis, wanted all of the great corpora-tions dissolved. The fervor for antitrust legislation would wane sharply during World War I and would not be revived after the armistice. Ulti-mately, governmental control over business activities derived more emphati-cally from taxing policies rather than from antitrust activity.

AN ETERNAL TRUTH: TAXES

Despite the pundit's barb that there are two events in life no one can escape—taxes and death—taxes, and particularly federal taxes, were negli-gible or nonexistent before World War I. The taxes that did exist were largely state, county, or municipal, and they usually fell on property. Fed-eral revenues throughout the nineteenth and early twentieth centuries de-rived primarily from land sales and the tariff. During the Civil War federal excise taxes on liquor and tobacco were raised to produce new revenues, and a federal income tax and an inheritance tax were created. These un-popular taxes increased federal income, but most of the war costs were funded by borrowing. In 1867 congress lowered the income tax rate, in 1870 it repealed the inheritance tax, and in 1872 it ended the income tax. For the remainder of the century federal revenues from import duties, land sales, and excise liquor taxes generally exceeded federal expenditures. Thus the advent of the modern graduated income tax system had less to do with the necessity for federal income than it did with social justice.

Farmer organizations in the nineteenth century persistently advo-cated a graduated federal income tax as a means to transfer the burden of taxation to those who held personal property, such as stocks and bonds, and who paid no taxes on those earnings. This would allow for the reduc-tion or elimination of the tariff. Progressives regarded the income tax, in part, as the imposition of stewardship on the wealthy, an exercise in equity, and a device for strengthening the central government. Congress had ap-proved an income tax bill in 1894, to become effective on January 1, 1895,

The floor of the New York Stock Exchange before the opening of trading during the "Great Bear Market" in 1923. (Courtesy: New York Stock Exchange Archives.)

but the Supreme Court ruled in *Pollock v. Farmer's Loan and Trust Company* that the income tax was unconstitutional. As the Spanish-American War and growing obligations of the United States abroad imposed new financial burdens on the federal government, national defense supporters and social justice advocates joined in supporting new revenue bills. In 1909 Congress approved an "excise Tax on the privilege of doing business," which more accurately was a corporate income tax. The Supreme Court decided that the corporate tax was an excise tax and did not violate the Constitution's prohibition on direct taxation. Congress also approved, subject to ratification by the states, an amendment to the Constitution authorizing an income tax on individuals.

The Sixteenth Amendment allowing Congress to "lay and collect taxes on income, from whatever source desired," was ratified on February 25, 1913, and Congress soon approved a bill levying personal and corporate income taxes. The initial rate was 1 percent for all single wage earners with incomes in excess of $3,000 or for married couples with incomes over $4,000. With 60 percent of the households earning less than $2,000 as late as 1929, the tax affected relatively few Americans, and those few only indifferently. Personal income tax receipts in 1913 reached $28 million, and corporate receipts only $32 million. Federal expenditures remained generally stable at $500–$750 million between 1900 and 1917, when mobilization for World War I began. In 1918, federal disbursements exceeded

$18 billion, but they then declined rapidly, averaging somewhat over $3 billion between 1921 and 1931. Between 1921 and 1929 the Republican administrations of Warren Harding, Calvin Coolidge, and Herbert Hoover virtually ended antitrust activities, and their secretary of the treasury, Andrew Mellon, persuaded Congress to cut the income tax. A vast reduction in federal activities produced smaller demands for revenues. Federal expenditures began to rise during the Depression and averaged somewhat over $7 billion yearly between 1934 and 1940. In the short run, war rather than the Great Depression was the prime stimulus for higher taxation, but in launching vast social welfare programs the New Deal initiated a new dimension of fiscal responsibility for the national government. The Great Depression, the New Deal, and finally World War II created new and ultimately pressing needs for additional federal revenues. Compared to the post–World War II era, federal taxation was nominal in the period between the wars.

ANDREW MELLON

Andrew Mellon served as secretary of the treasury under Presidents Harding, Coolidge, and Hoover. He was widely regarded in the 1920s as the "greatest Secretary of Treasury since Alexander Hamilton." Born in Pittsburgh, Pennsylvania, in 1855, Andrew William Mellon attended the institution that became the University of Pittsburgh before entering the lumber business. In 1874 he joined his father's bank and, in 1882, became president of T. Mellon and Sons. As a banker Mellon helped in the financing and formulation of Alcoa Aluminum, Gulf Oil Company, Union Steel, and many other firms, and he often obtained substantial stock interests for his contributions to their organization. Henry Clay Frick and Andrew Mellon founded the Union Trust Company of Pittsburgh in 1899, and, in 1902, T. Mellon and Sons became Mellon National Bank.

Andrew W. Mellon (1855–1937). Banker, financier, and secretary of the treasury. (Courtesy: *Dictionary of American Portraits.*)

When Warren G. Harding appointed Andrew Mellon secretary of the treasury in 1921, Mellon was sixty-five years old and one of the three wealthiest men in the nation. His biographers describe him as frail and slight, a shy, quiet man who wore dark clothes, a black tie, and drooping black socks. He kept his coat buttoned and smoked black-paper cigarettes. One reporter described him as a "tired double-entry bookkeeper who is afraid of losing his job"; another said he reminded him of "a dried up dollar bill that any wind might whisk away." His energy and impact on the economy belied his seeming physical frailty.

As treasury secretary Mellon reduced expenditures for almost every department of the government, and especially the budgets of the regulatory agencies. He vigorously opposed additional government spending for veterans' bonuses, public works, and public services. He supported disarmament as a money-saving necessity. He generally reduced government expenditures and paid off a substantial portion of the national debt while reducing taxes.

The wartime excess-profits tax was repealed. The corporation tax was lowered to 2.5 percent, and the maximum personal income tax was reduced from 65 to 32 percent. In 1925 Andrew Mellon personally saved $800,000 in taxes due to these reductions. Not only were taxes lowered, but Mellon also allowed numerous loopholes in the tax laws that provided special benefits to wealthier citizens. By the end of the 1920s it was estimated that 60,000 families at the top of the economic ladder possessed as much wealth as the 25 million families at the bottom. It was this disparity, which Andrew Mellon abetted, that led to the cry for a "new deal" in 1932.

DEPRESSION, NEW DEAL, AND TAXES

The Great Depression provoked a massive reliance on the federal government and collective action that progressivism could never have generated. The depression symbolized the apparent collapse and failure of the business leadership and its creed of democratic individualism and opportunity. Over a period of six weeks following the stock market crash on October 29, 1929, stock prices lost 40 percent of their value, and some corporate stocks became worthless. President Herbert Hoover and Congress responded to the crisis by creating the Reconstruction Finance Corporation, which made federal loans available to banks and businesses. The Federal Farm Board was authorized to make direct purchases of surplus farm commodities for the federal government, and President Hoover urged labor not to strike and manufacturers to maintain production and employment. But the depression worsened. Corporate profits disappeared and $5.6 billion in losses accrued in 1932. Unemployment climbed from a meager 3.2 percent in 1929 to 25 percent in 1933, and it remained in excess of 15 percent throughout the decade. The "withered leaves of industrial enterprise lie on every side," President Franklin D. Roosevelt observed at his inauguration, and the unscrupulous money changers have "fled from their high seats in the temple of our civilization."

Roosevelt's New Deal proposed to bind the nation's wounds and develop programs to preclude future economic catastrophe. Business leaders, whose malfeasance many believed had contributed to the coming of the Great Depression, had in fact been deeply involved in the construction of government-economic relations in the 1920s and participated in good measure in shaping many New Deal programs.

George N. Peek, for example, a businessman who had much to do with the development of federal farm legislation, became a New Deal administrator. Peek had joined Deere and Company in 1893 as a clerk in the credit manager's office of a branch firm. At the age of 28 he was picked as general manager of the ailing John Deere Plow Company. Sales and profits soared under Peek's direction. In 1909 he served on a committee to plan the reorganization of Deere and Company, and two years later the various branches and affiliates of John Deere, such as Moline Wagon Company and Union Iron, were being managed through a central holding company of which Peek had become vice-president for sales.[10]

During World War I Peek served on Woodrow Wilson's War Industries Board under Bernard Baruch. He advised cooperation among industries; conservation to avoid the wasteful use of materials, labor, and capital; standardization; price fixing "under certain circumstances"; and continuing government-business cooperation. When the war ended Peek became head of a new industrial board to supervise demobilization, but his ideas on government price controls soon clashed with other federal departments and the board ceased operation. Peek returned to the implement business as head of the Moline Plow Company.[11]

When farm prices collapsed in 1920, and the agricultural depression worsened throughout the decade, Peek and his associate and friend Hugh S. Johnson developed a plan for governmental assistance and regulation to restore farm prosperity. Considered in Congress between 1924 and 1928 as the McNary-Haugen Bill, it was passed on two occasions only to be vetoed by President Calvin Coolidge. The plan would have created a commodity marketing cooperative, made available low-interest government loans to farmers, and guaranteed a fixed price for farm products. The fixed price would be based on a "parity" figure derived from the relationship of agricultural and industrial price structures between 1909 and 1913. President Herbert Hoover substituted the Agricultural Marketing Act for the parity price scheme but retained the feature of low-cost governmental loans to farmers and accepted, in emergencies, the outright purchase of farm commodities by government agencies at prevailing market, but not parity, prices.

After the stock market crash in 1929 the farm depression deepened. Upon becoming president in 1933 Franklin Roosevelt accepted a new version of the parity pricing idea that substituted a government-owned commodity corporation for the cooperative marketing association planned by Peek. The Agricultural Adjustment Act (AAA) marked a new and unique collaboration between the federal government and a major sector of the private economy. Under the AAA the government guaranteed farm prices at parity levels and in return farmers accepted production and marketing controls. Supplemental legislation, such as the Kerr-Smith Act that taxed tobacco produced by farmers who did not sign AAA contracts, forced compliance where such was not obtained voluntarily. In a broad sense the government established supplies and controlled demand; thus the farm economy became intensely regulated. Farmers generally cooperated with business leaders such as Peek, Johnson, Otto Kahn of Kuhn, Loeb and Company, and Bernard Baruch in developing the outlines of the new farm policy; farmers have since remained generally supportive of federal farm programs.

The National Recovery Administration (NRA) also offers a classic example of the liaisons between government and business that developed in the New Deal era. Raymond Moley, a former professor of political science, unwrapped the basic idea of the NRA in a speech before the U.S. Chamber of Commerce in 1932, and the chamber endorsed the scheme with some enthusiasm. Moley advised establishing codes of fair competition for business combined with hour and wage laws for labor and fair prices for consumers. Subsequently, the National Industrial Recovery Act of 1933 required industry, labor, and government representatives to develop codes of competition that provided for minimum prices, production quotas, and minimum wages and maximum hours. Section 7a guaranteed the right of collective bargaining by labor. The NRA, headed by George N. Peek's former business associate Hugh S. Johnson, employed legal action and moral persuasion with its "Blue Eagle" label to enforce the agreements. Consumers were told that buying at the sign of the "Blue Eagle" was tantamount to being a patriotic citizen.

The NRA proved detrimental to most small businesspersons, laborers, and many consumers. Codes of fair competition tended to reflect the interests of the industry rather than those of consumers and workers. Price fixing and marketing quotas received government sanction. Small businesses, unable to participate in the program, lost customers. By 1935, when the Supreme Court struck down the NRA on the grounds that the delegation of congressional power to the executive to write legally binding codes was unconstitutional, public opposition to the program had mounted. The NRA was allowed to die a peaceful death.

The Supreme Court decision of 1936 striking down the Agricultural Adjustment Act, on the other hand, did not meet with the approval of the administration or farmers. Substitute legislation, the Soil Conservation and Domestic Allotment Act, allowed farmers to collect government subsidies under the guise of soil conservation, and in 1938 a new AAA reinstated the basic commodity-control parity price program without the previously offending provision for a processing tax to pay for it. The government now assumed full responsibility for the farmer's fiscal welfare.

New Deal financial legislation, frequently characterized as being antibanker had, perhaps, some negative elements, but it actually provided more help than hindrances to the community. As we have seen, President Roosevelt halted a bank panic two days after taking the oath of office by declaring a nationwide bank holiday. This action technically closed banks for four days, but actually most remained closed until they could sort out their financial condition and be certified by specially appointed bank examiners. Congress granted special authority for this procedure in the Emergency Banking Act passed a few days later. Banks that could be stabilized with an infusion of capital received government loans from the Reconstruction Finance Corporation. Those that were insolvent never reopened. Of those closed by the "holiday," 90 percent resumed business. The Glass-Steagall Banking Act and the Banking Act of 1935 strengthened Federal Reserve Board control over the reserve requirements of member banks and gave the board greater independence. These acts, supported by most of the banking community, provided government support to a discredited banking system and restored consumer confidence.

Other important financial legislation regulated the national stock exchanges. The Securities Act of 1933 required corporations trading their stock on national exchanges to register with the FTC and provide full financial information to the commission. In 1934 Congress created the Securities and Exchange Commission (SEC), which assumed the security registration functions of the FTC. Companies could not sell securities in interstate commerce or use the mail service to sell securities unless registered with the SEC. Officers and directors of corporations were required to disclose their personal holdings, and securities brokers and dealers also had to register and provide individual financial information. The act authorized the commission to regulate sales and exchanges of securities, and it empowered the board of governors of the Federal Reserve System to prescribe margin requirements for the sale and trade of securities, the *margin* being the collateral or cash required for a stock purchase. A 10 percent margin enables a buyer to purchase $10,000 in stock for a $1,000 investment, the remaining $9,000 being in the form of a "call loan" or brokers loan, at a "call rate" determined by the board of governors. Thus, a government agency provided not just regulation, but coordination and uniform standards for the securities industry.

Generally, the first New Deal, that is the programs and policies of the Roosevelt administration between 1933 and 1935, stressed cooperative business-government planning. The administration worked toward recovery and relief rather than reform or a restructuring of the social order. A growing sentiment critical of the liaison between businesspersons and the New Deal, a people increasingly desperate because of the slow economic recovery, and continuing high unemployment and impoverishment forced Roosevelt into a more controversial position. On the one hand, opponents such as Huey P. Long called upon the New Deal to end the rule of big business and to "Share-Our-Wealth," while on the other hand probusiness supporters such as Herbert Hoover, Al Smith, the Du Ponts, and the American Liberty League attacked Roosevelt's regimentation and regulation. The result was a second New Deal, which severed some of the business-government connections and which developed a greater responsibility for social welfare.

The second New Deal, which began in 1935, was ushered in by advisors who rejected the role business had thus far assumed in formulating economic policy. Legislation stressed aid and assistance to the individual rather than to industry. The National Labor Relations Act gave a decisive endorsement to collective bargaining and union shops by organized labor in direct conflict with the interests of industry. The Social Security Act of 1935 created government pensions for the aged. The act provided for three kinds of assistance—benefit payments for dependent children and the blind and crippled, unemployment insurance, and retirement annuities for the employed. Benefits were to be funded by taxes upon the employees earnings and on the employer. The Wealth Tax raised the maximum tax that the government could impose on individual incomes from 50 to 75 percent and was regarded by many as an important step in the redistribution of American income, although in retrospect little such redistribution occurred. The Works Progress Administration poured federal dollars into programs for the unemployed. The Fair Labor Standards Act of 1938 established a minimum wage, a maximum work week, and restrictions on child labor. Organized labor especially achieved a distinct advantage from the second New Deal and Roosevelt's shift in orientation.

THE UNIONIZATION OF INDUSTRY

Although industrial laborers enjoyed improved salaries and working conditions during World War I and the postwar boom years, the depression halted and reversed labor's progress. Intense competition within industry adversely affected labor. Assembly line speed-ups, the firing of older and higher-paid employees, arbitrary firings, lay-offs (as during Henry Ford's retooling for the Model-A in 1927–1928), and generally adverse employee relations produced increasing dissatisfaction among workers. The depression compounded labor's problems. Moreover, the strike, labor's most effective device for improving benefits, worked best in good times, when least needed, and was least effective in hard times when unemployment was high and factories were closing.

The New Deal provided some relief for industrial labor through Section 7A of the National Industrial Recovery Act, which guaranteed the right of collective bargaining under the codes of fair competition. Although unionization continued to be resisted in many businesses, and was sometimes countered by industry organizing workers into "company unions," labor made some strides in collective bargaining in 1933 and 1934. The International Ladies' Garment Workers Union and the Amalgamated Clothing Workers, for example, made enormous gains in membership, and by 1935 the business and political climate had become more favorable to external organization. The National Labor Relations Act (Wagner Act) provided a powerful new stimulus to unionization by establishing the National Labor Relations Board (NLRB) to monitor union elections and to control antiunion actions by employers.

Despite the improved political climate for the unionization of the auto industry, labor itself could not agree on the method of organization. The American Federation of Labor (AFL) faced an internal conflict over whether to attempt to organize autoworkers en masse in an industrial union or to use their traditional organization of skilled craft groups. Supporters of the industrial-union position pointed out that only 5 percent of the autoworkers could be termed skilled craftsmen, and that no effective union organization of the industry could proceed without incorporating the unskilled or semiskilled masses of workers. Traditional craft union advocates feared that the skilled workers would be overwhelmed by the nonskilled and that the "craft principle" would be jeopardized. John L. Lewis, head of the United Mine Workers (UMW), and William Green, president of the AFL, both supported the industrial-union structure for the auto industry, but in 1935 the industrial union advocates were forced to accept a decision that an automobile workers union would serve under the protective jurisdiction of the AFL for a provisional period. It was at this convention that the rift in the ranks of labor was symbolized by John L. Lewis's right hook to the jaw of William L. Hutcheson of the Carpenters' Union, an advocate of the traditional craft organizational structure.

At the close of the convention John L. Lewis and industrial union advocates established a Committee for Industrial Organization (CIO), which Lewis chaired. Despite an order from the executive committee of the AFL that it disband, the CIO proceeded to organize and recruit new membership. The United Automobile Workers (UAW) held its first national convention in May 1936, and it voted to join the CIO. In August 1936, the AFL suspended CIO affiliates from membership in its ranks, and two years later the committee became the Congress of Industrial Organizations, thus dividing the labor movement. Even while battling the AFL, Lewis and the CIO pressed ahead in their efforts to organize the automobile industry.

FORD MOTOR COMPANY AND THE RIVER ROUGE REVOLT

Efforts to organize the automobile industry met stiff resistance from the companies and "sandbagging" from rival union organizations. Government interceded with limited success. During the UAW strike at General Motors in 1937, which directly involved 48,000 workers in eighteen plants but which affected 126,000 workers in twenty-five cities, the governor of Michigan and the U.S. Department of Labor attempted to bring representatives from labor and management together to discuss issues. Management refused to negotiate until sit-down strikers left their plants. Finally, the union agreed to evacuate if General Motors met certain conditions. On February 11, 1937, the long and bitter ordeal was settled. General Motors recognized the UAW as the bargaining agent for its employees. Union confrontations with Ford Motor Company, however, which also began in 1937, became increasingly violent and nonproductive.

Norman Smith, "a hulking, unkempt, gentle-faced organizer," had been beaten by Ford-hired guards at Memphis. At the River Rouge plant in Detroit, Ford company goons beat CIO organizers pitilessly. Ford Motor Company, by threats and intimidation, and by offering company inducements to laborers, staved off union organizers until 1941. But that year, near the site of the River Rouge violence, Norman Smith announced, a few minutes after midnight, a strike—and called for a picket line.

The strike was provoked by Ford Motor Company, but not planned by union leaders. Eleven employees, key CIO personnel, had been fired by the River Rouge plant management. The CIO leaders asked to discuss the firings with Ford officials; management refused. While CIO bosses debated behind closed doors what action to take, the rank and file of employees in the River Rouge plant began work stoppages. By the time CIO leaders were ready to make a decision, events were out of their hands; there could be no retreat from a strike already in progress. The strike officially began at 12:15 A.M.

The 85,000 workers at the River Rouge plant rebelled against Henry Ford and in a sense against their own leaders. Ford eventually accepted all of the union's demands in return for its pledge that there would be no more trouble and that court cases pending against Ford would be dropped. Finally, Ford agreed to allow labor to put a union label on Ford cars. Successful unionization of the automobile industry derived in good measure from the legal and psychological support offered the union by the New Deal and the National Labor Relations Act. Labor had in one sense become a new "countervailing" power in the national economy.

Following Christmas, 1936, the United Auto Workers staged sit-down strikes in General Motors plants in Cleveland and Flint. Organizational activities and violent strikes spread to other plants so that, by mid-February 1937, first General Motors and then Chrysler Corporation capitulated and accepted union contracts with CIO-affiliate UAW as the exclusive bargaining agency for their workers. Ford Motor Company resisted unionization vigorously and sometimes violently. Walter Reuther, who became head of UAW, narrowly escaped assassination, and strike breakers and sabotage were utilized. But in the end, with war drawing near (1941), Ford Motor Company also accepted a union contract.[12]

The Progressive Era, the Great Depression, and the New Deal produced distinctive changes in the business environment. During the Progressive Era a new relationship developed between business and government. Whereas in previous decades government had been the handmaiden of business and industrial interests, under the leadership of Theodore Roosevelt and Woodrow Wilson government assumed regulatory authority over many phases of commerce. But this authority, particularly during the 1920s, tended to reflect only the interests and concerns of business. The depression subsequently dispelled both the moral and economic ascendancy of the business elite; nevertheless the first New Deal stressed government-business cooperation in the pursuit of relief and recovery. Although government regulations sometimes moved to that indefinable point where they became government controls, the controls, albeit governmental, generally remained in the hands of business leaders or their partisans.

The second New Deal denoted a transition in government-business relations, but by no means a revolution. It was less a "determined, stalwart, eloquent fight against business domination," than the displacement of at least some business leaders in government policy roles by professional bureaucrats and managers. Government assumed a broad general-welfare obligation through Social Security and farm programs, and it exerted far greater controls over business and private individuals through new taxing and spending authority. Perhaps most significantly, the depression and the New Deal facilitated the expansion of organized labor. By the eve of World War II both government and labor emerged as new and powerful social and political forces with which business had to contend. Government and labor would prescribe the terms on which business was to be conducted, and they became countervailing powers within the national economy.

NOTES

1. Earl Latham, ed., *John D. Rockefeller, Robber Baron or Industrial Statesman?* (Lexington, Massachusetts: Heath, 1949), p. v.

2. See *Historical Statistics of the United States, Colonial Times to 1970,* Series K240–250, p. 482; Series K407–413, p. 498; Series D735–738, p. 165; Series F1–5, p. 224.

3. U.S. 63rd Congress, Special Sess., *Senate Document 3,* reprinted in Henry Steele Commager, *Documents of American History* (New York: Appleton-Century-Crofts, 1968), pp. 82–84.

4. Robert H. Wiebe, *Businessmen and Reform: A Study of the Progressive Movement* (Cambridge: Harvard University Press, 1962), p. 212.

5. Ibid., pp. 211–224.

6. Harold F. Williamson, Ralph L. Andreano, Arnold R. Daum, and Gilbert C. Klose, *The American Petroleum Industry—II: The Age of Energy, 1899–1959* (Evanston, Illinois: Northwestern University Press, 1963), pp. 466–468.

7. Ibid., pp. 468–70.

8. Ibid., pp. 702–722.

9. Testimony of Willard P. Mueller, *Economic Concentration, Overall and Conglomerate Aspects,* Hearings before the Subcommittee on Antitrust and Monopoly of the Committee of the Judiciary, U.S. Senate, 80th Congress, 2nd Sess. (Washington, D.C.: Government Printing Office, 1964), p. 115.

10. Gilbert C. Fite, *George N. Peek and the Fight for Farm Parity* (Norman: University of Oklahoma Press, 1954), pp. 22–29.

11. Ibid., pp. 29, 37.

12. See Alfred D. Chandler, Jr., ed., *Giant Enterprise: Ford, General Motors, and the Automobile Industry* (New York: Harcourt, Brace & World, 1964), pp. 9–20, 194–229.

SUGGESTED READING

BERNSTEIN, IRVING. *The Turbulent Years: A History of the American Worker, 1933–1941.* Boston: Houghton Mifflin, 1970.

CHANDLER, LESTER V. *America's Greatest Depression, 1929–1941.* New York: Harper & Row, 1970.

DANIEL, PETE. *Breaking the Land: The Transformation of Cotton, Tobacco, and Rice Cultures Since 1880.* Urbana: University of Illinois Press, 1985.

FAULKNER, HAROLD U. *The Decline of Laissez-faire, 1897–1917.* New York: Rinehart Pub., 1951.

FINE, SIDNEY. *The Automobile under the Blue Eagle.* Ann Arbor: University of Michigan Press, 1963.

FUSFELD, DANIEL R. *The Economic Thought of Franklin D. Roosevelt and the Origins of the New Deal.* New York: Columbia University Press, 1956.

HAWLEY, ELLIS W. *The New Deal and the Problem of Monopoly: A Study in Economic Ambivalence.* Princeton, New Jersey: Princeton University Press, 1966.

KOLKO, GABRIEL. *The Triumph of Conservatism: A Reinterpretation of American History, 1900–1916.* Glencoe, Illinois: Free Press, 1963.

LINK, ARTHUR S. *Woodrow Wilson and the Progressive Era, 1910–1917.* New York: Harper & Row, 1954.

MOWRY, GEORGE E. *The Era of Theodore Roosevelt and the Birth of Modern America, 1900–1912.* New York: Harper & Row, 1958.

O'NEILL, WILLIAM L. *The Progressive Years: America Comes of Age.* New York: Dodd, Mead and Co., 1975.

SCHLESINGER, ARTHUR M., JR. *The Crisis of the Old Order, 1919–1933.* Boston: Houghton Mifflin, 1957.

SOBEL, ROBERT. *The Great Bull Market: Wall Street in the 1920s.* New York: W. W. Norton & Co., 1968.

WIEBE, ROBERT H. *Businessmen and Reform: A Study of the Progressive Movement.* Cambridge: Harvard University Press, 1962.

——. *The Search for Order, 1877–1920.* New York: Hill & Wang, 1967.

17 War and Business

In his farewell address as president in 1961, Dwight D. Eisenhower expressed deep concern about the connections between "immense military establishments" and the arms industry that pervaded the entire society—"economic, political, even spiritual." The "military-industrial complex," as he labeled this powerful structure, dominated the universities, the scientific community, and all levels of government. The president cautioned, "In the councils of government, we must guard against the acquisition of unwarranted influence, whether sought or unsought, by the military-industrial complex. The potential for the disastrous rise of misplaced power exists and will persist."[1] Journalists, economists, historians, and politicians have enlarged upon this moderate Republican critique of the economic imbalance created by a worldwide arms race to erect an ideology highly critical of the relationship between the military establishment and business.

The emergence of the interrelationship of business and the federal defense apparatus parallels trends from the 1880s to the present. Modern warfare has led to larger and more complicated economic and political structures that attempt to use bureaucracy in order to achieve monumental tasks. The effort to mobilize Americans to fight World War I by utilizing the administrative and technical skills of private industry created a vast state-managed defense system with an enormous business structure producing military goods for that particular market.[2] While substantial military spending gives rise to firms that are wholly defense oriented, supplying those military demands may also produce new public-sector industries and create competition for those firms with monopolistic positions in the existing economy. That the Nike-Hercules missile system of the 1960s required 1.5 million parts and 80,000 working drawings and blueprints suggests the need for business-military cooperation as defense needs became increasingly complex in the twentieth century. The specialized requirements of the military, and its effect on business, can be seen in the emergence of a modern navy in the late nineteenth century.

THE NAVY AND THE ARMS TRUST

Beginning in the 1880s the United States entered the naval arms race with Great Britain, Germany, France, and Japan. The search for colonial acquisitions, the efforts to dominate trade routes, and the need for protected coaling stations reflected the rise of imperialism in the late nineteenth century. In this period the nation was blessed with huge federal budget surpluses. Captain Alfred Mahan and others pointed to our aged, obsolete, decrepit navy that contained fewer modern ships than could be found in the Chilean fleet, and the Congress began to direct funds toward shipbuilding. The Department of the Navy turned to civilian shipyards and steelmakers to construct our first modern armored vessels, thus initiating the so-called military-industrial complex. Armor plate for battleships, which required heavy machinery to make, had only one potential buyer, the federal government. Entry into the manufacture of armor plate was limited to firms already in the steel business that possessed capital to build specialized facilities. The steel corporations offered to produce armor plate for the unusually high price of $545 per ton because of the substantial costs of manufacture.

As early as 1889 Bethlehem and Carnegie Steel acquired rights to a French process that added nickel to steel to produce a superior armor plate. Technological improvements by the mid-1890s made an even higher quality product available for the naval race. By the turn of the century only three American steel companies participated in the market—Bethlehem, Carnegie, and Midvale—and each depended upon Canadian nickel as the vital ingredient for the armor plate. A European cartel established an armor plate price of $540 per ton that U.S. producers soon accepted. Shortly after 1900 the Carnegie Steel Company became part of U.S. Steel Company, organized by J. P. Morgan and Company. Morgan gained control of the Canadian nickel output, and Morgan partners were also deeply involved in restructuring Bethlehem Steel prior to World War I. In 1915 Morgan and U.S. Steel acquired control of Midvale Steel and Remington Arms Company, thus creating an armament trust under the direction of the Morgan interests.

By the time of World War I, J. P. Morgan and Company controlled the armor plate industry and the nickel supply vital to its production. Profits on the nickel alone proved substantial. In order for the U.S. Navy to be competitive with the fleets of other major powers, and to protect the colonial possessions in the Caribbean and the Pacific, it had to have armor-plated ships, and Morgan's cartel provided the plate—at a high price. Businesspersons, labor union representatives, congressmen, naval offices, and university and religious leaders, all advocated a modern fleet for a variety of reasons.[3] The Department of the Navy and the Morgan interests helped form an alliance—a military-industrial complex—which would grow and mature during World War I.

BUSINESS AND WORLD WAR I

The crisis of 1917 brought the United States its first experience at total economic mobilization. The rapid deployment of materiel and troops to France required that a major share of the nation's industrial production be diverted to the war effort. The Wilson administration turned to business leaders to organize the procurement of supplies for the war machine. Little preparation had been made between the outbreak of the war in Europe in 1914 and mobilization efforts in the United States, which began in 1916. The Army Appropriations Act of that year created a Council for National Defense that would organize civilian advisory boards to develop mobilization plans. The council determined that private companies should supply munitions rather than expand federal munitions facilities, thus turning to the private sector from the outset. Leading the way in the mobilization effort, the council tapped hundreds of industrial leaders to serve on the advisory committees. Experts from industry served as "dollar-a-year" men, providing the government with advice without requiring the individuals to make undue financial sacrifices. Nevertheless, the army's general staff resented the involvement, or "interference," by civilians in their procurement procedures. The result was economic havoc as the army spent over $14 billion in three years through its inefficient supply system. Despite the efforts of the National Defense Council, the implementation of an orderly mobilization plan failed. The War Industries Board, created in July 1917, was an attempt to centralize all economic planning in one body. But it, too, failed to harness effectively the nation's productive capacity. Not until spring 1918 did President Wilson obtain sufficient authority from Congress to conduct the war effort with some degree of order.

The Great War was forcing a vast expansion of state involvement in the economy, and a civilian administrative army filled Washington as never before. New federal agencies, including the Committee on Public Information (propaganda), the Food and Fuel Administration (food and heat), and the War Industries Board (the total economy), conducted the war effort. The War Industries Board (WIB), containing some of the leading figures of several industries including Bernard Baruch of Wall Street, Robert S. Lovett of the Union Pacific Railroad, and Robert S. Brookings, a retired millionaire, acted as a clearinghouse to facilitate production of military and civilian goods in the most efficient and expeditious manner. When Baruch became chairman in March 1918, the WIB began to move more vigorously, and with the passage of the Overman Act on May 20, 1918, it became the most powerful agency for conducting the war.[4]

The "dollar-a-year" business leaders on the WIB and its subordinate bodies labored to organize each industry to maximize production; they coordinated businesses and forced former competitors to cooperate. In many cases the businesses did not fare well financially. Ford Motor Company, for example, which manufactured airplane motors, tractors, ambulances, trucks, tanks and even antisubmarine boats, was forced to cut back drastically on automobile production. Profits fell from $57 million in 1915–1916 to $31 million in 1917–1918. After taxes Ford made profits of $4.4 million on defense work; it could have earned much more if civilian production had continued without interruption.[5] Nevertheless, the patriotic fervor of the war effort aided the WIB's program to harness the productive capacity of firms such as Ford on behalf of the government. Ironically, the Wilson administration, which had entered office with a strong antitrust program and had enacted the Clayton Anti-Trust Act in 1914, simply ignored that aspect of progressivism by ending competition in an effort to defeat the Kaiser. The result was far greater federal involvement in national economic planning than had ever occurred before, and enhancement of the trend toward larger organizations in the total society. The precedent established by the experience placed military procurement in the hands of civilians in the War and Navy Departments who had strong ties to industry. The links between the military and big business welded by the experiences of 1916–1918 continued after the Armistice.

BETWEEN THE WARS, 1919–1941

From the Armistice to Pearl Harbor, plans for future mobilization were developed by the business community and the armed forces. During these years Congress ordered the War Department to work with industry and used defense appropriations to guarantee that the directive was followed. The defense budgets, although small, cemented ties between business and the military. Unlike the World War I period when the army, in particular, cooperated only reluctantly with civilians in the mobilization effort, the interwar years saw the beginnings of full cooperation between the military and industry.

The National Defense Act of 1920 reorganized military procurement through new supply bureaus with civilian leadership. A joint Army-Navy-Munitions Board coordinated procurement for the services. Thousands of business leaders assisted the War Department throughout the 1920s and 1930s as mobilization plans were drafted and redrafted. Some businesses felt that such service enhanced the probability of selling products to the government; others saw participation as an opportunity to make more efficient use of national resources. After numerous efforts to develop plans for mobilization and the massive purchasing a major war would require, the secretary of war presented the Industrial Mobilization Plan that was approved by Congress in 1930. Based on World War I experiences, the plan relied on joint military-civilian committees to control the economy. The proposal recognized that modern warfare required total planning of the economy and subordination of the military to civilian mobilization agencies. Even the antiwar Nye Committee of the 1930s accepted the interdependence of some industries—shipbuilding, for example—and the military. Clearly the defense establishment had to work closely with the emerging aviation industry.[6]

THE AVIATION INDUSTRY, 1919–1939

World War I created the aviation industry—and later almost killed it. There were no significant U.S. aircraft manufacturers in 1914; total national output was 49 planes. Yet the demands of war, first from the Allies, then from the U.S. Army for American flyers, led to the construction of more than 14,000 planes in 1918. Hundreds of small plants built motors and airplane parts and assembled the components. In all, the industry received $365 million in contracts before production was abruptly cancelled in 1918 with the Armistice. Although the aviation companies had produced an incredible number of planes, and employed 20,000 people, only $5 million in capital could be found in the entire industry. It soon fell on hard times as government surplus planes flooded the market. Throughout the 1920s and 1930s the plane builders struggled to survive on a few military and civilian orders. An industry that produced an expensive, high-quality, technologically innovative product with a small number of potential customers needed stability, and a consequence was the merger of many producers into a few large firms such as Douglas, Consolidated, and North American Aviation. Unlike the aviation industries in Western Europe, companies in this country did not receive direct government subsidies despite the demonstrated military importance of aircraft in World War I. While the federal government in 1926 did authorize 1,600 planes for the army and 1,000 for the navy, the limited funds for procurement led to much smaller acquisitions. Indeed, federal purchases fell in the 1930s, and only foreign orders in the last year of the decade saved several of the firms from bankruptcy. By 1939 the industry ranked forty-first among all businesses and was producing 6,000 planes yearly. Its success or failure was directly linked to military needs.[7]

In that year there were four major plane builders—Douglas, Boeing, Curtiss-Wright, and North American—and two engine manufacturers—Curtiss-Wright and Pratt and Whitney. Yet because of the complex technological interdependence of the firms, no oligopoly existed. In addition, the low capital requirements made it easy for new companies to enter the market, as Republic did in 1939. Military and civilian aircraft needs varied enormously, allowing each firm to specialize in one or two planes or motor types. Some, such as Sikorsky, concentrated entirely on one market, in this case the Flying Boat. The diversity in the industry proved very important after December 7, 1941.

BUSINESS AND THE COMING OF WORLD WAR II

As war clouds gathered in Europe and Asia after 1931, American business leaders vocally opposed any involvement by the United States. "The net result of war always is a loss," declared one spokesman, and another industrialist claimed that "private enterprise needs peace for profits."[8] As late as 1939 business executives opposed war more vigorously than the general public. At the same time most business leaders fought the Embargo Act, which drastically limited trade with countries at war or in war zones; they favored a *laissez faire* policy with regard to trading with belligerents. When war broke out in Europe in September 1939, business affirmed its desire for peace. Some of the opposition to war reflected traditional isolationism, but most industrial leaders saw war as an interruption of economic recovery in a time of ever-expanding federal control. A change in attitude developed in support of a new national defense program in 1940–1941, but until Pearl Harbor most businesspersons did not favor American involvement in the hostilities. This was particularly true of small businesses.

GENERAL ANILINE AND FILM COMPANY

The I. G. Farben chemical combine became an adjunct of the German rearmament effort in the 1930s—and a willing partner in Hitler's plan to make the Third Reich independent of foreign rubber and oil sources. In the United States I. G. Farben's most valuable property, General Aniline and Film Company (GAF), was controlled by a Farben holding operation based in Switzerland. General Aniline and Film produced dyes and photographic supplies, being second only to Eastman Kodak in the latter field. The Farben interests had lost the rights to thousands of patents in the 1920s as a consequence of World War I, and the company wanted to hide its control of GAF should war come again.

Nevertheless, the Treasury Department and other federal agencies moved quickly after the spring of 1940 to establish clear ownership of GAF by I. G. Farben, labeling GAF a Nazi front. On April 24, 1942, the government seized GAF as an alien property. When the war ended, the "Swiss owners" of GAF sought to reclaim the company. At the same time several American firms, either in the dye-stuffs business or wishing to enter it, sought to purchase GAF from the federal government. Claims by Standard Oil Company of New Jersey that it had purchased GAF before 1941 were rejected by the government. For decades claims and counterclaims reached federal courts as minority stockholders, "Swiss investors," and others sought to acquire title to what had become a major American industrial firm. Remington Rand, W. R. Grace and Company, and others made offers to purchase GAF, but no clear title could be established.

Finally, during the administration of John F. Kennedy, Prince Radziwill, the president's brother-in-law, served as liaison between the European claimants and the federal government to arrange a settlement. The president signed a law in October 1962 that allowed the sale. On March 9, 1965, General

Aniline and Film was sold at auction for $329,141,926 to a syndicate which then sold shares to the public. The European interests realized $122 million from the sale. Thus the seizure of GAF under the alien property law led to the creation of a large independent giant in the chemical and dye-stuffs industry.

In its early efforts to build up the nation's defenses after 1938, the federal government wanted massive results in the shortest possible time. While President Roosevelt and the War and Navy Departments gave lip service to the need to mobilize small business, such firms lacked the capital and experience to do little more than serve as effective subcontractors. Between June 1940 and December 1941 three-fourths of the basic military contracts awarded went to the nation's one hundred largest firms. In addition, over $13 billion had been allocated by the government to build new plants for the latter companies. Yet when the facilities of the largest corporations reached capacity by 1942, the War Production Board had no alternative but to turn to smaller businesses. The federal Smaller War Plants Corporation had $150 million to lend to such firms to help them respond to defense requirements, but even this program made little headway in redirecting defense contracts to smaller corporations.[9] The government's dependence on large-scale output by major firms can be seen in the enormous production figures of the World War II years, and in the rise of new industrial giants such as Henry J. Kaiser.

WAR PRODUCTION AND HENRY J. KAISER

The demands of war brought an end to the Great Depression, created a modernized industrial plant, and led to a substantial rise in productivity and real wages. The coming of the Lend-Lease program in March 1941 initiated the shift to military output. The War Management Commission saw the 8 million unemployed of 1939 disappear, and by 1942 eagerly sought submarginal workers for defense plants. The Defense Plant Corporation, a federal agency, funded two-thirds of the new factories added during the war years. Even with 14 million men and women in uniform, construction, mining, and manufacturing more than doubled production between 1939 and 1944. In five years productivity increased by 25 percent. The industrial economy provided the war effort with 296,000 airplanes, 11,900 ships, 86,000 tanks, and almost 3 million vehicles. A highly regulated and controlled economy exceeded all expectations of the military planners.

Federal fiscal policy helped maintain a dual civilian-military economy. War expenditures reached $350 billion, and the national debt rose to $260 billion, but much of the cost was paid from higher taxes. Increased taxes held down inflationary pressures and helped to limit "excess" profits on defense contracts. By 1944 federal taxes absorbed one-fourth of the national income, and federal expenditures represented half of all spending. The Office of Price Administration (OPA) effectively regulated consumer prices and rents, so that in six years (1939–1945), consumer goods prices rose only 28 percent despite the pressures created by shortages and the 50 percent rise in disposable income.

Not all businesses profited equally from war-related expansion. Firms that could convert to military production found new business, but those companies able to produce only for a civilian market were hurt badly. Some industries could convert more rapidly because of the nature of their output or because of access to capital. A few businesses closed, unable to survive in the wartime economy. Other entrepreneurs seized the opportunity to build industrial empires, and few as successfully as Henry J. Kaiser.

Kaiser entered the world of business as a road builder prior to World War I. He became a regional highway contractor in the Northwest and in the 1930s joined with five other construction firms to build the Hoover (Boulder) Dam. In combination with other firms he participated in constructing the Bonneville Dam, the San Francisco–Oakland Bay Bridge, tunnels in the Rockies, and dry docks on the Pacific coast. In 1940 when a British mission came to the United States seeking contractors to build Liberty ships to replace vessels being sunk by German submarines, Kaiser formed a consortium to build the ships. He eventually constructed seven shipyards with fifty-eight shipways where vessels were produced on an assembly-line basis with prefabricated parts. Welding processes replaced rivets as Kaiser sought and found ways to speed production. His yards soon launched a ship a day, initially taking twenty-seven days to build a vessel, and then constructing one in four days. The 197,000 workers in Kaiser yards built 1,490 vessels at 25 percent less than the average cost at the other shipyards. Kaiser simply applied his construction concepts to shipbuilding, a business he initially knew nothing about.

To construct the ships he needed steel, and he persuaded the federal

Henry J. Kaiser inspects his shipyard at Richmond, California, in 1943.   (Courtesy: Kaiser Aluminum Company.)

government to loan him money to build the first steel plant west of the Rockies at Fontana, California. Meanwhile, Kaiser produced cement, built military installations, and manufactured munitions. The various Kaiser firms did a $5 billion business in five years, earning profits of $40 million, or less than 1 percent. Kaiser had entered the war as a construction and engineering firm; in 1945 it emerged with skills and managerial expertise to enter many new endeavors.

After 1945 Kaiser vastly expanded its cement production, invested more money in the Kaiser Steel plant at Fontana, which became profitable in 1950, and entered the primary aluminum business. New Kaiser factories produced gypsum board, appliances, auto parts, chemicals, and aircraft. The postwar building boom led Kaiser to enter the home-construction field and later to develop a resort community in Hawaii. The only major failure experienced was the abortive attempt to manufacture automobiles. Kaiser Industries became a global conglomerate after 1945, and it was the instigator of one of the nation's most successful health-care plans, Kaiser Foundation Medical Care Program. It, too, grew out of Kaiser's World War II experiences. By 1967, if all Kaiser enterprises had been grouped together, it would have been the nation's thirtieth largest industry.[10]

The Kaiser story is unique, but similar experiences between 1940 and 1945 created capital, technology, and managerial skills that were utilized after V-J Day to build major new firms. Nowhere was this more evident than in aviation, and later aerospace.

WORLD WAR II AND THE ALUMINUM MONOPOLY

In 1939 one company produced aluminum in the United States—Aluminum Company of America (Alcoa). That year Alcoa sold 164,000 tons of the metal. Thirty years later, largely as a result of World War II, there were eight domestic producers who sold more than 3.3 million tons of aluminum per year. The war had created a tremendous need for aluminum, particularly for aircraft and other military purposes, and the federal government terminated Alcoa's monopoly by building aluminum plants and selling them or leasing them when the war ended. Experiences during the war showed many new ways aluminum could be used, and extensive research by the industry led to additional products, especially in the consumer market.

Commercial aluminum production had begun in France in 1855, but the cost was $115 per pound! By 1886 new refining methods drastically reduced costs and production began to climb. Not until 1907 was Alcoa formed; it employed the electrical production of a power plant at Niagara Falls, New York, to smelt its ores. Through its patents on the basic refining process, Alcoa established a monopoly in the business and cooperated fully with an international aluminum cartel. The monopoly continued despite a federal antitrust suit initiated in 1937. But by the time the monopoly charges had been upheld in a federal court in 1940, other firms already were entering the market, primarily Reynolds Metals Company, a lead and foil manufacturer for tobacco products.

Between 1941 and 1945 as military requirements for aluminum soared,

The Reynolds Metals plant at Lesterhill, Alabama, put in operation in 1941, enhanced the war effort and competition in the aluminum industry.   (Courtesy: Reynolds Metals Company.)

Alcoa sought to remain the major producer. Although it increased production 50 percent from 1940 to 1941, Alcoa could not meet all federal needs, and the Defense Plant Corporation, a federal agency, began to build aluminum plants and lease them to Reynolds and other firms not previously in the industry, as well as to Alcoa. When the war ended, the government sold as "surplus" its most efficient plants, and 40 percent of the capacity went to competitors of Alcoa. Henry J. Kaiser entered the aluminum business, and Reynolds expanded its plant capacity. By 1958 other major metals companies had become primary aluminum producers. Thus, war needs served to break Alcoa's monopoly far more effectively than a federal court antitrust decision. The new aluminum firms, through their research labs, created additional products and reduced raw-aluminum prices, leading to vast expansion of tonnage and sales. At the end of the 1960s Alcoa had about 34 percent of the market, Reynolds about 25 percent, and Kaiser 20 percent. Thus World War II had had a significant impact on one of the major metals industries, and the nation and its consumers were the beneficiaries.

AVIATION: WORLD WAR II AND AFTER

President Franklin Roosevelt, in May 1940, proposed that the aviation industry develop the capacity to produce 50,000 planes per year, and that a procurement program be enacted to provide the armed services with 50,000 military aircraft. He proposed a gigantic increase in output in a very short period of time. New plants, designs, and personnel had to be acquired, and existing facilities converted; it was necessary to transform the industry from a "job-shop mentality" to an assembly-line concept. Because of the vast array of parts, subassemblies, and firms involved, one aircraft might require 20,000 or more drawings and blueprints. Yet the nation needed an incredible number of planes, and very quickly. Following a series of conferences between plane builders and government officials, a division of responsibilities for motors, airframes, instruments, and landing gears was devised, and prime and subcontractors were licensed to make assemblies and parts. The industry terminated competition as demand greatly exceeded productive capacity. The goal established by Roosevelt in 1940 was easily exceeded when 86,000 planes were built in 1943 and over 110,000 in 1944.

The enormous increase in output could be attributed to the vast expansion of plant facilities as the federal government built huge factories at Willow Run, Michigan; Oklahoma City; and elsewhere to produce planes on assembly lines. The government benefited from the economies of scale gained by such prodigious production. An order for 1,200 B-24s in 1942 cost $238,000 per aircraft; an order for 4,500 more in 1944 cost $137,000 each, or a savings of almost half a billion dollars on the second contract. While aircraft manufacturers often provided planes designed by competitors, there was some degree of specialization. Lockheed, North American, and Republic tended to build fighter planes, while Douglas constructed transports and Boeing produced bombers. By 1945 the industry's capacity was extraordinary by any measure.[11]

The end of hostilities, however, posed severe problems for aviation. How would surplus planes be disposed of, and how would the government dismantle the huge facilites that only total war could utilize? The terrible depression the industry experienced in the immediate post–World War I years had to be avoided. Further, the federal government wanted to stimulate developments in aviation to maintain U.S. superiority in the air. Government planners, military procurement officers, and the industry urged that a program to foster development of new aircraft be devised and that a high level of capacity be maintained.

The fall-off in aviation construction was indeed dramatic. The end of hostilities saw contracts valued at over $21 billion canceled, and by 1947 the industry sold only $1.2 billion in planes and equipment yearly. The sixty-six plants of the war years had been phased down to only sixteen operating facilities. Many manufacturers who had been primarily automobile builders or subcontractors left the industry, leaving the prewar firms to cope in a diminishing market.

The obvious superiority of jet-powered aircraft caused the air force to pursue a research and development program as vigorously as appropriations allowed. The XP-80A jet fighter of 1945 whetted the appetite of the generals who saw their air force of 243 groups disintegrate to less than one ready squadron by December of that year. They recognized that the major aviation firms had the plants and technological skills to develop far more sophisticated jet planes, and they eagerly sought funds to build such aircraft. Moreover, the industry, ready to engage in such projects, was more fiscally stable than at any time in its previous history. In 1945 the fifteen largest companies had $620 million in working capital and only $13 million in bank debts. Lockheed, Republic, Convair, and Northrup designed and built jet bombers and fighters at a very slow rate until 1953; however, as a whole the industry began to lose money each year, over $115 million in 1947 alone. As a result, the federal government initiated a program to support the airplane manufacturers.

AVIATION AND THE COLD WAR

After 1947 the Truman administration actively sought to integrate aviation into the national defense program. The administration brought the industry's leaders and the military establishment together to forge an alliance eagerly supported by small businesspersons and local politicians. Some aviation executives who feared federal involvement were persuaded that the industry needed military support for research and development related to both military and civilian production. Although they had eagerly sought federal subsidies prior to 1940, the maturation of the industry and the acquisition of capital and production facilities during World War II made such aid seem far less significant or necessary. The development of strategic bombing and atomic weapons made future defense planning heavily dependent on aviation, however, and President Truman sought to create a working relationship between the Pentagon and its plane builders.

Ironically, military planners feared civilian control over procurement, and so they often opposed Truman's plans; the air force, specifically, did not aid the administration's efforts. The president issued an order in 1947 for the creation of a new aviation policy. Also, to help bring the industry and the military together, some political leaders urged development of aircraft with both civilian and military purposes. Yet some of the industry's leaders often ignored military needs as long as the civilian market kept their facilities active.[12] The issue of defense spending and the aviation industry became involved in local and regional politics because of the impact of federal contracts on business and employment. Members of the House and the Senate eagerly sought positions on military appropriations committees in order to direct federal aviation programs to plants in their states and districts. The political sector thus became deeply involved in aviation development in the Cold War.

The Korean War stimulated the aircraft industry as military demands increased markedly. It was not necessary to erect giant new plants, since many World War II facilities could be used. The stimulus did not last long, however, and after 1955 some plane builders had to return to dependence on civilian work. Business and pleasure aircraft sales doubled between 1955 and 1963, and commercial jet transports entered the market after 1958. Yet total military sales continued to dwarf civilian purchases, although the defense market shifted drastically after 1950 with a new emphasis on missiles and aerospace projects.

By 1958 missiles accounted for a quarter of the aviation industry's sales. Technological and construction changes were monumental, and the companies could use little of the missile-related facilites for civilian purposes. Aviation concerns that did not make the transition to missiles, or later to the space program, often left the aerospace field as technological changes made their products obsolete. Military purchases of aircraft fell from 5,203 units in 1956 to 2,700 units in 1969, creating a "boom or bust" cycle in the industry and some spectacular financial disasters as a result. As the firms sought to obtain and fulfill military contracts, especially for missiles, they hired more engineers and scientists so that as early as 1952 over 20,000 of the nation's 90,000 professional researchers in those fields were employed by these concerns. High overhead expenditures and technologically advanced manufacturing facilities placed the industry under severe strain. Despite the conventional wisdom that federal defense contracts were always highly profitable, there were tremendous risks involved as well.

When the Korean War ended in 1953, the aviation companies had been restored to their World War II position as major factors in the industrial economy. Sales the next year reached $4.5 billion, and profits were $170 million. Several companies, however, withdrew from the industry or nearly failed financially because of the volatile nature of the military and civilian markets. Unlike demobilization after World War II, sales to the Pentagon remained substantial as the shift to jet aircraft continued. After the Russians exploded a hydrogen bomb in 1953, the government made missiles an immediate priority, and General Dynamics, Martin, Douglas, Boeing, and Lockheed became deeply involved in aerospace. Other firms— Fairchild and Grumman—decided not to compete in this new technologically sophisticated field. Several of the companies entered general defense contracting to gain a balance of products rather than depending on one or two, fearing the impact of a canceled contract. Others sought partners in less cyclical industries. Martin merged with Marietta Corporation, maker of cement, lime, and rock products; North American merged with Rockwell-Standard, a diversified machine manufacturer. The space program after 1961 added yet another dimension to the industry, but even in its peak years it did not equal military aircraft sales in dollar value.[13]

The Kennedy and Johnson administrations purchased second-generation missiles, and the Vietnam War brought additional aircraft sales, but the industry was still subject to enormous economic vacillation. Aerospace suffered a series of severe shocks in the 1970s. Douglas, for example, which received little benefit from Vietnam War sales, tried to reap the rewards of the burgeoning commercial jet market but over-expanded and soon faced massive financial problems. Several large loans failed to alleviate the financial stress, and in 1967 it was absorbed by McDonnell. Thus a major defense contractor acquired a largely civilian plane builder to balance sales and share technology. Similarly, Lockheed almost went bankrupt after 1971 when its engine supplier, Rolls Royce, failed and simultaneously the cost of developing its L-1011 Tri-Star soared. Already having lost $200 million on a federal contract for the scandal-ridden C-5A transport, and with the Cheyenne helicopter contract

Lockheed F-104G, developed by a seven-nation consortium in the early 1960s.
(Courtesy: Lockheed Corporation.)

canceled, Lockheed approached bankruptcy. The federal government saved this prime defense contractor with huge loan guarantees, the fourth such effort on behalf of an aerospace company since 1945.

Aerospace sales peaked in 1968 at nearly $3 billion, and the 1970s found the industry with tremendous overcapacity. As the federal government reduced appropriations for defense and space programs, the industry fell on hard times. Space contracts declined from $6 billion in 1966 to $3 billion in the mid-1970s. This capital-intensive business saw its products rising in price even as its market shrank, and yet efforts at diversification had largely failed. As a captive industry to its largest customer, it could not shelter itself from either the vagaries of national defense policy changes or the tremendous ebb and flow of the civilian market. As a result there was little stability in the aerospace industry.

THE MILITARY-INDUSTRIAL COMPLEX

Ironically, the warning issued by President Eisenhower in January 1961 also marked the dawn of an extensive growth era for the military-industrial complex. The complex grew rapidly during the administrations of John F. Kennedy and Lyndon B. Johnson. Of the one *trillion* dollars spent for military purposes between 1945 and 1971, about 50 percent was appropriated between 1961 and 1969. The Department of Defense and the Pentagon decided to increase the number of combat divisions, intercontinental ballistics missiles, and carrier task force groups in 1961–1963, which required vast new expenditures. Kennedy used the so-called "missile gap" as a major issue in the 1960 election, and certainly the Sputnik scare of 1957 served to spur military spending. The Department of Defense became the industrial manager for the military production divisions of General Electric, Lockheed, General Dynamics, and other major defense contractors.

Severe criticism of the appropriations for the expanding war in Vietnam, as well as civilian needs at home, led to a substantial reduction in defense appropriations under Presidents Nixon, Ford, and Carter. The proportion of the national budget for defense spending fell from 32 percent in 1970 to 24 percent in 1979. If the military-industrial complex represented the tremendous power in Washington that its critics claimed it possessed in the 1960s, it failed to obtain the same level of fiscal support from the Congress. Defense appropriations in constant dollars declined precipitously between 1953 and 1974, with the exception of the Vietnam War years, and defense spending as a percentage of the GNP also fell. In effect, the so-called warfare state economy waned after 1963 as military and defense spending as a percentage of GNP declined from 14 percent in 1953 to 9.1 percent in 1963, and to 5.8 percent in 1974.[14] Obviously, the nation's military defense still rested on an alliance of private capital and professional military leaders under the direction of the federal government, but an enormous shift in priorities had taken place.

The reduction in military expenditures terminated with the end of the Carter administration. Elected on a pledge to enhance dramatically the American military presence around the globe and to modernize the armed forces, Ronald Reagan initiated an unprecedented peacetime arms buildup. In fiscal year 1980 the military and veterans agencies received $155 billion, or 22.7 percent of federal spending. In fiscal year 1987 the amount was $308.9 billion, some 27.8 percent of the budget. That amount represented 6.4 percent of the GNP. In some years the Pentagon received increases in excess of 16 percent, and much of the government's expenditures for research and development passed through the military. Congressional and public outcries against such huge sums grew louder by the end of the decade, and defense contractors again began to talk about diversification.

Military needs continued to represent a significant aspect of the total economy, and many firms existed in no small measure as a result of defense contracts. But as has been seen, war or military purchases often produced instability in industry and severe negative financial consequences. Yet defense requirements also enhanced the rise of new industries, such as aviation and aerospace, and ended monopolistic positions, as in aluminum. To simply damn, or praise, the military-industrial complex does not penetrate the mixed consequences of the interactions of war and business.

NOTES

1. Robert L. Branyan and Lawrence H. Larsen, *The Eisenhower Administration, 1953–1961: A Documentary History* (New York: Random House, 1971), II, p. 1375.

2. Robert D. Cuff, "An Organizational Perspective on the Military-Industrial Complex," *Business History Review* 52 (Summer 1978), pp. 250–267.

3. Johannes R. Lischka, "Armor Plate: Nickel and Steel, Monopoly and Profit," in Benjamin F. Cooling, ed., *War, Business and American Society: Historical Perspectives on the Military-Industrial Complex* (Port Washington, New York: Kennikat Press, 1977), pp. 43–58.

4. Robert D. Cuff, *The War Industries Board: Business-Government Relations during World War I* (Baltimore: Johns Hopkins University Press, 1973).

5. James J. Flink, *The Car Culture* (Cambridge: MIT Press, 1975), p. 97.

6. Paul A. C. Koistinen, "The 'Industrial-Military Complex' in Historical Perspective: The Interwar Years," *The Journal of American History* 56 (March 1970), pp. 819–839.

7. John B. Rae, "Financial Problems of the American Aircraft Industry, 1906–1940," *Business History Review* 39 (Spring 1965), pp. 99–114.

8. Roland N. Stromberg, "American Business and the Approach of War, 1935–1941," *The Journal of Economic History* 13 (Winter 1953), pp. 58–78.

9. Jim F. Heath, "American War Mobilization and the Use of Small Manufacturers, 1939–1943," *Business History Review* 46 (Autumn 1972), pp. 295–319.

10. *The Kaiser Story* (Oakland, California: Kaiser Industries Corporation, 1968).

11. G. R. Simonson, "The Demand for Aircraft and the Aircraft Industry, 1907–1958," *The Journal of Economic History*, 20 (September 1960), pp. 361–382; John B. Rae, *Climb to Greatness: The American Aircraft Industry, 1920–1960* (Cambridge: MIT Press, 1968).

12. Donald J. Mrozek, "The Truman Administration and the Enlistment of the Aviation Industry in Postwar Defense," *Business History Review* 48 (Spring 1974), pp. 73–94.

13. Charles D. Bright, *The Jet Makers: The Aerospace Industry from 1945 to 1972* (Lawrence, Kansas: The Regents Press of Kansas, 1978).

14. James L. Clayton, "The Fiscal Limits of the Warfare-Welfare State: Defense and Welfare Spending in the United States since 1900," *The Western Political Quarterly* 29 (September 1976), pp. 364–383.

SUGGESTED READINGS

BERNSTEIN, BARTON J. "The Debate on Industrial Reconversion: The Protection of Oligopoly and Military Control of the Economy." *The American Journal of Economics and Sociology* 26 (April 1967): 159–172.

BOLTON, ROGER E. *Defense Purchases and Regional Growth.* Washington, D.C.: The Brookings Institute, 1966.

BORKIN, JOSEPH. *The Crime and Punishment of I. G. Farben.* New York: Free Press, 1978.

CLAYTON, JAMES L. "The Fiscal Limits of the Warfare-Welfare State: Defense and Welfare Spending in the United States since 1900." *The Western Political Quarterly* 29 (September 1976): 364–383.

COOLING, BENJAMIN F., ED. *War, Business and American Society: Historical Perspective on the Military-Industrial Complex.* Port Washington, New York: Kennikat Press, 1977.

CUFF, ROBERT D. "An Organizational Perspective on the Military-Industrial Complex." *Business History Review* 52 (Summer 1978): 250–267.

———. *The War Industries Board: Business-Government Relations during World War I.* Baltimore: Johns Hopkins University Press, 1973.

HEATH, JIM F. "American War Mobilization and the Use of Small Manufacturers, 1939–1943." *Business History Review* 44 (Autumn 1972): 295–319.

KOISTINEN, PAUL A. C. "The 'Industrial Military Complex' in Historical Perspective: World War I." *Business History Review* 41 (Winter 1967): 378–403.

———. "The 'Industrial-Military Complex' in Historical Perspective: The Interwar Years." *The Journal of American History* 56 (March 1970): 819–839.

MROZEK, DONALD J. "The Truman Administration and the Enlistment of the Aviation Industry in Postwar Defense." *Business History Review* 48 (Spring 1974): 73–94.

PURSELL, CARROLL W., JR., ED. *The Military-Industrial Complex.* New York: Harper & Row, 1972.

Rae, John B. *Climb to Greatness: The American Aircraft Industry, 1920–1960.* Cambridge: MIT Press, 1968.

———. "Financial Problems of the American Aircraft Industry, 1906–1940." *Business History Review* 39 (Spring 1965): 99–114.

Simonson, G. R. "The Demand for Aircraft and the Aircraft Industry, 1907–1958." *The Journal of Economic History* 20 (September 1960): 361–382.

Stromberg, Roland N. "American Business and the Approach of War, 1935–1941." *The Journal of Economic History* 13 (Winter 1953): 58–78.

18 Government Regulatory Agencies

The depression, the New Deal, and progressive legislation culminated in the creation of a new relationship between the federal governnment and the economy. Government assumed an obligation to intervene in the economy through large-scale public spending, by creating incentives and opportunities for private investment, through taxation policies, and by establishing and enforcing guidelines for business transactions and the uses of private property. It was assumed that government could or should act whenever the social benefits exceeded the benefits that might be derived by the private sector acting independently. Despite its expanded role, however, by 1940 government still remained a relatively unobtrusive factor in the private lives and businesses of most Americans. Government spending accounted for only 9 percent of the GNP. World War II, more than the New Deal, led to the intrusion by government into the daily activities of consumers and businesses.

World War II markedly increased government participation in economic decision and brought direct involvement in the pricing and distribution of goods and services. The War Production Board allocated the use of raw materials and industrial facilities. The War Shipping Administration assigned shipping quotas and made actual consignments of freight to American and British merchant ships. The Office of Price Administration established wage and price controls, and government-imposed rationing determined the distribution of many consumer goods. In 1943 the Office of War Mobilization became the parent agency of the war-time regulatory boards. The next year the federal government accounted for almost half of all expenditures. For a time the public economy virtually supplanted the private sector.

Although reconversion was quickly effected after World War II, the federal government retained and even broadened its authority to establish "economic stabilization through government supplementation of private activity." The Employment Act of 1946 contained four major provisions. The first acknowledged the responsibility of government to "promote free competitive enterprise and the general welfare" and "maximum employment, production and purchasing power." The second required the submission of an annual economic report to the president. The third created the three-person Council of Economic Advisors. And the fourth established a joint committee of Congress to supervise the report. The act recognized the role of government in maintaining economic stability, and preventing market disasters such as occurred in 1929, and helping assure full employment and production levels.[1]

The cold war and the Korean War reinstated many of the "emergency" economic powers characteristic of World War II. Expanded defense and welfare spending broadened the role of government and, if they did not already exist, created the elements of a new political economy wherein the allocation of goods and services in the free marketplace became more regularly supplemented by governmental allocation of goods and services. Yet, despite the massive growth of the structures and agencies of government, and rising expenditures, the private sector of the economy outpaced the growth of government. By the 1960s government still accounted for a modest 20 percent of the GNP. A new era of regulatory expansion had begun, however, and would accelerate in the 1970s.

In that decade the budgets of federal regulatory agencies rose from $866 million to over $5.5 billion while their staff increased threefold from 27,000 to 87,000 people. The costs of all federal regulatory policies that affected private businesses—for example, mandatory pollution control devices in cars—reached an estimated $90 billion per year. In 1980 government regulations added $600 to the price of an average automobile, $2,000 to the price of an average home, $22 to the cost of an average hospital bill, and seven cents to the price of a pound of hamburger.[2]

Such data has served as powerful ammunition for those opposed to federal regulation and growing intervention in the economy. But government regulation is neither inherently wrong nor "bad." Regulations aid in the achievement of both national and business objectives. Regulations can be cost-efficient in that food and drug standards, environmental-pollution standards, and safety regulations can reduce injury and illness and contribute positively to higher productivity and a better quality of life.

Regulation does involve real cost, however, much of which is hidden. The enormous paperwork generated both by the staffs of the regulating agencies and by the businesses themselves in response to the regulations is expensive. Delays in obtaining permits or approval for production, marketing, or construction can be very costly. Expenditures for meeting pollution-control requirements and occupational health and safety regulations approached 6 percent of the total capital expenditures by the private sector of the economy in the last half of the 1970s. Outdated regulations, such as requiring truckers to make return trips empty because they were not able to enter the freight market in certain areas, can be a very real expense. Minimum wages can increase the pay of employees and also reduce the number of jobs and raise the costs of goods and services to the consumer. Taxation, of course, is a very real cost of regulation.

Economist Milton Friedman asserts that 40 percent of personal income is "disposed of on our behalf by government at federal, state, and local levels combined."[3] Income, excise, sales, fuel, and inheritance taxes determine the allocation of a good portion of the GNP. Thus, says Friedman, Americans are not truly "free to choose" how they might spend their earnings. Moreover, even on that portion remaining after taxes, regulations often determine what we may or may not buy and what price is to be paid. Yet the Americans who have freely chosen regulations and taxes are also free to reduce them. The problem is not simply regulation and taxes; rather it is *how much* regulation and the level of taxation. The issue involves a social-cost–social-benefit analysis; there are no permanent solutions or guidelines.

The proliferation of critics; the popularity of conservative economists, such as Milton Friedman; the expansion of programs such as the Center for the Study of American Business, American Enterprise Institute, the Center for Education and Research in Free Enterprise; and the election in 1980 of

United States Marshalls seize spoiled eggs at a bakery supply house. (Courtesy: Food and Drug Administration.)

a president committed to cutting costs and to "deregulation," indicated a growing public belief that government programs and regulations can produce diminishing if not negative returns. Historically, Americans have accepted restrictions on some of their individual liberties in exchange for the protection of other rights. The law ultimately secures to the individual one's right to property. Beginning at the turn of the twentieth century, government was increasingly utilized to improve the efficiency of the free-market system. The pure food and drug laws, banking regulations, the Federal Reserve System, and the securities and exchange statutes sought to make the business environment more efficient and more equitable. Some economists and business leaders believe that welfare capitalism, or political direction of the marketplace, became a conscious policy of the federal government in the 1930s, while others contend that the climate of public opinion toward the free-enterprise system changed markedly in the 1960s, when some activists not only urged increased government welfare spending and regulation but also attacked the concepts of private property, profits, self-interest, and price competition.[4] These negative views of governmental regulation and its intent gained greater support as the number of federal agencies and their authority grew rapidly in the last twenty years.

THE GROWTH OF FEDERAL REGULATORY AGENCIES

Only six federal regulatory agencies existed in 1900, the two largest being the ICC (Interstate Commerce Commission) and the Patent and Trademark Office. By 1930 eight more federal agencies had appeared, to include the Federal Reserve System and the FTC (Federal Trade Commission). During the decade of the 1930s ten new regulatory agencies were established by Congress including the FCC (Federal Communications Commission), CAB (Civil Aeronautics Board), SEC (Securities and Exchange Commission), and FDIC (Federal Deposit Insurance Corporation). Twenty-eight commissions and agencies, such as the Animal and Plant Health Inspection Service, Coast Guard, and Customs Service, administered the nation's regulatory policies until 1960. The Atomic Energy Commission (Nuclear Regulatory Commission), Small Business Administration, and Federal Aviation Administration are among the more prominent agencies formed after World War II. Beginning in the 1960s the creation of new regulatory agencies and commissions accelerated, and by 1980 the number of federal regulatory bodies doubled, twenty being created in the decade of the 1970s alone.[5]

The Center for the Study of American Business notes that "the growth in regulation has constituted not merely an intensification of regulatory activities, but also a dramatic shift in purpose and scope. A substantial portion of federal regulatory controls now affects not only specific industries . . . but all sectors of the private sector of the economy."[6] Characteristic of the new agencies that relate to all sectors of the economy is the Environmental Protection Agency (EPA).

The Environmental Protection Agency

Established in 1970, the EPA was given the responsibility for the enforcement of the following legislation:

Water Quality Improvement Act of 1970 (84 Stat. 94)

Clean Air Act Amendments of 1970 (84 Stat. 1676)

Federal Water Pollution Control Act Amendment of 1972 (86 Stat. 819)

Federal Insecticide, Fungicide and Rodenticide Act of 1972 (86 Stat. 975)

Marine Protection, Research and Sanctuaries Act of 1972 (86 Stat. 1052)

Noise Control Act of 1972 (86 Stat. 1234)

Provisions of the Energy Supply and Environmental Coordination Act of 1974 (88 Stat. 246)

Safe Drinking Water Act of 1974 (88 Stat. 1661)

Resource Conservation and Recovery Act of 1976 (90 Stat. 95)

Toxic Substances Control Act of 1976 (90 Stat. 2005)

Clean Air Act Amendments of 1977 (91 Stat. 685)

Aviation Safety and Noise Abatement Act of 1979 (94 Stat. 50)

Comprehensive Environmental Response, Compensation and Liability Act of 1980 (P.L. 96-510)[7]

Essentially, the work of EPA is to establish standards and enforce pollution controls through regulation and surveillance in areas relating to air, water quality, solid wastes, pesticides, toxic substances, drinking water, radiation, and noise. There are few human activities over which EPA does not have some authority. Its greatest involvement has been in the establishment of emission standards and automobile safety, industrial-emissions control, pesticide regulation, and water-pollution controls. The EPA budget rose from $71 million in 1970 to over $1.5 billion by 1982. Its operations directly affect virtually every business and individual.[8] While the EPA has its critics and detractors, it also has a strong coterie of admirers. The latter believe that the social benefits of EPA activities outweigh the fiscal costs to business, consumers, and taxpayers.

Occupational Safety and Health Administration

A recently established agency that caused rigorous public complaints is the Department of Labor's Occupational Safety and Health Administration (OSHA). Authorized by the Occupational Safety and Health Act of 1970, OSHA is viewed by many as a mindless bureaucracy, or perhaps bureaucracy run amuck. The agency is empowered to set standards to protect workers in businesses with more than ten employees against safety and health hazards, conduct workplace inspections without prior notification, and require certain reporting and posting procedures. OSHA's initial budget of $37 million in 1973 rose to an estimated $235 million in 1982, while personnel increased from approximately 1,700 to 3,000.[9] The costs of regulation were less for the agency doing the regulating, however, than for the industries regulated.

OSHA has, among other things, mandated chemical toilets in forests, specified the height of fire extinguishers above floors, and defined a "floor hole," and "floor opening," and a "step." Major business expenses now include staff and supplies required to complete OSHA reports. One of the problems has been that businesses are often unable to anticipate costs created by new regulations, such as the decision to require catalytic emission systems in smokestacks, or decisions to ban a pesticide. Success or failure of a firm, and certainly profits and losses, increasingly hinge upon a decision by a federal agency that may or may not be cognizant of the existence of the company or its products. The smaller firm is particularly vulnerable. Moreover, little cost-effective analysis has been conducted to evaluate the efficiency or effectiveness of such regulations. Work-related injuries and illnesses, for example, have declined little since OSHA began operation, although there has been far more effective reporting of such injuries and illnesses. Other federal regulatory agencies, such as the Food and Drug Administration (FDA), have clearly established records that demonstrate social benefits and cost effectiveness.

FOOD AND DRUG ADMINISTRATION

The FDA was created by Congress in 1906, primarily in response to unsanitary conditions in the nation's food industries and to control the sale of dangerous or ineffective medicines. Its legislation essentially required the correct labeling of food and drugs and the inspection and certification of food industries by this agency located in the U.S. Department of Agriculture. As was noted previously, a "pure food" certification from the federal government protected domestic markets and export sales to Europe. Government certification remains a critical factor in the successful marketing of food products and protects the public from contaminated foods.

The 1906 act reflected the willingness of individuals and firms to accept restrictions on certain liberties in exchange for the protection of

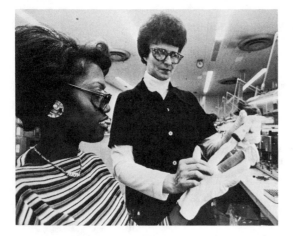

Inspection of protective clothing and equipment is part of the work of OSHA. (Courtesy: Occupational Safety and Health Administration.)

other rights. Thus consumers cannot buy and firms cannot sell tainted or adulterated food products. In return for the limitation of their "freedom" to buy or sell, individuals receive greater personal health security, and firms benefit from consumer confidence in their products.

Under the original legislation, regulation of food and drug products involved "ex post facto" action. That is, a product could be declared impure or mislabeled only after it entered the market. This resulted occasionally in some real public-health crises, such as in 1938 when a sulfanilamide elixir caused sickness and death among consumers. The Federal Food, Drug and Cosmetic Act of 1938 sought to prevent such disasters by requiring pre-market clearance to include extensive testing of new drugs. This, of course, has not entirely eliminated "mistakes," but premarket clearance has undoubt-edly reduced their number. Premarket clearance has, however, also in-creased the time-lag between the point when new drugs and products are developed and when they may enter the market, thereby increasing the costs of research and development and deferring profits to the firm.[10]

The speculative risks of drug companies are especially high. The phar-maceutical industry develops an estimated 30,000 chemical compounds for each one approved for prescription use. As one research institute has noted, "Many new drugs are discovered or developed, but few are cleared for marketing."[11] Research, testing, and FDA approval frequently require a decade before a new product enters the market, thus returns on invest-ments are extremely delayed, and once on the market drugs may have only seven or eight years of the seventeen-year patent life remaining. And, even more likely, they may be replaced on the shelf by a new product from a competitor. Nevertheless, such delays in market approval serve the pur-pose of providing greater assurances of the safety and effectiveness of drugs. Ironically, early release on the market in other countries can provide evidence of problems if any develop. On the other hand, delayed release increases costs, can contribute to the perpetuation of suffering or illness, and can also indirectly create real economic loss. Current debate over FDA regulations generally concerns methods of expediting or improving testing and release rather than the question of whether the agency should or should not regulate.

Legislation approved by Congress since World War II has amended and extended FDA authority to include medical devices as well as drugs. Activities of the FDA were enlarged under the authority of such acts as the Food Additives Amendment (1958), Color Additives Amendment (1960), Drug Amendments of 1962, Fair Packaging and Labeling of 1966, and the Radiation Control for Health and Safety Act of 1968. Since 1970, FDA annual budgets have risen from $168 million to about $350 million.[12]

THE FEDERAL GOVERNMENT AND HEALTH CARE

The FDA is on the periphery of a $200 billion health-care industry that absorbs approximately 9 percent of the total GNP. Modern medicine—that is, medical practices adopted for the most part since World War II—has greatly extended the lives and improved the quality of life of most Americans, but medical care has become enormously expensive. New drugs, beginning with the sulpha drugs of World War II and followed by antibiotics and immunization programs such as the Salk polio vaccine, have saved lives and prevented suffering for millions. The polio vaccine alone not only eliminated a major crippling disease but also dramatically reduced real economic loss. The installation of x-ray equipment in most doctor's offices and hospitals has been essentially a post–World War II phenomenon, contributing greatly to better medical treatment. Artificial joints, transplants, and literally spare parts for the human body have become available. The initial excitement and marvel of heart transplants and bypass surgery have within a decade given way to the routine. All of this has developed at enormous costs, yet those costs, when measured against life and health, may have been small. However, is the health-care system cost efficient? Do we get the most for the dollars spent and invested?

Government regulations presume that our society has failed through the free-market system to maximize health-care output per dollar of expenditure. Examples of that failure are the large proportion of untreated elderly citizens and the very young; the concentration of doctors in urban centers rather than in rural areas where they may be more needed; and the lack of adequate nursing homes. Conversely, there may be situations where the public is getting too much medical care in the form of unnecessary operations, drugs, or treatments. Government health-care programs and

Patent medicines and traveling medicine shows prevailed before the passage of the Pure Food and Drug Act.   (Courtesy: Food and Drug Administration.)

regulations are intended to reallocate health-care resources in a more efficient and socially desirable way.

The public portion of health-care expenditures rose from about 13 percent in 1940 to over 42 percent in 1970. Most of the public expenditures are related to Medicare and Medicaid programs. Approved by President Lyndon B. Johnson in July 1965, medicare capped almost a half-century of debate and controversy. Medicare, incorporated under the Social Security Administration and since 1977 administered by the Health Care Financing Administration, provides hospital and medical insurance. Money to pay for the programs comes from contributions paid by workers, employers, and the self-employed at a rate (in 1978) of 1.1 percent on earnings up to $17,700. Expenditures under the insurance programs have grown at an alarming rate. For the 1973–1974 fiscal year the hospital insurance fund paid out $7.8 billion and the medical program spent $2.9 billion. Three years later, 1976–1977, the hospital insurance costs were $58.7 billion, and the medical reimbursements were $7.5 billion and rising. It has been estimated that more than half of the increase in health-care expenditures was due to increases in the price of those services. Or, put another way, the prices of health-care services have increased more rapidly than prices in any other area of the economy. But the quality of health care, it may be reasonably argued, has risen more than proportionately.

Concern has grown that the rapid escalation in the costs of medical care, both public and private, has not yielded commensurate benefits. It is extremely difficult to measure the economic benefits of health care, but there is some evidence that public policy has contributed to the misallocation of health-care expenditures. For example, because individuals do not pay the full cost of treatment at the time it is received, they are more inclined to purchase those services. Thus, subsidized medical care creates new or abnormal demands on medical services.[13]

Government shares other indirect costs of health care. For example, federal programs provide research grants; award low-cost loans for hospital construction; contribute heavily toward the education of doctors, pharmacists and medical technicians; allow deductions by taxpayers for medical care and medical insurance; and make direct payments for Medicare. These subsidies, some economists believe, contribute to the problems of the health-care system. Price has been eliminated or at least diminished as a factor in determining the allocation of medical resources. Thus regulation by government authority, or by the medical industry, replaces the free market. Regulatory agencies have attempted, usually ineffectually, to control expenditures within the health-care industry, but efforts to reduce expenditures have often created new costs in other areas.

Federal and state health regulations operate on four different levels. One level is to control entry into the health-care market through the licensing of physicians, pharmacists, nurses and other medical-care personnel as well as medical facilities. Some state legislatures have experimented with establishing maximum hospital and treatment rates—that is, with price controls such as have been established for public utilities. Another approach, the inspection and review procedures as conducted by Professional Standards Review Organizations (PSROs), have proved costly and nominally effective. But the most widely used mechanisms are health-maintenance organizations created under federal matching-grant programs. The National Health Planning and Resources Development Act of 1974 required participating states to adopt "certificate of need" (CON) programs and state and local health-planning agencies. The theory or motive behind the program was to create greater cost efficiency in federal health expenditures such as in hospital construction.[14]

Funding of new hospital construction cannot be obtained until a certificate of need is issued by an authorizing agency. The theory is to reduce unnecessary hospital or medical construction on the grounds that such facilities impose excess burdens on the taxpayer and consumer. There is also the assumption that once medical facilities, needed or not, are built, they will be used and that use then creates an additional and unnecessary expense for the consumer and taxpayer. Much the same reasoning enters into the control of student admissions into medical schools. Controls on the entry and licensing of foreign medical school graduates, and even on the allocation of specialists being trained in the medical schools, seek to eliminate waste, duplication, and inefficiency in medical practice. The result, of course, is that medical care becomes proportionately more scarce, and more expensive, and the cost-saving efforts produce spiraling medical-care expense. Two researchers in this field have concluded:

> Regulation and consumer welfare can be dichotomous or in conflict: Excessive hospitalization, unnecessary laboratory tests, and surgery that is not mandated, for example, not only maintain medical costs at an artificially high level but—it can be argued—constitute inferior or inappropriate treatment for the affected individual patients. . . . Thus, prior screening of patients to justify hospitalization, concurrent (in-hospital) review of hospitalization and treatment, and retrospective review, have all been employed for the related, although frequently conflicting purposes of guaranteeing the quality of medical services and controlling their costs.[15]

In other words, government or bureaucratic efforts to reduce expenditures create additional costs that are met with new regulations and regulatory machinery that create new fiscal burdens. Bureaucratic growth seems to be an axiom that applies to the broad range of regulatory agencies as well as to the health-care agencies. It is clear, however, that the Public Health Service has at times effectually provided direction and coordination for an otherwise disparate and independent medical services industry in order to meet epidemics or threatening diseases. One of the current crises that has placed the Centers for Disease Control (CDC), a division of the Public Health Service, in a leadership role, more so than in a regulatory role, is the acquired immunodeficiency syndrome (AIDS).

AIDS became the number one health priority of the Public Health Service (PHS). In June 1986 at a planning meeting in Coolfont, West Virginia, the Public Health Service estimated, using Centers for Disease Control projections, that by the end of 1990 there will have been 279,000 cases of AIDS and 179,000 deaths. As of September 30, 1987, the CDC has received reports of 42,354 cases of AIDS and 24,412 deaths.

The CDC has taken a leadership role in a number of other AIDS-related areas. For example, in late 1986 there was growing disagreement between groups of individuals advocating mandatory AIDS virus antibody testing and others opposing any testing except under conditions of strict confidentiality or anonymity in order to protect against possible acts of discrimination. The CDC convened the "Conference on the Role of AIDS Virus Antibody Testing in the Prevention and Control of AIDS" on February 24–25, 1987 and assembled public health experts and other appropriate officials to discuss the medical, public health, social, legal and ethical issues surrounding testing. Utilizing the information gained, the CDC developed recommendations for the increased use of human immunodeficiency virus (HIV) antibody counseling and testing.

CDC now possesses the major elements for a comprehensive AIDS prevention and control program i.e., information/education activities directed to the general public, school and college-age youth, persons at increased risk, and health workers; expanded counseling and testing activities primarily for those at risk; and health education/risk reduction activities directed to those at risk or infected.

The prevention and control of AIDS requires the partnership of federal, state and local governments, private and public organization, and the entire medical community. CDC has supported this partnership through direct technical and financial assistance to State, local, and territorial health authorities, and private and public nonprofit organizations.

ENERGY AND GOVERNMENT

The federal government has had a long-term and growing role in developing national energy resources and policies. The OPEC oil embargo of the mid-1970s was not solely responsible for the expansion of federal energy-related programs and regulations, although the energy shortages certainly accelerated those programs, as one scholar of the subject notes: "Throughout the twentieth century, government has taken a growing role in attempting to fashion policy and institutions that will assure the continued development of energy resources while encouraging their more efficient use."[16] Even before 1850, when wood was the greatest energy source in America, government policy promoted low-cost energy through easy access and acquisition of land and timber. When coal supplanted wood as the primary fuel in the late nineteenth century, government policy provided cheap entry into and exploitation of coal reserves. Only when petroleum began to replace coal in the early twentieth century did conservation acts and labor regulations begin to control access to coal. Similarly, throughout most of the twentieth century, government has facilitated and encouraged the utilization of low-cost fuel. In some respects it continues to do so, except that policy is now tempered with the understanding that energy supplies are exhaustible and that the United States is dependent on foreign suppliers.

In the late nineteenth and most of the twentieth century the ICC, and perhaps the U.S. Attorney General's office, which handled federal antitrust actions, served as the major regulatory agencies of the energy industry. In 1920 the Federal Power Commission (FPC) was established to regulate interstate distribution of hydroelectric power. It has authority to license private hydroelectric facilities and regulate the service and rates of public utilities selling electricity in interstate commerce at wholesale prices, that is, as a primary distributor. The Natural Gas Act of 1938 extended FPC authority to include natural gas pipelines, utility systems, and producers selling natural gas interstate. In the 1950s the FPC gained and began to exercise the authority to set natural gas prices. A very low pricing policy encouraged rapid expansion in the residential and industrial use of natural gas during the next several decades. According to business historian Joseph A. Pratt, the long-run result of the FPC's low-price policy was to dry up available supplies of natural gas. Economics, some argued, rather than politics should have determined energy prices. By 1981, legislation providing for acceleration of the deregulation of natural gas began to move through Congress.

In the 1960s and 1970s, as with other federal agencies, the FPC received a host of new, legislatively mandated functions. The Clean Air Act (1967), National Environmental Policy Act (1969), Emergency Petroleum Allocation Act (1973), and Energy Policy and Conservation Act (1975) extended the services and obligations of the agency. In 1977 the Department of Energy Organization Act restructured the FPC, making it the Federal Energy Regulatory Commission under the auspices of the newly created Department of Energy. The organization of a separate Department of Energy marked the institutionalization, if it did not already exist, of a greater role by federal agencies in the development and distribution of energy.

In one area of energy development the federal government exercised preemptive authority—in the licensing and control of all nuclear-power facilities. The Eightieth Congress (1946) created the five-person Atomic Energy Commission (AEC) with exclusive authority to conduct research in and develop nuclear energy. In 1975 the AEC was superceded by a Nuclear Regulatory Commission (NRC). Nuclear energy, needless to say, became one of the most controversial topics of the post-World War II era.

Because of its dominant role in the nuclear industry the federal gov-

"Trailer City" occupied by inspectors from the Nuclear Regulatory Commission at Three Mile Island, Pennsylvania. (Courtesy: Nuclear Regulatory Commission.)

ernment's programs in this field became the targets of vigorous opposition by antiwar protestors, environmentalists, and consumer-advocate groups. Ralph Nader, the preeminent consumer advocate of the era, and John Abbotts coauthored a volume entitled *The Menace of Atomic Energy* (1977) that stated the strong concern many Americans have over the development and utilization of atomic power. Said the authors, "The atomic industry was imposed upon the American people through a sequence of actions by the government, reactor manufacturers and utility monopolies."[17] Congress meanwhile delegated its responsibilities to the Joint Committee on Atomic Energy, "which may as well have been composed of the board of directors of General Electric, Westinghouse, and Commonwealth Edison," claimed the same critics.[18] The consumer advocates argued that nuclear energy required the concentration of political and economic power, which was inherently wrong. Worker and consumer exposure to radioactivity, the real threat of serious reactor accidents, not to mention leaks such as occurred at Three Mile Island in 1979, and environmental hazards made nuclear power inherently dangerous and uneconomic. "Radioactive violence is silent and long range," and "atomic energy [is] a profound challenge to the civic mind, since its silent violence circumvents the normal human senses of the exposed population."[19] Nader and other antinuclear advocates urged the utilization of alternative energy sources such as solar power.

RALPH NADER

Ralph Nader is unique in the United States as a consumer advocate. *Progressive* magazine salutes him as "Citizen of the Republic" because of his selfless defense of the rights and safety of the public, but many businesspeople, and particularly the management of General Motors, have referred to him in less kindly terms. In 1965 Nader published a book entitled *Unsafe at Any Speed:*

The Designed-in Dangers of the American Automobile. Nader attacked the auto industry in general for its emphasis on profits and styling as opposed to safety and efficiency. The Chevrolet Corvair, a General Motors product, he identified as particularly unsafe and ill-conceived. Within two years Nader's book had sold half a million copies, and the Corvair was passing into oblivion. Subsequent tests have tended to discount the engineering defects attributed to the Corvair, especially the later models, but Nader's book and vigorous criticism did cause substantive changes in automobile engineering and in safety standards.

Nader was instrumental in the passage of the National Traffic and Motor Vehicle Safety Act of 1966. Subsequently he waged publicity campaigns designed to inform the public of safety hazards in automobiles, including defective seat belts, fuel tanks, and emission-system designs. During his campaigns for auto safety Nader became subject to alleged harassment and intimidation by General Motors, which produced suits and countersuits. Nevertheless, his popularity with the general public continued to grow as did contributions to his organizations.

In the 1970s Nader turned his expanding staff into investigations of hazards in the mining industry, the safety standards of natural gas pipelines, the indiscriminate use of x-rays in dental examinations, and health standards in meat-processing plants not inspected under interstate commerce authority. Nader became the bane of many businesspeople and a blessing to many consumers as he emerged as one of the most controversial individuals in contemporary society. For all of his criticisms, however, he did not attack the business system as inherently wrong, but rather in the older progressive tradition he championed the individual against the arbitrary use of power by government or by large corporations.

A Princeton University Phi Beta Kappa, Nader completed his law studies at Harvard University in 1958. He began private practice in Hartford, Connecticut, and lectured at the University of Hartford on a part-time basis. In 1964

Ralph Nader (1934–   ). Reformer, lawyer, and consumer advocate.   (Courtesy: Ralph Nader)

he became a consultant in the Department of Labor, where he gathered much of the material used in the writing of his book on auto safety. Through his writings, lectures, and occasional teaching, and surrounded by a young staff of lawyers and investigators, Nader created his own distinctive business that served as a product-testing laboratory and a marketing-analysis group.

Inasmuch as the energy industry, whether petroleum or nuclear, is heavily controlled by government regulations and policy—and because the administration and Congress are constantly subjected to pressure by various groups, including industry—energy policies are continuously being revised. Constant policy changes affected the developmental costs of the Alaskan oil fields and the construction of nuclear reactors. Federal regulation of the energy field has both long-run and short-run economic consequences for business and consumers.

Debate about the role of the federal government in business and the economy has occurred since the United States was conceived. It has been a generally healthy and productive dialogue. There is no question but that the role of government in shaping and directing economic growth and allocating income has grown markedly. As a consequence, there has been a corresponding outcry from those who would return to a policy of *laissez faire* and a totally free market, conditions that have actually never existed in this country. It is simply not true that the American economy flourished best, and that more Americans lived better lives, in the days when government regulations and interference were less significant. It is true, however, that regulations can be a burden as well as a blessing, and that their social benefits must be measured against their social costs.

NOTES

1. 60 Stat. 33, approved February 20, 1946.

2. Murray L. Weidenbaum, "The Forgotten Consumer: Hidden Costs of Government Regulation," in National Federation of Independent Business, Public Policy Discussion Series (1977), n.p., adapted from Weidenbaum, *Government-Mandated Price Increases* (Washington, D.C.: American Enterprise Institute for Public Policy Research, 1975).

3. Milton and Rose Friedman, *Free to Choose: A Personal Statement* (New York: Harcourt Brace Jovanovich, 1980), p. 65.

4. Svetozar Pejovich, ed., *Governmental Controls and the Free Market: The U.S. Economy in the 1970s* (College Station: Texas A&M University Press, 1976), pp. 7–8.

5. Ronald J. Penoyer, ed., *Director of Federal Regulatory Agencies*, 3rd ed. (St. Louis, Missouri: Washington University, Center for the Study of American Business, 1981), pp. 1–4.

6. Ibid., p. 4.

7. Ibid., p. 37.

8. Ibid.

9. Murray L. Weidenbaum, "Time to Control Runaway Regulation," *Reader's Digest* (June 1979), pp. 98–102.

10. *Proposals to Reform Drug Regulation Laws, 1979, 96th Congress, 1st Sess.* (Washington, D.C.: American Enterprise Institute, October 1979), pp. 2–6.

11. Ibid., p. 2.

12. Penoyer, ed., *Directory of Federal Regulatory Agencies,* p. 69.

13. Penny Hollander Feldman and Richard J. Zeckhauser, "Some Sober Thoughts on Health Care Regulation," in *Regulating Business: The Search for an Optimum* (San Francisco: Institute for Contemporary Studies, 1978), p. 101.

14. Ibid., pp. 100–101.

15. Ibid., p. 102.

16. Joseph A. Pratt, "Natural Resources and Energy," in Glenn Porter, ed., *Encyclopedia of American Economic History* (New York: Charles Scribner's Sons, 1980), pp. 211–212, and see pp. 202–213.

17. Ralph Nader and John Abbotts, *The Menace of Atomic Energy* (New York: W.W. Norton & Co., 1977), p. 12.

18. Ibid.

19. Ibid., p. 11.

SUGGESTED READINGS

ARGYRIS, CHRIS, and others. *Regulating Business: The Search for an Optimum.* San Francisco: Institute for Contemporary Studies, 1978.

DAVIS, DAVID HOWARD. *Energy Politics.* Second edition. New York: St. Martin's Press, 1978.

DAVIS, LANCE E., and DOUGLASS C. NORTH. *Institutional Change and American Economic Growth.* Cambridge, England: Cambridge University Press, 1971.

FRIEDMAN, MILTON, and ROSE FRIEDMAN. *Free to Choose: A Personal Statement.* New York: Harcourt Brace Javanovich, 1980.

KLARMAN, HERBERT E. *The Economics of Health.* New York: Columbia University Press, 1965.

KOLKO, GABRIEL. *Railroads and Regulation: 1877–1916.* Princeton, New Jersey: Princeton University Press, 1965; reprinted, New York: W. W. Norton & Co., 1970.

MACAVOY, PAUL W. *The Economic Effects of Regulation.* Cambridge: MIT Press, 1965.

NADER, RALPH, and JOHN ABBOTTS. *The Menace of Atomic Energy.* New York: W. W. Norton & Co., 1977.

PEJOVICH, SVETOZAR, ed. *Governmental Controls and the Free Market: The U.S. Economy in the 1970's.* College Station: Texas A&M University Press, 1976.

PENOYER, RONALD J.,ed. *Directory of Regulatory Agencies.* Third edition. St. Louis: Washington University, Center for the Studies of American Business, 1981.

PORTER, GLENN. *Encyclopedia of American Economic History.* Two volumes. New York: Charles Scribner's Sons, 1980.

SIMON, WILLIAM E. *A Time for Truth.* New York: Reader's Digest Press, 1978.

19 Retailing

By the end of the 1980s McDonald's employed more people than the United States Steel Corporation. America, that great manufacturing giant, producer of huge industrial machines, had become known as the maker of Big Macs. Almost half of all Americans employed in nonagricultural jobs were working in service industries and retail trade. During the economically "stagnant" 1970s the nation created over 10 million jobs, but more than 7 million were in services and trade, that is, in those businesses that engage in the distribution, marketing, and maintenance of consumer products. And, in the 1980s, almost two-thirds of the new jobs were generated by small businesses. These numbers reflected the massive shift of the nation's economy from manufacturing to services at all levels. Just the *increase* in employees alone in restaurant, health, and business services in the 1970s exceeded the *total* employment in the steel and automobile industries. As golden arches replaced blast furnaces as the symbols of American enterprise, the roles of the service and retail sectors of the economy became increasingly important. The great advances in consumer spending that began after World War I had created mass markets for family and household goods. New technology and efficient national distribution systems produced a cornucopia of products based on synthetic materials, electricity, and electronics that were sold to families with rising per capita incomes. New forms of retail stores based on unique administrative structures and innovative advertising methodologies moved and marketed these products. Department stores, grocery chains, variety and drug stores, discount stores, and franchised service and retailing operations made phenomenal changes in the economy in the twentieth century.

The sweeping alteration of one of the principal sectors of the economy began with the increasing expenditures for consumer durable and nondurable goods in the era following World War I. The steady increase in the use of prepared foods and ready-made clothing corresponded to the same urges that led to purchases of radios, refrigerators, vacuum cleaners, electric irons, and many other small appliances. The rate of growth in employment opportunities in the trade and retail sectors surpassed that of manufacturing between the turn of the century and the stock market crash in 1929, a further indication of the maturation of the national economy. Many manufacturers entered consumer markets with new products, formulated national advertising schemes to create name brands, and sought retail and wholesale outlets for these products. As per capita income continuously reached record heights, that demand led to more expensive goods in much greater variety. Manufacturers studied the marketplace to increase mass sales and sought the best outlets for new products. Retailers specialized in one line of product, or larger stores offered comprehensive outlets for merchandise. The nation's great wealth provided a solid basis upon which a consumer-oriented society would be built.[1] One means to market the proliferation of goods flowing from the factories was the department store.

DEPARTMENT STORES

The retail distribution of consumer commodities changed very little from the colonial era until after the Civil War. Most town and city dwellers purchased goods from general stores or from retail outlets that sold a narrow range of specialty items. To go "shopping" in one of America's large cities in the 1830s meant laboriously walking from store to store selecting goods; in small towns or crossroad villages one store, often with relatively high prices, sold a broad range of products, but only one type or style of each. The retail marketplace changed abruptly during the next century as the department store became the major urban merchandiser, as chain stores spread across the nation into smaller cities and larger towns, and as mail-order houses with huge catalogues of commodities brought greater choices and lower prices to the residents of rural America.

The evolution of the department store began with the pioneer effort of Alexander T. Stewart in New York in 1846. Stewart operated a large dry goods business, both wholesale and retail; the latter, called the Marble Dry Goods Palace, offered a central location, many departments, numerous services, and a low mark-up on the goods that he sold for cash only. Stewart generated a high-volume business through extensive and aggressive advertising, and he centralized all the nonselling functions within the store. By the 1860s Stewart's business, both wholesale and retail, was so large that he

Alexander T. Stewart (1803–1876). Merchant whose department store became the model for large-scale retailing. (Courtesy: *Dictionary of American Portraits.*)

generated 10 percent of all the imports into the port of New York. His retail sales alone reached over $8 million by 1865. One of Stewart's customers, Mrs. Mary Todd Lincoln, redecorated the White House with goods from his store. Organized by departments, he placed under one roof all the items sold by dozens of specialty stores and offered attractive surroundings with a competitive pricing policy. With considerable pride, shoppers would declare of recently purchased items, "I got it at Stewart's." The innovations that Stewart developed were expanded upon and refined by John Wanamaker in Philadelphia, R. H. Macy in New York, and Marshall Field in Chicago.[2] Soon similar department stores could be found in major cities all across the nation.

The growth of urban markets, aided by improved transportation and communication, made the retail trade a major factor in national income. Retail sales and employment expanded as modern marketing methods and advertising techniques enhanced the role of department stores and other merchandisers. Wholesalers had to adopt new policies to supply the larger retail outlets, and manufacturers hired additional salespeople to reach this new marketplace. Distributors, such as Alexander Stewart, moved goods into these markets at phenomenal rates; Stewart distributed $42 million in goods in 1870 and employed 2,000 people in his firm. Many of the larger department stores also distributed commodities in their geographical region with wholesale volumes greatly exceeding retail sales. The vast number of products flowing out of their warehouses and into railway cars and express wagons caused the distributors to create managerial structures not unlike those used by the retail portions of their businesses.

As the department stores increased in number and size, they began to reduce the role of the wholesaler, or to assume that function themselves. They bought manufactured goods from the factory and sold directly to the consumer, thereby eliminating the middleman, reducing costs and prices, and stimulating sales. Simultaneously, the department stores cut into the business of specialty shops scattered through the cities by providing delivery services and guaranteeing the return of unsatisfactory merchandise. In larger urban areas some of the department stores began to open branches, and some, like John Wanamaker, created branch outlets in other cities. The expansion of the leading department stores laid the basis for the rise of chain stores in the twentieth century.[3]

Department stores like Carson, Pirie, Scott in Chicago, I. Magnum in San Francisco, and Bullock's in Los Angeles followed the lead of Wanamaker's and Macy's, who added new consumer lines to their dry goods. Departments soon sold jewelry, shoes, furniture, carpets, and toys. The success of these areas led to additional departments selling silverware, china, flowers, books, stationery, and finally household appliances. These new departments enhanced total sales to allow for even higher volumes; and profits were made on volume, not mark-up. With substantial cash flowing into their newly acquired registers, the department stores could pay manufacturers cash for their products. Advertising and cutting prices moved "slow" goods to maintain the high rate of stock turnover that led to greater profits. The huge three- and four-story department store in the heart of the city became the leading symbol of urban mass-consumer markets in this country, just as the mail-order houses became the "department stores" for rural Americans.

MAIL-ORDER HOUSES

The small-scale mail-order business existed early in American history, but in the 1870s the giant mail-order firms became significant factors in the distribution of goods. The small town and crossroad village general store could not compete with the mail-order firms with their extensive catalogues and low prices. The expansion of postal delivery services, especially Rural Free Delivery (RFD) and parcel post, provided the means for the mail-order houses to move goods from their enormous warehouses to their customers. The numerous express companies continued to play a major role as did the telegraph, but the postal system made mail orders feasible for most customers. In the last three decades of the nineteenth century farmers believed they were overcharged by local stores and suppliers, particularly if they purchased on credit, and in their anger they turned to the mail-order catalogues, which often offered merchandise of higher quality at less cost. The mail-order innovators found a vast potential market and an efficient delivery system emerging almost simultaneously.

In 1872 Aaron Montgomery Ward and his brother-in-law formed the Original Grange Supply House to sell goods to farmers through the mail. Their initial endeavor had the support of the Patrons of Husbandry (the Grange). A former employee of Marshall Field, Ward issued a single-page list of commodities as his first catalogue. Within twenty years the catalogue had grown to over 500 pages with 24,000 items, and sales exceeded $1 million yearly. The success of Montgomery Ward produced competitors, and in 1893 Sears, Roebuck was founded. It too grew rapidly, especially with the coming of Julius Rosenwald as head of the firm in 1895, and by 1906 Sears did an annual business of $38 million. Richard

Sears and Alvah Roebuck began by selling watches through the mail, but their lines of merchandise expanded rapidly. When Roebuck retired and Rosewald entered the company with fresh ideas and capital, more lines were added and sales reached a phenomenal volume. The growth of the firm meant that an entirely new administrative structure had to be created to move hundreds of thousands of items from manufacturer to consumer efficiently and profitably.

The leaders of Sears, Reobuck organized the company into departments that specialized in particular lines of goods. The managers of the departments determined which products would be purchased from the manufacturers. The catalogue division established policy for marketing, and warehouse managers developed procedures for inventory control and the distribution of orders received. The structure allowed for huge volume and lower profit margins and prices. Sears surpassed Montgomery Ward to become the nation's leading mail-order firm. Its success produced an angry outcry from rural merchants, but labor, agricultural, and consumer groups forced Congress to expand parcel post service in 1912 to allow more families access to the wares of Sears and Wards.[4] The mail-order firms successfully reduced the cost of living and raised living standards for millions of rural families.

But what strategy would Sears and Wards adopt when their customers began to emigrate from the farms, villages, and small towns to the smaller cities and to metropolitan America? World War I and its aftermath accelerated tremendous demographic changes as millions of people moved to the urban centers. Sears attempted to cope with its changing business by establishing warehouses in Dallas and Seattle, but its managers faced greater problems than simply geographical dispersal. The recession of 1920–1921 left Sears with an inventory of over $100 million, and only a personal pledge of $20 million from Julius Rosenwald prevented collapse of the firm. Then in 1924 Rosenwald brought Robert E. Wood into the Sears management, and an entirely different strategy was adopted. A former army quartermaster and official in the building of the Panama Canal, Wood had studied the *Statistical Abstract of the United States* and understood that the decline of rural America meant disaster for Sears. The answer, he believed, was to enter retail marketing, establishing stores in urban America where the population growth was occurring. Sears would remain in the mail-order business but would also open an entirely new activity as a retail merchandiser. Wood's theory had already been rejected by Montgomery Ward, where he had been an executive before joining Sears. Beginning the next year Wood opened 8 retail stores; within only four years he had created 324 stores of various sizes. The stores stocked part of the catalogue lines and included catalogue departments where the full range of goods could be ordered and picked up. Wood closely studied urban growth patterns, highway and street plans, and carefully selected sites for his retail stores. Obviously, the automobile played a major role in the development of the general strategy and in the tactical decisions as well. The retail stores pushed what Wood called the big ticket items, such as refrigerators and other electrical appliances, in the consumer-oriented 1920s. Montgomery

Julius Rosenwald (1862–1932). An executive of Sears, Roe-buck, who developed its marketing strategies. (Courtesy: *Dictionary of American Portraits*.)

Ward, following the same pattern as Sears, soon became a major retailer as well.[5] Sears and Wards became part of an even larger trend in the twentieth century, the rise of the chain stores.

CHAIN STORES

Demography and economic change also proved significant in the emergence of chain stores, whether their main business was dry goods or groceries. As the number of households in urban centers increased, they turned to stores to provide what self-sufficient farm families had produced for themselves. The percentage of women in the labor force increased dramatically, meaning fewer foods were canned or preserved and fewer clothes were made at home. The large department stores in the major cities met the needs of some of the growing hordes of urbanites, and their branches reached out to rising suburbs. But what of the medium or smaller city and their retail sales potential? To a great extent that market was tapped by the chain stores.

The J. C. Penney chain is illustrative of this new form of retailer. Started in 1902 as a chain of cash department stores, the firm became a giant merchandiser. James Cash Penney opened the Golden Rule store in Kemmerer, Wyoming, to sell dry goods. After reaching a volume of $29,000 the first year, he opened a second store; and, after forming a third, he bought out his partners in 1907. Penney continued to open additional dry goods stores in small towns until in 1917 he had 71 outlets and sales reached $3.6 million. The greatest period of growth came during and after World War I as sales volume produced by 475 stores in 1923 exceeded $62 million. Part of the growth of the chain can be attributed to Penney's strategy of giving each store manager one-quarter of that store's profits. Penney would have more than 1,400 stores by the mid-1930s, many invading the territories of Sears, Wards, and the great department stores. Reversing the Sears strategy, Penney's would later open a mail-order division. And, like the other dry goods chains, Penney's would open charge accounts, which its founder had believed to be immoral. Penney's moved from dry goods to full-scale department stores in 1962 as it became, after Sears and Wards, the nation's third largest retailer with over 3,000 stores.[6]

Most of the dry goods chains followed the same process as Penney's, though rarely with the same degree of success. Supervision of far-flung branches was difficult; finding honest and efficient managers sometimes proved impossible; coordinating purchases, distribution, and sales, as well as large advertising campaigns, taxed executives. But slowly structures evolved that allowed for control of the chains and sustained volume merchandising. Regional chains gradually became national in scope by growth or through mergers. As the chains grew, their administrative structures evolved with buyers who specialized in particular acquisitions, regional sales supervisors to coordinate the branches, and large accounting departments to monitor inventories and cash flow. All the chains sought to move higher and higher volumes of goods into larger urban markets, a pattern that led to the development of enormous shopping centers and malls.

The concept of the shopping center could be traced back to the bazaars of the ancient Middle East, but one of the earliest modern urban centers was the Galleria Vittorio Emmanuele in Milan, Italy. Built by British capital in 1867, this huge glass-domed structure covered the intersection of two major thoroughfares, linking stores and shops with a well-lighted, weather-protected arcade. In the United States suburban sprawl, the expanding ownership of automobiles, and the increasing number of chain and department stores led to the creation of shopping centers away from the downtown areas. The first major planned center was built in

J.C. Penney (1875–1971) and a drawing of his first store in Kemmerer, Wyoming. (Courtesy: J.C. Penney Company.)

Kansas City by the J. C. Nichols Company in 1922. A beautifully land-scaped center with an attractive and harmonious architectural style, the Country Club Plaza would serve as a model for similar centers that mush-roomed across the nation after 1945. Shopping center developers obtained large mortgages from major insurance companies to build enclosed malls with massive parking lots. The shopping centers would include one or more department stores and numerous chain stores and franchised outlets. Some of the regional malls contained 1 to 2.5 million square feet of space. The immediate impact of the malls in smaller cities and large towns was to destroy previous retail marketing patterns, producing decay, if not death, in the older center of town. Many of the department store chains built the malls or helped to finance them. Macy's, for example, owned five centers outright and half interest in three more. The shopping malls replaced old neighborhood structures as the enclosed centers provided skating rinks, art shows, symphony concerts, restaurants, motion pictures, and, in some loca-tions, even hotels. As they became the focus of community life, the malls grew in number to 20,000 by 1977 with $300 billion in sales, or half of all retail sales in the country.[7] The malls emerged as the chain stores came to dominate all areas of the retail economy following a pattern established by the great grocery stores.

Wal-Mart and Sam M. Walton

Wal-Mart Stores Incorporated became the nation's third-largest retailer in the 1980s, surpassed only by Sears, Roebuck and Company and K-Mart Cor-poration. Its dramatic success in less than twenty years could be attributed to the vision, evangelistic enthusiasm, and merchandising skills of its founder, Sam Moore Walton. Walton parlayed a small group of dimestores into a chain of 1,200 discount stores that transacted $13 billion in sales in 1987 with a 7.5 percent profit margin. Two years before *Forbes* declared Walton to be "the Richest Man in America" with $3.6 billion in Wal-Mart stock. Family-held stock generated $11 million in dividends that year, all produced by stores in communities of 25,000 people, sometimes less. Scattered across the South and Midwest, the Wal-Mart stores represented the most recent technology, real estate expertise, and extraordinary merchandising.

Born in Kingfisher, Oklahoma, in 1918, Sam Moore Walton graduated from the University of Missouri in 1940 and became a trainee with J.C. Penney. After World War II he opened a dimestore in Arkansas and in 1962 operated nine Ben Franklin stores. When that chain did not encourage his deep discounting concept, he opened his first Wal-Mart and by 1970 had 51 stores in operation. Walton went public that year, and in 1972 Wal-Mart was listed on the New York Stock Exchange. His stores catered to the needs of small-town residents and appealed to customers with discounted prices on nationally known brands. Walton made every effort to sell only products produced in the United States.

A quiet, shy man, Walton kept the corporate headquarters in Bentonville, Arkansas. There he literally led managers in cheers during executive commit-tee meetings. On the road four or five days a week, Walton visited stores, addressed some of the 200,000 employees, scouted for sites for new stores, and met with suppliers. That same commitment and enthusiasm has been dedicated to his fifty Sam's Wholesale Clubs, with sales of $2.7 billion in 1987, and to the "hypermarkets," a combination of food and nonfood stores in a supercenter. Operating in only 24 states, Wal-Mart seemed poised to pass K-Mart and possibly even Sears as the nation's leading retailer, according to some analyists. Walton demonstrated that huge volumes in merchandising can be achieved outside of the nation's metropolitan centers.

GROCERY CHAINS

The first of the major grocery chains emerged in the 1860s in New York City. George F. Gilman and George Huntington Hartford operated 26 stores in lower Manhattan selling tea exclusively. In 1869 the name Great Atlantic and Pacific Tea Company was adopted, and additional stores were opened in the northeastern part of the country. The firm had expanded west to St. Paul and south to Norfolk by 1880, with over 100 stores in operation. The next twenty years saw the A&P cover nearly the whole country, and its lines grew to include coffee, cocoa, sugar, and other baking products. The firm bought directly from manufacturers and food processors, sold in volume at low mark-up, and competed very effectively against neighborhood and village general stores. Much of the success of the A&P had been its credit policy and delivery services. While A&P proved quite profitable, and a large chain had been developed, a significant part of the grocery market remained outside its business. Young John Hartford, son of George Hartford, convinced his elders in the company to allow him to open a cash-and-carry outlet in 1912, which proved to be an enormously profitable operation. Soon the new cash-and-carry division was established across the nation with stores opened at the rate of 50 per week. Vast volume sales meant lower prices from food processors, with a corresponding growth in retail sales. The chain had 14,000 outlets in operation by 1925, but the small, low-rent, one-person stores were already becoming obsolete. The combination store, or supermarket, offered not only coffee, tea, spices, and baking goods but also fresh meat and produce and a full range of canned and packaged foods. A major marketing decision led A&P to reduce its outlets to just over 4,000 and to convert its old tea stores to full-range, self-service, grocery supermarkets.[8] The alteration in marketing strategy reflected changes in consumer buying habits, mobility produced by urban growth, expanded automobile ownership, and competition from other grocery chains.

To increase profits on various food lines, the Atlantic & Pacific acquired or built food-processing plants and began to market its own brand name items called Ann Page. The chain operated over thirty bakeries, which provided bread, pastries, and confectionary items, and twelve coffee-roasting plants supplied A&P label coffees. The A&P also operated a cheese warehouse, salmon canneries, and even a laundry to clean uniforms.

An early A&P Tea Outlet and delivery wagon. (Courtesy: The Great Atlantic & Pacific Tea Company.)

Its research division developed a new variety of big-breasted chickens and worked with poultry specialists to increase egg production. The A&P published *Woman's Day,* a service magazine that boasted of a multimillion circulation without subscriptions. The management also decided not to blanket the nation with stores and avoided competing in some parts of the West and South, a decision that reflected the strength of grocery chains in those areas.

Regional grocery firms provided A&P with stiff competition after 1900. The Kroger Company, Jewel Tea, Safeway, First National Stores, and others introduced new lines of food products and merchandising techniques. By focusing on the distribution of goods, they established mechanisms to move high volumes of perishables from processors to consumers quickly and efficiently. Decentralized regional management structures were given these responsibilities. The smaller chains also contributed new marketing and advertising schemes. Clarence Saunders, a Memphis grocer, pioneered the self-service concept in 1916 at his Piggly Wiggly store. The customer moved through the store past counters and shelves where goods were displayed, and then to a clerk who priced and boxed the selections. Saunders not only replaced the clerks who had previously gathered the food products for the customer, but he also exposed the customer to many other items and found that sales grew as a result.[9] Soon Kroger, Safeway, and other chains adopted the concept. By the 1930s the self-service supermarket became the basic means for the distribution of food products as the grocery chains came to dominate the industry. Similar chains emerged among variety and drug stores.

VARIETY AND DRUG CHAINS

Simultaneously with the rise of the grocery stores there emerged chains of variety or "dime" stores, and later came the drug store chains. Before the development of these chains the retail outlets used by most consumers were owned by independent merchants who obtained their goods from wholesalers or distributors. As the chains were formed, many manufacturers refused to sell to them directly in order to protect their distributors and the independents. Though there were enormous differences in the volume of orders, they also attempted to charge the chains the same prices. As the chains grew in size and strength, however, they forced many manufacturers to sell to them directly and at lower prices. The chains then cut retail prices, causing considerable economic harm to the independent operators. Consumers turned to the chains that offered not only greater variety but also lower prices. The chains used their profits to improve the appearance of their stores, to find and develop the best locations, and to engage in regional or even national advertising campaigns. The chains did not offer charge accounts or deliveries, but consumers still went to them for a wide assortment of goods. The system employed by the chains moved products rapidly and efficiently into the consumer market, and sales reflected their widespread acceptance.[10]

One of the first merchants to employ these methods of retail marketing was Frank W. Woolworth. After serving as a clerk in a dry goods store in upstate New York, Woolworth opened a five-and ten-cent store in Lancaster, Pennyslvania, in 1879. He believed that a store which offered a variety of miscellaneous smallware priced at five to ten cents would attract customers. On the first days of business he sold $127.65 of his $410.00 inventory. Success was not instantaneous, however: His first three branch stores failed. But a store in Scranton succeeded, and by 1881 yearly sales reached $18,000. Woolworth believed that he needed good locations for a number of stores to create high-volume sales. By 1895, with 25 stores, sales reached $1 million and two years later he opened his first dime store in New York City. Woolworth purchased several smaller chains, but major expansion came in 1911 when his 318 stores joined with five other groups to form F. W. Woolworth Company with 596 outlets and combined sales of

$52 million. The company located its headquarters in New York City and in 1913 opened the fifty-story Woolworth Building. The Gothic-style sky-scraper became known as the Cathedral of Commerce, a symbol of the chain's financial success; Woolworth paid for the building—$13.5 million—

F.W. Woolworth's gothic office tower in New York City.   (Courtesy: F.W. Wool-worth Co.)

in cash. The Woolworth chain would send its stores with their distinctive red signs across the nation, and by the 1960s some 2,500 stores were in operation in the United States, with others in Great Britain, Canada, and Mexico.[11]

The success of Woolworth in marketing low-price consumer goods attracted the attention of other merchants who began to form similar chains. S. H. Kress & Company, S. S. Kresge, John G. McCrory, and other firms emulated the dime stores of Woolworth, and in many communities the stores often stood in the same block of Main Street. The goods soon included items priced in excess of a dime or a nickel, but the concept of smallwares remained constant until the 1930s. The variety stores stressed notions, toys, small hardware, inexpensive fabrics, and household items. Rows of counters displayed the goods, which were placed in small bins separated by wood or glass dividers. Clusters of counters were presided over by a clerk with access to a cash register. The clerks maintained inventories and the displays under direction of the store managers. Some of the larger variety stores added candy counters and then "soda fountains" that attracted additional customers for the variety goods. The dime store chains enhanced the standard of living by making available a wide range of consumer goods at popular prices.

The great drug store chains paralleled the rise of the variety stores but at a later date, emerging only after the turn of the century. Typical of the drug chains was that founded in 1909 by Charles Walgreen in Chicago, the owner of a small neighborhood drug store. When he attempted to open a second store, friends told him there were already too many drug stores. Walgreen replied, "Chicago may have too many drug stores, but it hasn't enough *Walgreen* drug stores!" Walgreen's marketing methods were not unlike those of the grocery and variety chains. He emphasized good locations, low prices, high volume, effective advertising, and quality pharmaceuticals. He often carried goods in the stores that competed directly with the variety chains, but he also had drugs, health, and bath items that they did not stock. Walgreen's added small electrical appliances in the 1920s to broaden their consumer appeal. By the time of his death in 1939, Walgreen had built a chain of almost 500 stores with sales of over $70 million. His marketing methods had been followed by the Louis K. Liggett stores and those of the Skilleran, Owl, Eckerd, and other drug chains.[12]

The mass marketing of consumer goods through chain distribution came to dominate the retail sector of the economy early in this century. Cigars, shoes, jewelry, and other products served as the basis for chains. The Thom McAn stores marketed shoes in over 800 outlets by the 1960s, with G. R. Kinney, a division of Woolworth, operating even more shoe stores. The concepts employed were the same even though the consumables differed. By the 1950s the large grocery, variety, drug, shoe, and jewelry chains had achieved great successes, but a new approach to mass marketing arose that threatened all, and doomed some, of the chains: The discount store offered yet another approach to high-volume sales.

THE DISCOUNTS

The explosion of discount stores in the 1960s could not have taken place without the so-called fair trade laws. These laws attempted to prevent unfair competition by price cutting—that is, large chains could purchase goods in volume and then cut prices to the point where they eliminated competition. Many manufacturers also wanted to establish and maintain retail prices for their goods to maximize profits for their retailers. Ironically, in the Great Depression several major drug store chains endorsed fair trade laws because deep discounting was harming their financial stability. Virtually all the state governments, and in 1937 the federal government, passed laws authorizing the maintenance of minimum or fair prices for goods. Manufacturers legally established minimum retail price agreements that outlets for their products were generally forced to sign. The laws stated that even those who refused to accept the agreements were bound by the conditions. While few grocery items were "fair traded," most drugs, appliances, dry goods, and other consumables were marketed under minimum-price agreements. Price wars abated after the laws became effective, and until 1951 the statutes were sustained by federal and state courts. In that year, however, the United States Supreme Court ruled that retailers who refused to sign such agreements could not be bound by minimum prices. Efforts to close this loophole failed, and state and lower federal courts began to invalidate the concept of fair trade.[13]

Before 1951 a few firms in larger cities offered appliances, luggage, and furniture at less than fair trade prices, but they made little impact on retail sales. With the demise of the fair trade rules, however, large operations began to offer a wide range of products with discounts of 15 to 25 percent on standard prices for name brand merchandise. Efforts by manufacturers like General Electric and Westinghouse to prevent discounted pricing failed as low-margin retailing began to spread across the nation. The discount operators, who would accept margins of less than 25 percent if volume could be raised to a very high level, opened giant stores with as much as 150,000 square feet of floor space where large and small appliances, dry goods, sports equipment, toys, drugs, and even groceries were offered at reduced prices. Vast parking lots surrounded the stores, which were established along major urban thoroughfares. Korvettes, Arlans, Two Guys, GEM, Spartan, and other discount chains operated over 2,500 outlets by 1962, and the average discount store had developed a sales volume of more than $2.5 million yearly.

The success of the discount stores forced many of the established chains and department stores to open similar operations or create new divisions as discounters. Woolworth, for example, opened Woolco stores as discounts. The declining Kresge variety stores created the K Mart division of full-fledged discount department stores, and it proved so successful that the chain abandoned its old name and adopted the new one. Grocery chains created new stores that eliminated elaborate displays and offered goods from cardboard boxes with limited or no fresh meat or produce items. Not all the the chains found discounting profitable, however; the W.

T. Grant Company declared bankruptcy after overexpansion and unfavorable locations brought this great variety store chain to financial disaster. Several of the larger discount chains also declared bankruptcy as the volume of sales failed to reach levels necessary to maintain deep discounts on all items.

The discount stores began to select locations in suburban areas where population growth rates were higher and where families with larger disposable incomes were moving. They took advantage of the fact that the new suburban branches of downtown department stores rarely had the traditional "bargain basements," leaving a large void in their normal operations. The early discounters replaced their drab, inexpensive stores with cleaner, brighter surroundings, but they avoided the elaborate and expensive decor of the traditional department stores. They often leased floor space to other firms to sell items not carried by the discount chain. By the end of the 1970s such stores numbered almost 10,000 with yearly sales approaching $50 billion. They turned their inventories an average of four times each year, twice the rate of the department stores. The K Mart stores soon rivaled Sears, Roebuck as the nation's biggest retailer, having surpassed J. C. Penney by 1977. The revolution in retail merchandising brought on by the discount stores represented part of a major change in consumer spending practices and alterations in the service sector of the national economy. General prosperity, middle-class affluence, two-income families, and greater mobility created demands for a whole range of new services and products.[14] Joining the discount stores as purveyors of these goods and services were the chains of franchise outlets that also spread across the nation.

THE FRANCHISES

The aspirations of many Americans to "be their own boss" became realities after 1945 with the boom in franchising. The spread of small franchised businesses dramatically altered marketing of some products—as well as American dietary patterns. A franchise contract allowed an individual to do business under the name and corporate image of a national firm that often had many of the attributes of a chain. In return for use of the corporate name and access to its product line, the small entrepreneurs agreed to operate in a prescribed manner, sell only the specified products, pay an initial fee for the franchise, and return the franchiser a percentage of the sales. The franchise holder often obtained capital through the firm and had the risks of entering a new business somewhat reduced. Initially the capital required for most franchises was relatively small, but as the decade of the 1980s arrived, some large-scale franchises required an investment of half a million dollars or more. While fast-food franchises of infinite variety attracted national attention, franchises also emerged in electronics, bookstores, handicrafts, toys, clothing, and many other product lines and services. The Rexall drug chain pioneered in retail franchising early in the century, and other chains such as Western Auto and Ben Franklin had developed similarly. But the urge to create an independent business, and the capital required to initiate the business, came largely after World War II. Many national companies began to foster the franchise concept in order to create new markets for their products. B. F. Goodrich found in franchised tire operators a means to greatly expand tire sales, and then the company purchased the Rayco seat cover and accessory chain to extend the sales potential of its franchises. Even Sears, Roebuck and Montgomery Ward began to franchise their catalogue order stores. The franchise business soon became a major factor in the retail sector of the economy.

RAY KROC AND THE GOLDEN ARCHES

At the ripe old age of 52, suffering from arthritis and diabetes, Ray Kroc devised a fast-foods concept that made him a millionaire many times over. He had been a paper-cup salesman and had marketed mixers for soda fountains, but as sales of the latter declined he sought another livelihood. In 1954 he visited one of his malt-mixer customers in San Bernardino, California, primarily because it had purchased eight machines that would mix forty milkshakes at one time—obviously, it had to be a thriving hamburger drive-in. He discovered a large operation limited to burgers and drinks at low prices; the volume was large and steady. At first he saw this as a prototype to which more mixers could be sold, but after talking to Dick and Maurice McDonald, the owners, he saw a far greater potential. The McDonalds stressed cleanliness, efficiency, and an assembly-line process for cooking. Orders were filled in seconds. Kroc suggested expansion, but the McDonalds wanted to open only one more outlet, not the dozens Kroc envisioned. When Kroc then suggested franchising other McDonalds, they told him they already had eight franchises in California and Arizona, but that the quality of the operations varied, and this reflected negatively on their own drive-in.

Kroc then proposed that the McDonalds allow a third party to franchise the other operations who would guarantee that only high-quality restaurants could hold the franchises. He volunteered to be that third party and returned home to Chicago to formulate his plans. Kroc carried a contract from the McDonalds to organize the chain that gave him $950 for each franchise opened plus 1.9 percent of all their gross receipts; 1.4 percent for Kroc and .5 percent to the McDonald brothers. The contract guaranteed that all the franchises would look exactly like the San Bernardino drive-in, to include its golden arch. Kroc continued to sell mixers, but meanwhile he also developed his own McDonalds in Des Plaines, a Chicago suburb in 1955. After resolving some legal problems—the McDonalds had forgotten to tell Kroc they had previously sold a franchise for Cook County, Illinois—Kroc began to earn a substantial return on his hamburger operation. He franchised 37 sites by 1957, and in the next two years opened 164 more. Soon investors were approaching him eager to build golden arches, and Kroc gave up his mixer business. He stockpiled sites for franchises in advance by purchasing vacant lots on busy streets, and he acquired some $170 million in properties for the firm. When the McDonald brothers decided to retire, Kroc bought them out for $2.7 million, and then he went public with a stock sale. Shares offered at

$22.50 in 1963 rose to $50.00 in a short period. As the franchises grew in number, the total hamburgers sold climbed into the hundreds of millions.

Kroc's McDonald chain became the model for fast-food franchises across the nation. McDonald franchises required $250,000 in capital to start with, but the rate of return was higher than the industry average. Franchise holders had to meet stringent requirements for food quality, hours of operation, cleanliness, and constant maintenance and improvement of the site. Kroc's timing was excellent, as more families and individuals began to eat meals outside of the home. His franchises all promised the same basic menu and same format with prices most consumers could afford. There were 9,410 McDonalds in operation by 1986, with some 159,000 employees. In addition to opening new stores abroad, McDonald's expanded its product line to include breakfasts, salads, and ice cream in its domestic outlets. The nation's premier fast-food chain, McDonald's, and its founder, Ray Kroc, had helped to alter the nation's eating habits.

In the most common arrangement, an operating franchise was granted in which the small-scale entrepreneur ran a business in an exclusive territory with the direct assistance of the parent company. It was possible for the successful franchise holder to acquire additional franchise locations and create, in effect, a chain within the chain. Not all franchise operators achieved that level of success, and the industry was plagued with dishonest contracts or franchises for products either faulty or with sales volume so low that profit levels were minimal or nonexistent. Nevertheless, the opportunity to form their own business appealed so strongly to thousands of Americans that the franchised store became a significant factor in the consumer marketplace.[15]

Some of the franchise operations were based on technological change and the development of new products and services. For example, the explosion in technology in electronics, particularly in television and sound equipment, created a vast market. In 1963 Charles Tandy, a Fort Worth businessman, bought the nine Radio Shack stores and then began to market the franchises nationally. He provided a large number of selected electronic products with high turn-over for mass markets. Radio Shack advertised heavily, placed stores in large shopping malls and in small towns, and ordered products from manufacturers with the Radio Shack brand name. The chain mushroomed, and by 1980 had 7,500 stores. The growing sophistication of consumer-oriented calculators, computers, copy machines, and word processors brought Xerox and IBM into the retail market with each of these giants opening specialty outlets to market their products.

Not all large corporations which entered franchising profited from the experience. In the highly competitive fast-foods industry few achieved profit levels comparable to McDonald's. Ralston-Purina found its Jack-In-The-Box chain less profitable than its pet-food operations; General Foods lost money on its Burger Chef franchises; and Heublien saw Kentucky

Fried Chicken absorb profits earned from its other lines. While more and more Americans ate outside of the home, capitalizing on that trend depended not only upon packaging popular food items, but also upon marketing them. Large firms and their franchise holders discovered that to do both profitably was difficult.

Service industries represented a growing segment of the national economy in the last three decades. The distribution, marketing, and maintenance of consumer products occupied a significant fraction of all workers. Increases in consumer spending, and a growing discretionary aspect of that spending, laid the basis for the rise of the service industry. But, as the discretionary segment of family income declined because of high rates of inflation and rising taxes, the various elements in the service sector came under severe competitive pressures, and some major retailers perished. Nevertheless, the economy remained clearly oriented toward the consumption of durable and nondurable goods through mass marketing, a trend as old as Alexander Stewart's Marble Dry Goods Palace.

NOTES

1. Thomas C. Cochran, *200 Years of American Business* (New York: Basic Books, 1977), pp. 113–114.

2. Harry E. Resseguie, "Alexander Turney Stewart and the Development of Department Store, 1823–1876," *Business History Review* 39 (Autumn 1965), pp. 301–322.

3. Alfred D. Chandler, Jr., *The Visible Hand: The Managerial Revolution in American Business* (Cambridge: Harvard University Press, 1977), pp. 223–227.

4. Ibid., pp. 229–233.

5. Alfred D. Chandler, Jr., *Strategy and Structure: Chapters in the History of the American Industrial Enterprise* (Cambridge: MIT Press, 1962), pp. 225–237.

6. Godfrey M. Lebhar, *Chain Stores in America, 1859–1962* (New York: Chain Store Publishing Corp. 1963), pp. 15–18; Robert Hendrickson, *The Grand Emporiums* (Briarcliff Manor, New York: Stein & Day, 1979), pp. 143–149; Norman Beasley, *Main Street Merchant: The Story of the J. C. Penney Company* (New York: Whittlesey House, 1948).

7. Hendrickson, *The Grand Emporiums*, pp. 268–283.

8. Lebhar, *Chain Stores in America*, pp. 24–26; Tom Mahoney, *The Great Merchants* (New York: Harper Brothers, 1955), pp. 172–187; Roy J. Bullock, "The Early History of the Great Atlantic & Pacific Tea Company," *Harvard Business Review* 11 (April 1933), pp. 289–298, and "A History of the Great Atlantic & Pacific Tea Company since 1878," *Harvard Business Review* 12 (October 1933), pp. 59–69.

9. Lebhar, *Chain Stores in America*, p. 34.

10. Chandler, *The Visible Hand*, pp. 233–235.

11. Hendrickson, *The Grand Emporiums*, pp. 115–123; John Kennedy Winkler, *Five and Ten: The Fabulous Life of F. W. Woolworth* (New York: R. M. McBride and Company, 1940).

12. Lebhar, *Chain Stores in America*, p. 20.

13. Ibid., pp. 112–119.

14. Hendrickson, *The Grand Emporiums*, pp. 188–204.

15. Harry Kursh, *The Franchise Boom* (Englewood Cliffs, New Jersey: Prentice Hall, 1968), pp. 4–9, 22–24, 30–40.

SUGGESTED READINGS

BEASLEY, NORMAN. *Main Street Merchant: The Story of the J. C. Penney Company.* New York: Whittlesey House, 1948.

BULLOCK, ROY J. *"The Early History of the Great Atlantic & Pacific Tea Company." Harvard Business Review* 11 (April 1933): 289–298.

———. "A History of the Great Atlantic & Pacific Tea Company since 1878." *Harvard Business Review* 12 (October 1933): 59–69.

CHANDLER, ALFRED D. JR. *Strategy and Structure: Chapters in the History of the American Industrial Enterprise.* Cambridge: MIT Press, 1962.

———. *The Visible Hand: The Managerial Revolution in American Business.* Cambridge: Harvard University Press, 1977.

EMMETT, BORIS, and JOHN E. JEUCK. *Catalogues and Counters: A History of Sears, Roebuck and Company.* Chicago: University of Chicago Press, 1950.

HENDRICKSON, ROBERT. *The Grand Emporiums.* Briarcliff Manor, New York: Stein & Day, 1979.

KURSH, HARRY. *The Franchise Boom.* Englewood Cliffs, New Jersey: Prentice Hall, 1968.

LEBHAR, GODFREY M. *Chain Stores in America, 1859–1962.* New York: Chain Store Publishing Corp., 1963.

MAHONEY, TOM. *The Great Merchants.* New York: Harper & Brothers, 1955.

RESSEGUIE, HARRY E. "Alexander Turney Steward and the Development of the Department Store, 1823–1876." *Business History Review* 39 (Autumn 1965): 301–322.

WINKLER, JOHN KENNEDY. *Five and Ten: The Fabulous Life of F. W. Woolworth.* New York: R. M. McBride and Company, 1940.

20 | Multinational Corporations

The roots of multinational companies in the American economy extend back to the English and Dutch trading companies of the sixteenth and seventeenth centuries. Throughout the colonial period and into the nineteenth century American entrepreneurs established branches overseas to buy local products and to sell American exports. Some of these traders invested in foreign businesses, thus establishing the basis for contemporary multinational enterprises. A *multinational* is a firm that does business in two or more foreign countries. These are businesses with direct investments, as opposed to those that simply operate sales offices in another country, and they are involved in the development and management of business enterprises abroad. American investors placed large amounts of capital in other countries well before World War I, and much of that capital was in manufacturing as well as extraction industries and utilities. American investment abroad increased throughout the 1920s, declined during the Great Depression, and then grew rapidly after 1945. Ironically, in the latter period individuals and firms from other countries accelerated simultaneously their investments in the United States. By the 1960s the multinationals had become the most powerful private economic organizations in the world, and they dominated nearly all of the technologically advanced industrial economies.[1] A phenomenon of the last three decades has been the growing impact of the non-American multinationals on the economy of the United States and its implications for the future. Although the American multinationals had been the largest in number and size, the rise of multinationals in many countries altered world market conditions and built even stronger interrelationships between national economies around the globe.

THE BIRTH OF MULTINATIONALS

The transition from simple trading to direct investment in foreign businesses occurred by the mid-nineteenth century. Representatives of American firms abroad began to take a deeper interest in production facilities and transportation in order to increase trading possibilities. The American government tacitly encouraged international commerce through its foreign diplomatic offices, even as businesspersons began to invest in railroad and telegraph schemes as well as mining and agricultural projects. Individual American emigrés placed capital in Canadian paper and cotton mills, Mexican transportation facilities, Hawaiian agriculture and trade, and Russian railroads. These were generally high-risk operations engaged in by only the most adventuresome investors. While the capital invested was relatively small, the seeds for future activity had been planted. At the same time other Americans, particularly investment bankers and railway promoters, sought British, French, Dutch, and German investment capital for American development. By 1857 direct, long-term foreign investment in the United States reached a quarter of a billion dollars in value. The multinational enterprise was a two-way street well before the Civil War.

In the three decades following Appomattox, American investments abroad grew rapidly as did the amount of foreign capital placed in the United States. The coming of faster transportation in the form of steamships and better and more reliable communication by ship and by cable, in addition to the maturation of local firms into national enterprises, accelerated the rise of the multinational. Companies with national structures began to apply their newly developed sales methods in international markets, then to invest in mining and manufacturing facilities abroad, not unlike their branch plants scattered across the United States. While the emphasis on marketing American-made products predominated, direct investments began to accelerate, particularly in Canada, Mexico, and the Caribbean. For example, when I. M. Singer sought to increase the sales of its sewing machines, it established branch offices with foreign agents. Problems with patents, poor representatives, and difficulties with remittances from Great Britain led Singer to build its first factory abroad in Scotland. Meanwhile, Singer representatives covered much of the world so that by 1874 half of Singer's sales were outside of the United States. The plant at Glasgow, Scotland, tripled in size, and another factory was opened in Canada even as worldwide sales grew. By the end of the 1880s Singer could be described as a multinational firm. The Singer experience would be repeated by Standard Oil, General Electric, National Cash Register, and others.[2]

Singer sewing machine central agency. São Paulo, Brazil, in 1912.   (Courtesy: The Singer Company.)

Many of the enterprises that expanded abroad produced goods superior in quality to those manufactured elsewhere. Technological advances in the United States created markets for locomotives, locks, guns, elevators, cash registers, harvesters, and refined petroleum products. As economies of scale multiplied, American manufacturers cut prices, causing European companies to protest that the Americans were "dumping" goods on their domestic markets. The charge was not true; American companies could and did produce export goods at lower prices even when transportation charges were added. Initially, these firms sold through agents, then installed branch managers, and then, as business increased in volume, investments would be made in manufacturing or assemblying facilities. Profits from sales and marketing would be reinvested directly with new administrative offices to manage them, thus creating a multinational enterprise.

By the 1890s American firms in five distinct areas had become significant multinationals—communications, electrical apparatus, chemicals, petroleum, and insurance. American firms deployed cable communications from the United States to western Europe and Latin America, enhancing the investment activities of other companies. Alexander Graham Bell's telephone became a major export as networks were established in Europe, Asia, and Latin America. In another area of American technological achievement, electricity, Western Electric established a manufacturing plant in Belgium as early as 1882, the first of many such operations. Affiliates of Edison Electric brought incandescent lights to Great Britain, France, and elsewhere, simultaneously creating markets for their generators and other products. Chemical and drug firms introduced a wide range of new pharmaceuticals and related products worldwide, establishing plants abroad. George Eastman discovered that quality control could best be established by having facilities in foreign locations rather than by shipping film, developers, and related goods. Standard Oil, of course, moved rapidly into international activities, acquiring foreign firms with distributing, production, and refining networks. And American insurance companies sold policies in Europe, Canada, Latin America, and Australia by the 1800s; they then invested premiums in foreign real estate and securities. Symbolically, the American Chamber of Commerce formed an organization in Paris in 1894. From simple efforts to broaden markets for American-made goods, foreign business activity led to the rise of the modern multinational firm.[3]

Around the turn of the century American investment abroad accelerated as the corporate giants created between 1897 and 1914 sought monopoly or oligopoly not only at home but also overseas. Europeans spoke of an American invasion as firms from the United States purchased subsidiaries, opened new facilities, or initiated international cartels. From the Sherwin-Williams slogan that their "paints cover the earth" to the Guggenheim's announced intent to seek mining properties in all parts of the globe, American investors sought to place substantial amounts of capital outside the United States. The depression after 1893 also encouraged firms to market surpluses abroad. The new industrial giants created in the era of mergers applied their marketing and manufacturing skills to international sales and found that substantial profits often resulted.

The federal government adopted new postures in foreign affairs that encouraged the growth of international trade and investment, such as the Open Door Policy in China, the acquisition of a colonial empire in the aftermath of the Spanish-American War, the development of the Panama Canal, and the interventionist policy in Latin America as proclaimed in the Roosevelt Corollary. As the United States emerged as a world power it could, and did, encourage foreign investment; but, as has been seen, American enterprises had been involved abroad for four decades previously, and rarely did particular policies toward individual countries provide specific aids to investment. The industrial giants could, however, depend on helpful and friendly foreign policies emanating from Washington.[4]

ADAPTING TO FOREIGN BUSINESS CLIMATES

In the years before 1914 American firms investing overseas had to make substantial adjustments in their assumptions and business practices. Conditions in the nation in which they planned to invest were often far more influential in the decision-making process than American foreign policy. The multinationals, or potential multinationals, still looked to export markets for their goods being produced in this country. They also invested heavily in facilities to produce raw materials abroad for export to the United States and other markets. These firms had to take cognizance of foreign competition and business practices. While the domestic business climate was strongly antitrust, European firms preferred the creation of combinations or cartels to forestall competition. As a result, many businesses established highly restrictive international agreements on production, patents, export quotas, sales territories, and output. Where American technology or economies of scale were overwhelming, wholly owned subsidiaries were established that totally dominated foreign markets, a practice illegal at home under the Sherman Anti-Trust Act but not so in most other countries. When foreign governments sought to protect home industries from the Americans, the companies from the United States often purchased interests in those industries to gain a market. Political and diplomatic factors, as well as economic conditions, shaped American investment policies abroad.[5] And it should be kept in mind that many of the investments proved to be less than successful. When an American firm introduced ice cream to the British market, it failed—the product simply did not appeal to the consumers. Nevertheless, American direct investment abroad stood at almost $3 billion by 1914.

WILLIAM H. LEVER

Why a sketch of William H. Lever, a British industrial leader who died in 1925? The First Viscount Leverhulme of the Western Isles created the firm of Lever Brothers, which became half of the British-Dutch multinational Unilever, one of the earliest and most successful multinationals to operate in the United States. A successful grocer in the north of England, the thirty-year-old Lever decided in 1881 to enter a new field. He developed a hard hand soap with a high concentration of palm or copra oil that produced much more lather than hard soap made from tallow. Quickly it became a popular product in Great Britain. He cut and wrapped the soap in a distinctive paper, a marketing innovation, and advertised the product extensively. A mass-produced consumer good, Sunlight soap became the model for additional Lever products. His business flourished, and by the 1890s he developed a large export trade. The next step was the creation of factories abroad in continental Europe, the British colonies, and the United States. Needing additional capital, he transformed the firm into a public business even as his marketing methods created even larger sales and profits. Lever, who also saw the possibilities of margarine as a cheap substitute for butter, allied his firm with Dutch margarine manufacturers. Despite opposition by dairy farmers and other food processors, margarine became a widely used staple, and Lever marketed that product worldwide along with soap.

Lever entered the United States through an American subsidiary, Lever Brothers, and marketed lines of soap, detergents, and toilet articles. In 1897 and 1899 he purchased soap factories in Boston and Philadelphia. Public reaction to his major products, Sunlight and Lifebuoy, was negative initially, and Lever dropped the latter and added Lux, which became a major seller following an intensive advertising campaign. Additional products—Lux Flakes and Rinso—made Lever Brothers a well-known manufacturer in the United States, and few consumers even knew that the vegetables shortening Spry and other Lever brand names were produced by a British firm.

William H. Lever (1851–1925). English industrialist and founder of Lever Brothers. (Courtesy: Unilever Limited.)

Unilever plants around the globe manufactured a wide variety of goods for household consumption. Food products included margarine, ice cream, cooking fats, and frozen and canned foods. Lever produced a large number of toilet article products including toothpaste, shampoos, and of course soap, and subsidiaries manufactured paper and plastic products and packaging materials.

By 1979, worldwide sales by Unilever in seventy-five countries reached over $10 billion as the multinational produced foodstuffs and soaps in plants in Australia, Great Britain, Canada, France, Germany, and the United States. The two owners of Unilever, Unilever Ltd. of London and Unilever N.K. of Rotterdam, independently operated the subsidiaries abroad, but a closely intertwined directorate clearly linked the various branches. For all practical purposes, this multinational operated as if there were only one company, and the American subsidiaries—Thomas J. Lipton, Good Humor, and Lever Brothers—were tightly coordinated by the parent companies.

Because of their geographical proximity, generally friendly governments, untapped raw resources, and economic underdevelopment, three areas—Mexico, Canada, and the Caribbean—were of particular importance to American investors. Between the 1870s and 1912 Americans invested more money in Mexico than any other country, and Canada ranked second. The regime of Porfirio Diaz in Mexico City eagerly sought capital from the United States, which was placed in railroads, mines, ranches, and petroleum. The railways opened the rural countryside to further investment as the Diaz administrators sought to enhance the nation's economy and their private purses. Soon American developers gained sizable landholdings and mining interests. After 1900 American firms dominated the Mexican petroleum industry. The "tranquility" in Mexico ended in revolution in 1911 with the overthrow of Diaz; the subsequent period was rife with political turbulence, assassination, and economic chaos. Eventually the Mexican government expropriated the petroleum companies, most of the railways, and much of the land. After 1914 investors refused to risk additional capital in Mexico, and Canada became the leading nation for placing American funds outside this country.[6]

Canada became a dominion in 1867, and its newly united government sought investment capital. Vast distances required extensive railway development, and raw resources, mainly copper, nickel, and timber, could only be exploited with substantial capital investment. A politically stable Canada friendly to the United States encouraged the shift away from Mexico, and by the first two decades of the twentieth century, American investors had put money into not only railways, mining, and lumber but also petroleum, utilities, and manufacturing plants. Some firms served only Canadian markets, but others sought to use their Canadian subsidiaries to penetrate markets in the British Empire. Canadian-produced goods received preferential tariffs in the British economic system and paid lower duties than American products. In Canada, unlike Mexico, many of the ventures had Canadian partners, and few of the businesses established by Americans were wholly owned by citizens of the United States. The presence of American firms in Canada would grow rapidly through and following World War I.[7]

American investment in the Caribbean came largely after the Spanish-American War. Investors placed capital in railways, mines, petroleum, sugar plantations, and other agricultural ventures, primarily bananas. Political instability, disease, untrained workers, and competition with British, German, and French investors made this a high-risk area for American firms. The fortunes of the United Fruit Company are illustrative of the gambles involved in the region.

UNITED FRUIT COMPANY

Formed in Boston in 1899, United Fruit initially developed sugar holdings in Cuba. Andrew Preston, president of United Fruit, moved quickly to establish the firm in the region and soon owned or leased 300,000 acres of land in Costa Rica, Nicaragua, Honduras, Santo Domingo, Jamaica, and elsewhere. Using the company's $20 million in capital, Preston established banana plantations at most of the sites, which also produced citrus, coconut, rubber and cacao as well as raising cattle. United Fruit gradually reduced its purchases from independent producers and acquired many of their properties. Its landholdings grew to over 850,000 acres. As the operations expanded, the local governments encouraged United Fruit by reducing export duties and by providing land at very low prices.

Under Preston's guidance United Fruit built and operated its own fleet of ships to take the produce to Europe and the United States, and it soon began to construct railways to serve its plantations and ranches. Preston took advantage of technical advances in refrigeration in constructing his warehouses, ships, and freight cars. By 1902 United Fruit imported over 90 percent of all the bananas brought into the United States. The transportation network moved the highly perishable bananas quickly and efficiently to American ports. The need for rapid communication in the scattered empire led to the establishment of a subsidiary to operate a radio network. To develop its lands, United Fruit invested $190 million in drainage, water, and sewer systems, as well as roads, hospitals, and company towns. The size and scope of its operations simply dominated the small and underdeveloped countries in which it operated. Preston formed a "banana empire" throughout the region that created fear and distrust among the local people. More than once United Fruit would be blamed when U.S. Marines arrived to occupy national capitals to restore order, collect taxes, and install a new and friendly government. Thus, United Fruit came to be directly linked by many Latin Americans with the Roosevelt Corollary and "Yankee imperialism."[8] In this region, as elsewhere, economic and political developments in the United States and in the countries where investments were made shaped the nature and size of each venture.

THE MATURATION OF THE MULTINATIONALS

A firm basis had been laid by the time of World War I for significant expansion of American investment abroad. Failures in Mexico, and in China, had been more than offset by successes in Canada and Western Europe. The initial activities in Latin America outside of Mexico gave promise of a high rate of return. Worldwide experiences taught entrepreneurs the need to view each country as unique, and to develop a broad range of strategies to deal with different host governments and business practices. Yet despite the almost global involvement of American firms, in 1914 investments abroad were less than those of Great Britain, France, and Germany, representing only 7 percent of the nation's GNP. Some of the country's largest firms had become multinationals, however, and they would be emulated by others. Advanced American technology and entrepreneurship were prime factors in spurring investment overseas and the formation of multinational enterprises.

World War I proved to be a watershed in the evolution of the American multinational firms. In the decades that followed they invested more heavily, opened new operations, and began to replace or triumph over their European competitors. Before the war the American companies successfully challenged the British only in Mexico, the Caribbean, and parts of Central America. By the beginning of World War II, the Americans dominated the Western Hemisphere as well as some countries in Africa and the Middle East. The multinationals grew, integrated, and diversified as they spread across the world. The government of the United States actively supported these efforts throughout the 1920s and 1930s. The proliferation of the multinationals and their components, as well as their vast economic power, often produced mixed responses from foreign governments who saw such economic developments and American foreign policy inexorably linked even when they were not.[9]

FROM 1920 TO 1940

World War I greatly disrupted established American investments in Europe, but the war also served to stimulate interest in business opportunities on the continent. Economic dislocation created by the war allowed U.S. firms to penetrate postwar European markets more rapidly. Also, while the Europeans had fought, Americans firms added to their direct investments in Asia and Latin America. The Americans moved quickly to develop larger overseas operations in mining, food processing, and petroleum to satisfy new markets created by the war. But there were losses as well as gains. The revolutions in Mexico and Russia, especially the former, cost American investors heavily. Destruction in Europe during the war eliminated some American holdings. The Armistice also brought out latent strains of nationalism; many governments sought to restrict American penetration of their home markets and to rebuff American efforts to again dominate markets they had previously controlled overseas. Nevertheless, multinationals headquartered in the United States stood ready to enter the 1920s with renewed enthusiasm for expansion abroad.

The Wilson administration—and later those of Harding, Coolidge, and Hoover—passed legislation favorable to American investment overseas. It altered tax laws, provided commercial and legal information about foreign investment, and engaged in diplomatic negotiations to stimulate receptivity to American investment. The world depression of 1920–1921 only temporarily slowed expansion of the multinationals, and as the domestic economy boomed again after 1923, so did overseas investment. While Secretary of Commerce, and then president, Hoover worried about foreign competition stimulated by U.S. overseas investment and about the loss of technological advantages, his fears failed to dampen the ardor of firms committed to direct foreign investment. American businesspeople actively sought markets in China, Latin America, Europe, and Canada. Petroleum companies expanded their involvement in the Middle East, and Ford Motor Company built plants in Japan and even Turkey. General Motors purchased Vauxhall in England, Opel in Germany, and enlarged its operations in Canada. As these firms expanded, they took with them the ideas of mass production, efficient management, and standardization—hallmarks of American business practices.

THE COCA-COLA COMPANY

Any American tourist abroad desperate for a palatable cold drink has no problem finding the ubiquitous "Coca-Cola" sign. The very first Coca-Cola was served at a soda fountain in Atlanta, Georgia, on May 18, 1886, and the new drink rapidly became part of the national and international scene. Asa G. Candler bought all rights to the product in 1888, and the Coca-Cola Company soon distributed the drink nationally through an elaborate marketing system. The company then began to sell its syrup in Canada in 1900; by 1928 sales in Toronto equaled those in New York City, and within two years sales in Montreal vied with those in New Orleans. A subsidiary was formed in Canada, thus opening the way for development of a multinational.

The Candler family sold the firm for $25 million in 1919, and four years later leadership passed to Robert W. Woodruff, who was determined to expand operations around the world. Woodruff believed that if the product could be marketed aggressively with a guarantee that it was potable and "refreshing," the sales potential would be unlimited. The same marketing techniques used in the United States were employed abroad with Coca-Cola selling bottling rights to business leaders who would build plants to manufacture the product. Coca-Cola sold the franchise holders the syrup made from its secret formula. The company, which spent massive sums advertising Coca-Cola, found some markets easy to penetrate and others, such as the British Isles with its habitual attachment to formal tea and coffee times, difficult. Nevertheless, sales abroad expanded so much that by the 1970s more than half of the Coca-Cola consumed was outside of the United States.

Built solidly on the concept of locally owned and operated bottling plants, international sales of Coca-Cola were not as susceptible to expropriation and nationalism as wholly owned subsidiaries of some American firms. Of the 13,000 employees in plants overseas, approximately 99 percent were citizens of the country in which the plant was located. Coca-Cola called its multinational policy "partnership in industry." As a result, "Cokes" could be purchased from more than 4 million retail outlets in the world.

Until 1954 Coca-Cola remained the firm's sole product. Subsequently it entered the citrus, tea, and coffee markets and introduced other flavored

Coca-Cola delivery truck in Egypt in 1950. (Courtesy: The Archives. The Coca-Cola Company.)

drinks and instant foods. These were also marketed internationally. Because of the need for pure water in its manufacturing and bottling operations, Coca-Cola had long been interested in water purification and desalinization. The acquisition of Aqua-Chem in 1970 made the firm one of the leaders in research and development of pure water facilities. This endeavor added to Coca-Cola's world operations with the creation of water plants in thirty-five nations. The Coca-Cola trademark became the most widely known in the world, and its principal product was labeled in eighty languages. The licensing and franchising procedures used by Coca-Cola as it became a major multinational served as a model for other American firms with similar products to market abroad.

Throughout the 1920s more American firms invested larger sums in increasingly diversified operations overseas. Firestone created rubber plantations in Liberia while oil companies pursued petroleum in Rumania, Saudi Arabia, and the Dutch East Indies. American utility firms built electrical, telephone, and radio networks around the globe. As this expansion progressed, some firms developed relationships with three or more countries, creating highly complex organizations and investment structures. For example, Eastman Kodak's subsidiary in Great Britain established branches in Africa, the Middle East, and Asia. Many Canadian affiliates of American companies had operations in third or fourth countries. These arrangements often aided U.S. efforts to penetrate markets in the British Empire. The British, French, Germans, Swiss, Dutch, and Italians passed laws limiting investments by foreigners and preventing them from exercising their voting rights to the securities they owned. Yet despite efforts to resist American multinationals, they continued to increase their operations, and as long as the domestic economy boomed, they advanced abroad.[10]

The 1929 stock market crash and the coming of national and international depression in the 1930s greatly reduced the previously rapid rate of growth among the American multinationals. When the United States enacted the protectionist Smoot-Hawley Tariff in 1931, European nations retaliated, thus further reducing international trade. As armed conflicts broke out overseas during the decade, American multinationals suffered losses, withdrew from some markets, and redirected their interests toward "safe" nations or regions. Revolutions in Latin America, currency export controls by nations trying to cope with depression, and devaluation of currencies harmed efforts to maintain operations in many countries. Some American firms simply abandoned overseas branches and markets. Actions by the Roosevelt administration to stimulate foreign trade as part of an effort to aid the domestic economy did not generally prove beneficial to the multinationals. Even where operations remained profitable, many nations simply refused to allow funds to be transferred out of their country. As the world moved closer to war, the risks for investments abroad increased and enthusiasm and confidence within the multinationals declined. A major exception existed in the petroleum industry, where American firms became even more involved in Europe, the Middle East, and Asia and the number of oil companies with overseas operations also grew. Ironically, throughout the decade there had been increasing investments by European and other foreign interests—both firms and individuals—in the United States.[11]

WORLD WAR II AND THE FIRST POSTWAR DECADE

From September 1, 1939, until V-J Day in August, 1945, the multinational firms saw their investments abroad destroyed by military action, threatened by expropriation, and often isolated beyond direct managerial control because of travel and communications problems. While investments in Canada and part of Latin America remained profitable, these were the exceptions. Firms from the United States expanded petroleum and mining operations in Latin America, and American airlines replaced German and Italian carriers in the hemisphere, but success stories among the multinationals were few. Strongly supported by the U.S. government, American oil companies replaced British domination of Middle Eastern oil, especially in Saudi Arabia. However, the share of the GNP represented by foreign investment fell to 3.4 percent in 1946, the lowest figure in this century.

Peace, industrial reconversion, the coming the the Cold War, and economic expansion at home deeply affected the multinational enterprises after 1945. Once the United States accepted responsibility for rebuilding the economies of Western Europe and Japan with the Marshall Plan, the government spurred anew the enthusiasm of the multinationals. After the adoption of the policy of containment with the Truman Doctrine and the creation of the North Atlantic Treaty Organization, opportunities for investment abroad, especially for defense-related businesses, grew at an extraordinary rate. This is not to say that the federal government celiberately sought to use private investment to dominate world trade and markets, but it was part of a broader policy to block aggression by the Soviet Union, stabilize the economies of Western Europe, and counter the rise of communist revolutions in the emerging third world. Unfortunately, American diplomats and politicans often confused the latter with nationalism and efforts to end colonialism.

While the Departments of State and Commerce actively promoted American foreign investment, it also negotiated the General Agreement on Tariffs and Trade, which sought to reduce trade barriers. Some U.S. firms felt that the government's policies served to hinder their activities. Export licenses were required for trade with the Soviet bloc, and antitrust suits against firms such as General Electric found the companies guilty of participation in international cartels. The judgments forced divestiture of foreign holdings and termination of patent and trade agreements. Alcoa (Aluminum Company of America) was forced to separate from its Canadian subsidiary. These facts do not support the views of some historians and economists that the Cold War came into being because the U.S. government sought to establish American economic domination of the postwar world. The coming of socialism to Britain, fears of communism in France and Italy, and unfavorable currency restrictions initially limited investment abroad to reestablishment of prewar affiliates and subsidiaries.[12]

By the mid-1950s conditions for expansion by the multinationals improved markedly. The petroleum companies led the way with huge investments in the Middle East, South America, and Indonesia. The colonial British, French, and Dutch governments had departed, or had been forced by revolutions from Africa and Asia, and economic prosperity had returned to most of Western Europe. The end of the Korean War and the beginning of the summit conferences suggested that the most dangerous threats to world peace were lessening. American corporations saw the improvement of national economies abroad and emergence of mass-consumer markets as opportunities to employ techniques not unlike those used in this country. Because of these factors, the next two decades would witness a vast proliferation of investment abroad and the creation of many multinational firms of extraordinary economic size and power.

THE MULTINATIONAL EXPLOSION

For more than two decades following the mid-1950s, American business generally prospered, expanded, diversified, and sought new international markets. The commitment to research and development in some areas accelerated even as most firms sought to streamline internal structures and make their managements more efficient. System analysis, new products, greater capital expenditures, and growing markets for securities heightened the expansion of American industry. Conditions in the domestic economy provided a solid basis for more intensive and extensive pursuit of business abroad. Total value of American direct investments overseas rose from almost $32 billion in 1960 to over $227 billion in 1981 and to $1.7 *trillion* in 1987.[13] At the same time, spurred by a reorientation of American foreign policy, investment outside of Western Europe and the developed countries also increased rapidly.

The government of the United States created several agencies for economic development abroad and actively participated in international organizations that served the same purpose. The Agency for International Development extended loans to firms desiring to invest in less-developed countries. The United States Import-Export Bank not only encouraged investment but also made transfers of funds much easier. The United States actively participated in the International Bank for Reconstruction and Development and the Inter-American Development Bank. Both organizations stimulated the expansion of the multinationals. Further, the government put other countries on notice that if American firms had their properties expropriated without adequate compensation, then all aid from the United States would be terminated. The gradual reduction of foreign aid programs made this threat increasingly hollow, however, and the growing deficit in the balance of payments caused the American government to moderate its enthusiasm for overseas investments. Regardless, the attitudes and actions of foreign governments still were far more crucial to the multinationals than policies of the American government. The French government under Charles de Gaulle restricted American business opportunities there even as the Japanese virtually closed entry into their economy. Nevertheless, the multinationals continued to expand in size and strength as direct foreign investments grew faster than the domestic economy.

The multinationals moved away from agriculture and utilities as strong strains of nationalism in host countries made these areas often subjects of expropriation. Manufacturing became the principal endeavor as American technology could be applied to the production of new products and the development of new markets. In chemicals, electronics, and mass-marketed consumer goods, firms from the United States had distinct advantages over most other nations save Japan. American industries that fell behind technologically, like steel, had few overseas operations except for the extraction of raw materials. On the other hand, the technologically sophisticated firms moved abroad vigorously. Control Data, for example, opened branches in Spain, Portugal, Greece, Mexico and Hong Kong. As in the pre–World War II era, the firms from the United States saw the establishment of international manufacturing facilities as a way to enhance the marketing of commodities in those nations. But they also sought to penetrate additional markets, and did so aggressively.

In order to surmount fears of American economic domination and to avoid the impact of strident nationalism, many multinationals turned to joint ventures with firms in the host country or became junior partners in existing firms. The joint ventures spread risks and were viewed far more favorably by foreign governments and their peoples. The growing employment of foreign nationals in the overseas operations accelerated the search for more direct and efficient management of those joint ventures. Many firms reorganized their international divisions and made products the basis upon which their structures rested. The domestic division producing the product would assume responsibility for that product overseas as well. There was, then, an integration of foreign and domestic operations at a lower level while overall policies were still being made at the corporate level. Market orientation replaced the supply orientation of the pre-1939 multinationals.

By the end of the 1970s a greater diversity of American investment abroad developed. Manufacturing remained the major sector, but despite expropriations, turmoil, war in the Middle East, and the price restrictions of the Organization of Petroleum Exporting Countries (OPEC), investment in petroleum and petrochemicals abroad soared. American retailers such as Sears, Roebuck expanded their international operations, as did hotel chains like Hilton, Sheraton, and Holiday Inn. Banks in the United States established branches abroad in profusion, indicating again the importance of the multinationals and of world trade to the domestic economy.

THE IMPACT OF THE MULTINATIONALS

The total effect of the multinationals on the American economy grew more significant each year. The third largest industrial unit in the world, after the United States and the Soviet Union, was the American subsidiaries abroad. As concern for the balance-of-payments deficit heightened, the multinationals pointed to their role in stimulating sales of American exports and to the continued flow of foreign capital into this country. The exports, they argued, create jobs in the United States even as their plants abroad produced goods that competed with American-made products. The multinationals agreed that American technology was being exported but noted that they often gained access to foreign technology, especially in Western Europe and to some extent in Japan. To charges that they were part of international cartels, and thus artificially raised prices, the multinationals responded that they actually stimlulated international competition. The multinationals contended that by contributing to economic growth abroad, they were making their host countries less dependent upon American military and economic aid. There is no general agreement on these factors, but the debate does suggest the depth of concern in the United States and abroad about the power of the multinationals and the degree to which they are involved in American foreign policy.

In general, the host nations benefited economically from the stimulus of investments by the multinationals. Exports by these firms improved the host nation's balance-of-payments situation and created local capital. The host country also gained new technology and additional trained scientists, technicians, and managers. There was, of course, the fear, and sometimes the reality, of interference by the American multinational in the government of the host nation or the use of American foreign policy to protect or enhance the position of the firm.

Canadians came to resent the power of American companies when they controlled almost half of that nation's industrial plants. Similarly, the British watched with some alarm as subsidiaries of American firms came to dominate one quarter of that nation's exports. American firms held four-fifths of the computer market in West Germany and Italy, almost half the automobile production in the former, and almost 40 percent of the pharmaceuticals in the latter. Only in Japan, China, and the Soviet bloc had market penetration by American firms been highly restricted. Perhaps the most dramatic achievement had been the general replacement of the countries of Western Europe by the United States as the primary investor abroad.[14]

Throughout this century the growth of the American multinationals was neither constant nor of the same pattern. Investments in agriculture and utilities declined even as capital placed in manufacturing, mining, and petroleum escalated. Some markets were lost, Cuba, for example, but whole continents, such as much of Africa, opened to American multinationals after 1945. Many of the branches and subsidiaries abroad profited to the degree they were able to stand alone as separate entities, with security ownership their last major tie to the American parent. Firms such as International Telephone and Telegraph generally were forced to abandon utilities and shift their capital to large-scale investments in manufacturing in the host country. United Fruit, suffering from the rise of nationalism in Central America, expropriation, the vagaries of American dietary habits, and antitrust action at home, largely removed itself from agriculture and railways and became a wholesaler and shipper. Indeed, United Fruit became only a division of a much larger conglomerate, United Brands. Clearly, both the attitudes of the host government and the business practices and methods of the multinational have been major factors in their successes or failures.

The American firms that were most aggressive and that had technologically advanced products penetrated foreign markets with the greatest degree of success. Ironically, the same held true of foreign multinationals that entered the United States.

FOREIGN MULTINATIONALS IN AMERICA

From the colonial period to World War I, the primary investors in the United States from outside the country were the British. By the year 1900 the size of the British investment dwarfed that of the second nation, the Netherlands, tenfold. And, at the outbreak of war in 1914, of the $6.7 billion in foreign-owned investments, the British held $4.2 billion. Their funds had been invested in ranches, railroads, mining, flour milling, lumber, insurance, and real estate. The French, Germans, Dutch, and Swiss placed capital in the United States as well, but the British dominated foreign investment. Most of the capital from abroad was used to purchase stocks, bonds, and real estate, and while these were direct investments, they did not usually represent the creation of manufacturing branches or subsidiaries of foreign firms in this country.

During the next three decades the size of foreign investments in the United States declined as many of the Western European nations became debtors to America. Foreign investment peaked in 1940 at $8.1 billion, nearly all in security portfolios, and fell to $7.7 billion by 1950. This trend was sharply reversed over the next twenty years as direct foreign investment reached $20.7 billion in 1974, partially as a result of the growing presence of foreign multinationals, and would rise to $89.8 billion in 1982, and to an incredible $1.54 *trillion* in 1987.

The prosperity of the American economy, the huge mass-consumer market, and relatively few restrictions on business, as compared with many nations, made this country very attractive for long-term investment and the creation of American subsidiaries. First British, then Dutch and German, and finally Japanese firms entered the United States. Declining security values on the American stock exchanges and the dramatic fall of the dollar against other currencies made some firms tempting targets for foreign takeover, a cheap means to enter markets in the United States. British investors acquired larger holdings in petroleum, banks, department stores, and grocery chains. Baskin-Robbins became part of Allied Brewing of Great Britain; Miles Laboratories was purchased by Bayer of Germany; and Libby, McNeil & Libby was acquired by Nestle of Switzerland. Although no single foreign multinational came to dominate a particular market, the presence of multinationals was felt in several areas of the economy, especially banking.[15] As recently as 1982 the United States remained a creditor country with a $136.9 billion investment surplus, but foreign purchases of

Rendering of new Toyota plant in Georgetown, Kentucky, 1988. (Courtesy: Toyota Motor Manufacturing, U.S.A., Inc.)

securities and real estate led to a net debt of $368 billion by 1987. Britain remained the largest foreign investor, with the Netherlands second and Japan third. Foreigners had come to own about 5 percent of the nation's assets. The United States entered the twentieth century as a debtor nation and appeared to be about to enter the twenty-first in the same condition.

JAPANESE MULTINATIONALS

Where only 44 Japanese firms entered foreign manufacturing markets between 1914 and 1945, some 90 became multinationals between 1962 and 1964, and more than 200 firms opened operations abroad between 1968 and 1970. A major philosophical change among the largest Japanese firms occurred as they moved from emphasizing exports to the production of commodities abroad.

The extraordinary increase in the size and scope of Japanese multinationals came in less than a decade. The Japanese moved into many areas, but primarily textiles, timber, and steel. The Japanese multinationals initially concentrated their investments in the developed countries, especially Canada, and to a lesser extent in the United States. Most of the facilities created were designed to serve markets in the host country, the large Japanese soy plant in Wisconsin being a prime example. Of the products made by Japanese multinationals abroad, 75 percent were sold in the host country and only 5 percent were shipped to Japan, with 20 percent sold to third countries. These figures suggest that construction by Japanese firms of automobile plants in the United States would exacerbate competition, not reduce it for the benefit of American car companies.

American multinationals found competition with Japanese multinationals very difficult. The Japanese successfully entered the textile and steel markets in Brazil, for example. Japanese steel firms displaced companies from the United States in much of Latin America. Because Japanese exports of consumer products, such as television sets, had been aimed at markets in developed countries from the outset, the Japanese had the technological expertise to build plants for the manufacture of these commodities abroad and already had a reputation for high quality and dependability. Thus, Sony established a plant to make color television sets in southern California. Another electronics firm, Matsushita, bought Motorola's television division to enhance its Panasonic label. The creation of Japanese-owned manufacturing facilities in the United States did not reach the dollar level of the Western European nations, but the rate of investment was extraordinary. By 1979 the Japanese had invested $3.4 billion.

As Japanese investment in the United States accelerated, state and local governments vied with each other to attract these new outlays. Kentucky won a Toyota plant, Indiana a Subaru-Isuzu facility, and Ohio a Honda factory. States offered reduced or no taxes, job training programs for workers, and other incentives. Japanese capital was also sought for office buildings, hotels, and shopping centers, and the level of investment reached remarkable levels in California ($5.3 billion) and New York ($2.5

billion), with six other states showing at least $1 billion in Japanese-owned assets. Japanese investors purchased $150 billion in stocks and bonds in 1986 alone, and while few American firms came under complete Japanese control, such as Scripto, some companies found that substantial stock positions were held by Japanese investors. As this trend continued, a poll in 1988 showed that 78 percent of the American people wanted a limit placed on what foreigners could buy.[16]

THE GLOBAL ECONOMY

The rapid growth of the world's multinational firms produced additional interdependence among national economies. America's dominance of the multinationals declined, indicative of the rise of multinationals in Western Europe and Japan. As recently as 1971 the United States had 58 of the world's largest multinationals, but that number fell to 49 in 1979. Of the world's 500 largest firms, the United States had 219 in 1979, compared with 280 only eight years earlier. Japan stood in second place with 71 companies, while Great Britain had 51 and West Germany 37. In many nations the fears of American firms expressed only a decade earlier all but disappeared as their own multinationals grew at an even faster rate than their U.S. competitors when they adopted many of the manufacturing and marketing techniques of their American counterparts. By 1985 of the 20 largest industrial companies in the world, 13 were headquartered in the United States, but of the top 50 firms, only 22 were in the United States and 6 were located in Japan. Competition between the multinationals also increased as national or state trading companies in the Soviet bloc entered international markets. Some observers argued that the multinationals were displacing the traditional role of trade in the world economy.

In automobiles, steel, and more recently in computers and aircraft manufacturing, the industrial multinational giants of the United States faced global competition. While public attention focused on imports and their effect on employment, there was little concern expressed about the continuing loss of export markets. With one-quarter of all corporate profits generated by sales overseas, the long-range impact of foreign multinationals in the world market was an even greater threat to the economy of the United States than the flood of Japanese cars, computers, and television sets. The multinationals had become a significant factor in the "planetization" of the world economy.

NOTES

1. Much of the information in this chapter is based on the outstanding studies of multinational firms by Mira Wilkins. These works are indispensable guides to the rise and maturation of American multinationals. See *The Emergence of Multinational Enterprise: American Business Abroad from the Colonial Era to 1914* (Cambridge: Harvard University Press, 1970), and *The Maturing of Multinational Enterprise: American Business Abroad from 1914 to 1970* (Cambridge: Harvard University Press, 1974).

2. Wilkins, *The Emergence of Multinational Enterprise*, pp. 35–45.

3. Ibid., pp. 47–69. See also Alfred D. Chandler, Jr., *The Visible Hand: The Managerial Revolution in American Business* (Cambridge: Harvard University Press, 1977), pp. 368–369.

4. The debate among scholars on the role of big business in the creation of American imperialism has produced a vast body of literature. Exceptionally clear statements of the issues can be found in Walter LeFeber, *The New Empire* (Ithaca, New York: Cornell University Press, 1963); Ernest R. May, *Imperial Democracy* (New York: Harcourt, Brace & World, 1961); Charles S. Campbell Jr., *Special Business Interests and the Open Door Policy* (New Haven, Connecticut: Yale University Press, 1951); Carl P. Parrini, *Heir to Empire: United States Economic Diplomacy, 1916–1923* (Pittsburgh: University of Pittsburgh Press, 1969); and David Healy, *U.S. Expansionism: The Imperialist Urge in the 1890s* (Madison: University of Wisconsin Press, 1970).

5. Wilkins, *The Emergence of Multinational Enterprise*, pp. 70–79.

7. Hugh G.J. Aitken, John J. Deutsch, and others, *The American Economic Impact On Canada* (Durham, North Carolina: Duke University Press, 1959), provides a broad view of American investment practices.

8. A full range of interpretations concerning United Fruit can be found in Frederick U. Adams, *Conquest of the Tropics: The Story of the Creative Enterprises Conducted by the United Fruit Company* (Garden City, New York: Doubleday, 1914); Thomas P. McCann, *An American Company: The Tragedy of United Fruit* (New York: Crown Publishers, 1976); and Charles M. Wilson, *Empire in Green and Gold: The Story of the American Banana Trade* (New York: Henry Holt and Co., 1947).

9. Wilkins, *The Maturing of Multinational Enterprise*, pp. 3–45.

10. Ibid., pp. 111–163.

11. Ibid., pp. 167–205; for the importance of overseas operations to the American multinational, see Mira Wilkins and Frank Ernest Hill, *American Business Abroad: Ford on Six Continents* (Detroit: Wayne State University Press, 1964).

12. Wilkins, *The Maturing of Multinational Enterprise*, pp. 258–310.

13. Ibid., p. 329.

14. Ibid., pp. 327–408. For European views, see also, Georges Peninou and others, *Who's Afraid of the Multinationals?* (Westmead, Hampshire, England: Saxon House, 1978).

15. William G. Kerr, "Foreign Investment in the United States," *The Dictionary of American History* (New York: Charles Scribner's Sons, 1976), pp. 62–67; Walter Damm, "The Economic Aspects of European Direct Investment in the United States," in Sidney E. Rolfe and Walter Damm, eds., *The Multinational Corporation in the World Economy* (New York: Praeger, 1970), pp. 35–51.

16. M. Y. Yoshino, "The Multinational Spread of Japanese Manufacturing Investment since World War II," *Business History Review* 48 (Autumn 1974), pp. 357–381.

SUGGESTED READINGS

BROWN, COURTNEY C., ed. *World Business: Promise and Problems.* New York: Macmillan, 1970.

CARSTENSEN, FRED V. *American Enterprise in Foreign Markets: Singer and International Harvester in Imperial Russia.* Chapel Hill: University of North Carolina Press, 1984.

FRANKO, LAWRENCE G. "The Origins of Multinational Manufacturing by Continental European Firms." *Business History Review* 48 (Autumn 1974): 277–302.

McCRAW, THOMAS K., ed. *America Versus Japan: A Comparative Study.* Boston: Harvard Business School Press, 1986.

PENINOU, GEORGES. *Who's Afraid of the Multinationals?: A Survey of European Opinion on Multinational Corporations.* Westmead, Hampshire, England: Saxon House, 1978.

ROLFE, SIDNEY E., and WALTER DAMM, eds. *The Multinational Corporation in the World Economy.* New York: Praeger, 1970.

STOREY, DAVID J., ed. *The Small Firm: An International Survey.* New York: St. Martin's Press, 1983.

VERNON, RAYMOND. *The Economic and Political Consequences of Multinational Enterprise: An Anthology.* Boston: Graduate School of Business Administration, Harvard University, 1972.
———. *Sovereignty at Bay: The Multinational Spread of U.S. Enterprises.* New York: Basic Books, 1971.
WILKINS, MIRA. *The Emergence of Multinational Enterprise: American Business Abroad from the Colonial Era to 1914.* Cambridge: Harvard University Press, 1970.
———. *The Maturing of Multinational Enterprise: American Business Abroad from 1914 to 1970.* Cambridge: Harvard University Press, 1974.
YOSHINO, M. Y. "The Multinational Spread of Japanese Manufacturing Investment since World War II." *Business History Review* 48 (Autumn 1974): 357–381.

21 Profits and Losses

Business in America is the product of centuries of historical development, and history provides useful insights into the dynamics of the American business system. These are the dynamics of change, of people and places, of events and opportunities grasped and sometimes lost. Business in America is in the process of constant change, and yet it never wholly disentangles itself from the past. Business at any time is people making a living, or seeking to make a living, through the production, sale, or exchange of goods and services for a profit. Thus, Christopher Columbus has something in common with Gerard Swope, James J. Hill, and James Ling. Business must constantly weigh changing external elements—resources, weather, technology, government (foreign and domestic), demography—in the decision-making process.

As Christopher Columbus discovered, people in business must work within the political, economic, and social, context of their times. They interact with government. They are affected by changing technology. They are subject to environmental controls and resource limitations. Energy resources change, and the supply varies even as technology provides new sources or processes for energy conversion. The entrepreneur must operate within the constraints of both the primary or natural environment and the secondary or man-made environment. The secondary environment determines how business may or may not be conducted, but business in turn shapes the secondary environment. The energies, efforts, and ideas of people in business change the values and lifestyles of the society and the character of their government.

The most important element in business at anytime has been the individual. That person, who may be variously a proprietor, entrepreneur, inventor, manager, or salesperson, is the crucial element in the inception and operation of a business. Yet there is no typical business leader. There seem to be no clear definitions of character, aptitude, or training required to be successful in business. There are men and women of varying talents who successfully organize and manage small and large businesses, and it is not axiomatic that the small businessman or woman aspired to create a large enterprise. Personalities in American business are diverse, incongruous, and occasionally exciting, though usually not. They are in every instance decision makers, managers, and capitalists seeking a profit. The history of American business demonstrates that people are the source of economic change and that change is the cumulative product of the activities and ideas of millions of individuals engaged in the business system. Business is intrinsic to the quality and style of American life.

A capitalistic society that provides incentives to individuals, including profits, property, and security in owning that property, is necessary to the achievement of success in business. Thus one of the dynamics of the American business system is the socioeconomic environment in which that business operates. That environment changes over time and clearly affects the form of business ventures. During the era of exploration and discovery business opportunities were ordinarily with trade, and most often on an international basis. As older empires crumbled, trade between the new United States and the rest of the world became circumscribed and troublesome. The American colonial merchant lost the protective British mercantile umbrella that created some opportunities but denied others. For most of several decades between 1776 and 1815, American merchants were virtually denied access to European markets. In this period there was a rather clear formulation of a distinctive American system of doing business. The seeds for the industrial revolution and an American system of manufacturing were sown, and the concept of the modern corporation took form. Society firmly adopted individualism, personal liberty, and rights in property as essential values.

During the next phase of economic development three major forces— the westward movement, urbanization, and industrialization—were concurrent and interrelated factors. The production, sale, and exchange of goods and services occurred over an expanding geographic area. Manufacturing increasingly required the importation of raw materials from more remote places and the shipment of finished products to distant markets. The structure of business and the supporting social system became larger in order to accommodate the greater size and diversity of business activity. Businesses spilled across state lines and became first regional and then national phenomena. It was the age of the individual and the entrepreneur. Opportunities and resources abounded. Government received a social mandate to facilitate the expansion of business activity; that mandate provided that government should help business, but not interfere. If national banking was a constraint, then the bank should be abolished. If railroads must be built, governments on every level should facilitate that work. The production of food and fiber was aided and abetted by easy access to land. The Civil War was an interlude, and in some respects an aberration, in the prevailing scheme of business expansion, but it was also a product of that expansion. Slavery was incompatible with the ideal of democratic opportunity; states rights was a deterrent to regional and national business activity.

As business spilled across state lines and became regional and national in scope, the structure of business and its relationship to state and local governments changed. By the last quarter of the nineteenth century the corporation had replaced the individual proprietor and partnership as the dominant force in the economy, but the corporation by no means dispossessed the small businesspeople or their firms, which increasingly came to serve as the specialists in the interstices of the business world. Small businesses could do some things more efficiently and effectively than the large. They could, for example, provide the feeder airlines linking the national systems, and the stores, shops, gasoline stations, agencies, and dealerships that made big business work. And, most importantly, the small businesses provided much of the inspiration, new ideas, and supporting ideology for big business.

Big business in the later nineteenth and early twentieth centuries was characterized by the expansion of basic institutional structures, by innovation, and by adaptation to changing social and political situations. The great age of railroad construction and development peaked by the turn of the twentieth century. The ubiquitous automobile began to putter along country lanes and through city streets, bringing an exiciting new age of subdivisions, urban sprawl, supermarkets, franchise stores, and interstate highways. Several hundred automobile companies vied for a seemingly inexhaustible market. There was Studebaker, Packard, Chrysler, Ford, General Motors—and then their number declined. And one day there would be Datsuns, Volkswagens, and Toyotas.

Modern life and a growing commerce required ever-larger energy sources. Petroleum superseded coal, but the demand for the older fuels never ended. What responsibility did the government have to provide or to facilitate the production of energy? Government tried subsidies, allotments, regulation, and on occasion direct competition with private corporations. Over the years energy companies, whether petroleum, coal, or electric-based, became larger and usually developed national and international production and marketing structures.

Insurance also found a home in the modern, urban-industrial automobile age. From humble and often speculative tontine origins, the modern insurance company became a giant financial intermediary. Insurance became the service industry of the business system, designed to protect the property and the lives of the American people. In conjunction with the giant insurance corporations there developed a veritable army of independent agents, appraisers, and salespeople, the small businessmen and women who kept the giant enterprise alive and well.

Essential mechanisms in the expansion of the American business system were money and banking. That industry from the beginning united public and private interests in a sometimes unholy and occasionally unworkable alliance, but it accomplished some remarkable things. State banking vied with federal banks, and private banks with chartered banks. New York and eastern banks seemingly achieved a hegemony over the nation by the late nineteenth century. Questions of democratic opportunity brought about banking reforms and a Federal Reserve System. Banks themselves began to evolve under the stress of competition and the changing needs of society. Checks, credit cards, and electronic transfers replaced cash in daily transactions. Banks, like insurance companies and savings and loan institutions, became larger and more sophisticated financial enterprises that generally did an increasingly better job of financing businesses. Government, especially following the financial catastrophes of the Great Depression, became more closely identified as an insurer, financier, and regulator of banks, and it came to have a growing responsibility and participation in foreign trade and overseas investment.

As was true with the banking, insurance, and transportation industries, foreign commerce had ancient roots in America. As colonies, America served long as a source of raw materials for British factories, and as a marketplace for British goods. But as was true in other enterprises, foreign commerce in the modern era became increasingly complex and political. The U.S. government, its army, navy, and embassies, became the overseas representatives of American business interests. As some American businesses began to establish branches and factories in other countries, the larger businesses of those countries did the same in the United States. By the post–World War II era the multinational corporation had become a formidable new business structure wherein business had simply outgrown the confinement and service capabilities of national governments. The multinational corporation seemed new and different, and yet there were ties to the distant past—perhaps to the conquistadors or the Hudson Bay Fur Company, or perhaps the Panama Canal Company and the Virginia Company.

That which was obvious to the conquistador and the New England merchant has again become a part of the American business consciousness. American business and financial interests are interdependent with the world economy. For example, the near energy monopoly created by OPEC in 1971–1973 generated crude-oil price increases of almost 1,700 percent. Petroleum that had sold for $2 per barrel rose to $32.50 in 1981. Despite the fact that petroleum collapsed to $12–$16 per barrel after 1985, the consequences of the earlier "oil boom" and OPEC embargo continued to unfold.

The United States and Western nations transferred billions of dollars of their wealth to OPEC and other oil-producing areas. Even within the United States there was a transfer of wealth to oil-producing states. Subsequently, much of the money from abroad returned to the United States as investment capital in banks and businesses. American financial institutions, managing much of the world's money, invested this capital in domestic business expansion and often as loans to governments of third-world developing nations, particularly those whose "development" related to petroleum production. By 1986 almost one trillion dollars had been loaned by American institutions to foreign borrowers.

Concurrent with this frenetic financial activity of the 1970s and early 1980s, American public and private spending soared, creating tremendous inflationary pressures. Growing trade deficits and recurring federal budget deficits generated by defense and welfare spending and the rising costs of servicing the federal debt compounded the development of serious economic problems in an economy that had since World War II experienced almost uninterrupted expansion and good health.

By 1985, for the first time in almost one hundred years, the United States was importing more industrial products, including automobiles, machinery, and other capital goods, than it exported. At the same time, employment in American manufacturing industries declined sharply. The steel industry, for example, produced 88 million tons of steel in 1985, compared to 130 million tons fifteen years earlier, and the number of steel workers employed dropped by almost two-thirds. Agricultural exports, which expanded each year after World War II, continued to rise through the 1970s but stabilized by 1980. Imports of consumer goods also rose sharply. Total imports reached $91 billion in 1984, compared to imports of $8 billion in 1965. The following year (1985) the United States achieved a $150 billion trade *deficit*. It was also in that year that the United States became a debtor nation, which it had not been for seventy years.

Even as businesses, individuals, and governments attempted to adjust to the new financial crises generated by inflation, energy shortages, and budget and trade deficits, conditions affecting business and financial decisions changed rapidly. Federal policies designed to combat inflation and to conserve energy produced few of the desired results. Stagflation, characterized by high interest rates, rising prices, and declining real economic growth, gripped the nation. Nevertheless, the steady inflow of foreign capital, particularly the "petro-dollars" from Saudi Arabia and the profits of Japanese industry, cast an aura of well-being in the nation's financial centers, but they provided little relief for business and consumers.

The general public's perception of crisis was probably greater than that of the financial centers. Disaffection and concern with the economy led to the election of Republican President Ronald Reagan and the implementation of new austerity measures characterized by tax and spending reductions, deregulation, free trade, and tight monetary policies. These measures in turn contributed to rising unemployment, seemingly larger trade deficits, larger budget deficits, and declining economic growth. The recession of 1981–1983 waned with a reviving economy, a stronger dollar, declining unemployment, and inflation markedly curbed from near 13 percent levels of the late 1970s to a more manageable 3–4 percent level. And petroleum prices began to decline as conservation and alternate energy sources, as well as OPEC disunity, began to take effect. By 1986 petroleum had plummeted to $12.50 per barrel. The result was yet a new round of financial destabilization.

Consumers, of course, benefited. So did the broad economy as the flow of dollars to OPEC eased. But the flow of dollars to petroleum-dependent states such as Texas, Oklahoma, Lousiana, and even Alaska, also dwindled, creating recession there. Even greater financial difficulties struck the third-world developing nations. Mexico, for example, owed $98 billion, most of it to American banks, and most of it secured by crude petroleum valued at $32 per barrel. Governments became insolvent. At home, many businesses and individuals, as well as state governments whose revenues depended heavily on petroleum, became destitute. Soon, the banks and financial centers who were their creditors followed suit. Thus, the repercussions of the OPEC embargo continued to unfold in the late 1980s.

Banks, savings and loan institutions, and other financial agencies associated with energy loans or even the more general stagflation loans (made on overvalued properties at high interest rates) began to absorb huge losses. Fewer than 10 banks failed each year in the United States between 1943 and 1981. Yet a total of 138 banks failed in 1986 alone; 184 closed in 1987, and even more in 1988.

The developing financial crisis struck the stock market on October 19, 1987. The Dow Jones industrial average dropped 508 points, followed three days later by a 77-point decline, and by another 156-point drop on October 26. Program trading (computer triggered), lower corporate profits, tight money, and the renewed threat of inflation and growing trade deficits were among the explanations for the most severe financial shock since the stock market collapse in October 1929. But in the 1980s, unlike the era of the Great Depression, the stock market weathered the storm, and the FDIC protected the savings of depositors. Despite the market collapse and bank failures, the American business system remained strong and intact.

The crises of the 1980s were all a part of the process of a substantive financial and economic realignment and adjustment that had been underway within the United States, and indeed in the world economic order, since 1971, if not before. The 1980s, in fact, had parallels in the experiences of the 1780s when the American economy tore itself from the British hegemony, or the 1880s when statistically America made the transition from an agriculturally dominated economy to an industrial economy. Although never the same, one decade of American business experience can never be wholly divorced in style, in content, or in the character of the people, or in the nature of the environment, from that of another decade. Although change is itself one of the most consistent elements of the business environment, American business has been founded on a value system that has remained remarkably stable over three centuries.

Throughout the ebb and flow of over three centuries, Americans maintained a fervent support for business so long as it implied democratic opportunity, personal liberty, and the right to acquire profit and property. They also retained a healthy skepticism and vigilance to maintain those liberties and rights. The self-made man became a national hero even as the corporation very nearly became the antithesis of individualism and personal liberty. Ultimately the corporation and big business came to terms with populistic tendencies in America. Government became bigger than big business, and its agencies became the watchdogs and often the guardians of the public. Intermittently Americans became uneasy with the corporate image, and taxes would be raised, labor unions protected, regulatory commissions established, and consumer advocates listened to. And sometimes, too, they lowered corporate taxes and provided low-interest loans and subventions to aid commerce. When inflation and regulation seemingly began to throttle business expansion, Americans and Congress began to talk about and then act on deregulation. While Americans may have questioned and challenged the role and activities of big business and giant corporations, they rarely questioned the central ideas of capitalism. Unjust profits were wrong, but the notion of profits remained acceptable. Corporations could be guilty of misconduct, but as business entities they had every right—and the legal, moral, and constitutional support of the American people—to exist. Thus, Americans have tended to preserve the marketplace and the business system as primarily responsible for the production and distribution of goods and services; but the federal government has always had a role, and more recently a growing one in that process.

Generally Americans have accepted the idea that one must justify one's existence by being a producer. So long as business involved primarily the sale and exchange of goods and services, there was some skepticism of the businessperson's worth. To acquire wealth without being a creator or producer of goods was to live off of the labor and production of others. Benjamin Franklin was among those who equated commerce with cheating. But the technological revolution and the changing social order began to alter the perception of business. No longer exclusively a shopkeeper or merchant, the manufacturer was a producer of goods. Soon the understanding of services as a product began to include even the merchant under the umbrella of the American system of enterprise. Despite concern about Robber Barons and the growth of giant corporations, the United States constantly became more business oriented; and, as it did so, its social and political structures became more intertwined with the structures of business. Business leaders enjoyed a vast public confidence. Men and women in business regularly represented the people in Congress and filled executive offices, state legislatures, and local governing bodies. Government became increasingly a patron, regulator, and partner in business enterprise, but it was on occasion an uneasy alliance, for government very clearly imposed contraints on individual opportunity and freedom or independence of choice.

Business itself tended toward becoming bigger. Large businesses competed in national and international markets. Size became cumbersome in many instances, and internal organizational structures of a firm moved toward diversification and decentralization even as ownership and management became separate entities. The success of big business hinged upon the innovative and organizational abilities of its directors and managers. Chance events, such as foreign wars and revolutions, oil embargoes, crop failures, and droughts, made success a sometimes fleeting thing. Increasingly effective competition from manufacturers and retailers in Japan and Western

Europe for international and even domestic markets created a new crisis of self-confidence. Traditional American leadership in basic manufacturing enterprises has been sorely challenged. Unlike the first decades after World War II, American business and economic power are no longer preeminent. Nevertheless, the world of business became bigger and more complicated, and business opportunities, including new markets and new products, expanded rapidly.

Society bred generations of risk-takers, entrepreneurs who set new goals or objectives and created the organizations and raised the capital to pursue those objectives. Electronics, computers, pharmaceuticals, housing, travel, food services, and sales were among those industries that attracted millions of Americans to business. Between 1960 and 1970 alone the economy experienced a net increase of over 500,000 corporations, 20,000 partnerships, and 300,000 proprietorships. Business receipts rose from $1 to $2 trillion dollars, and by 1980 the total number of business enterprises exceeded 12 million. Certain industries, such as petroleum and automobiles, experienced growing concentrations. Relatively few firms held the great bulk of the financial resources of American manufacturing. Although the large corporations seemed to be getting bigger, many new companies were constantly joining the ranks of, or displacing, some of the older firms at the top levels of business enterprise.

Thousands of new products were marketed that did not even exist decades earlier. While the world of business brought a vast array of new goods and services to American life, it simultaneously created a crisis in the quality of life. Demands for energy resources accelerated. Urban blight, pollution, and overcrowding existed alongside a wide range of material goods. Society became more depersonalized, and individuals found great difficulty in sustaining their uniqueness. As President Woodrow Wilson observed long ago, our life contains good things in rich abundance, but evil has come with the good. The problems of society, however, also create opportunities, for if there were no problems and no wants there would be no innovation and no social progress. One of the dynamics of the American business system may indeed be its problem-creating–problem-solving character. Business, by any measurement, and the men and women in business, have been the vital force in the life of the nation. For, the business of America *is* business.

Index